Mary Louisa Georgina Petrie

Clews to Holy Writ

Or, the Chronological Scripture Cycle

Mary Louisa Georgina Petrie

Clews to Holy Writ
Or, the Chronological Scripture Cycle

ISBN/EAN: 9783337099619

Printed in Europe, USA, Canada, Australia, Japan

Cover: Foto ©Lupo / pixelio.de

More available books at **www.hansebooks.com**

CLEWS TO HOLY WRIT

OR, THE

CHRONOLOGICAL SCRIPTURE CYCLE

A SCHEME FOR STUDYING THE WHOLE BIBLE IN ITS
HISTORICAL ORDER DURING THREE YEARS

BY

MARY LOUISA GEORGINA PETRIE, B.A.

(MRS. ASHLEY CARUS-WILSON)

NINTH THOUSAND

London
HODDER AND STOUGHTON
27, PATERNOSTER ROW

MDCCCXCIV

Printed by Hazell, Watson, & Viney, Ld., London and Aylesbury.

TO ADELINE,

DUCHESS OF BEDFORD,

ONE OF THE FIRST

OUTSIDE OUR COLLEGE BY POST TO ADOPT

THE C.S.C. SCHEME,

AND THE FIRST TO SUGGEST

ITS ISSUE IN THIS FORM FOR A WIDER PUBLIC,

I Dedicate

MY LITTLE BOOK.

PREFACE TO THE SIXTH THOUSAND

THE reception which my little volume has had from the reviewers and the public has been most gratifying to the author of a first book. The few adverse criticisms were based on the idea that I was daring enough to attempt the difficult, if not impossible, task of setting forth an authoritative scheme of Biblical chronology. Preparation of this book has, on the contrary, led me to doubt if an undisputed date can be assigned to any single event in Scripture history. Modern research has not yet replaced the generally condemned old chronology by a generally accepted new one. Hence it seemed best, in a popular book, to use the "received chronology" as a convenient working basis, indicating that it is only approximately true anywhere, and in many places very doubtful.

My marriage, on August 31st, 1893, to Professor Ashley Carus-Wilson, of McGill University, Montreal, has changed both my name and my address, and puts it out of my power to admit any new students into the College by Post, at any rate until the summer of 1894. All letters referring to it should be addressed to "The Secretary of the College by Post," at Hanover Lodge, Kensington Park. Letters intended for me should go to Canada. We are arranging to lend the MS. answers to the questions to the many leaders of Scripture classes, etc., who are using this book, on payment of a subscription of at least 2s. 6d. to the Prize Fund of the College by Post.

MARY L. G. CARUS-WILSON.

September, 1893.

PREFACE.

"WILL you as a young student help another young student?" The request was made by the founder of the "Christian Women's Education Union" to me in my early college days, when I had only matriculated and all the hardest part of my work for the University of London lay before me. So I began an informal correspondence with two or three other girls whose schoolroom days were over, and who were isolated from educational advantages. A few months later, casual mention in the *Girl's Own Paper* of this brought such scores of applications for the proffered aid that the organisation now known as the COLLEGE BY POST came suddenly into being.

Born thus in the summer of 1881, it has grown steadily since. University College, London; Westfield College, Hampstead; Girton and Newnham Colleges, Cambridge; Somerville and Lady Margaret Halls, Oxford; the Ladies' College, Cheltenham, and kindred institutions for higher education of women have contributed able teachers glad to share with others what they have themselves received to a staff on which 200 have now been enrolled.

From all parts of the United Kingdom, from the Continent and the Colonies, students representing many different conditions of life and degrees of education, to the number of 3000, have entered our classes. We do not prepare for any public examinations, but many who have small opportunity of availing themselves of professional tuition are eager to continue self-culture of various kinds under definite guidance through correspondence. We would fain lead them to prefer wise books to foolish ones; to enrich their lives by caring for history, literature, and science, when continuing to learn ceases to be a duty imposed from without and one is free to arrest or foster further intellectual growth. And since the most important history, the noblest literature, and the highest knowledge should always come first, every one of our students undertakes to give half an hour a day to Bible study on some regular system. Some do this merely because it is the condition of receiving gratuitous instruction in other subjects. But these soon find that to know the Bible aright is to love it above all other books. And an ever-increasing number who do not need our teaching in other subjects join Scripture classes only, and continue Scripture study year after year when marriage or pressure of other fresh claims on time has made secular study with us impossible. During more than six years we availed ourselves of four plans of Bible reading, each of which joins us to organisations of larger extent than our own, and each of which has its peculiar advantages: (*a*) The Lectionary of the Church of England, by which the Old Testament is read once and the New Testament twice in the year. Four chapters a day are, however, too large a portion for thorough study, save in the case of those who have abundant leisure. (*b*) (*c*) The two Bible Unions shaped some sixteen years ago by two clergymen of the Church of England, and now numbering many thousand adherents all over the world— viz., the Bible and Prayer Union, which reads the Bible straight through in three years and three months at the rate of one chapter a day; and the Christian Progress Union, which reads the Old Testament and New Testament straight through together, in rather more than two years and a half. Both are clear and simple plans, but tend to ignore the historical connection of the books of the

Bible with each other. (*d*) The Bible study plan, varying from year to year, of the Young Women's Christian Association. This, as a rule, is only adopted by those few of us who are connected with the practical work of that good society.

No one of these schemes completely meets our special needs as students; and my desire to add a fifth scheme took shape during a long ramble among the moors and mountains of Argyllshire in August 1887. Surely the most intelligent and profitable method of studying the Bible is to read it in the chronological order of the events it relates and the books it contains, so far as that can be ascertained. Thus we can illustrate the story of what was done by the poetry and other literature which explains the motives and sets forth the results of those deeds " in order " (Luke i. 3, Acts xi. 4). This rearrangement will produce fresh interest in the narratives; fresh proof of their power, and irresistible evidence of their authenticity as history; fresh light on the will of God when we see the truths He has revealed, not as isolated things, but as parts of a whole set forth in regular progression, from the dim dawn of the first promise in Eden to that bright noontide when the Eternal Son came in the Father's Name to reveal God to man perfectly.

Such was the idea embodied in the CHRONOLOGICAL SCRIPTURE CYCLE. Those who first adopted it began work with MS. papers on February 1st, 1888, and henceforth the number of C.S.C. classes rapidly increased. Then many whose lives are too busy to admit of their joining our classes, who are engaged in Bible teaching at home or in missionary work in distant lands, asked for the set of C.S.C. pamphlets which had been prepared in the first instance solely for our own students.

That there is a real need for such aid as we seek to give among the more thoughtful Bible readers of to-day, who cannot easily obtain or use the larger works of modern scholars, is indicated by these facts. In little more than four years our students and their friends have subscribed for 3000 sets of pamphlets; and the scheme is now being followed by 50 out of 60 of our Scripture classes, as well as by nearly 1700 individual Bible readers. To many Holy Writ has thus become not only interesting but fascinating; and the promised half-hour has grown into an hour at the expense of less absorbing secular studies.

This volume forms the third edition or fourth thousand of the C.S.C. Papers. In revising them I have been much indebted to my colleagues in the COLLEGE BY POST for hints and criticisms founded upon experience of the practical work of our C.S.C. classes. Of other friends whose larger knowledge has in various ways aided my responsible task, special mention must be made of the Principal of St. John's Hall, Highbury. Throughout I write for the plain reader who knows no language but English. Should more erudite persons use "Clews to Holy Writ," I trust they will forgive explanations of far from recondite things, recommendations of popular and inexpensive books, and studious avoidance of learned allusions and deep and difficult questions.

And now, as with sails trimmed anew my humble craft speeds out to sea from its inland lake, I pray God that this effort to help my fellow-students, not discoursing from a pulpit, but meeting them on common ground, may be used to stir many others up to fresh study of His inexhaustible and everlasting Word.

MARY L. G. PETRIE.

CONTENTS.

	PAGE
PREFACE	vii
INTRODUCTION	1
GENERAL PLAN OF THE CHRONOLOGICAL SCRIPTURE CYCLE	9

FIRST TERM.
THE DAYS OF THE PATRIARCHS 19

SECOND TERM.
THE DAYS OF MOSES 39

THIRD TERM.
THE DAYS OF DAVID . . 60

FOURTH TERM.
THE DAYS OF SOLOMON . . 78

FIFTH TERM.
THE DAYS OF THE PROPHETS . . 95

SIXTH TERM.
THE DAYS OF JEREMIAH . 118

SEVENTH TERM.
THE DAYS OF EZRA 138
THE SIX CENTURIES FROM JUDAH'S FALL TO THE BIRTH OF CHRIST 164

		PAGE
THE PSALMS IN THEIR HISTORICAL SEQUENCE .		. 170

EIGHTH TERM.

THE DAYS OF THE SON OF MAN . . .	. 213
THE GOSPELS IN THEIR HISTORICAL SEQUENCE .	. 244

NINTH TERM.

THE DAYS OF S. PAUL . . .	. 278
SECOND SERIES OF QUESTIONS	. 309
GENERAL INDEX . .	. 335
INDEX TO THE PSALMS . . .	. 337

INTRODUCTION.

"The word of the Lord was precious in those days; there was no open vision."—1 SAM. iii. 1.

"The Bible is an interpretation of the eternal, intelligible to every man through all time in the language in which he was born."—DR. WESTCOTT, *Bishop of Durham.*

"Let us read every word, ponder every word, first in its plain human sense: then if, in after years, we can see any safe law or rule by which we may find out its hidden meaning, let us use it, and search into the deep things of God, not from men's theories, but from His own words."—CANON KINGSLEY.

GOD is silent now as He was in the days of Eli, and for us there is no open vision. In one sense, indeed, He is ever revealing Himself as "the thoughts of men are widened with the process of the suns." With fresh insight into Nature we gain fresh knowledge of His ways, while the course of History is constantly showing us more and more of His will concerning man. But His supreme revelation was when He "spoke unto us in His Son," whom the heaven has now received until the times of restoration of all things (Acts iii. 21, R.V.); and since that Divine voice is heard no longer among us, most "rare" and "precious" is the Book that contains its words, with all the Prophetic teaching that led up to them and all the Apostolic teaching that flowed out of them (Heb. i. 1, ii. 3, 4). We are Christians because we believe in Christ, not because we believe in the Bible. Our faith is centred in a Person, not in a book. But, being Christians, we prize and study the Bible, because we can abundantly prove that in the Gospels we have the authentic record of Christ's life and teaching, that He has set His seal upon the Old Testament as "the Scriptures of the prophets which cannot be broken" (Matt. xxvi. 56; John x. 35; *cf.* Rom. i. 2), and that the whole New Testament is the work of men to whom He promised that His Holy Spirit should teach them all things and bring all that He had said to their remembrance (John xiv. 26). The Bible tells us of a Living Christ, and is interpreted to us by the Living Spirit of God who once moved its writers (2 Peter i. 21). Therefore it stands alone among the "sacred books" of the world in being itself living, not dead. Too often, however, it has been treated as if it were dead. No book is more read and less studied; no book has been more grievously misunderstood, since the Jews who reverenced the paper on which it was written rejected Him of whom it spake. For it is read more devoutly but less intelligently than other books. And so we hear those who are eager and well-informed on other subjects confess that, while they make some acquaintance with the New Testament, they cannot find the Old Testament interesting. How could they, when they hardly read it at all, or else, like Browning's half-learned, but wholly self-satisfied preacher in "Christmas Eve and Easter Day," "hug the book of books to pieces," reading it piecemeal and haphazard, isolating it from its New Testament elucidations, and never inquiring into those circumstances of time and place without knowledge of which any record of the past loses most of its meaning? Should we venture to treat any other book whose author we respected in such a way? Others again read as a compendium of theology or a philosophical dissertation, what is really a collection of Literature in its four most attractive forms: Biography, that is, portraits of the heroes who make history; Letters, that is, the most spontaneous utterances of human thought; Poetry, that is, the loftiest utterances of human thought; and, above all, History, that is, "philosophy teaching by example."

In these days secular history is being re-written by men with highest gifts of thought and expression. Instead of retailing trivial anecdotes, small personalities, crude statements of character, and partisan arguments, they show which were really the important events of the past, what led up to them, and what new developments of national life and human progress may be derived from them. The materials for secular history are contradictory, fragmentary, and in many ways unsatisfactory. But the materials for sacred history contain all we need know, if not all that would gratify our curiosity. Its writers, under Divine guidance, were unbiassed and absolutely truthful. (Occasional trifling confusions of names and numbers, which are inevitable in writings preserved for hundreds of years in MS., cannot affect the historic worth of the Scriptures for any candid reader.) Rightly read, this history shows explicitly what can only be found implicitly in other histories, how from age to age, in spite of man's weakness and wickedness, the purposes of God are carried out.

Yet, instead of tracing the march of events by aid of chronology and geography, the handmaids of all history, and using the field-glass that shows each part in relation to the whole, we take the microscope for minute investigation of words and phrases; we revel in whimsical applications of morsels of misunderstood narrative: using for instance, I quote facts, Gen. xliii. 27 and 1 Sam. xxi. 8 (last clause) as texts for exhortations that might have been fitly based upon Rom. vi. 6 and Rom. xii. 11; and thus treat the Bible as the fashionable folks of the Regency in Louis XV.'s reign treated the fine and valuable engravings whose figures they cut out to paste on fans and fire-screens. We can prove anything from Holy Writ when we regard it as a long string of "texts" whose dates and contexts may be ignored—*e.g.*, that God does not exist, from a sentence of Psalm xiv. 1.

Sometimes indeed we read it straight through, content to pass from the history of Esther to that of Job, who lived more than 1000 years earlier; from the end of Judah's Captivity in Daniel to the latter days of the kingdom of Israel in Hosea; from Obadiah's denunciation of Edom's exultation over the fall of Jerusalem to Jonah's message 200 years before to Nineveh, which had been swept away ere Jerusalem was attacked; from S. Paul in his Roman prison writing to the Colossians to S. Paul at Corinth, eleven years back, writing to the Thessalonians. Then we complain that the prophets are uninteresting, and S. Paul's teaching hard to understand!

The first "clew" (or guiding thread) to a right understanding of Holy Writ is to realise that it is an organic whole, to which each of its parts has a definite relation; the second clew is to ascertain that relation. Not that we are to substitute a vague "general idea" of the Bible for a close study of its details. Every flower in it, as Luther quaintly says, is a garden, and every tree a forest. But we must first find out where, when, by whom, and under what conditions, a passage was penned, and what it could have meant for those who originally read it, before we go on to ask what meanings its words may be made to include for us. Of course this will involve some trouble, but while God does make provision for our unavoidable ignorance, He does not make provision for our uncalled-for indolence. The good we each get from the Bible must depend upon the amount of earnest effort we put into our reading of it. Often, because we will not make that effort, we are half-hearted and unstable in the faith, when we might be whole-hearted and strong.

The whole Bible must always be looked at in its two complementary aspects of *Unity* as a *Divine* Book on the one hand, and *Diversity* as a *Human* Book on the other.

Observe (*a*) *Unity of Authorship*. Throughout God speaks, and He changeth not (James i. 17). The same Lord who said to Adam, "Thou shalt not eat of it" (Gen. ii. 17), said to S. John, "Fear not" (Rev. i. 17). But very different was the knowledge of the Apostle from that of our first father. From Eden to Patmos, God's revelation of Himself was gradual, as men were able to bear it (John xvi. 12; 1 Cor. iii. 2). "Truth is one, and right is ever one," sings Edmund Spenser; but humanity, educated by God, is ever making progress, and so His teaching, though one, was not uniform. From age to age there was a continuous advance, not from less to more true, but from simple to complex manifestations of truth, each of which must therefore be considered in connexion with its own period. And though the Canon was closed 1800 years ago, the Bible is a book of progress still, for its meaning can never be exhausted. Its Divine Author still leads us into all the truth, and each generation may learn more from its pages than the last. Many things are clearer to the average Christian of to-day than to the most enlightened Christian of bygone times, as those of us who read the religious books of the remote past know well.

(*b*) *Unity of Time*. Its history covers 3700 years, but

is most unequally distributed over that period. More than 2000 years is compressed into nine chapters of Genesis; while the 40 years from 1491 to 1451 fills more than 140 chapters; the 48 years from 1064 to 1016 fills more than 130 chapters; the week of our Lord's Passion fills 25 chapters; the last 15 years of S. Paul's life 100 chapters, reckoning his Epistles.

(c) *Unity of Place.* Find on the globe Rome, the Black Sea, the Persian Gulf, and Sinai. The area enclosed by a curved line drawn through these four places is the scene of the whole Biblical history. By far the greatest part of it is concerned wholly with a little strip of coast, scarcely 140 miles long, between Sidon and Gaza.

(d) *Unity of Subject.* The Bible is not a history of the world, but of God's Kingdom on earth, and of His testaments or covenants (see 2 Cor. iii. 6, 14, R.V. margin) with a Chosen People whom He called, redeemed, and trained, in order that He might come to them bringing full salvation. The Old Covenant was with Israel in anticipation of His first coming; the New Covenant is with the Church in anticipation of His second coming.

Hence the structure of the Old Testament corresponds throughout to that of the New Testament. In each we have (1) God's Revelation and Covenant. See *Pentateuch* and *Gospels*. (2) What was therefore done, *i.e.*, History. See *Joshua to Esther* and *Acts*. (3) What was therefore taught, *i.e.*, Doctrine. See *Job to Malachi* and *Romans to Revelation*. The curse which closes the Old Testament (Mal. iv. 6) passes into the blessing which closes the New Testament (Rev. xxii. 21). Moreover "the New Testament is latent in the Old Testament; the Old Testament is laid open in the New Testament." Each is the necessary complement of the other, and we cannot neglect the Old Testament without in the end losing our hold upon the New Testament. This is well brought out in Dr. Saphir's " Christ and the Scriptures" (Morgan & Scott, 1s. 6d.).

The Old Testament is the Divine introduction to the New Testament. Israel's history is the key to the history of the whole world; and since it is typical throughout of the history of the Church, it has a peculiar application to ourselves (1 Cor. x. 11).

The Scriptures have one theme, for they refer to one Person. Throughout "they contain the display of His excellences, and are the lively picture of His matchless beauty" (*Archbishop Leighton*).

The whole subject of the inspiration of the Bible is handled in a very helpful way in the first chapter of Dr. Westcott's "Introduction to the Study of the Gospels" (Macmillan, 10s. 6d.).

We turn now to the human side of the Bible, and consider its diversity.

(*a*) *Diversity of Authorship.* "The Bible is authoritative, for it is the Voice of God; it is intelligible, for it is in the language of man." Its authors were *penmen*, not mere *pens*. The Old Testament contains 39 books, all written in Hebrew (except Ezra iv. 8—vi. 18, vii. 12-26; Jer. x. 11, and Dan. ii. 4—vii. 28, which are in Aramaic), during rather less than 1100 years (1490 to 397), by 26 widely different authors whose names we know (viz., Moses, Samuel, David, Solomon, Asaph, Heman, Ethan, Agur, Ezra, Nehemiah, and the sixteen Prophets), and doubtless by others also. The New Testament contains 27 books, all written in Greek, during rather less than 50 years, by nine authors, viz., SS. Matthew, Mark, Luke, John, Paul, Peter, James, Jude, and the author of Hebrews. With the possible exception of S. Luke's two books, it was all written *by* Israelites, though not *for* Israelites only.

Questions too complex to be entered upon fully here have recently arisen as to the date and authorship of various portions of the Bible. That, for instance, Deuteronomy was *written*, not merely *discovered*, in the reign of Josiah; that the second part of Isaiah is from the hand of a much later prophet than the first, are hypotheses fascinating to some minds. But they are only hypotheses, not proved facts, and wider knowledge has frequently overthrown hypotheses which seemed equally plausible. The arguments in favour of the earlier dates assigned for generations to these books are so strong that, until more convincing evidence than any as yet brought forward can be given for setting those dates aside, the most accurate and judicious scholars hesitate to treat such hypotheses as if they belonged to the region of knowledge and not of conjecture.

We must avoid on the one hand rash assumption that traditional views are wrong; and on the other hand equally rash assumption that all traditional views can hold their own. That Job is a contemporary biography, or that Joshua was written by him whose name it bears, is neither proved nor provable; in either case it is possible, but not probable, and the question is not of vital importance. That all the four Gospels were written before the end of the first Christian century, and are therefore contemporary biography, has in our own days been established upon evidence to which our fathers had no access, and to this question the gravest issues belong.

(*b*) *Diversity of Method.* More and more clearly from age to age God has made known to man His truth by history, type, prophecy, sign, vision, and parable, " by divers portions and in divers manners" (Heb. i. 1, R.V.). The Bible may be the history of one nation only, but that, as the one unmingled race of high antiquity, has the most persistent of nationalities, and the longest of histories, and is connected with almost every other important nation in the world.

Nowadays it is said in some quarters that the Bible is in peril from " Higher Criticism," and certain good people, whose piety is greater than their intelligence, echo the assertion, and deprecate criticism altogether. The faith of unstable souls is indeed in peril from a criticism that errs in not being high enough. But from criticism of the right kind the Bible has everything to gain, and if we are wise we shall read it in the fullest light our own age can throw upon it. Ignorance, not knowledge, is the real foe; and just as the Church gains fresh strength in times of persecution, so Holy Writ wins fresh appreciation in times when it is being tried (Psalm cxix. 140, R.V. margin). For when unassailed, it is also in great measure unstudied; whereas the labours of scholars in various departments have lately, as never before, shown the unity and beauty of its literary structure, and the minute accuracy of its historical narratives. And when we cease to read into it what it does not say, and clearly ascertain what it does say, we discover again and again that its statements are in harmony with the latest results of scientific research.

Moreover, living in days of worldwide missionary effort and worldwide missionary success, we can assert as the Christians of past times could not assert, that the Bible, written in a remote age and an obscure country, has proved its Divine origin by its power to win human hearts of every race and to transform human lives in every clime as no other book ever did or ever could do. S. T. Coleridge, that profound thinker, says that for him the most convincing proof of its Divine origin is that it finds him at deeper depths of his being than any other book. These are matters that claim our earnest consideration. For in the near future (I quote Bishop Phillips Brooks, preaching from Matt. xxii. 37, on "The Mind's Love for God") "there will be an ever-increasing demand for thoughtful saints; for men and women, earnest, lofty, spiritual, but also full of intelligence, knowing the meaning and the reasons of the things they believe, and not content to worship the God to whom they owe everything with less than their whole nature."

By the Word we are quickened, that is, made alive (Psalm cxix. 50), by it we grow (1 Peter ii. 2), by it we become strong (1 John ii. 14). There is no surer sign of bodily sickness than lack of appetite for wholesome food. There is no surer sign of spiritual sickness than lack of appetite for that which is sweeter than honey (Psalm xix. 10; Jer. xv. 16; Ezek. iii. 1-3). Does the Christian life seem unreal? Is the Christian faith beset with difficulties amid the conflict of human opinions and the clatter of controversies and arguments? Is this your bewildered query concerning the Son of God, as concerning a Being, awful, distant, vague, "Who is He that I may believe on Him?" (John ix. 36).

"Have ye not read?" (Matt. xix. 4), "Understandest thou what thou readest?" (Acts viii. 30). Take comfort in the knowledge that all may read and all may understand, for all who ask may have the guidance of Him through whom the Scripture not only *was* but *is* inspired to be the living and life-giving Word for every age and every race (Luke xi. 13; James i. 5).

The Chronological Scripture Cycle.

FIRST TERM.
The Days of the Patriarchs.

The Chosen Family. B.C. 4004—1490. *From the Creation to the erection of the Tabernacle* . . . . p. 19.

SECOND TERM.
The Days of Moses.

The Chosen Nation. The Tabernacle and the Theocracy. B.C. 1490—1256. *From the erection of the Tabernacle to the Midianite Oppression* p. 39.

THIRD TERM.
The Days of David.

The Chosen Nation under one King. B.C. 1256—1018. *From the Midianite Oppression to the choice of a site for the Temple* . . . p. 60.

FOURTH TERM.
The Days of Solomon.

The Chosen Nation Centre of an Empire. The First Temple. B.C. 1018—915. *From the choice of a site for the Temple to the accessions of Jehoshaphat and Ahab* . . . . p. 78.

FIFTH TERM.
The Days of the Prophets.

Decline and Fall of the Kingdom of the Ten Tribes. B.C. 915—697. *From the accessions of Jehoshaphat and Ahab to the death of Hezekiah* p. 95.

SIXTH TERM.
The Days of Jeremiah.

Decline and Fall of the Kingdom of Judah. B.C. 697—588. *From the death of Hezekiah to the Fall of Jerusalem* . . . . p. 118.

SEVENTH TERM.
The Days of Ezra.

The Restoration and the Second Temple. B.C. 606—397. *From the Fall of Jerusalem to the close of the Old Testament Canon* . . p. 138.

EIGHTH TERM.
The Days of the Son of Man.

The Gospel preached to the Jews. B.C. 6—A.D. 51. *From the coming of Christ to the Conference at Jerusalem* . . . . p. 213.

NINTH TERM.
The Days of S. Paul.

The Gospel preached to the Gentiles. A.D. 51—97. *From the Conference at Jerusalem to the close of the New Testament Canon* . . p. 278.

GENERAL PLAN

OF THE

CHRONOLOGICAL SCRIPTURE CYCLE.

DIVIDING the Bible, which contains 1189 chapters, into nine portions of about 132 chapters each, we read it through in 3 years, 36 months, 1095 days, or nine terms of four months, taking one chapter a day and an extra chapter in the course of every 12 days.

The section for each term is headed by (*a*) A title showing the main subject of the term's reading; (*b*) The dates marking off its period of history; (*c*) The names of the books and parts of books to be read; (*d*) A motto for the Bible student, taken from these books; (*e*) A tabular scheme of the term's reading. It consists of nine chapters, each of which may be read either in connexion with the rest of the section or with the corresponding chapters of the other sections: that is, either historically or topically, as we divide the Bible into nine successive sections, or take a ninefold view of it from beginning to end.

"Clews to Holy Writ" is not a commentary to be merely read through, but a series of suggestions which mean little for those who do not work each out for themselves, studying every section closely and constantly, and looking up all passages referred to.

The chapters in each section are as follows :—

I. GENERAL SUMMARY, gathering up the threads of our story, and ascertaining the main events and most striking lessons of our period as we glance backwards and forwards.

II. BOOKS TO BE READ, indicating their literary characteristics and keynotes, and marking off from the *history* which relates the *action* of the period, the *poetry* which utters its best *thought*. We do not read the Bible only for the intellectual enjoyment of its many literary charms, but we shall enter into its higher aspects all the better for not ignoring these.

III. PERIODS AND DATES.—Here we arrange the order of our reading in detail, and map out our whole period into forty well-defined shorter epochs. Where exact dates are out of the question, approximate dates are given, and here and there we disregard the actual order of time in order to round off an important subject. Very numerous careful statements of hours, days, weeks, and years in Holy Writ show the importance attributed to chronology by its writers.

IV. GEOGRAPHY.—Here we connect each chapter of history with particular places, whose physical characteristics are swiftly sketched.

V. HEROES.—The biographical interest of any period centres round the makers of its history. We are apt to think of Bible characters as mere abstractions rather than "men of like passions with us." Hence we must endeavour to realise the individualities of those who long years ago strove with the power of evil and were strong in the grace of God, that we may take to ourselves the practical lessons of their lives, which will be given as a rule through New Testament quotations for the first seven, and Old Testament quotations for the last two terms.

VI. THE COMING MESSIAH.—It has been well said that the best key to the mystery of the written Word is the mystery of the Incarnate Word. So, beginning at Moses, we trace the dominant theme of the Bible (Luke xxiv. 27), its one great Hope of ever-growing brightness, brought at each crisis in the providential history of the world within narrower limits, and illustrated by fresh details. There are two kinds of Messianic prophecy.

(*a*) *Types*, or prophecies in picture or action. "Type" means "likeness," and Scripture types are "likenesses" of good things to come, or earthly shadows of heavenly substances. We discriminate typical (1) Persons—*e.g.*, Moses; (2) Things—*e.g.*, Manna; (3) Ordinances—*e.g.*, the Day of Atonement; (4) Offices—*e.g.*, Prophet, Priest, and King; (5) Events—*e.g.*, the Exodus; (6) Acts—*e.g.*, the burial of Jeremiah's girdle. These last are often called Signs. Observe, that although we may use types to illustrate and confirm doctrines, we cannot prove doctrines from them; also that search for new and far-fetched types often leads us astray. There are quite enough unmistakable ones to afford study for our whole lives. Here again the Bible is its own best explanation.

(*b*) *Predictions*, or prophecies in words or speech, which are either (1) Direct, *i.e.*, referring only to Christ (*e.g.*, Zech. ix. 9); (2) Indirect, having a primary historical fulfilment in some one who partially realised what Christ realised wholly (*e.g.*, Psalm lxxii.). "While the words of the Psalms and Prophecies not only admit of, but even demand, germinant and springing developments, they are primarily applicable to events and circumstances of their own days" (*Calvin*). Their ultimate fulfilments grow out of primary fulfilments which it must be our first business to understand, but neither contradict nor supersede them.

These Predictions fall into three classes—viz., those fulfilled at the first Advent, those to be fulfilled at the second Advent, and those that have a double fulfilment in both.

The evidence of miracle is strongest in the age when the miracle is wrought; the evidence of prophecy is strongest in the age most remote from its utterance. Yet even the earliest Christian apologists appeal, especially in argument with Jews, to prophecy rather than miracle (see Blunt's "Christian Church of the First Three Centuries," chap. vii.). For us the progress of events, and the greatly increased knowledge of the past now possessed, give the prophetic aspect of Scripture a special importance. But we must remember that Predictions are not mere adjuncts of revelation, attached to it from without, in order to prove it to us, but essential parts of it. The Scripture record is nearly always twofold. The Prophet looks forward, and says, "It shall be," ere the Historian looks backward and says, "It was" (comp. Gen. xv. 13, 14 with Exodus). Its Prophecy is History anticipated, its History is Prophecy fulfilled; but while its History ceases 1800 years ago, its Prophecy looks on to the end of the world.

In our eighth term we open the New Testament as if

we had never opened it before, to discover how far the Messiah of History realises, and how far He transcends, the Messiah of Prophecy whom we have learned to know. "And by the title of Christ or Messiah, so slowly defined, so variously interpreted, so gloriously fulfilled, God teaches us to find the true meaning of all history, teaches us at all times to wait, to watch, to hope" (*Westcott*).

VII. GOD'S REVELATION OF HIMSELF TO MAN.— "Revelation is not the sum of the happiest guesses, or wisest observations and reflections, which devout and thoughtful men have made regarding God ; but it is the sum of what God Himself has imparted to the minds of men to guide and rule their thoughts about Him" (*Dr. Marcus Dods*). Man seeking God is the origin of other religions. God seeking man is the origin of the Christian religion. Slowly and gradually, as we shall see, did God make Himself known by new Names and new dealings with men. Yet our revelation of "the glory of the Eternal Trinity" is not only in harmony with, but was dimly adumbrated by, the earliest manifestations of the God of Israel.

VIII. MAN'S RELATION TO GOD IN WORSHIP.—The history of religion is the history of man's response to these manifestations. This will lead us through Sacrifice and Prayer in their most general form, to the Mosaic Ritual, the Tabernacle, the two Temples, and the organisation of the Church. Here too we notice the ever-recurring tendency to some form of idolatry.

For the first two terms illustrative passages are indicated. After this we come to periods fully elucidated by contemporary Psalms. In the later sections we note how sacred history is corroborated by secular history.

IX. THIRTY-TWO QUESTIONS.—These are not intended as a test of memory at the end of the term's reading, but of observation and thought from day to day. Many of them are planned to suggest topics and modes of research. At first sight they may seem full of unknown things, but though some are more difficult than others, the most difficult are less difficult than they appear. That they demand care and accuracy rather than much previous knowledge has been proved by the following fact. In our classes, although the best papers are always sent in by those who take the most pains, they are not always sent in by those who have had most educational advantages.

Every examination paper follows out the term's reading in order, and winds up with some questions glancing through the whole of it. Early in each term, those Students of the College by Post who have sent in answers to the questions of last term receive the loan of a MS. containing the complete Answers to compare with their own and copy. They thus get the full benefit of the questions they were not successful over themselves as well as the benefit of having their work corrected by our teachers. These Answers are not always exactly in the same form as those expected from students. A mere reference sometimes stands for the statement asked for, and in order to supply information not readily accessible to students, explanations or quotations are added in other cases to the actual reply.

The figure at the end of each question represents the marks to be gained by answering it completely. The maximum of marks for each term's paper is 400, and for all the nine papers, 3600.

Most of those who have been through the C.S.C. once wish to go through it again. At their request a second series of questions and answers more advanced than the first has been prepared (see p. 309). These should in no case be attempted until the first series has been worked out.

Some of those who have found the C.S.C. course useful and stimulating are helping me to form a Prize Fund, by means of which we are able to reward those of our students who work out all the nine papers well. Those who obtain over 3000 marks choose as a First Class prize a book or books to the value of 10s. 6d.; those who obtain over 2400 marks choose a Second Class prize to the value of 7s. 6d.; and those who obtain over 1800 marks choose a Third Class prize to the value of 5s.

The names of prize-winners are published in my annual Letter to our Students.

Over 100 students have already won these rewards, and the number promises to increase steadily. Possibly some readers of "Clews to Holy Writ" who are independent of such aid as our classes give, and desire to encourage systematic Bible study, may feel kindly disposed to contribute towards these hardly earned and greatly appreciated prizes.

Let me conclude with twelve practical suggestions to C.S.C. students, and to others who adopt the C.S.C. scheme. I will word them abruptly for the sake of brevity.

What we read. . . . . Heb. iv. 12; 2 Peter i. 20, 21.
Why we read . . . . Luke i. 4; 2 Tim. iii. 16, 17.
How we should read. . . { Acts xvii. 11; Prov. ii. 4, 5; 1 Cor. ii. 13; James i. 21; 1 Thess. ii. 13.

We must (Critically,   *in order to know* What to Believe.
 read { Devotionally   "   "   Whom to Love.
the Bible (Practically   "   "   How to Live.

I. Provide yourself with the following books :—
(*a*) The Authorised Version of the Bible, with references.
(*b*) The Revised Version, which may now be had for tenpence. This is most helpful to the student, not only because of its greater accuracy and marginal information, but also in discriminating poetry from prose, and substituting for the little "verses" that are so largely responsible for the "collection of texts" view of Scripture, a first-rate system of paragraphs. Read the two prefaces to it carefully.

Look out the A.V. references, and study the daily chapter in both A.V. and R.V. Striking differences between them might be underlined in the latter.

(*c*) Helps to the Study of the Bible (Frowde, Clarendon Press, 1*s*. and 3*s*. 6*d*.). This you need not get if you already have "The Oxford Bible for Teachers." It is referred to here as "Oxford Helps."

Those who wish for more books will find the following useful :—
(*a*) "The Bible Handbook," by Dr. Angus (Religious Tract Society, 5*s*.).
(*b*) The Student's Old Testament History and The Student's New Testament History (each 7*s*. 6*d*., Murray).
(*c*) Concise Dictionary of the Bible, 21*s*., or smaller Bible Dictionary, by Dr. Smith, 7*s*. 6*d*. (Murray), or Cassell's Bible Dictionary, 7*s*. 6*d*.

(*d*) Student's Edition of the Speaker's Commentary, in six volumes (7*s*. 6*d*. each, Murray).

(*e*) Bishop Ellicott's Commentary for English Readers, in eight volumes (21*s*. each, Cassell).

(*f*) A good Concordance, say Eadie's Cruden.

But unless you can give much more than half an hour a day to C.S.C., you will find your whole time occupied by right use of the three books named as absolutely necessary, and of "Clews to Holy Writ." A single chapter will claim more and more of your time with growing interest and knowledge. If you not only "read," but "mark, learn, and inwardly digest" (four distinct processes), you will probably feel inclined to diminish rather than increase the quantity of your reading as you improve its quality.

II. Pray daily ere you read your chapter, in such words as Psalm xxv. 4, 5, or Psalm cxix. 18, or Eph. i. 17-19, for the Holy Spirit's aid. Could we have greater help towards understanding a difficult book than the power of speaking constantly with its author?

Pray also after you have read, for every precept may be turned into petition, and every promise into praise.

"Young men," Professor Beck of Tübingen used to say to his students, "let me remind you that theology without the Holy Spirit is not only a cold stone, but absolute poison."

III. Mark one striking text in each chapter, and look at yesterday's marked text ere you begin to-day's reading. There are many advantages in using always one copy of the Bible, so mark it neatly or you may regret not having done so hereafter.

IV. Find for each Old Testament chapter a New Testament quotation or allusion or precept or illustration. The references will help you here.

V. Ask daily after you have read your chapter, "What does it teach me concerning (*a*) God, (*b*) Man, (*c*) Christ, who is the Son of God, the very image of God's substance as the Incarnate God; who is the Son of Man, made like unto His brethren in all things as the Divine Man?" Ask also what practical lessons you may gain from it for your own daily life. Treat the Bible as a matchless temple, wherein we may increase our awe and excite our devotion to God (I quote Robert Boyle's fine simile). For we suffer great spiritual loss when we regard it merely as an arsenal for weapons of defence and offence; when we only take our own views to it for confirmation and other people's views to it for condemnation. Controversy is both easier and more exciting than humble search for truth, and therefore it pervades so much of the so-called "religious" writing and talking of the day. But if we would really benefit by the study of God's Word, we must, as Bible readers, avoid this spirit of contention altogether.

Of the three kinds of study indicated in the table above, "Clews to Holy Writ" deals mainly with Critical study, not because we regard it as the most important, but because the Bible must appeal to the intelligence ere it can appeal to the heart and will. Critical study is a means to a higher end which we do not ignore, but lead up to—viz., those Devotional and Practical applications of our study in which others can help us least, since we must each of us make them for ourselves, if they are to be worth anything.

VI. Commit to memory at the rate of one or two verses a day, some specially beautiful and important passages in the term's reading. We cannot store up what we take in too carefully, since we know not how soon we may be called upon to give it out.

VII. The C.S.C. scheme is not meant to be tried for a term or two, but to be followed throughout. Hence all should begin at the beginning, and do each month's reading in the month and each term's in the term. If one term's work is interrupted, another term should be given to it, as it is far better to extend the whole course over more than three years than to break the continuous chain of study; for each section takes all the preceding sections for granted and is closely linked with the following sections. The tabular schemes should be used throughout together with the chapters headed "Periods and Dates." As the course is planned for *any* three years, particular months cannot be considered, but since three years contain thirty-six months, and the Bible contains 1189 chapters, the average number of chapters read each month will be $\frac{1189}{36} = 33$, as shown in the arabic numerals on the tabular schemes. A second chapter can be read on any day that there is more time and when the first chapter is very short or a mere list of names.

VIII. Set up a note book or a sheaf of loose sheets fastened at the corner, for working out subjects as you read, and accumulating material for answers to the questions, which should be before you throughout the term.

IX. Towards the end of the term, begin to prepare a fair copy of your answers. Boiling down several pages of notes into a few lines of terse and concentrated information is a most instructive process. Let it become familiar to you, for you will lighten your teachers' work not a little by sending them concise, clearly arranged, and clearly written answers instead of diffuse and confused ones.

X. Answer some questions if you cannot answer all, and remember that since no answer can win more than maximum marks, nothing is gained by giving *more* than you are asked for. Write on both sides of the paper, leaving a margin, and number your answers in the margin. Give your name and address at the end of your paper. It will be corrected if it reaches your teacher at the time appointed.

XI. Remember (1) That if the chapter is difficult, the difficulties will probably disappear as you read on. There are few which cannot be traced, if we are honest, either to Prejudice, Presumption, Ignorance, or Carelessness. "When two texts contradict one another, a third will be found to reconcile them," was the helpful rule of the Rabbi Ishmael. (2. That if the chapter seems barren, your Biblical knowledge and spiritual insight is still imperfect, and also that forced applications are a fruitful cause of errors. (3) That to the reader of devout heart and holy life God reveals what is hidden from mere ability and learning (John vii. 17, Matt. v. 8).

XII. Finally, will you pray for all who are following this scheme that to them, as well as to you, the C.S.C. may be not only an intellectual interest, but a means of growth in grace and in the knowledge of our Lord and Saviour Jesus Christ?

FIRST TERM.

THE DAYS OF THE PATRIARCHS
THE CHOSEN FAMILY.

B.C. 4004—1490.

Genesis. Job. Exodus. (132 *chapters.*)

"Moses took the book of the covenant, and read in the audience of the people."—EXOD. xxiv. 7.

1st MONTH (33).
    Genesis I.—XXXIII.

2nd MONTH (33).
    Genesis XXXIV.—L.
    Job I.—XVI.

3rd MONTH (33).
    Job XVII.—XLII.
    Exodus I.—VII.

4th MONTH (33).
    Exodus VIII.—XL.

I. GENERAL SUMMARY.

THE keynote of Gen. i. is *God said.* As regards Nature, His will is fully carried out (Psalm xxxiii. 9).

The keynote of Gen. iii. is *Hath God said?* As regards Man, His will is thwarted (Eccles. vii. 29). Gen. iii. 17-19 is the declaration, not of a threat or of an arbitrary punishment, but of an inevitable result, brought about by man himself, and working in accordance with God's great natural laws. Far heavier would have been the doom of living on for ever, sinful and idle.

The rest of the Bible unfolds the Divine plan whereby God's purpose is notwithstanding accomplished, and man redeemed. Throughout God calls, tests, and chooses for special privilege not Cain, but Abel; not the rest of mankind, but Noah's family; not Japhet the elder, but Shem the younger (Gen. x. 21, ix. 26); not the eldest brother Haran's son, but the younger brother Abraham (Isa.

li. 2); not Ishmael, but Isaac; not Esau, but Jacob; not Reuben, but Joseph (1 Chron. v. 1, 2); not Manasseh, but Ephraim (Gen. xlviii.); not Aaron, but Moses (Exod. iv. 16); not Nadab and Abihu, but Eleazar (Num. xx. 28).

From the whole race God chose one family, whose training is described in Genesis. When it had suffered so severely that it had become utterly helpless, God sent a twofold message through Moses; to Israel, a promise, "I will deliver you," which was received with faith and worship; to Pharaoh, a command, "Let My people go," signified by (1) Word, (2) Signs, (3) Judgments; and received with (1) Scornful refusal, (2) Defiant imitation, (3) Unwilling recognition of the Divine power, and notwithstanding continued hardness of heart (Job xxxiii. 14; Isa. xxvi. 9). Then God brought that family from Africa to Asia; from the garden of Egypt to the desert of Sinai; from slavery to freedom; and not only a great nation, but "History itself was born on that night when Moses led forth his countrymen from the land of Goshen" (*Bunsen*).

This chosen nation (Deut. vii. 6; Amos iii. 2; Rom. ix. 3, 4) were not the substitutes for, but the representatives of, all mankind. They were not blessed merely for their own sake, so their national history, unlike any other national history, is of interest and importance for all the world.

II. Books to be Read.

(See "Oxford Helps," § v.)

This term we read one great poem, and two of the historical books of Moses, which contain four archaic fragments of Hebrew verse and two magnificent odes—viz.,

(*a*) Lamech's Sword-song (Gen. iv. 23, 24).

(*b*) Noah's Prophecy concerning his sons, an epitome of universal history (Gen. ix. 25-7).

(*c*) Jehovah's Prophecy concerning Rebekah's sons, an epitome of Israel's history (Gen. xxv. 23).

(*d*) Isaac's Prophecy concerning his sons, an amplification of (*c*) (Gen. xxvii. 27-9, 39, 40).

(*e*) Jacob's Benediction, giving the destinies of the Twelve Tribes (Gen. xlix.).

(*f*) Moses' Song of Victory, in three stanzas, the grandest national hymn ever sung to the glory of Jehovah and to liberty, and the first specimen of responsive choral music (Exod. xv. 1-18).

Genesis is not only the oldest complete book in the world, its earlier chapters appear to embody records far more ancient than Moses, going back to the very beginning of human history (Luke i. 70). About these there is nothing distinctively Hebrew, their simplicity of treatment and subject belongs to the dawn of civilisation, and they have interesting features in common with the earliest Egyptian and Chaldean literature. It is not, however, a mere compilation of old annals, but a religious history, whose unity and symmetry show that it was penned throughout with a definite design. Genesis falls into twelve natural divisions beginning Gen. i. 1, ii. 4, v. 1, vi. 9, x. 1, xi. 10, xi. 27, xxv. 12, xxv. 19, xxxvi. 1, xxxvi. 9, and xxxvii. 2, all save the first headed by " These are the generations [*i.e.*, "offspring": comp. Matt. iii. 7, A.V. and R.V.] of——." The first five portions refer to General, and the last seven to Church History; and their relative lengths are very significant. Its keynote is *Called and chosen* (Matt. xxii. 14; 1 Peter iii. 9).

Job, undoubtedly an historical character, probably lived before Moses, as his patriarchal length of days indicates; and after Abraham, since his friends refer to the destruction of Sodom. The question whether the Book of Job is a veracious record of his actual words, brought by Moses from Midian, or a truthful general picture of his character and life, shaped by a poet of Solomon's age and made the groundwork of a lesson for all time, does not affect its canonicity. All Scripture is divinely inspired and true in the highest sense. But its loftiest truths are clothed not in the barely literal, but in the poetical form that contemplates everything in its permanent and typical aspect. Whatever view we take of the date and authorship of Job, we read it now to fill the century that divides Gen. l. from Exod. i.; because it illustrates individual before we pass to national religion, the Patriarchal before we pass to the Mosaic age, God's dealings with a Gentile before we pass to His dealings with Israel. Its keynote is *Fear the Almighty and Incomprehensible; Trust the All-Wise and All-Loving*

(Rom. xi. 33, viii. 28, v. 3, 4). Natural instinct, strengthened by simple faith in God, connects happiness with goodness. Obedience to God's law must lead to the blessedness He means His creatures to enjoy. This is our *first thought*, exemplified in the speeches of Job's friends and in Psalm i. Experience of the imperfections and contradictions of life shows that too often the wicked prosper and the righteous suffer. How then can God be all-wise, all-powerful, and all-loving? This is our *second thought*, and this is what Satan tempted Job to think. Mature conviction, growing out of closer study of God's law and man's nature, teaches us that through man's free-will the mysterious power of evil makes exceptions to God's law, which is a general law connecting goodness and happiness. This is our *third thought*, and third thoughts are best and truest. We may go on to say concerning these exceptions:—

(1) God's ways are past our comprehension, but we have good cause to believe that His wisdom, power, and love are infinite. This is the answer to the problem given in Job.

(2) In the next life all wrong will be completely redressed. This answer is suggested in Psalm lxxiii.

(3) The righteous may not be happy, but they are blessed even in the midst of sorrow.

> "Ill that Thou blessest is our good,
> And unblest good is ill;
> And all is right that seems most wrong,
> If it be Thy sweet will."—*Faber*.

This answer is suggested in Psalm xvii. 14, 15. In the Fourth Term we shall have a striking example of "unblest good," and in the Seventh and Ninth Terms of "blest ill." But these two last answers could not be fully worked out until after the anguish of the Cross and the glory of the Resurrection. Job remains true as one solution, no longer the only solution, of the problem.

It falls into five sections:—

(*a*) i.—ii. Prose Prologue stating the Problem concerning Affliction. The trouble and temptation of unproved Job.

(*b*) iii.—xxxi. Discussion of the Problem from the human point of view, by Job who regards Affliction as an unfathomable mystery ("Wherefore hidest Thou Thy face?" xiii. 24); and by his three friends who, as dogged defenders of the traditional popular belief, regard Affliction as a punishment for sin ("Who ever perished, being innocent?" iv. 7).

(c) xxxii.—xxxvii. Exposition of the Problem from the point of view of one divinely enlightened, by Elihu who regards Affliction as a merciful discipline for our instruction ("God, who teacheth us more than the beasts," xxxv. 11).

(d) xxxviii.—xlii. 6. Solution of the Problem by Jehovah Himself, who shows that Affliction is a test of integrity towards and trust in Him ("Though He slay me yet will I wait for Him," xiii. 15, is followed by "My servant Job . . . him will I accept," xlii. 8).

(e) xlii. 7-17. Prose Epilogue. The blessing of proved and trustful Job.

Exodus continues Genesis, begins the national history of Israel, and contains the first portion of the Mosaic Law. Its keynote is *Redeemed of the Lord* (Luke i. 68; 1 Peter i. 18, 19; Gal. iv. 4, 5).

According to a continuous stream of credible testimony from the earliest days of Israel's history, we have attributed the Pentateuch to the fifteenth century before Christ, and no book has had more external evidence to its authorship. One school of modern critics, however, professing to be guided by internal evidence, declares that its account of the Creation is unscientific, and contradicts facts ascertained by recent investigations; that its records are legendary; and that instead of being contemporary history, it is a compilation made many centuries after Moses. We cannot enter into the question at length, but one or two suggestions may be made in passing.

(1) It is one thing to have a reasonable faith, another to be able to answer all the hard questions concerning it that could be asked.

(2) If, as regards isolated passages, there are difficulties in believing the Bible to be a Divine and human book, there are still more serious difficulties in believing it to be a merely human book as a whole, which is the alternative.

(3) Gen. i. was not intended to satisfy the scientific

curiosity of the learned few, but to instruct the mass of mankind, for whom it would have been utterly unintelligible had it been written in technical scientific terms.

(4) When the exact translation is ascertained, and the rash interpretations of prejudiced opponents of the faith and also of half-learned apologists for it are swept away, this oldest of all books proves to be almost the only non-scientific book in the world that does not contain one incorrect statement about natural facts; while at the same time it accounts for things that science confesses itself unable to account for. See Liddon's "Elements of Religion," Lecture II. (Longmans, 1s. 6d.).

(5) Geology shows that the general order of the Creation must have been that of Gen. i.

(6) Ethnology points to the Euphrates Valley as the probable cradle of the race, and traces its dispersion thence under conditions entirely compatible with those described in Genesis.

(7) Archæology proves, from records of the past long hidden, but now uncovered in many unexpected ways and places, the minute accuracy of the Biblical description of ancient Egypt.

(8) The Ordnance Survey of the Sinaitic Peninsula examined, some 25 years ago, the geography of the Exodus and the Wanderings, demonstrating that the story in the Pentateuch could only have been written by a contemporary and eye witness.

(9) Many converging arguments show that it is not only possible but probable that the Deluge took place.

Before all this positive evidence of an early date, ingenious speculations as to a late date based mainly on linguistic considerations that may be entirely fallacious, do not look very satisfactory. To those who wish to pursue these subjects further, I recommend Sir J. W. Dawson's "Modern Science in Bible Lands" (Hodder & Stoughton, 6s.), the work of an eminent scientist who speaks with authority; and I know of no more profound or masterly treatment of the relation of modern science to revelation as a whole, than "Can the Old Faith live with the New?" by Dr. George Matheson, of Edinburgh (Blackwood, 7s. 6d.).

III. Periods and Dates.

The whole history of the human race, now nearly 6000 years of age, may be divided into three great periods according to three successive phases of God's dealings with man. Each is about 2000 years long.

(*a*) *The Patriarchal Dispensation*, or Probation of all men under the Law of Conscience, during which God manifested His Power. B.C. 4004 to 1921, from Adam to Abraham (Gal. iii. 16), 2083 years.

(*b*) *The Jewish Dispensation*, or Probation of one Chosen People under the Law of Moses, during which God manifested His Righteousness. B.C. 1921 to A.D. 70, from Abraham to the Fall of Jerusalem, 1990 years.

(*c*) *The Christian Dispensation*, or " Times of the Gentiles " (Luke xxi. 24), under the Law of Christ, during which God manifests His Love. A.D. 70 onwards.

Some would, however, bring (*a*) down to 1491, *i.e.*, to Moses (see Rom. v. 13, 14), and would date (*c*) from B.C. 625, *i.e.*, from the founding of the Babylonian Empire, the first of the mighty Gentile powers that prepared Christ's way. In this case (*b*) overlaps both (*a*) and (*c*).

The scanty records of the 2514 years we study this term leave its chronology uncertain. Here we follow the commonly received dates as given in " Oxford Helps," § vii.

430 years (*i.e.*, 1921—1491) is spoken of in Exod. xii. 40, 41, as the whole period of the sojourning or pilgrimage of the Chosen Family, during which Abraham and his children were homeless wanderers. S. Paul reckons 430 years (Gal. iii. 17) from the promise given in Ur to the law given at Sinai. Rather more than 400 years elapsed between the vision of Gen. xv. (which foreshadowed the whole history of Israel) and the Exodus (Gen. xv. 13 ; Acts vii. 6).

(1) B.C. 4004—2348 (1656 years). From the Creation to the Deluge. *Probation of the whole human race.* **Gen. i.—viii.**

(2) B.C. 2348—1921 (427 years). From the Deluge to the Call of Abraham. *Probation of the descendants of Noah.* **Gen. ix.—xi.**

(3) B.C. 1921—1491 (430 years). From the Call of

Abraham to the Exodus. *Probation of the Chosen Family.*
  (*a*) 1921—1706 (215 years). The Sojourning in Canaan. **Gen. xii.—xlv.**
  (*b*) 1706—1491 (215 years). The Sojourning in Egypt. **Gen. xlvi.—l.; Job; Exod. i.—xii.**
(4) B.C. 1491—1490 (one year). From the Exodus to the erection of the Tabernacle. *Redemption of the Chosen People.*
  (*a*) From Passover to Pentecost, 1491 (seven weeks). The great Deliverances. **Exod. xiii.—xviii.**
  (*b*) From Pentecost 1491, to Passover, 1490 (10 months and 10 days). The Revelation at Sinai. **Exod. xix.—xl.**

IV. GEOGRAPHY.

(See "Oxford Helps," Maps I., II., III., IV., and VIII., and §§ ix., xxx.)

Geology demonstrates that before the Deluge a considerable portion of what is now the Persian Gulf was land. Immediately after the Deluge, a considerable portion of what is now land was swallowed up by the Persian Gulf. Through this once high and well-wooded, then submerged, and now low and marshy country, flows a broad tide, fed by four great rivers—viz., the Euphrates; the Hiddekel, or Tigris; the Gihon, or Choaspes, watering not the African, but Nimrod's Cush; and the Pishon or Pasitigris rising in mountains rich in mineral products, and descending through a fertile country where the beautiful Persian capital of Shushan (Esth. i. 2) afterwards was (see Map VIII.). Here our story begins, for here (as Sir J. W. Dawson shows in an argument too long to quote) was *Eden*; hither, as to their cradle, Noah's descendants made their way southeastwards (Gen. xi. 2) from the mountains where the Ark grounded; and hence therefore, according to Indian, Persian, and Chaldean tradition, mankind originated. In the plain of Shinar also they built the city whose name runs all through the Bible from Gen. x. to Rev. xviii.

Prof. Sayce identifies Mugheir immediately to the west of

Erech with *Ur* whence Abraham set forth. Others, however, identify Ur with Orfah or Edessa in Mesopotamia, much higher up the river, which an abundant spring and high crag prove even now to have been a well-watered and well-protected place for an early settlement. He went on to *Haran*, the headquarters of Laban's family, whence the two great caravan routes to the Euphrates and Tigris diverge; and then to *Damascus*, the oldest city now existing; and through Palestine (whose geography we take next term) to *Egypt*, a most fertile, thoroughly cultivated, and thickly populated country, which was to the wandering tribes of Asia then what Italy has since been to Gauls and Goths. For it was the home of the earliest civilisation in the world, which archæology traces back beyond B.C. 3000; of a race skilled both in the fine and the mechanical arts, loving nature, honouring women, deeply impressed with the seriousness of life on both sides of the grave, and exercising an influence, whose whole power we are only now beginning to estimate, upon the two nations of antiquity, the Hebrews and the Greeks, to whom we ourselves owe most. The Valley of the Nile (which is the true Egypt) is unlike any other part of the world. It has neither Alpine grandeur nor pastoral softness, nor variety of plain and upland, meadow and forest. Its hills have neither heather nor pine upon them, in its rainless sky there is neither cloud nor mist. The Nile (worshipped as "The Hidden One," because until the middle of this nineteenth century its source was a mystery) rises once a year and covers the whole valley and plain, so that from desert to desert, river and country are one (Amos viii. 8, R.V.). Thus the soil is renewed and fertilised for its three annual harvests. Egypt is the land of light, of glowing sunshine, and of moonshine and starshine so brilliant that night is but a softer day. From the time that Israel's ancestors went down thither, it has drawn men of every clime with a resistless fascination.

From Egypt, the scene of our story shifts to the *Wilderness* (Hos. xi. 1; Jer. ii. 2), not an uninhabited place, for two powerful nations, the Kenites and the Amalekites, were there; but a place wild and desolate, and shut out from the rest of the world. As Israel advanced, the mountains closed round them: they found themselves in an avenue of lofty rocks at the end of which, rising immediately out of the level plain, towered massive Sinai, like a huge altar in a vast sanctuary, whence every form of life, animal and vegetable, was withdrawn. To them the rugged and desolate grandeur of the scene must have suggested that they had reached the end of the world, as they waited there for the revelation of their God.

V. HEROES.

Keynotes
{ *Abraham*, 1 John v. 4.
Joseph, 2 Peter i. 5-7.
Job, James i. 12.

We see in *Abraham* the great Bedouin sheikh, the prince of the desert, leading a vast caravan of servants, flocks, and herds, and wandering homeless for exactly a century in the land promised to his heirs; the saint whose unflinching loyalty won him the title of "God's friend," and who, putting God first in all the relations of life, became also "the father of the faithful": in *Joseph* the able statesman, vicegerent of the greatest monarch of his age, wielding almost absolute power in a highly civilised foreign land, fearing God, and therefore fearing nought else: in *Job* the patriarch dwelling amidst his own people, as father and ruler of a pastoral tribe, proved in the fire of manifold temptations, to the glory of God and the comfort of God's suffering servants in all ages.

The Bible gives us much valuable teaching through contrasted types of character. Besides these almost perfect heroes we have the mixed character of *Jacob*, erring greatly, and yet through the teaching of adversity proving that

"Men may rise on stepping-stones
Of their dead selves to higher things."—*Tennyson*.

Mark these seven stages of his life: (1) Gen. xxv. 31, (2) xxvii. 35, (3) xxviii. 20-22, (4) xxxi. 5, (5) xxxii. 10, (6) xxxii. 28, (7) xlix. 18. Side by side also with the three ancestors of the Chosen People, who inherited the blessing, are three others, and the more nearly these are related to those in the flesh the more widely are they separated from them in the sight of God. From the beginning the wheat and tares grew together, and men often found it hard to discriminate them (Matt. xiii. 30). *Lot*, Abraham's nephew, who is called a righteous man, started at God's command for the Promised Land. Mercy as well as judgment was predicted for his descendants in the end (Jer. xlviii. 47, xlix. 6), and Ruth, one of them, was Christ's ancestor. But, more worldly than Abraham, he compromised his religion for the sake of wealth, enjoyed neither happiness nor influence in this world, lost all he had in it, barely saved his own soul "as through fire" (1 Cor. iii. 15), and was forefather of nations expressly shut out from the Lord's congregation (Deut. xxiii. 3). *Ishmael*, Isaac's half-brother, whose personal character is not described, was received into covenant with God (Gen. xvii.), and his descendants have never been destroyed. But he and they were outcasts, and are regarded as representatives of those who have only a form of religion according to the spirit of bondage, instead of its living power according to the spirit of adoption (Gal. iv.). *Esau*, Jacob's twin brother, who is called a profane person, was born heir to God's blessing. He despised his birthright, bartered it away, and defied God by marrying heathens. Thus he turned the greatest blessing into the most irreparable loss. God hated him (Mal. i. 3), and called his descendants "the people of My curse" (Isa. xxxiv. 5). So we first learn the lesson that S. Paul finally sums up in his Epistle to the Romans. There is nothing arbitrary in God's ways: the greater the privilege, the greater the responsibility. By abusing the blessings He freely bestows we earn curses that were never intended for us.

VI. THE COMING MESSIAH.

"*Your father Abraham rejoiced to see My day.*"

John viii. 56.

Many histories look back to a golden age which is past and gone. Jewish history looks forward (Heb. xi. 40 ; Acts xxvi. 6, 7). And just as we teach children first from pictures, and afterwards from the printed page, so early in the Old Testament we find many Types and few Predictions, and later on many Predictions and few Types. All the six kinds of Types occur this term; but leaving *ordinances, acts,* and *offices* to be considered with the Mosaic Law generally, we note as typical *events*, the offering of Isaac and the Exodus; as typical *things*, Jacob's Ladder (access through Christ, Eph. ii. 18), the Pillar of Cloud and Fire (presence of Christ, Matt. xxviii. 20), the Manna (Christ the Bread of Heaven, John vi.), the Smitten Rock (Christ's gift of Living Water, John iv.); and as typical *persons*, Adam, Enoch, Noah, Melchizedek, Isaac, and Joseph. The first of these, a type by contrast, is worked out below; the working out of the last, a type by comparison, forms one of our Questions.

THE FIRST ADAM (1) Was created in the image of God. (2) Was of the earth. (3) Became a living soul. (4) Was made to have dominion over all. (5) Was appointed to subdue the earth. (6) Was overcome by desire of pleasure in a garden. (7) Yielded to the lust of the flesh, the lust of the eyes, and the vainglory of life (Gen. iii. 6; 1 John ii. 16). (8) Excused himself when justly accused. (9) After the fall God pronounced judgment on the Serpent, judgment on the Woman, judgment on the Man; of sorrow, weariness, and death (Gen. iii. 14-19). (10) By his one trespass death reigned.

THE SECOND ADAM (1) Is the very image of God's substance (Heb. i. 3). (2) Is of heaven (1 Cor. xv. 47). (3) Became a life-giving spirit (1 Cor. xv. 45). (4) Is Lord of all (Phil. ii. 11). (5) Will subdue all things (1 Cor. xv. 25). (6) Overcame by endurance of pain in a garden (Matt. xxvi. 36-44). (7) Conquered the lust of the flesh (Luke iv. 3), the lust of the eyes (Luke iv. 5), and the vainglory of life (Luke iv. 9). (8) Was silent when unjustly accused (Matt. xxvii. 12). (9) Destroyed the serpent (Rev. xii. 9, 10); was born of woman (Gal. iv. 4); endured sorrow (Isa. liii. 3, 4; Matt. viii. 17), weariness (John iv. 6) and death (Psalm xxii. 15). (10) By His one act of righteousness grace reigned unto eternal life (Rom. v.)

Observe these parallels also:—

Gen. i. Heaven and earth created.	Rev. xxi. Heaven and earth renewed.
Gen. ii. God with man in a garden.	Rev. xxi. God with man in a city.

Gen. ii. Eat not lest thou die. John vi. Eat and live.
Gen. iii. Tree of life withheld. Rev. xxii. Tree of live given.
Gen. viii. Earth destroyed by water. 2 Peter iii. Earth destroyed by fire.
Gen. xi. Confusion of Tongues. Acts ii. Gift of Tongues.

To us, all these Types speak far more plainly than they did to those who first saw them, but to that age were also given nine Predictions of growing fulness and clearness. The Coming One would be the descendant of Eve, of Seth, of Noah, of Shem, of Abraham, of Isaac, of Jacob, of Judah. (1) Gen. iii. 15. An enigmatical prophecy that he (or they) who are born of woman should suffer from, and yet in the end triumph over, the power of evil. (2) Gen. ix. 26, 27. A dim announcement of blessing to Shem, and to Japhet through him. (3) Gen. xii. 3 ; (4) Gen. xviii. 18 ; (5) Gen. xxii. 18 ; (6) Gen. xxviii. 14. Definite promises of blessing through Abraham's descendants to all nations. (7) Gen. xlix. 10. A promise which for the first time centres in one Person, a ruler descended from Judah. (8, 9) Job xix. 25-7 ; Job xxxiii. 23, 24. Trustful aspirations rather than direct predictions, and made outside the Chosen Family, therefore on a different footing from the others, even if we regard this as their chronological place.

Besides types and predictions, there are in the Old Testament three special lines of preparatory revelation concerning the Divine Nature of the Coming One, not to be associated with the expectation of the Messiah, until, in the course of many ages, as we shall see, the conception of the Messiah rises above that of a merely human deliverer. The Divine Son is called (1) the Wisdom of God (1 Cor. i. 24), anticipated by Prov. viii. (2) The Word of God ; the opening statement of Genesis that in the beginning God created through His Word, is repeated and filled with new meaning as the opening statement of S. John's Gospel. (3) The Messenger or Angel of God (Mal. iii. 1 ; Job xxxiii. 23, R.V. ; John xx. 21 ; Heb. i. 2). All through the Old Testament we see an Angel of God's Presence (or Countenance), who is worshipped as God and yet seen of men ; who is not only commissioned by Jehovah, but represents Him so directly and fully that when He speaks or acts God

Himself is felt to speak or act. Comparison of John i. 18, x. 30; 2 Cor. iv. 6; Acts vii. 38; 1 Cor. x. 4, 9 (R.V. margin); Jude 5 (R.V. margin) leads to the inevitable inference that in this Angel there is a mysterious foreshadowing of the Incarnation. More than half the allusions to Him occur this term. See Gen. xvi. 7, 13, xviii., xxi. 17-19, xxii. 11, 12, xxxi. 11, 13, xxxii. 24, 29, 30 (*cp.* Hos. xii. 4, 5), xlviii. 15, 16; Exod. iii. 2, 6, 14, iv. 5, xiv. 19, xxiii. 20-23, xxxii. 34, xxxiii. 2, 14; Num. xxii. 23, 32, 35; Josh. v. 15, with vi. 2; Judg. ii. 1, v. 23, vi. 11, 12, xiii. 3, 6, 18; comp. Rev. xix. 11-13; 1 Kings xix. 7, 9; Isa. lxiii. 9; Zech. i. 11, iii. 5, xii. 8. "There was One designated, not as an epithet but as a description of his being, *the Angel of the Lord*, in whom God accustomed His creatures to the thought of beholding Himself in human form. Whether it was God the Son who so manifested Himself beforehand (this was the common belief of the early Fathers) or not, yet there was One, known as *the* Angel of the Lord, distinct from and above all the rest." (*Pusey.*)

VII. GOD'S REVELATION OF HIMSELF TO MAN.

Wrong ideas about God lie at the root of every form of error and superstition (Psalm l. 21; Acts xvii. 29). Hence the need of His gradual self-manifestation. This came first, through the negative declaration that He is invisible and incomprehensible (Deut. iv. 14-19), whose result was that to the heathen world Israel seemed to have a religion without a God. But "let those who wish to understand the hidden wisdom of the Second Commandment, study the history of ancient religions. No argument can prove that there is anything very wrong in all these outward signs and symbols. To many people we know they are even a help and comfort. But history is sometimes a stronger and sterner teacher than argument, and one of the lessons which the history of religions certainly teaches is this, that the curse pronounced against those who would change the invisible into the visible, the spiritual into the material, the Divine into the human, the infinite into the finite, has come true in every nation on earth." (*Max Müller.*) Secondly, God manifested Himself through that positive declaration of His attributes which forms the Old Testament Creed

(Exod. xxxiv. 5-7). To Israel, unable to know Him in His absolute and unapproachable majesty, and forbidden to make unworthy representations, each fresh and lasting revelation came in a new Name, gathering up what was shown of God's character, working, and will from age to age. Throughout the Old Testament we shall trace these names, and observe the different circumstances under which different names are used. Here we note the four earliest :—

(1) ELOHIM, a title, meaning "the Mighty One" and translated "God," is used in those passages which speak of the God of nature, and of the world as under a general Divine influence (*e.g.*, in the account of the Creation and of heathen nations). It is a plural word, understood and used as a singular. This had a present reference to the polytheism (worship of many gods) of the nations around, showing that the God of Israel united in Himself all the various powers and attributes of Deity. It had also a future reference to the Christian doctrine of the Trinity, foreshadowed in Gen. i. 26, iii. 22, xi. 7. The singular of Elohim forms part of many names (*i.e.*, "Daniel"), and we find it in Matt. xxvii. 46, and know it well in its Arabic form, "Allah."

(2) EL SHADDAI, meaning "God Almighty," the above title qualified, was the special, but not the only name by which God was known to the Patriarchs, in whom He sought to create and to cherish the sense of personal dependence on a strong Helper. It only occurs in the Pentateuch and in Ezek. x. 5, but we find Shaddai (*i.e.*, the Almighty) in Num. xxiv. 4, 16, and often in Job.

(3) ADONAI, a title, meaning "lords" (plural of majesty), translated "Lord," and probably the same word as the name of the Egyptian god "Aten"; is used in Gen. xv. 2, xx. 4, etc., and occurs in many proper names.

(4) JEHOVAH, a proper name, meaning "He Who Is" (Rev. i. 8; Heb. xiii. 8), used in those passages which speak of the God of the covenant, and of the world as under a supernatural overruling Power demanding our adoration (*e.g.*, in the history of the Chosen People). It is "a declaration of the simplicity, unity, and self-existence of the Divine Nature, exactly opposite to all the multiplied forms of idolatry, human, animal and celestial, that prevailed, so

far as we know, everywhere else" (*Stanley*), and "a manifestation of the Eternal who makes Himself known in time' (*Westcott*). In the French Bible it is well translated by "L'Eternel." It was occasionally used in Patriarchal times (Gen. iv. 1, 26), but its frequent use dates from the Exodus. Kuenen reckons that about 190 Old Testament personal names are compounded with it, including those of fourteen out of the nineteen kings of Judah. The contexts in which it and Elohim respectively occur should always be noted (*e.g.*, Psalm xix. 1, 14). In later times a feeling of reverence (founded on Lev. xxiv. 16), which became a superstition, led the Jews to replace Jehovah by Adonai. Hence our English Bible translates it LORD and sometimes GOD (R.V. Preface, p. 2). In Psalm lxviii. 4, lxxxix. 8 (R.V.); Isa. xxxviii. 11 (R.V.), etc., we have a shortened form, which also occurs in Hallelu-*jah*. The name Ehyeh (Exod. iii. 14, 15, R.V. margin) is from the same root, and has the same meaning.

Summing up, we may say, outside Israel God is anonymous, to Israel He is Jehovah, to the Church He is Father, Son, and Holy Ghost (*Saphir*).

VIII. MAN'S RELATION TO GOD IN WORSHIP.

Ever since Adam left Eden men have tried to approach God through Sacrifice. This may be of two kinds:—

(*a*) A thank-offering for God's favour in the past, or a gift to secure His favour for the future, generally in the form of fruits of the earth. Such was the sacrifice of Cain, who worshipped Elohim the Creator, as the type of the Deist, and whose form of religion finally degenerated into mere nature worship. It was, however, not only the incomplete character of his offering, but the spirit in which it was offered that caused its rejection (Prov. xv. 8).

(*b*) An expiation for sin, generally in the form of an unblemished creature whose blood is shed (Heb. ix. 22). Such was the sacrifice of Abel, who worshipped Jehovah, and looked for the coming Redeemer, as the type of the Christian, and whose form of religion finally degenerated into worship of subordinate redeemers and intercessors. All the various religions of the world go back to those two primæval altars; and since animal food is first permitted in

Gen. ix. 3, Gen. iii. 21 may indicate that sacrifices, such as Abel's, were divinely instituted. Elsewhere also in Genesis we find the germ of those Mosaic institutions which we shall consider next term.

The offering of Isaac is sometimes misunderstood, and criticised as if it were an example of human sacrifice for sin. So far from sanctioning, it condemns such sacrifice. For (*a*) Abraham had committed no particular sin, and apprehended no special danger. (*b*) It was not a sacrifice to atone for sin, or to propitiate God, but a *burnt offering*, the meaning of which throughout the Bible is dedication of oneself to God, and perfect obedience to His will. It was not made in the spirit of Mic. vi. 6, but of Acts xxi. 13. (*c*) Isaac is a type of humanity devoted to death, but not actually slain. The ram, divinely provided and slain in his stead, is a type of the Lamb of God.

Prayer is first mentioned in Gen. iv. 26; we have the first specimen of prayer for others in Gen. xvii. 18, xviii.; and of prayer for oneself in Gen. xxxii. (omitting Lot's hasty request in Gen. xix. 18, 19). No grander examples could be given of its true nature, and of its power with God. (See "Oxford Helps," § xii.)

PASSAGES ILLUSTRATING GENESIS.—1 Chron. i. 1—ii. 6; Psalm cv. 1-23; Josh. xxiv. 2-4; Neh. ix. 7, 8; Hos. xii. 2-5, 12; Acts vii. 2-16; Heb. xi. 3-22.

PASSAGES ILLUSTRATING EXODUS.—1 Chron. ii. 18—viii.; Psalm cv. 24-45; Josh. xxiv. 5-7; Neh. ix. 9-20; Hos. xii. 13; Acts vii. 17-44; Heb. xi. 23-9; 1 Cor. x. 1-11; Psalm lxxvii. 14-20, lxxviii. 1-54, lxxxi., cxiv., cvi. 7-13, 19-23, cxxxv. 8, 9, cxxxvi. 10-16; Judg. v. 4, 5; Hab. iii. 3-13; Isa. lxiii. 11-14.

Here we pause, but if we have entered into our First Term's reading we cannot stop here. We are but half through the career of a man who has had a greater influence upon the world than any other man we could name, except S. Paul. We reserve the full consideration of his character and work till we finish the story of his life next term. The Chosen People are wandering in the Wilderness. What will their destiny as a nation be after this long training? The Tabernacle has been set up. What is the nature and meaning of the worship for which it is established?

IX. QUESTIONS

(See pp. 13, 18.)

[Questions I., VII., XI., XIV., XXIII., XXIV., and XXVIII. may be answered with help of any books. The other 28 questions should be answered with the help of a reference Bible and the R.V. only.]

I. Explain fully the meanings of these words as shown by their derivations :—Bible, Scriptures, Canon, Testament, Pentateuch, Genesis, Exodus. (14.)

II. Classify the books of the Bible in four groups, as (*a*) History, (*b*) Biography, (*c*) Letters, (*d*) Poetry. (4.)

III. Give *three* references to prove each of these statements :—(*a*) God spoke through Old Testament writers, (*b*) God spoke through New Testament writers ; (*c*) Christ insisted upon the importance and authority of the Old Testament, (*d*) The first Christians studied it diligently. (12.)

IV. Specify the three acts of *creation* recorded in Gen. i. What further act of creation is mentioned by S. Paul ? (4.)

V. Show by Old Testament and New Testament references that the world and all in it was created by God the Father, God the Son, and God the Holy Ghost. (6.)

VI. On what were the first three curses pronounced ? (3.)

VII. What brought about the Deluge ? State its extent and duration. What were the dimensions of the Ark ? What did it contain ? Name three new precepts and two promises given after the Deluge. (20.)

VIII. Illustrate Heb. xi. 9 by a brief summary of Abraham's wanderings in Canaan, noting his four chief halting-places. (12.)

IX. Discuss the character of Abraham, with special reference to New Testament allusions to him, and justify from Scripture his two titles, (*a*) Friend of God, (*b*) Father of the Faithful. (14.)

X. Prove that Abraham's immediate ancestors, and also that his descendants in Egypt, worshipped false gods. (3.)

XI. Name four important descendants of Esau in the New Testament, in whom his striking but cruel, worldly, and unstable character was reproduced. How was the prophecy that he should first serve, and then have dominion over his brother, fulfilled in his descendants ? (6.)

XII. Consider Joseph as a type of Christ in character and circumstances. (14.)

XIII. Name the first two possessions of Abraham's family in Canaan. To whom did they ultimately belong? (6.)

XIV. Reconcile Gen. xlvi. 27 and Acts vii. 14. (6.)

XV. Mention two incidents in the life of Ephraim. (4.)

XVI. How old was Noah's father when Adam died? How old was Abraham's father when Noah died? How old were Jacob and Esau when Abraham died? How old was Joseph when Isaac died? (12.)

XVII. On how many occasions are we told of God speaking to man in Genesis? To whom did He speak? (15.)

XVIII. What allusions to Job are there in Scripture outside the Book of Job? Find a New Testament quotation from Job. (3.)

XIX. Summarise the four parts of Elihu's discourse. (14.)

XX. Quote two passages proving that Amram was a pious man. (N.B. He is not actually named in either.) (2.)

XXI. Give the seven reasons Moses gave for not going before Pharaoh, and God's answers to them. How many interviews had Moses with Pharaoh? (14.)

XXII. What were the four compromises Pharaoh tried to make? Give the names of the magicians who withstood Moses. (6.)

XXIII. Make a list of the ten plagues of Egypt, showing the object or victims, duration, significance, and immediate result of each. (20.)

XXIV. Explain the following passages :—Gen. vi. 2, 6; Job iv. 18, xix. 25, xxvi. 5, 6, xxxi. 26, xxxvii. 16, xxxviii. 31; Exod. iii. 22, ix. 12. (30.)

XXV. Where, when, by whom, and with what result was the battle of Rephidim fought? (4.)

XXVI. Have we Biblical warrant for speaking of the *ten* Commandments? Show from Genesis that each of the ten was recognised before they were given on Sinai. (22.)

XXVII. Give the passages in which the first mention is made of the following :—(1) A Prophet, (2) a Priest, (3) a King, (4) a Covenant, (5) Believing in God, (6) a "Righteous Man," (7) Musical Instruments, (8) a Tombstone, (9) Money, (10) a City, (11) Egypt, (12) more wives than one, (13) written History, (14) the written Word of God. (14.)

XXVIII. What are the meanings of the following names? —Adam, Eve, Cain, Abel, Seth, Noah, Abraham, Sarah, Ishmael, Isaac, Edom, Jacob, Israel, Judah, Joseph, Ephraim, Manasseh, Moses, Abimelech, Pharaoh. (20.)

XXIX. How many New Testament allusions can you find to Adam, Eve, Cain, Abel, Enoch, Noah, Lot, Sarah, Hagar, Esau? (20.)

XXX. What do you know of the following?—Asenath, Bashemath, Deborah (of Haran), Eliezer of Damascus, Hur, Iscah, Jochebed, Kezia, Oholiab, and Shiphrah. (20.)

XXXI. Make a list of all the names of God that you can find in Genesis, Job, and Exodus. (30.)

XXXII. Give references for the following passages occurring in this term's reading :—(a) "Where art thou?" (b) "Be thou a blessing." (c) "Submit thyself." (d) "I withheld thee from sinning." (e) "I have filled him with the Spirit of God." (f) "Remember this day." (g) "Stand still." (h) "Go forward." (i) "I fear God." (j) "I am not worthy." (k) "I abhor myself." (l) "Teach Thou me." (m) "Let us make us a name." (n) "We desire not the knowledge of Thy ways." (o) "Come, let us slay him." (p) "For we are brethren." (q) "Who is on the Lord's side?" (r) "Am I in the place of God?" (s) "If a man die, shall he live again?" (t) "There is a spirit in man." (u) "God took him." (v) "God heard, . . . remembered, . . . saw, . . . took knowledge of them." (w) "The Lord is in this place." (x) "That rebel against the light." (y) "I have bought you this day." (z) "He that voucheth for me is on high." (26.)

For *Second Series* of Questions, see p. 309.

SECOND TERM.

THE DAYS OF MOSES.
THE CHOSEN NATION.
THE TABERNACLE AND THE THEOCRACY.

B.C. 1490—1256.

Leviticus. Numbers. Deuteronomy. Psalm XC. Joshua. Judges I.—V. and XVII.—XXI. Ruth. (136 *chapters.*)

"These words ... shall be upon thine heart, and thou shalt teach them, ... talk of them, ... bind them upon thine hand ... and between thine eyes, ... and write them upon the door posts."—DEUT. vi. 6-9.

5th MONTH (34).
  Leviticus I.—XXVII.
  Numbers I.—VII.

6th MONTH (34).
  Numbers VIII.—XXXVI.
  Deut. I.—V.

7th MONTH (34).
  Deut. VI.—XXXIV.
  Psalm XC. Joshua I.—IV.

8th MONTH (34).
  Joshua V.—XXIV. Judges I.—V.
  and XVII.—XXI. Ruth.

I. GENERAL SUMMARY.

GOD has redeemed the people whom He chose to be His own purchased possession. They did not deliver themselves by such a battle as Marathon, or Morgarten, or Bannockburn; He did for them what they could not do for themselves. In the Red Sea they have been baptised into Moses for a new life (1 Cor. x. 2). They have been claimed by God as His sons (Exod. iv. 22; Deut. xiv. 1; Hos. xi. 1). They have been made heirs of the Promised Land (Exod. vi. 8). Will they live the new life as obedient children, and enter into their inheritance? This is the question our second term's reading will answer sadly enough by showing that only two of the grown men who crossed the Red Sea also crossed Jordan (Num. xxvi. 64, 65). A like question confronts us, baptised into Christ as "children of God and inheritors of the kingdom of heaven," and redeemed not by the blood of the many lambs of the Passover, but by the precious blood of the one adorable and immaculate Lamb of God (Eph. i. 4-7). The solemn lesson drawn for us from Israel's unbelief in Heb. iii. is brought before us whenever we join in singing Psalm xcv. at the public worship wherein we claim our Christian privileges.

In Israel's Exodus, which revived worship of the True God and hope of the Messiah, when both were perishing, we see the roots of all that is most valuable in religion to-day. Recently discovered Egyptian records show us how the way was divinely prepared for this important event by the victorious campaigns in Western Asia of Rameses II., whose harsh but able features were seen by our contemporaries when his mummy was unrolled a year or two ago. His wars weakened the Canaanites, but also overstrained the resources of Egypt, and led, in the reigns of his weak successors, to counter-invasions, which depleted the garrisons that held Israel in subjection. It is possible that the Pharaoh of Exod. i. was Seti, son of Rameses I. That the Pharaoh of Exod. ii. 23 was Rameses II., son of Seti; and that the Pharaoh of Exod. v.-xiv. was Menephtah II., son of Rameses II., are widely received conclusions of modern archæology. See Dr. Kinns' "Graven in the Rock" (Cassell, 12s. 6d.), Prof. Poole's "Cities of Egypt" (Smith, Elder, 5s.).

Some profess to account for the most characteristic Hebrew institutions by the sojourn in Egypt, but M. Le Page Renouf entirely gainsays this theory. The following results of their bondage may, however, be certainly traced: —(a) An ever-recurring tendency to idolatry. (b) A preference for non-monarchical institutions which lasted 400 years. (c) A liability to leprosy, consequence of long exposure and hardship. Moreover, in fertile and cultivated Egypt they acquired the arts of civilisation and industry, and affliction welded them together into one nation. During more than half their sojourn there, however, they seem to have been wealthy and prosperous (Exod. i. 9).

The number who left Egypt must have amounted to between two and three millions in all, and if we would understand how a horde of unruly and craven bondmen were transformed into dauntless warriors who proved the most faithful generation in Israel's history, we must gain a clear idea of the exact sequence of events in the wilderness. Each incident there has its own particular place and its special relation to the whole, and no part of that whole was more fruitful than the 37½ years whose story occupies only five chapters. Then it was that the slave-generation died out (Psalm xc. 5-8) and the conqueror-generation grew up. The conquest began when they crossed the brook Zered (Deut. ii. 13), and ended when they occupied Galilee (which was to the Canaanites what Wales and Cornwall were to the Britons), or, in a larger sense, when David took Jerusalem.

God's command to exterminate the heathen, which first appears in Num. xxxi., has been misunderstood and therefore questioned. By their heinous sins, these heathen had forfeited the lives God gave them (Deut. ix. 5). The agents of His judgments were therefore no more murderers than are the executioners who carry out a legal sentence. Moreover, distance in time from heathen Europe, and in space from heathen Asia and Africa, causes us to have but a vague notion of what heathenism really is. The testimony of those who have studied it closely either in past or present forms proves that it not only permits and sanctions, but enjoins iniquities and abominations which Christian influence has made utterly hateful in Christian lands, even for those who do not confess the name of Christ. This heathenism came to a climax in the Canaanites and their neighbours, and in those pre-Christian days evil was so strong that toleration of those who habitually practised it would have been dangerous and even fatal. We, under different conditions, are commanded to hate sin, and love the sinner; Israel's only safety lay in hating the sinner as well as his sin. S. Chrysostom finds a key to this command in Psalm cxxxix. 21, 22, and it is further explained by our Lord's words in Matt. v. 38, 39, 43-5; Luke ix. 54-6. The political wisdom of a command which made Israel the instrument of deserved and inevitable punishment to these notorious idolaters was proved again and again by the long train of evils which followed upon their incomplete obedience to it. The Israelites fought not only for themselves, but for us. Just as the intellectual progress of mankind depended upon the victory of Greece at Marathon, so the future of morality and religion for the whole race depended upon the victory of Israel at Bethhoron.

We are apt to estimate the days after Joshua by those closing episodes of Judges, which account for the omission of Dan in 1 Chron. iv.-vii. and Rev. vii., and for the phrase "little Benjamin" in Psalm lxviii. 27. Three-quarters of the whole period seem, however, to have passed in a peace and prosperity which has little history, but which finds beautiful illustration in the story of Ruth.

II. BOOKS TO BE READ.

(See "Oxford Helps," § v.)

This term we read the three remaining books of Moses and his one Psalm, the history of his successor Joshua, half the story of the Judges, and the biography of Ruth. Glancing at their surface, this appears the least attractive of all the nine portions into which we divide the Bible. The first three books seem to be full of obsolete laws and ceremonies; Joshua seems full of barbarous exterminations and lifeless geography; Judges of petty strifes stirred up by evil passions. When, however, instead of carelessly reading, we search these Scriptures diligently, we find them rich in historical interest and spiritual instruction. And even the details that we are tempted to regard as wearisome and barren, teach us that we must stoop to individual names and minute particulars, if we would appreciate God's condescension and the reality of His special oversight of the children of men (Luke xii. 6, 7).

Moreover, they contain five short poems or fragments and four sustained songs all singularly attractive—viz.,

(*a*) The Aaronic Benediction of the people given at the close of the daily sacrifice (Num. vi. 24-6).

(*b*) Fragment from the Book of the Wars of the Lord concerning the crossing of Arnon, the first river they had come to since they left the Nile (Num. xxi. 14, 15).

(*c*) The jubilant Song of the Well, perhaps a common water-drawing chant in after-times (Num. xxi. 17, 18).

(*d*) A shout of triumph over the Amorites after their second victory (Num. xxi. 27-30).

(*e*) Stanza from the Book of Jashar of a Battle Ode commemorating their greatest victory (Josh. x. 12-15).

(*f*) The sevenfold Prophecy of Balaam touching Israel's destiny and finally glancing at the Gentile world beyond (Num. xxiii., xxiv.).

(*g*) The magnificent Song of Witness for God by Moses (Deut. xxxii.).

(*h*) The Benediction of the Twelve Tribes by Moses (Deut. xxxiii.).

(*i*) Deborah's ecstatic Pæan over Sisera, the only prophetic utterance between Moses and Samuel (Judg. v.).

This term also we make our first acquaintance with the Book of *Psalms* (see p. 170).

Leviticus, the shortest book of Moses, consists of God's own words to His people, excepting only chaps. viii.-x., xxiv. 10-16, 23. Its structure is as symmetrical as that of Genesis. In it God makes provision for man to draw near Him in worship. Its keynote is *Separated unto the Lord* (John xvii. 15; 1 Peter i. 15, 16, ii. 24).

Numbers describes that journey through the wilderness which has ever since been regarded as a parable of human life in its spiritual aspect of a *pilgrimage*. Its keynote is *Sinners against their own lives* (Prov. viii. 36; Jer. xxvi. 19, R.V.; Luke xiii. 34; John v. 40, 44).

Deuteronomy is to the other books of the Pentateuch what S. John is to the other Gospels, not merely repeating, but enlarging upon their theme, and showing its full significance. Its keynote is *Choose* (Matt. vi. 24; 1 John ii. 15; Heb. x. 38, 39): and it falls into seven portions:

(1) First address by Moses in the Arabah, i.—iv. 40; (2) Second address by Moses in the valley opposite Bethpeor, iv. 41—xxvi.; (3) Third address by Moses and the Elders at Ebal and Gerizim, xxvii.—xxx.; (4) The Charge, xxxi.; (5) The Song, xxxii.; (6) The Benediction, xxxiii.; (7) Appendix, probably by Joshua, xxxiv.

Joshua (which may be written by him whose name it bears, or by one of the elders who out-lived him, Josh. xxiv. 31) is the Book of the Wars of Israel, and the Doomsday Book of Israel also, and shows how their heritage was won and divided. Of course it must be illustrated by the map. Setting aside the somewhat doubtful sentiment which interprets Jordan as death and Canaan as heaven, we have here a parable of human life in its spiritual aspect of a *warfare*. Its keynote is *Be strong and of a good courage* (Heb. xiii. 5, 6; 1 Peter iii. 13, 14; Eph. vi. 13).

Judges is a mournful history of Israel's decline into anarchy and apostasy, when indolently enjoying their fertile land, they tolerated their foes, and strove with their brethren, and a national war degenerated into struggles of separate tribes against their immediate enemies. Its keynote is *Called out from the world, yet of the world* (James iv. 4; 1 Cor. xv. 33; 2 Peter ii. 20, 21).

Ruth, a prose idyll, is the first chapter in the history of the family of which Christ was a member. Its keynote is *In the world, yet not of the world* (Rom. ii. 10, 11; Matt. xix. 29). No other ancient history contains such vivid pictures of the life of the past as Judges and Ruth, and the mixed characters of this transition period have been well likened to those who made the history of the Middle Ages.

III. PERIODS AND DATES.

(See "Oxford Helps," § ix.)

We are still unable to fix exact dates, but may roughly map out these 234 years as follows:—(3) is fixed at 25 years in accordance with the statement of Josephus that Joshua, who died aged 110, was 35 years younger than Moses. Of this we cannot be quite sure, but it must be correct within a year or two. Josh. xiv. 7, 10 shows that Joshua's subjugation of the land occupied seven years.

(1) B.C. 1490--1452 (38 years). From the erection of the Tabernacle to the second arrival at Kadesh. *Probation of the Chosen People in the Wilderness.*

    (*a*) From Passover to Pentecost, 1490 (7 weeks). The close of the year of organisation at Sinai. **Lev.; Num. i.—x. 10.**

    (*b*) From Pentecost to Feast of Tabernacles, 1490 (4 months and 10 days). March from Sinai to Kadesh, and unsuccessful attempt to enter the Promised Land from the South. **Num. x. 11—xiv.**

(c) From the Feast of Tabernacles, 1490, to Passover, 1452 (37½ years). The Wanderings, probably in the neighbourhood of Seir. **Num. xv.—xix.**

(2) B.C. 1452—1451 (1 year). From the second arrival at Kadesh to the death of Moses. *Conquest of the Land of Gilead, east of Jordan.*

    (a) From Passover to end of Tebeth, 1452 (10 months). March from Kadesh to the Plains of Moab. Successful attempt to enter the Promised Land from the East. **Num. xx.—xxxvi.**

    (b) From Tebeth, 1452, to Passover, 1451 (2 months). Encampment in the Plains of Moab. Farewell address of Moses. **Deut.; Psalm xc.**

(3) B.C. 1451—1426 (25 years). From the death of Moses to the death of Joshua. *Conquest of the Land of Canaan, west of Jordan.*

    (a) Occupation of the Valley of the Jordan. **Josh. i.—viii.**

    (b) Occupation of Judæa and Samaria. **Josh. ix., x.**

    (c) Occupation of Galilee. **Josh. xi., xii.**

    (d) Settlement in the Promised Land. **Josh. xiii.—xxiv.**

(4) B.C. 1426—1256 (170 years). From the death of Joshua to the beginning of the Midianite oppression. *Israel under the first four Judges.*

    (a) Eight years' oppression of the Syrians on the north-east (1402—1394), and rule of Othniel. **Judg. i.—iii. 11.**

    (b) Eighteen years' oppression of the Moabites on the east (1354—1336), and rule of Ehud. **Judg. iii. 12-31.**

    (c) Twenty years' oppression of the Canaanites on the north (1316—1296), and rule of Deborah and Barak. **Judg. iv., v.**

    (d) Three undated episodes of the early days of the Judges, inserted between the histories of

Samson and Samuel, who were probably about the same age—viz., the origin of the idolatrous worship at Dan, **Judg. xvii., xviii.**; "the battle in Gibeah against the children of iniquity" (as Hosea calls it), whose details may be passed over, **Judg. xix.—xxi.;** and the story of Ruth, **Ruth.**

IV. Geography.

(See "Oxford Helps," Maps IV., V., and §§ ix., xxx., and xxxiii.)

A few days' journey along the shore of the Mediterranean might have brought Israel from Egypt into Palestine. But with their minds cankered and their bodies enfeebled by slavery they would have been unfit either to conquer or to re-people the land. They needed the free air of the desert to make them bold and hardy, and the discipline of their wanderings to train them in the fear of God. Moreover, they needed a time of withdrawal from the rest of mankind that their religious and social institutions might be fully organised, and that they might learn, as they could never have learned elsewhere, to depend wholly upon God. Modern travellers describe the scanty vegetation, inadequate rainfall, poor and scarce water, and absence of animal life in the wilderness in a way which plainly shows that Israel's needs must have been miraculously supplied. During the Wanderings, Kadesh, the only city named, seems to have been their headquarters.

Aaron died gazing back from Hor across the Wilderness to Egypt. Moses died gazing forward from Pisgah across Jordan to the Land of Promise; and already the rich forest and pasture lands east of Jordan (Deut. xxxii. 14; 2 Kings iii. 4; Psalm xxii. 12) had been subdued and assigned to tribes whose character was especially pastoral (Judg. v. 16).

Palestine proper lies between the Arabah or wilderness beyond the Dead or Salt Sea, the Jordan valley, the Lebanon mountains, and the Mediterranean, "the sea" or "the great sea" of the Scriptures, just as the Euphrates is "the river" or "the great river" (Num. xxxiv. 7; Deut.

xxx. 13; Psalm lxxii. 8; 1 Kings iv. 21). It is called (*a*) Canaan (Exod. xv. 15); (*b*) the Land of Canaan (Judg. xxi. 12); (*c*) Palestine or Philistia (Exod. xv. 14; Isa. xiv. 29, 31; Joel iii. 4; comp. A.V. and R.V.); (*d*) the Land of the Hittites (Josh. i. 4); (*e*) the Land of the Hebrews (Gen. xl. 15); (*f*) the Land of Israel (1 Sam. xiii. 19); (*g*) the Land of Jehovah (Hos. ix. 3); (*h*) the Glorious Land (Dan. xi. 41); (*i*) the Holy Land (Zech. ii. 12); (*j*) the Land (Ruth i. 1). It is 139 miles long from Dan to Beersheba, and 55 miles wide at its widest from Gaza to the Dead Sea—*i.e.*, it is about the size of Wales, and as mountainous as Switzerland; and for its beauty, variety, small extent, and great influence it may be compared to Greece. From north to south it falls into four parallel bands: (*a*) Seaboard, a maritime plain broken only by the spur of Carmel; (*b*) hill country from Lebanon to the desert, broken into two masses by the plain of Jezreel; (*c*) the deep trench of the Jordan valley; (*d*) from Hermon to the Red Sea, the hills of Gilead and Moab. Beyond these lie wide prairies.

The position of Palestine links it both to the East and to the West. For though it is in Asia, a broad and impassable desert separates it from the rest of that continent; and it looks towards Europe and Africa. In the Greek church at Jerusalem, a circle of marble pavement and short column marks that spot as the centre of the world. And it tells a truthful tale. Palestine is set in the midst of all the worldwide empires of history, including the British Empire of to-day (Ezek. v. 5); and it commands the Mediterranean, the one great highway of nations until the discovery of America. It became the cradle of the only literature which was written for all mankind, and which finds response in every human heart. Within its narrow borders every variety of scenery and temperature is illustrated; and the products of almost every region from the Poles to the Tropics may be acclimatised (Deut. viii. 7-9). There are found the mighty range of Lebanon, "the great white mountain," grim with eternal snow; the gentle uplands of Galilee; the rugged hills and rocky gorges of Judaea; coasts here shelving and there abrupt, washed by the sparkling waves of the Tideless Sea; the laughing Lake of Galilee fringed with flowers of every hue, and lovelier than even the far-famed lakes of Italy; the awful Dead Sea, whose leaden ripple breaks over the deepest depression on the whole surface of the earth; brooks overflowing and impetuous in winter that well-nigh vanish in summer; bubbling springs that can be identified to-day where cities are sought in vain; vineyards on very fruitful hills; corn as tall as a horseman, standing thick on fertile vale and plain; shadowy forest and sunny garden, sandy desert and arid steep. Still, off the beaten track, we find abundant proof that no country better repays cultivation, while so rich is it in wild flowers that from one blasted rock nearly 1000 lbs. of honey were lately taken (Psalm lxxxi. 16). We ask the travellers of to-day to give us their impressions of Palestine. They are at once enchanted with its surpassing natural beauty and depressed by the ruin and desolation which proclaims that it is under a long-enduring curse. See Henderson's "Palestine" (T. & T. Clark, Edinburgh, 2s. 6d.); Thomson's "The Land and the Book" (Nelson, 7s. 6d.); Stanley's "Sinai and Palestine" (Murray, 12s.); and the maps and publications of the Palestine Exploration Society.

The *Jordan*, never called "the *river*," like the Euphrates or Nile, but always spoken of by its significant proper name, which means "the Descender," is unlike any other stream on the face of the earth. It rises 1000 ft. above the Mediterranean, flows through the two lakes of Merom and Galilee, and empties itself into the Dead Sea 1300 ft. below the Mediterranean, having fallen 2300 ft. in a course of 150 miles. It never turns aside from its course due north and south, and never loses itself in ocean; its bed is so deep that its stream flows unseen almost to the end; its downward course in one long cataract is so rapid that no boat can swim upon it for more than half a mile, and it is as useless for navigation as it is for irrigation. No wonder the Canaanites were overcome with fear and amazement on beholding the vehement rush of such a river arrested where its tide is strongest, at floodtime (Josh. iii. 15, v. 1), when the Ark of God stood in its bed, as the Son of God was hereafter to stand there in prayer to be set apart for His work on earth, and acknowledged by a voice from the excellent glory of Heaven.

V. HEROES.

Keynotes
{ *Moses*, 2 Cor. xii. 15.
  Phinehas, Gal. i. 8.
  Joshua, 1 Cor. xvi. 13.

During forty years *Moses* grew from an exceeding fair child into a student at the most learned university, and a prince at the most brilliant court of his age. His wisdom must have been acquired at On, the mother university of the world; and, according to Josephus, he became general of the Egyptian army and won renown by his victory over the Ethiopians. Then having shown himself an ardent patriot, he endured, for another forty years, exile, through which he became acquainted not only with the desert in which he was to guide a nation, but with the will of God, which he was to declare as it had never been declared before (Psalm ciii. 7). Then after this long training he came forward for a third period of forty years, as the God-sent deliverer, dauntless leader, enlightened lawgiver, and victorious commander, judging sin, yet pleading for the sinner; bearing, believing, hoping, and enduring all things for his discouraged, disaffected, and erring people. And mighty not only in his works, but in his words, he was for the Hebrews the father both of poetry and history. He died at last with his heart's prayer ungranted, leaving others to enter into his labours, beholding from Pisgah the goodly land which he would not enter until, after a lapse of fifteen centuries, he talked upon another high mountain with the Christ of whom he wrote (Matt. xvii. 1-3; John v. 46). Abraham and David are both called prophets incidentally (Gen. xx. 7; Acts ii. 30). But never, either before or after, were the lofty thought of the prophet and the bold action of the ruler joined as they were joined in Moses. Beside Moses stood the eloquent Aaron (Exod. iv. 14), greater in office, less great in character; and the dignified Hur (husband of Miriam, according to Josephus), who seems to have been the head of those seventy elders in whom some trace the origin of the Sanhedrin (Exod. xxiv. 9, 14; Num. xi. 16).

For our other heroes, however, we take rather his minister Joshua, and his grand-nephew Phinehas. *Phinehas*, third high priest of Israel, is the first example of the uncompromising warrior-ecclesiastic, who will not only maintain truth, but punish error with the sword, whose staunchness is rewarded by that "covenant of everlasting priesthood," through which (if we except the period between Eli and Solomon) all the high priests of Israel were his descendants until the Fall of Jerusalem in A.D. 70.

Joshua is the first example of the God-fearing soldier, simple, straightforward, undaunted; strong, yet gentle; devout, yet practical ; one who had learned how to command by obeying ; as a servant, jealous for his master's honour ; as a ruler, jealous for God's honour ; never putting himself forward, never seeking aught for himself until all had received their portions, this greatest of Ephraimites stands forth as one of the few Old Testament worthies whose memory is blameless, and as the first who bore that name which was to become the Name above every name (Heb. iv. 8, R.V. margin ; Phil. ii. 9, 10).

VI. THE COMING MESSIAH.

"*Christ having come a high priest of the good things to come, through the greater and more perfect Tabernacle . . . through His own blood, entered in once for all into the holy place, having obtained eternal redemption.*"— Heb. ix. 11, 12 (R.V.).

No period is richer in Messianic Types. Moses is the one *person* to whom, as a Prophet, our Lord directly compares Himself; Aaron is His great type as a Priest; Joshua, His namesake, foreshadowed Him both as Servant of God and as victorious King ; and Boaz as the Kinsman Redeemer whom Job foretold.

The *Tabernacle*, God's holy dwelling-place set in the midst of the people, is a type of Christ as God Incarnate (Heb. viii. 2, 5, ix. 11, x. 5 ; Dan. ii. 34 ; Col. ii. 9 ; John i. 14, R.V. margin ; Rev. xiii. 6, xxi. 3). Each of its contents has spiritual significance. Its *Door* (John x. 9) and its *Veil* (Heb. x. 20) are typical ; Christ is foreshadowed in the *Table of Shewbread* as the Bread of Life and the King ; in the *Golden Candlestick* as the Light of the World and the Prophet ; in the *Altar of Incense* as the Intercessor and Priest ; in the *Ark* as the Fulfiller of all God's will ; in the

Mercy Seat as the Propitiation for our sins through whom we have our access to the Father (Eph. ii. 18). In the *Laver* we see our Regeneration through Him who came by water as well as by blood, to renew as well as to justify (Titus iii. 5, R.V. margin; 1 John v. 6); while the *Brazen Altar* points to the Cross, where He not only offered Himself as Priest, but suffered as Victim (Heb. xiii. 10-12).

Each of the five Sacrifices there made showed a different aspect of the one "full, perfect, and sufficient sacrifice, oblation, and satisfaction for the sins of the whole world." I give them in the order in which they were offered. The *Sin Offering*—made monthly and yearly for the congregation, and occasionally for individuals, partly burned on the altar, and, in two special cases, partly burned outside the camp, in other cases partly eaten by the priests; the only sacrifice whose blood was poured at the base of the altar, and the most fundamental of all—shows Christ's *Atonement* for the sin of the world, for "the fault and corruption of the nature of every man" (Article IX.), for our unconscious sinfulness (Isa. liii. 12; John i. 29; 2 Cor. v. 21). The *Trespass* or *Guilt Offering*—only made occasionally for individuals, partly burned on the altar, and partly eaten by the priests, and accompanied by confession, restitution, and a special ransom—shows Christ's *Expiation* for the particular sins of particular sinners, for our known sins (Isa. liii. 11; 1 John iii. 5, i. 7-9). The *Burnt Offering*—made daily, weekly, monthly, and yearly for the congregation, and occasionally for individuals, wholly burned upon the altar, the earliest kind clearly discriminated, the commonest, and the most comprehensive in its meaning—shows Christ's *Satisfaction* for man's rebellion and disobedience when He gave Himself up without blemish and without spot before God in perfect self-consecration as our Representative (Isa. liii. 10; John x. 17, 18; Eph. v. 2; Heb. x. 6-9). The *Meal Offering*—made daily and on special occasions for the congregation, and occasionally for individuals, partly burned on the altar, and partly eaten by the priests, and pervaded throughout by oil, type of the Holy Spirit; in one sense the earliest, since its name is given to the offerings of Cain and Abel, though only Cain's was, strictly speaking, a meal offering,—shows Christ's acceptable *Oblation* of a perfectly holy human character and life before men (Isa. liii. 9; Matt. iii. 17; 1 Peter ii. 22; Rom. v.). The *Peace Offering*—made both for the congregation and for individuals on many occasions, always after other sacrifices, partly burned on the altar, partly eaten by the priests, and partly eaten by the people—shows Christ's *Reconciliation* of man to God (Isa. liii. 5; Eph. ii. 14; Col. i. 20; John xiv. 27).

Summing up, these offerings embody three main ideas:— (*a*) *Expiation* in the Sin and Trespass Offerings, made *for* (*i.e.*, to obtain) communion with God, never accompanied by meat and drink offerings, and consumed in token of wrath. Sacrifices of this type were the creation of the Mosaic Law (Rom. iii. 20), though they had been imperfectly anticipated already. Their whole meaning is brought out for the first time in the Epistle to the Hebrews, after the great Antitype had died. (*b*) *Self-devotion* in the Burnt Offering. Christ dedicating Himself for us, we daily dedicating ourselves to Him (Rom. xii. 1), was its teaching, the deepest of all, which links all the five Jewish sacrifices together, and constitutes the chief difference between them and the heathen sacrifices. We see from the prophets also that this teaching was the one most often ignored. (*c*) *Thanksgiving* in the Meal and Peace Offerings (see p. 34). Burnt, Meal, and Peace Offerings were all made *in* (*i.e.*, having obtained) communion with God, were of a sweet savour, and were burned in token of acceptance. ("Consumed" and "burned" are here used to represent two quite different words in the Hebrew.)

Note in conclusion these three special sacrifices, with their New Testament explanations:—(*a*) The annual Peace Offering of the *Paschal Lamb*, 1 Cor. v. 7. (*b*) The annual Sin Offering of the *Goat for Azazel*, Heb. ix. 7. (*c*) The occasional Sin Offering (made but seven or nine times in all Israel's history, said the Rabbis) of the *Red Heifer*, Heb. ix. 13.

At the base of the whole Levitical worship lay the conception that only Blood, the material vehicle of that immaterial thing which we call Life, can atone for (*i.e.*, cover) human sin, whose inevitable result is death. Thus it taught that nothing short of the Death of Christ could retrieve man's Fall (Lev. xvii. 11 ; Heb. ix. 22 ; Acts xx. 28 ; 1 Peter i. 15-20). Before He came, the Jews clearly recognised the reference of their sacrifices to the coming Messiah, and since He was rejected by them, sacrifice has disappeared from their worship.

For the meanings of the High Priest's Robes, and of the other *ordinances and acts* of the Mosaic ritual, and for fuller working out of those suggested above, reference must be made to the New Testament, and especially to the Epistle to the Hebrews, an inspired commentary upon the Mosaic Law that students would do well to learn by heart at the rate of $2\frac{1}{2}$ verses a day, if possible, in the course of this term. One typical *event* of our period is referred to by Christ (John iii. 14), and another by S. Paul (1 Cor. x. 4).

Lastly, this term's reading contains two Predictions.

(*a*) Num. xxiv. 17-19, wherein, looking forward to the future triumph of the Hebrew race and their King, the heathen seer, like Caiaphas hereafter, condemned himself. This had partial fulfilment in David's conquest of Moab ; its complete fulfilment will be when Christ rules as King (Matt. ii. 2 ; 1 Cor. xv. 25). (*b*) Deut. xviii. 15-19. This occurs in a book which proved the sheath whence Christ thrice drew the sword of the Spirit for His own use (Matt. iv.), and was expounded by Him of Himself when He taught as a Prophet (John v. 45-7 ; Acts iii. 22). All that was permanent in the new relation established by Moses between God and Man is here transferred to a future Lawgiver.

VII. God's Revelation of Himself to Man.

This term's reading speaks less of new names of God, and more of a new relation of God to man. As the unconscious freedom and innocence of childhood gives place to the deeper seriousness and independence of manhood, so the direct and familiar, but occasional intercourse of God with the Patriarchs ceased when Moses no longer spake face to face with Him. Joshua was the first man who received for his guidance a copy of the Scriptures, which are mentioned for the first time in connexion with him (Exod. xvii. 14; Josh. i. 8).

This fuller revelation was associated with a sterner law. Jehovah was the unseen King and Head of Israel then, just as Christ is the unseen King and Head of His Church now. Theocracy (government by God) is a word used by the Jewish historian Josephus, and commonly applied to the 400 years between the Exodus and the reign of Saul. Strictly speaking, however, Israel's constitution was a theocracy always, whether its human ruler was a prophet like Moses, or a priest like Eli, or a king like David. God was always their supreme King (1 Sam. xii. 12; Isa. vi. 5, xxxiii. 17), and they were called then, as the Church is called now, to be His special people for a special reason (1 Peter ii. 9).

Observe how the threefold form of the Aaronic Benediction anticipates a clearer revelation of the Triune God (Num. vi. 24-6).

VIII. Man's Relation to God in Worship.

Two cardinal truths were uttered at Sinai:

(*a*) That the people of Israel were set apart as a holy nation, which explains why the Ceremonial Law was given at first to separate them, and abrogated later on when their privileges were to be shared by others.

(*b*) That their God was "eternal, incorruptible, invisible," which explains but does not excuse their besetting sin.

The various laws of Moses may be classified under three heads. (1) *Moral*, referring to our duty to ourselves. All sin wrongs ourselves in the first place, while most sins wrong others also. These laws are the same in all ages (Matt. v. 17-48). (2) *Political*, *Civil*, and *Criminal*, referring to our duty to our neighbour. Of these laws, changed social conditions have altered the details though not the principles (Mark x. 5). (3) *Religious* and *Ceremonial*, referring to our duty to God. These laws, so far as they referred to outward observances, were modified after the more perfect manifestation of God in Christ. (Contrast Lev. xi. and Deut. xiv. with 1 Tim. iv. 4 and Rom. xiv. 20, 21.)

In spite of the written Law, a people constantly engaged in war or agriculture would have sunk into ignorance and barbarism had not a leisured and learned class not wholly dependent on their own toil been set apart to teach it to their fellows (2 Chron. xxxi. 4). Such were the Levites (see Exod. xxxii. 26-9, which explains the contrast between Gen. xlix. 5-7 and Deut. x. 8, 9, xxxiii. 8-11). They had neither political power nor personal wealth, and were free to devote themselves to the maintenance of public worship. In time they became chroniclers and psalmists also.

The Israelites proved too "carnal" (1 Cor. iii. 1) to understand the worship of an unseen God and King. Hence Idolatry became their great national sin until the Babylonian Captivity. There were two kinds of idolatry, which must be carefully distinguished throughout the Old Testament.

(*a*) Transgression of the First Commandment, worshipping false gods instead of or together with Jehovah. This apostasy formed the sin of Israel at Shittim (Num. xxv.), of Joash the Abiezrite (Judg. vi.), and of King Ahab.

(*b*) Transgression of the Second Commandment, worshipping Jehovah, the one Creator, under the symbolic likeness of a created thing (2 Kings xviii. 22, xvii. 41). These unlawful "aids to devotion" formed the sin of Israel at Sinai (Exod. xxxii.), of Micah (Judg. xvii.), and of King Jeroboam I.

PASSAGES ILLUSTRATING LEVITICUS, etc.—1 Chron. ii.-viii.; Neh. ix. 21-31; Psalm xliv. 1-3, lxxviii. 55-8, xcv. 8-11, cvi. 13-18 and 24-48, cxiv., cxxxv. 10-12, cxxxvi. 16-22; Micah vi. 4-9; Acts vii. 45, xiii. 18-20; Hebrews. Whitfield's "Tabernacle, Priesthood, and Offerings of Israel" (Nisbet, 5*s*.) deals with the symbolism of the Mosaic ritual in a simple and popular way.

Again we pause, but what we have read only stimulates us to read on. When and how will a strong nation be formed out of this chaos of warring tribes? Will the Israelitish dodecarchy give place to monarchy as the English heptarchy did? Will Shiloh continue to be the capital, and Ephraim the leading tribe? Will the struggle with their heathen neighbours for independence, nay for existence, pass into an assured mastery over them? Who is this David, whose ancestry has been so fully described?

IX. QUESTIONS.
(See pp. 13, 18.)

[Questions I., II, XII., XXI., and XXIV. may be answered with help of any books. The other 27 questions should be answered with the help of A.V. and R.V. only.]

I. Draw, with fine pen and ruler :—

(*a*) A ground plan of the Tabernacle, showing the relative size and position of the Court, the Holy Place, and the Holy of Holies, and also their contents.

(*b*) A ground plan of the Camp of Israel, showing the positions of the three companies of Levites and of Moses and Aaron with regard to the Tabernacle, and stating the leader, number, and charge of each; and secondly, the positions of the twelve tribes, naming their leaders. Mark the points of the compass on both plans. (25.)

II. Quote one description of the wilderness from the Psalms, and two from the Prophets, which indicate the hardships of those who wandered there. (3.)

III. Enumerate seven occasions on which the Israelites murmured. (7.)

IV. Show from several passages that they transgressed the First as well as the Second Commandment in the wilderness. (6.)

V. Quote a conversation between Balaam and Balak on the subject of the sacrifices that are pleasing to God, and prove from the Second Book of Kings that human sacrifice was not unknown among the Moabites. (4.)

VI. Give the total number of the children of Israel (*a*) in B.C. 1706; (*b*) in B.C. 1490; (*c*) in B.C. 1452. Which tribe increased and which tribe decreased most between 1490 and 1452? (8.)

VII. "Let me die the death of the righteous!" Was this aspiration fulfilled in the case of the man who uttered it? (2.)

VIII. Quote three New Testament precepts enforcing each of the Ten Commandments. (30.)

IX. "Of all the ancient lawgivers, Moses alone endeavoured to mitigate the evils of slavery as a domestic institution" (*Milman*). Point out some of these mitigations. (8.)

X. Name the five kinds of animals that might be offered in sacrifice, stating for which of the five kinds of sacrifice each was available. (8.)

XI. Mention (*a*) The one offering that need not be unblemished; (*b*) the one fast appointed by Moses. (2.)

XII. What were the three great annual festivals? By what various names are they called? How were they observed? What was their significance in relation to (*a*) The seasons of the year; (*b*) the history of Israel; (*c*) the Gospel of Christ? What additional annual festivals were instituted after the Captivity? (30.)

XIII. "Nazirite" means "one separated." From what was the Nazirite separated? Name some famous men who were Nazirites. (6.)

XIV. Point out the differences in privilege, garb, function, etc., between the high priest and the priest, and between the priest and the Levite. (10.)

XV. Find in the Gospels or Acts of the Apostles an exemplification of each of the following passages:— (1) Exod. xxx. 7, 8; (2) Exod. xxxviii. 26; (3) Lev. x. 6, xxi. 10; (4) Lev. xi.; (5) Lev. xii. 3; (6) Lev. xii. 8; (7) Lev. xiii. 45, 46; (8) Lev. xiv. 3, 4; (9) Lev. xx. 10; (10) Lev. xxiii. 3; (11) Deut. xvi. 16; (12) Deut. xix. 15; (13) Deut. xxi. 23; (14) Deut. xxiii. 25; (15) Deut. xxv. 1-3; (16) Deut. xxv. 5. (16.)

XVI. In Deuteronomy, Israel is bidden to *remember* twelve times. Give references, and name the things to be remembered. (11.)

XVII. Quote a verse in Deuteronomy where God is called Israel's Father. His love to us, and our love to Him is a thought running all through that book, which thus anticipates Christ's teaching. Trace this out carefully. (12.)

XVIII. Where is Moses called (1) a prophet, (2) a priest, (3) a king, (4) a leader, (5) a lawgiver, (6) a shepherd of God's flock, (7) a man of God, (8) a man mighty in his words and works? Show by a genealogical table his relationship to Levi and to Bezalel. What do we know to the discredit of one of his grandsons? (15.)

XIX. Dean Stanley suggests "heedless of self" as the exact meaning of the word rendered "meek" in Num. xii. 3. Discuss the character of Moses, showing how this trait was impressed upon all his actions from first to last. How often did he intercede successfully for his people? (12.)

XX. Mention a speech and two actions of Moses recorded in Hebrews and not in the Old Testament. What do we learn from the New Testament as to his motive in throwing in his lot with Israel? Consider Moses as a type of Christ. (15.)

XXI. The exhortation, "Be strong" occurs more than twenty times in the Bible. Give as many references as you can. (10.)

XXII. How and when was the curse in Josh. vi. 26 fulfilled? What New Testament allusions are there to Jericho? (4.)

XXIII. "They asked not counsel at the mouth of the Lord." What were the circumstances and the results of this omission? Give other instances of enterprises undertaken with and without prayer. (12.)

XXIV. Draw on card or drawing paper a map of Canaan as divided among the tribes, indicating the portion of each, and marking the six cities of refuge in red. Mark also the Sea of Chinnereth, the Dead Sea, the Arnon, the Jordan, the Kishon; Hermon, Carmel, Ebal, Gerizim, Tabor, Dan, Beersheba, Bethel, Jericho, Ai, Gibeon, and any other cities you please which are mentioned in this term's reading.

N.B.—Rule margins, latitudes, and longitudes; outline in pencil, then in ink with a very fine pen; then colour in transparent washes, and lastly print the names. (25.)

XXV. Sketch the character and career of Phinehas. In what words, six times repeated, is the character of Caleb summed up? (10.)

XXVI. Prove that the mother and grandmother of David's grandfather were not Israelites. (5.)

XXVII. Illustrate 1 Chron. v. 1, 2, by showing very briefly—(*a*) that up to the days of Samuel, Ephraim and Manasseh were the leading tribes; (*b*) that from Samuel to the Captivity, Judah was the leading tribe; (*c*) that Reuben made an unsuccessful attempt to claim the right of the firstborn. (15.)

XXVIII. Where, when, by whom, and with what result were the following battles fought?—Hormah, Jahaz, Edrei, Bethhoron, Merom, Megiddo. (24.)

XXIX. How many New Testament allusions can you find to Aaron, Joshua, Korah, Balaam, Rahab, Barak? (10.)

XXX. What do you know of the following?—Achsah, Adoni-bezek, Chilion, Eldad, Heber, Hobab, Jair the Manassite, Mahlah, Mishael, Shamgar, the Kenites, Chittim? (24.)

XXXI. Show how the following attributes of God are revealed in this term's reading:—Living, Holy, Jealous. Where is He called the Rock five times, and in what book is He called "God of the spirits of all flesh" twice? (5.)

XXXII. Give references for the following:—(a) "A mother in Israel." (b) "Children in whom is no faith." (c) "The land ye have rejected." (d) "Because ye believed not in Me." (e) "Every man in his place." (f) "Every man straight before him." (g) "Every man shall be put to death for his own sin." (h) "Be sure your sin will find you out." (i) "Wroth with me for your sakes." (j) "My son, give glory to the Lord." (k) "Let us go up at once." (l) "Whithersoever thou sendest us we will go." (m) "Come thou with us." (n) "A full reward be given thee of the Lord." (o) "I am come forth for an adversary." (p) "I am not among you." (q) "I dwell in the midst of the children of Israel." (r) "Thou shalt love thy neighbour as thyself." (s) "Thou shalt be altogether joyful." (t) "The Lord your God proveth you." (u) "That ye go not about after your own heart and your own eyes." (v) "It is not too hard for thee." (w) "The secret things belong unto the Lord our God." (x) "What hath God wrought!" (y) "He is thy life." (z) "He hath known thy walking through this great wilderness." (26.)

For *Second Series* of Questions, see p. 309.

THIRD TERM.
The Days of David.
The Chosen Nation under One King.
B.C. 1256—1018.

Judges VI.—XVI. 1 *Samuel.* 2 *Samuel I.—XXIII.* 1 *Chronicles I.—XX. Psalms II.—XXV. XXVII. XXIX. XXXI. XXXII. XXXIV. XXXV. XXXVIII.—XLI. LI.—LXIV. LXVIII.—LXX. LXXVIII. CI. CVIII.—CX. CXXXVIII. CXL.—CXLIII.* (146 *chapters.*)

"The law of the Lord is perfect, . . . the testimony of the Lord is sure, . . . the precepts of the Lord are right, . . . the commandment of the Lord is pure, . . . the judgments of the Lord are true and righteous altogether."—Psalm xix. 7-9.

9th MONTH (35).
  Judg. VI.—XVI. 1 Sam. I.—XVII. Psalms VIII., XIX., XXIII., XXIX. 1 Sam. XVIII. Psalms CXL., CXLI.

10th MONTH (37).
  1 Sam. XIX., XX. Psalms LIX., XIII., XI. 1 Sam. XXI. Psalms LVI., XXV. 1 Sam. XXII. Psalms XXXIV., CXLII., LVII., LII. 1 Sam. XXIII.—XXVI. Psalms LVIII., XXXV., LIV., VII., XVII. 1 Sam. XXVII.—XXXI. 1 Chron. I.—X.

11th MONTH (37).
  2 Sam. I.—V. 16. 1 Chron. XI. 1-9, XIV. 1-7. 2 Sam. XXIII. 8-39. 1 Chron. XI. 10-47, XII. Psalm LXXVIII.,

11th MONTH *Continued.*
  Psalm XVI. 2 Sam. VI., VII. 1 Chron. XIII., XV.—XVII. Psalms CI., XXIV., XV., CX., CXXXVIII. 2 Sam. V. 17-25, VIII.—XI. 1, XII. 26-31, XXI. 15-22. 1 Chron. XIV. 8-17, XVIII.—XX. Psalms XX., XXI., LX., CVIII., IX., II., XVIII. 2 Sam. XXII. Psalm LXVIII.

12th MONTH (37).
  2 Sam. XI. 2—XII. 25. Psalms LI., XXXII., VI., XXXVIII., XXXIX., XLI., XL., LXX., V. 2 Sam. XIII.—XV. 12. Psalms X., XII., XIV., LIII., LXII., LXIV. 2 Sam. XV. 13—XVII. Psalms CXLIII., LXIII., XXVII., LV., CIX., LXIX., XXII., XXXI., LXI., III., IV. 2 Sam. XVIII.—XXI. 14.

I. General Summary.

THE Promised Land has been claimed, but secure possession can only be won through conflict with all the neighbouring nations (see "Oxford Helps," § xxx.). *Syrians,*

Moabites, and *Canaanites* have already been defeated, and a preliminary encounter with the *Philistines* (Judg. iii. 31, x. 11) has taken place. Three greater struggles remain, whose story occupies us throughout this term.

At its beginning we find Palestine overrun by hordes of *Midianites* and *Amalekites* from the desert, and the Israelites fleeing for their lives to mountains and caves. Their signal deliverance from this extremity is often referred to afterwards (Psalm lxxxiii. 9-12; Isa. ix. 4, x. 26).

Eighty years later came the *Ammonite* invasion, and lastly the *Hundred Years War* with the *Philistines* (Gen. x. 14). A pastoral tribe of that name occupied the fertile plain of South-West Palestine in Abraham's days (Gen. xx., xxi.). By 1491 they had become a formidable military and commercial nation with five strongholds (Exod. xiii. 17, xv. 14) who had already given Israel cause to fear them (1 Chron. vii. 20-22, viii. 13). When their territory was assigned to Dan and Judah, they contested these invaders' succession and obtained the mastery for a period of forty years known as "the days of the Philistines" (Judg. xiii. 1, xiv. 4, xv. 11, 20). *Shamgar* and *Samson* began to deliver Israel from them (Judg. iii. 31, xiii. 5), and it was probably to avenge the crowning exploit of the latter that they put themselves in array against Israel at Aphek, and inflicted a defeat which seemed to destroy her national existence. This overthrow was referred to as "the day of the captivity of the land" (Judg. xviii. 30; Psalm lxviii. 18), and the catastrophe which desolated Shiloh can only be paralleled in Israel's history with the Fall of Jerusalem in B.C. 588 and in A.D. 70. Hence the murderous fury which Jeremiah's allusion to it provoked. The rout of Israel under priests whose "sin was very great before the Lord" was retrieved on the same spot twenty years later by the blameless prophet *Samuel* (1 Sam. vii. 13). Then Israel asked for a king to strengthen their hands, and God gave them *Saul* (1 Sam. ix. 16, xiv. 52). Central Palestine had now become a Philistine country, and its heirs had passed over Jordan again. He turned the tide of war, but because he rejected the word of the Lord his great victory at Michmash ended in defeat on the scene of Gideon's triumph over Midian. Final deliverance came through the faithful King *David*, who fought his first battle in 1064, and his last battle some thirty years later, against the Philistines. He carried the war into the enemy's country, captured their strongholds, and made them tributary (2 Sam. iii. 18, xix. 9). Not until the disastrous reign of wicked Jehoram (889—885) shall we meet with them again; but in " Palestine" (*i.e.*, " Philistia "), the most familiar name of the land of Israel, they left a lasting trace of their long domination.

David's wars were the summary and the conclusion of the whole contest (Acts vii. 45). The victories of Barak and Gideon over the *Canaanites* and *Midianites* were final; but it was David who, besides subduing the Edomites, finally vanquished the *Syrians, Moabites, Amalekites, Ammonites,* and *Philistines*. And so "the heathen perished out of God's land" at last (Psalm x. 16), and Israel became united, independent, and strong (Josh. xxi. 45).

Of the 330 years between Joshua's death and Saul's accession, 111 were passed by some portion, sometimes a large portion, of God's People in servitude. This was not part of God's plan for them, but the result of their own worldliness and disobedience, and pursuit of what they considered expedient and not of what was right. (Observe these four stages: Judg. i. 21, iii. 5, xxi. 25, x. 6.) They sought to serve their own true God and the false gods of their neighbours as well; they wanted to have both God and God's enemies for their friends (Psalm cvi. 34-6). Now those who live wholly for the world may be happy, though not in the highest way; those who live wholly for God must be happy in the highest way. But those who try to serve God and the world at once must be miserable. That is our lesson from those ancient wars. What was their result for Israel?

Nine hundred years elapsed between the Exodus and the Babylonian Captivity—viz., 400 years of irregular government by fifteen judges, and 500 years of monarchy. The progress and prosperity of the nation under David and Solomon fully justified the establishment of monarchy, which we have now to consider.

Two hundred years after the death of Moses they offered an hereditary crown to Gideon. He refused it, and the power of his son was too limited to warrant us in calling him the first King of Israel. 150 years later, under Philistine pressure, the need for a permanent guarantee of national unity again asserted itself with irresistible force. Different judges had ruled different tribes; Samuel for the first time ruled all Israel (1 Sam. iii. 20), and when Shiloh lay desolate and Jerusalem was still a Jebusite city, his abode at Ramah became the national centre. Events were ripe for more settled political institutions than the casual rule of men who claimed uncertain allegiance during their lives, and left certain confusion at their deaths (Judg. xvii. 6, xviii. 1, xix. 1, xxi. 25). Monarchy, though not established by Moses, was clearly contemplated by the Mosaic Law (Deut. xvii. 14-20). But wilfully and defiantly the people demanded a king, that they might be "like all the nations," ignoring their peculiar position as the People of God. And God, who sometimes allows us to mete out our own punishment when we importune Him to give according to our own will, not His (Psalm cvi. 15), gave them a king after their own heart of the tribe of Benjamin. When they had learned that "unblest good is ill," He gave them a king after His own heart of the tribe of Judah, and established his dynasty for ever (Acts xiii. 21, 22).

II. BOOKS TO BE READ.

(See "Oxford Helps," § v.)

This term our time is divided between four of the historical and one of the poetical books of the Old Testament. The larger number of appointed chapters does not represent more work. For we have already made some acquaintance with 1 Chron. i.-viii., and several of the following chapters are almost verbal repetitions of chapters in Samuel; many of the Psalms are very short, and four of them occur twice over. We are in the age of one of the greatest poets of the world, and, with two exceptions, the following poems are all from his hand:—

(*a*) The Song of Hannah, the earliest "hymn" properly so-called, a first outpouring of individual as distinct from national devotion (1 Sam. ii. 1-10; comp. Luke i. 46-55).

(*b*) David's Song of the Bow, from the Book of Jashar, the finest and the most ancient of all dirges, mourning Saul with the harp that had so often soothed him, and, full of charity as it is of poetry, saying nought but good of David's enemy, while commemorating David's friend, the mighty archer of the archer tribe, in words destined to be used by David's own tribe as they learned to handle the archer's weapon (2 Sam. i. 19-27).

(c) David's Elegy over Abner, a brief outburst of grief for the sudden and violent end of a great prince (2 Sam. iii. 33, 34).

(d) David's Song of Praise on the greatest day of his life, when he was at once conqueror and king, poet and musician. Two liturgical psalms, added to the Psalter after the Captivity, were founded upon it (Psalm cv. 1-15, xcvi., cvi. 47, 48), as our Prayer Book makes general use of the three canticles in S. Luke (1 Chron. xvi. 7-36).

(e) David's Song of Victory, recalling his conflicts with all his enemies from the first and most implacable, and ascribing his success wholly to God (2 Sam. xxii.; comp. Psalm xviii.).

(f) David's Last Words, one of his most notable psalms. It sums up all his life's experience of the faithfulness of God (2 Sam. xxiii. 1-7). (We read this next term, but note it now to complete the list.)

Sixty-one *Psalms*, all, save one, by David; see p. 180.

1 and 2 *Samuel* with 1 and 2 *Kings* are spoken of in the Septuagint as "the four books of Kings." They form one historical compilation based upon the writings of Samuel, Nathan, Gad, Isaiah, and others (1 Chron. xxix. 29), and, it seems, completed and finally edited by Jeremiah the prophet immediately after the Captivity. They were written by Prophets with all the freshness and fulness of contemporary records. They are political, military, and poetical, and contain the history of all Israel. Only they insert accounts of the reign of Saul, of David's wanderings and of his fall, and of the rebellions of Absalom and Adonijah. Their keynote is *The Throne of the Lord's Anointed* (John i. 41, 49, xii. 13, xviii. 33-7).

1 and 2 *Chronicles* are called in the Septuagint, "The history of the things left out." They are based upon the public records first instituted by David (1 Chron. xxvii. 24), but were edited after the Captivity, probably by Ezra the priest, some 150 years later than Kings. They cover the

whole period of the four Books of Kings, which they are evidently designed to supplement. In contrast to Kings, they were written by Priests and Levites, with the dispassionate judgment befitting records of events long past. They are ecclesiastical, genealogical, and prosaic, and contain the history of Judah (1 Chron. v. 2, xxviii. 4). Only they insert complete genealogies from Adam, complete statistics of David's kingdom, full descriptions of his preparations for the Temple, and henceforth of everything relating to its worship. Their keynote is *The Lord dwelleth in Jerusalem* (1 Chron. xxiii. 25, R.V.; Matt. v. 35; John iv. 20; Rev. xxi. 2, 3).

III. PERIODS AND DATES.

The chronology becomes more definite as this period of 238 years draws to a close, but several very perplexing questions are connected with it. S. Paul's statement in Acts xiii. 20 (but see R.V.) agrees with the result of adding up the periods of servitude and judgeship named in Judges, but it cannot be reconciled with the assertion in 1 Kings vi. 1, that 12 periods of forty years elapsed between the Exodus and the erection of the Temple. Some, therefore, regard this assertion as an erroneous interpolation and throw the Exodus back 140 years; others more reasonably recognise that the periods in Judges are not successive but overlap each other. For instance, Judg. xi. 26 indicates that Jephthah's rule began in 1152, and since Samson's cannot have begun later than 1136, Ibzan, Elon, and Abdon must have been contemporary in another part of Palestine with one or other of these two. Thus in a period only extending over 130 years, 450 years are accounted for.

(1) B.C. 1256—1136 (120 years). From the Midianite oppression to the beginning of Samson's rule. *Israel under eight Judges.*

    (*a*) Seven years' oppression of the Midianites and Amalekites in Central Palestine (1256—1249), and rule of Gideon, Abimelech, Tola, and Jair. **Judg. vi.—x. 5.**

    (*b*) Eighteen years' oppression of the Ammonites

on the east (1170—1152), and rule of Jephthah, Ibzan, Elon, Abdon (and Eli?) **Judg. x. 6—xii.**

(2) B.C. 1136—1096 (40 years). From the beginning of Samson's rule to the accession of Saul. *Israel under the last three Judges. "The days of the Philistines."*

    (*a*) 1136—1116. The rule of Samson and Eli, and defeat at Aphek. **Judg. xiii.—xvi.; 1 Sam. i.—iv.**

    (*b*) 1116—1096. The rule of Samuel and victory at Ebenezer. **1 Sam. v.—vii.**

(3) B.C. 1096—1056 (40 years). From the accession of Saul to his death. *Israel under Samuel and Saul.*

    (*a*) 1096—1064. The probation of Saul through prosperity. **1 Sam. viii.—xv.**

    (*b*) 1064—1056. The probation of David through adversity **1 Sam. xvi., xvii.; Psalms viii., xix., xxiii., xxix.; 1 Sam. xviii.; Psalms cxl., cxli.; 1 Sam. xix.; Psalm lix.; 1 Sam. xx.; Psalms xiii., xi.; 1 Sam. xxi.; Psalms lvi., xxv.; 1 Sam. xxii.; Psalms xxxiv., cxlii., lvii., lii.; 1 Sam. xxiii.—xxvi.; Psalms lviii., xxxv., liv., vii., xvii.; 1 Sam. xxvii.—xxxi.; 1 Chron. i.—x.**

(4) B.C. 1056—1018 (38 years). From the death of Saul to the choice of a site for the Temple. *Israel under David.*

    (*a*) 1056—1049. His reign at Hebron over Judah. **2 Sam. i.—iv.**

    (*b*) 1049—1036. His reign at Jerusalem over all Israel. His victories, glory, and prosperity. **2 Sam. v. 1-16; 1 Chron. xi. 1-9, xiv. 1-7; 2 Sam. xxiii. 8-39; 1 Chron. xi. 10-47, xii.; Psalms lxxviii., xvi.; 2 Sam. vi., vii.; 1 Chron. xiii., xv.—xvii.; Psalms ci., xxiv., xv., cx., cxxxviii.; 2 Sam. v. 17-25, viii.—xi. 1, xii. 26-31, xxi. 15-22; 1 Chron. xiv. 8-17, xviii.—xx.; Psalms xx., xxi., lx., cviii., ix., ii., xviii.; 2 Sam. xxii.; Psalm lxviii.**

    (*c*) 1036—1018. His sin and suffering. **2 Sam. xi. 1—xii. 25; Psalms li., xxxii., vi., xxxviii., xxxix., xli., xl., lxx., v.; 2 Sam. xiii.—xv. 12;**

Psalms x., xii., xiv., liii., lxii., lxiv., 2 Sam. xv. 13—xvii.; Psalms cxliii., lxiii., xxvii., lv., cix., lxix., xxii., xxxi., lxi., iii., iv.; 2 Sam. xviii.—xxi. 14.

IV. GEOGRAPHY.

(See "Oxford Helps," Maps V. and VI.)

We have already studied Palestine, the scene of all this term's events, and although Jerusalem is characterised as "the city where David encamped" (Isa. xxix. 1), there are several good reasons for postponing its topography to the reign of David's son, who was "King in Jerusalem" (Eccles. i. 1).

How much of the whole land which God promised was possessed by Israel? This geographical question now calls for solution.

By God Himself to Abraham, through Moses to Israel on leaving Egypt, and again through Ezekiel to Israel during the Babylonian Captivity, a territory was promised to the Chosen People, which was 2½ times as large as Great Britain and Ireland, or 300,000 square miles in extent. Speaking generally, it lay between the Nile and the Euphrates, the Mediterranean and the Persian Gulf or the Syrian Desert. Solomon for a short time ruled the whole of it as King of Israel and suzerain of Israel's neighbours. But, omitting the Trans-Jordanic provinces whose occupants soon ceased to have any close connexion with their compatriots, we find that what they actually possessed lay between Beersheba and Dan, the Mediterranean and Jordan, and was little larger than Wales. Did Israel's sin make void the promise, or will it be fulfilled hereafter? Jer. xxxii. 37-42; Amos ix. 15; Rom. xi. 29.

Careful comparison of the following passages with each other and the maps will show the exact boundaries:—
Gen. xiii. 14, 15, xv. 18; Exod. xxiii. 31; Num. xiii. 21, xxxiv. 2-8; Deut. xi. 24; Josh. i. 3, 4; 1 Kings iv. 21, 24, viii. 65; 2 Chron. vii. 8, ix. 26; Psalm lxxii. 8, lxxx. 11, lxxxix. 25; Isa. xxvii. 12 (R.V.); Ezek. xlvii. 13-21; Zech. ix. 10.

On the north, Mount Hor (that is, either Mount Casius on the Bay of Antioch, or the Lebanon Range generally), the entering in of Hamath to Zebad, and the River, or the Great River, that is, the Euphrates.

On the east, the Euphrates and Syrian Desert, or else the Orontes, Jordan, the Salt (or Dead) Sea, and Red Sea.

On the south, the deserts of Paran and Zin, called "the ends of the earth," to "the brook of Egypt" (that is, the Wadi l'Areesh or Rhinocolura). The Nile, or "river of Egypt," is only mentioned in Gen. xv. 18.

On the west, the Great, Hinder, or Western Sea, or Sea of the Philistines, that is, the Mediterranean.

V. HEROES.

Keynotes { *Gideon*, Phil. iv. 13, 17 (R.V.), *Samuel*, Eph. vi. 18. *David*, Eph. vi. 6.

Each of this term's heroes stands out sharply contrasted with a contemporary in a way that throws much light upon him. *Gideon* is the most heroic character in Judges, and he wrought the greatest deliverance there recorded. Mighty in faith, he recalls the past greatness of Joshua; courteous, forbearing, and humble, he anticipates the future grace of David. His disinterested patriotism finds a modern parallel in George Washington. He yields to none of the judges in dignity; Samuel only, who rose above his superstitious devotion, excels him in holiness. The crown he set aside was seized by the rash and unscrupulous *Abimelech*, the one judge who performed no public service.

Samson and *Samuel* were about the same age. Both were Nazirites from birth; both were raised up to deliver Israel, and received a special call and a special training for their work. Samson's extraordinary physical power enabled him to strike terror into the Philistines and encourage Israel, but his wayward inconsistency and uncontrolled passions wasted that power on isolated feats, and he carried out no organised plan of national defence and founded no national institutions. Samuel's extraordinary moral power was an outcome of the holy and consistent life of one who had served the Lord from his youth. He and S. John are the great Scripture examples of inward, silent, unbroken growth in grace from childhood, as Jacob and S. Paul are of sudden and decisive conversion in mature years. Note that the same religious surroundings which aided this growth in him only hardened the sons of Eli. Warrior, ruler, counsellor, intercessor, and prophet, Samuel was neither king nor priest nor poet. He was not, like Moses, the originator of new institutions, nor, like Jeremiah, the upholder of old ones. To him was committed the hardest task of guiding his country safely through a time of transition, when new conditions brought new needs. He was the last judge, and the first of that long succession of prophets who will claim our chief attention later on. And as the Levite son of Zacharias was forerunner of the Son of David, so the Levite son of Elkanah was forerunner of David.

Chosen of the Lord (2 Sam. xxi. 6, R.V.), endowed with the Spirit, with Samuel for his counsellor and David for his friend, *Saul* was favoured in all his circumstances. But his fierce Benjamite temper was ungoverned, his better impulses were guided by no steady principle, his religion did not influence his moral nature. Ever and always he did according to his own will, and sought what was right in his own eyes. God put him to a test less severe than those which Abraham and Gideon had undergone triumphantly. First, by a trial of endurance under pressure from the enemy (1 Sam. xiii.). In his rash superstition and impatience he broke through the restraint imposed upon him by Samuel. Secondly, by a trial of obedience under pressure from the people (1 Sam. xv.). In blind self-confidence he disregarded God's plain command to him. These failures proved him unfit for the trust committed to him, so, in mercy to Israel, God first took the kingdom away from his family, and secondly rejected him from being king. His third and crowning sin was asking counsel of one that had a familiar spirit in defiance of the law of Moses (1 Chron. x. 13, 14). Suicide, possibly completed by the hand of one of those Amalekites concerning whom he had sinned, was the dark close of a career that might have been full of light. So he perished, self-willed king of a self-willed people; and, though fits of madness came over him as they have come over more than one unhappy monarch whose imperious will has been unchecked by either principle or circumstances, we cannot assert that he was not responsible for his own destruction (2 Peter ii. 21).

David and S. Paul stand alone among the characters of Holy Writ in leaving writings through which we can look into their heart of hearts, and, of all the heroes of the Old Testament, *David* is the one we know best; 131 of its chapters have him for their theme or their author, and he is frequently mentioned in Scripture elsewhere. His daring courage, his quick sagacity, the prudence that never deserted him, his prompt resource in difficulty, his singular mixture of tenderness and severity, his inborn power to rule, his skill to plan and enterprise in carrying out his plans, remind us of the champions of the past. His intellectual gifts link him to the "wise men" of the age which succeeded his. For, while we speak of the rod of Moses, the spear of Joshua, the sword of Gideon, and the mantle of Samuel, we refer to the harp of David. As Moses the Prophet anticipated Samuel, so Moses the Psalmist anticipated David, who was the greatest of Israel's poets, and the first of all poets to give utterance to man's deep joy in nature's beauty and man's deep longings after communion with God. "David" means "beloved," and no one ever gave or received more passionate and devoted love than he, from the day the young hero of Ephes-Dammim was the nation's darling, to the day the aged king bowed the hearts of all as the heart of one man (1 Sam. xviii. 1, 3, 5, 16, 20, 22, 28, 30; 2 Sam. xix. 14). His was that highly emotional nature that feels pleasure and pain and is conscious of the good and evil in others to a very rare degree. The versatility and complexity of character and gifts which we note in many of the tribe of Judah reached their climax in David, and the training for his life work was unusually complete. The early years of pastoral solitude and meditation; the camp and court, first of Israel, then of Philistia the great military power of the day; the College of Prophets at Ramah, in which we may discover a germ of the universities of Christendom; the life of hardship and risk in the wilderness where David gathered followers, not as a mere rebel against Saul, but as an independent chieftain, destined to be king, fighting Israel's foes, and having with him Abiathar, the High Priest, and Gad, the prophet of God;—in all these he learned, above every other lesson, to know God, to trust Him wholly, and to commune with Him daily and hourly. "Servant of God" is the title given to him oftener than any other, which he shares with Moses and Joshua only of all Old Testament saints in the New Testament, the title in which S. Paul, the greatest of all the sons of Abraham, gloried. "The way of David" becomes as proverbial as "the way of Jeroboam" afterwards, and God, who rejected Saul, made with David an everlasting covenant (2 Sam. xxiii. 5).

But, it may be said, surely the shortcomings of David were even more grievous than those of Saul. When his throne was established in peace and prosperity, despite the generosity and chivalry, the self-control and faithful friendship which had hitherto distinguished him, he was hurried away into shameful sin against God and man. It is not enough to reply that we cannot judge a Jewish king by a Christian standard, since his temptations were greater and his restraints fewer than ours. His crimes would, it is true, have been thought little of by contemporary monarchs, but then he had the law of Moses. To his disregard of one clear precept in it (Deut. xvii. 17) may be traced not only all the evils and troubles in his own family, but his successor's apostasy and the consequent disasters to his house and to Israel. Yes, like Saul, David sinned, and many men have been more blameless than he. Yet few have been so good, for notwithstanding his sin it remained the habit of his life to fulfil God's will from his heart (1 Kings xv. 3-5; Acts xiii. 22), and therefore, unlike Saul's sins, his sins were followed by fullest acknowledgment, deepest contrition, and meekest endurance of the appointed chastisement. David's "heinous sin, hearty repentance, and heavy punishment" (to quote Fuller's expressive phrase) is recorded for our everlasting instruction. From the record we learn these three things. That the noblest intellectual gifts, the greatest religious privileges, the fullest knowledge of the truth, and the highest spiritual attainments cannot keep us from the most flagrant transgressions if we cease to depend humbly upon God and to use diligently all the means of grace (1 Cor. x. 12). That repentance means much more than penance and much more than remorse, and that "the forgiveness of sins," in which we so continually profess our belief, is free, final, and abundant (with Isa. xliii. 25 compare 1 Kings xiv. 7, 8). Lastly, we learn that in this life we must reap the natural consequences even of forgiven sin. David's own words of self-vindication in Psalm vii. 3-5 were terribly taken in earnest, although death, the legal penalty he had incurred, was remitted ; and from the Psalms he wrote beyond Jordan, ten years later, we perceive that there is anguish worse than death ; it can never be with us as it would have been if we had not sinned.

VI. THE COMING MESSIAH.
"How then doth David in the Spirit call Him Lord?"
Matt. xxii. 41-5 (R.V.).

Each of the "saviours" whom God gave Israel (Neh. ix. 27) was a more or less perfect Type of Him whom the angel named JESUS (Matt. i. 21). Gideon sets aside the crown, Jephthah gives his dearest a willing sacrifice to free her country from a terrible obligation, Samson dies with the Philistines. for Israel, Samuel prays without ceasing for his people. But "the good things to come" were most distinctly foreshadowed in "the man whom God raised on high" (with 2 Sam. xxiii. 1 comp. Acts v. 31) as His Anointed. The whole history of David is a type of the militant kingdom of Christ, and all his utterances in the Psalms find their deepest and highest application as the utterances of his greater Son (Luke xxiv. 44, and p. 177).

That our Lord would spring out of Judah had been already foretold. This term we learn to add "Son of David" to "Son of Abraham" (Matt. i. 1). Three Predictions in the historical books give more definite shape than had been given heretofore to the hopes which reached their highest pitch just 1000 years after David.

(*a*) 1 Sam. ii. 10, which makes first mention of the Lord's Anointed (Luke ii. 26 ; Acts iv. 26, 27, R.V.).

(*b*) 1 Sam. ii. 35. The original allusion is to Zadok, whose descendants held the high-priesthood till the Fall of Jerusalem in A.D. 70, but it finds complete fulfilment in Christ (Heb. ii. 17).

(*c*) 2 Sam. vii. 12-16; 1 Chron. xvii. 11-14. Here again the immediate reference is to Solomon, but even without David's own comments on the promise in 2 Sam. xxiii. 3-5, and in the Psalms, the words "for ever" show for the first time that the Messiah would not only be a King, but that He would be more than human (Isa. lv. 3; Luke i. 31-3; Acts ii. 30, 31, xiii. 34; Heb. i. 5). This being so, we may see in the "house for God's name" the earliest mention of the Church of Christ (1 Tim. iii. 15; Heb. iii. 6). Henceforth there was an ever-growing expectation of a second David greater than the first (Ezek. xxxvii. 24, 25; Amos ix. 11).

VII. God's Revelation of Himself to Man.

To the Patriarchs God was known as El Shaddai; to Moses as Jehovah. Now in a fresh crisis of His people's history, He reveals Himself again by a new name, Jehovah Sabaoth (1 Sam. i. 3, 11, xvii. 45), first publicly proclaimed by David on the day he brought up the Ark to Zion (2 Sam. vi. 2, 18, vii. 26; Psalm xxiv.). Sabaoth, like "host," is used both of the stars of the material heaven and of the angels of the invisible world, and this name means "Lord of Hosts or Armies," *i.e.*, of all the intelligent creatures who perform the Divine will in heaven and earth (1 Kings xxii. 19; Neh. ix. 6; Dan. iv. 35; Psalm ciii. 21; Matt. vi. 10; Luke ii. 13), and is translated in the Septuagint by a Greek word which in 2 Cor. vi. 18, and nine times in Revelation, is rendered "Almighty," but which should rather be rendered "All-sovereign." To the newly settled fabric of Church and State it was a pledge of victory and glory, and while it indirectly rebuked idolatrous worship of the host of heaven (Acts vii. 42), it answered to the wider range of vision opening on Israel with a new epoch of her civilisation. Jehovah Sabaoth remained the chief name of God throughout the monarchical period. It occurs over 260 times in the Old Testament and twice in the New Testament (Rom. ix. 29 ; James v. 4), and is used to-day all over Christendom when "the holy Church throughout all the world" echoes the songs of heaven in her grandest hymn of praise.

Observe how David's enumeration of the God of Israel, the Rock of Israel, and the Spirit of the Lord (2 Sam. xxiii. 2, 3) points on to future manifestation of the Three in One.

VIII. MAN'S RELATION TO GOD IN WORSHIP.

We have seen how the days when every man did what was right in his own eyes (Judg. xxi. 25 ; Deut. xii. 8, 28) ended in a corrupt priesthood, a desolate sanctuary, and a captive Ark. The Ark never returned to the dishonoured Tabernacle in ruined Shiloh, but during the succeeding age of political change and religious confusion both were carried from place to place, and worship seems to have been offered at each. Meanwhile the people relapsed again and again into the two forms of idolatry explained last term, and the practice of various unauthorised superstitions prevailed (Judg. xviii. 24-7 ; 1 Sam. xv. 23, R.V., xix. 13). But at length God chose a place for His abode (1 Chron. xxiii. 25, R.V. ; Psalm lxviii. 16, lxxviii. 67, 68, lxxxvii. 2, cxxxii. 13, 14), and it was the desire of David's heart there to build a House for Him who had so long been served in a roving tent.

How David prepared for that House, and how Solomon reared it, we shall learn next term.

IX. QUESTIONS.

(See pp. 13, 18.)

[Questions III., IV., V., VI., XV., XVI., XVII., XXV., and XXIX. may be answered with the help of any books. The other 23 questions should be answered with the help of A.V. and R.V. only.]

1. "The Lord sent Jerubbaal and Jephthah and Samuel." Complete the quotation, and show in a few words for what purpose each was sent, and how he carried out that purpose. (6.)

II. Make a chronological table of the fifteen Judges, stating where they ruled, how long they ruled, and what they did for Israel. Which of them are commended for their faith in the New Testament? (30.)

III. At what times and in what ways was the judgment upon Eli's house completely fulfilled? (5.)

IV. Prove from Jeremiah and the Psalms that Shiloh was desolated after the capture of the Ark. (3.)

V. Show without reference to the books bearing his name that Samuel was a prophet, acceptable to God, and a man of faith and prayer. (6.)

VI. What do we know to the credit of one of Samuel's grandsons? (4.)

VII. Give examples of the vehement vows that were one characteristic of the age between Moses and David. (8.)

VIII. Sketch briefly the history of Saul's persecution of David, and trace David's wanderings. (20.)

IX. Why did David commit his parents to the King of *Moab*? Did he keep the oath recorded in 1 Sam. xxiv. 21, 22? (4.)

X. Rehearse briefly the chief incidents in the career of Jonathan, and illustrate his faith, courage, patience, generosity, unselfishness, and piety. (15.)

XI. How may we account for the conduct of the men of Jabesh Gilead to Saul, and for that of Joab to Abner? (4.)

XII. Prove that each of the following tribes furnished Israel with at least one ruler between B.C. 1500 and B.C. 1000 :—Levi, Judah, Zebulon, Issachar, Dan, Naphtali, Manasseh, Ephraim, Benjamin. (12.)

XIII. How often was David anointed? (2.)

XIV. Give as full an account as you can of David's nephews, omitting Joab. (14.)

XV. Which of Solomon's great-grandfathers is particularly described in the Psalms? (3.)

XVI. Where is David called (1) a prophet, (2) a patriarch, (3) "David the King," (4) "a leader and commander," (5) "the man of God," (6) "the servant of God," (7) God's "firstborn," (8) God's "anointed," (9) "a man after God's own heart," (10) "one chosen out of the people," (11) "the sweet psalmist," (12) inventor of instruments of music, (13) "light or lamp of Israel," (14) father of the Messiah? On what occasion did he wear the dress and perform the office of a priest? (16.)

XVII. Find six New Testament references to David as inspired, and ten to him as the ancestor of the Messiah. On how many occasions was our Lord addressed as "Son of David"? What events in David's life are alluded to in the New Testament? (22.)

XVIII. What does "Samuel" mean? Show how the lives of Samuel and David illustrate the power of prayer. (15.)

XIX. Consider David as a type of Christ in character and circumstances. (15.)

XX. Briefly relate the history of the Ark of God from B.C. 1451 till it "had rest" in B.C. 1041. (15.)

XXI. Trace the application of 1 Chron. xvi. 20-22 to Abraham, Jacob, David, and the Ark. (8.)

XXII. "The Lord was with him." Find 14 passages in which this is said of David. (14.)

XXIII. Is there any evidence that Absalom's effeminate vanity caused his death? (2.)

XXIV. Name three heroes who slew lions. (3.)

XXV. Explain the Old Testament historical allusions in the following passages in the Psalms:—ii. 7, iv. 7, vii. 4, xi. 6, xxi. 3, li. 11, lv. 3, 12-14, lx. 6-9, lxi. 2, lxviii. 11, 29 R.V., lxxviii. 60-68, cx. 4. (28.)

XXVI. Show by New Testament quotations that these ten Psalms refer to Christ:—ii., viii., xvi., xxii., xxiv., xl., xli., lxviii., lxix., cx. (20.)

XXVII. By whom and to whom was the oldest letter whose contents are on record written? Who uttered the oldest parable, and who invented the oldest riddle extant? To whom was the first temple mentioned in Scripture dedicated? (4.)

XXVIII. Name the first instance of a foreigner holding high office in Israel, and the first instance of a ruler who owed his elevation wholly to popular suffrage. (4.)

XXIX. Illustrate Acts x. 35 by naming representatives of the nations whom God bade Israel destroy or shun among the friends and followers of David. (8.)

XXX. Where, when, by whom, and with what result were the following battles fought?—Harod, Oreb's Rock,

Karkor, Aroer, Aphek, Ebenezer, Michmash, Havilah, Ephes-Dammim, Gilboa. (40.)

XXXI. What do you know of the following?—Ahitub, Chimham, Gaal, Hushai, Ichabod, Ittai, Merab, Purah, Sheba, Ziba, the Cherethites, and Pelethites. (24.)

XXXII. Give references for the following:—(*a*) "Thy people offer themselves willingly"; (*b*) "I have looked upon My people"; (*c*) "The Lord seeth not as man seeth"; (*d*) "Who daily beareth our burden"; (*e*) "Go in this thy might"; (*f*) "God is gone out before thee"; (*g*) "God is for me"; (*h*) "Them that honour Me I will honour"; (*i*) "That they might set their hope in God"; (*j*) "God was entreated of them because they put their trust in Him"; (*k*) "I have no good beyond Thee"; (*l*) "Thou knowest Thy servant"; (*m*) "Strengthen me only this once"; (*n*) "O that Thou wouldest keep me from evil"; (*o*) "Blessed be the Lord that hath kept back His servant from evil"; (*p*) "Thou art worth ten thousand of us"; (*q*) "Thine are we, David"; (*r*) "With me thou shalt be in safeguard"; (*s*) "Thou shalt surely prevail"; (*t*) "The wicked shall return to Sheol"; (*u*) "Thou shalt not die"; (*v*) "The Lord sat as King at the Flood"; (*w*) "The host was secure"; (*x*) "But little lower than God"; (*y*) "The woman went in her wisdom"; (*z*) "I shall be satisfied." (26)

For *Second Series* of Questions, see p. 309.

FOURTH TERM.

THE DAYS OF SOLOMON

THE CHOSEN NATION CENTRE OF AN EMPIRE.
THE FIRST TEMPLE.

B.C. 1018—915.

2 *Sam.* XXIII. 1-7, XXIV., 1 *Kings* I.—XVI. 28, 1 *Chron.* XXI.—XXIX. 2 *Chron.* I.—XVI. *Song of Songs, Proverbs, Ecclesiastes, Psalms* I., XXVI., XXVIII., XXX., XXXVI., XXXVII., XLII., XLIII., XLV., XLIX., L., LXVII., LXXIII., LXXVII., LXXXI., LXXXII., LXXXIV., LXXXVI., LXXXVIII., LXXXIX., XCI., CXI., CXII., CXXVII., CXXVIII., CXXXI., CXXXII., CXXXIII., CXXXIX., CXLV. (123 *chapters.*)

"Blessed is the man . . . whose delight is in the law of the Lord."
—PSALM 1. 2.

13th MONTH (29).

Psalms XXXVI., XXXVII., CXXXIII. 2 Sam. XXIV. 1 Chron. XXI.—XXIX. 22. Psalms XXVI., XXVIII., XXX., CXXXIX., CXXXI., LXXXVI., CXLV. 2 Sam. XXIII. 1-7. 1 Kings I.—V. 1 Chron. XXIX. 23-30. 2 Chron. I., II., Psalms LXXII., XLV.

14th MONTH (31).

1 Kings VI.—IX. 9. 2 Chron. III.—VII. Psalms CXXXII., L., CXXVII., CXXVIII., LXXXI., LXXVII., LXXXII., XLII., XLIII., LXXXIV. 1 Kings IX. 10—X.

14th MONTH *Continued.*

2 Chron. VIII.—IX. 28. The Song of Songs.

15th MONTH (31).

Proverbs.

16th MONTH (32).

1 Kings XI. 2 Chron. IX. 29-31. Ecclesiastes. Psalms LXXXVIII., XLIX., LXXIII., CXI., CXII., XCI., 1 Kings XII. 1-19. 2 Chron. X. 1 Kings XII. 20—XIV. 2 Chron. XI., XII. Psalm LXXXIX. 1 Kings XV. 1-8. 2 Chron. XIII. 1 Kings XV. 9-24. 2 Chron. XIV.—XVI. 1 Kings XV. 25—XVI. 28.

I. GENERAL SUMMARY.

SAUL had been little more than the pastoral chief of amalgamated tribes, ruling Central Palestine only. David succeeded to a kingdom distracted by civil dissensions, without a capital, almost without an army, but loosely knit together, and everywhere surrounded by powerful and victorious enemies. He founded an hereditary monarchy, shaped its institutions, and left a compact and united state, not only independent but powerful, and rapidly rising to a prosperity that had every prospect of permanence. His kingdom became Solomon's empire, which extended over the whole territory promised to the Chosen Nation. For the first and last time it took its place among the great powers of the East, its history culminating just as Greek history was beginning. We may institute a threefold comparison between this Hebrew golden age and England's golden age under Elizabeth and James I.

(a) *Politically.* Just as the old world of the East and the new world of the West were thrown open to Elizabethan exploration, and the way was thus prepared for the "Greater Britain" of to-day; so eastern Ophir and western Tarshish were sought out by Solomon's subjects, which resulted in a vigorous foreign policy, far-reaching commercial enterprise abroad, and wealth and splendour hitherto unknown at home.

(b) *Intellectually.* Just as the widened Elizabethan horizon stimulated patriotism, and nourished our greatest English literature and earliest English research; so Israel's enlarged knowledge, new sympathies, and grander ideals found expression in a profounder and more highly finished literature, whose finest specimens we still have, and in a new interest in botany and natural history, of which only the record survives, since it is not the object of Holy Writ to chronicle scientific discovery of Nature's wonders.

(c) *Religiously.* Just as the outward ceremonial of our national worship was reconstructed in a more spiritual and less superstitious form in Elizabeth's days; so Israel reared an abode for God as worthy as human skill and lavished wealth could make it, and Solomon uttered Israel's creed in its highest form at the dedication of this long-desired House.

The main interest of this period, unlike that of the preceding, is ecclesiastical and political rather than personal, and its history forms the most secular chapter of the sacred record. Because the glory of Solomon was after the fashion of this world it passed away (1 Cor. vii. 31), and no story is more disappointing than the tale of how its fair promise was blighted. There are but three allusions to Solomon in the New Testament, and they are keys to his whole history. He attained much, yet he fell short of perfection, *politically*, in spite of his splendour (Matt. vi. 29); *intellectually*, in spite of his wisdom (Matt. xii. 42); *religiously*, in spite of the noble fabric he reared (Acts vii. 47, 48). Judged by Deut. xvii. 14-20, he violated every principle of the Hebrew Constitution; and he left an insecure throne, a discontented people, and formidable enemies upon his frontiers.

On the surface, the Disruption that took place immediately after his death was due to the thoughtless self-will of Rehoboam and the revolutionary ability of Jeroboam; ultimately, it was to be traced to national luxury, pride, self-confidence, and godlessness; also to Solomon's impoverishing lavishness; Egypt's jealousy of Israel's prosperity; and the revival of old tribal heartburnings as one result of David's sin (2 Sam. xx.). Rachel's children owned the most fertile tracts of Palestine; Shechem and Shiloh, chief seats hitherto of secular and religious greatness; and the historic cities of Jericho, Gilgal, Bethel, and Ramah. From them had sprung Gideon, Jephthah, Ehud, Jair, and Abdon, among the judges; Deborah and (by birth though not descent) Samuel among the prophets; Abimelech and Saul, the first kings; Joshua, Jonathan, and Abner. So they had always been inclined to resent the domination of Judah ere they broke into open and final revolt. Henceforth we deal with two struggling kingdoms, weak halves of what had once been a strong whole. The lesson plainly is that nations and individuals may miss an opportunity God will not give them again, if they reject His counsel for them (Luke vii. 30, R.V.; Psalm lxxxi. 13-16).

II. BOOKS TO BE READ.

(See "Oxford Helps," § v.)

This term two-thirds of our reading is literature, and only one-third history. In contrast to our Third Term, we read a smaller number of chapters than the average, because that literature demands special care and thought. The historical books we continue call for no further comment. For the thirty *Psalms* of this period, see p. 194.

Three other works depict in a threefold philosophy of life, the development of Solomon's character and of the thought of his age.

The Song of Songs is pure poetry, idyllic or pastoral as regards its subject, and lyric and dramatic (though scarcely a drama) as regards its form. (If the composition of the Book of Job, the nearest approach to an epic in the Bible, is rightly referred to Solomon's reign, all the three great species of poetry are represented in this age.) The only survivor of his 1005 songs, doubtless the finest of them all, this Song pictures the brilliant promise of Solomon's youth. It evidently describes ideal human love, and its keynote is *Love is strong, indestructible, and priceless* (2 Cor. v. 14; Rom. viii. 35-7; 1 John iv. 10, 11). It has been variously explained, but the following summary of its purport is at once reasonable and widely accepted :—

The scene of i. 2—iii. 5, and of viii. 5-14, is laid in a wooded district of Northern Palestine, where Solomon is spending part of the summer in tents; the scene of iii. 6—viii. 4 is the royal palace at Jerusalem. There are two chief speakers and three choruses—viz., Shelomoh or Solomon (1 Chron. xxii. 9), the King of Israel; Shulammith, a village maiden of Northern Palestine, whom he woos in the guise of a shepherd; Chorus of young men, his companions (iii. 6-11); Chorus of virgins, her companions (i. 2-4, i. 8, i. 11, v. 9, vi. 1, vi. 10, vi. 13, vii. 1-5, viii. 5 *a*); Chorus of Shulammith's brothers (viii. 8, 9). The King's 13 speeches are the following: i. 9, 10, i. 15, i. 17, ii. 2, ii. 7, iii. 5, iv. 1-15, v. 1, vi. 4-9, vii. 6-9, viii. 4, viii. 5 *b*, viii. 13. The rest is uttered by the Bride. The alternate speeches should be marked off before one reads the poem in the R.V., which gives each a separate paragraph. R.V. is to be preferred throughout for this book.

First Canto. The King seeks and wins the Bride and brings her to Jerusalem ("My Beloved is mine," ii. 16).

(*a*) i. 2—ii. 7. The Bride in the King's pavilion.
(*b*) ii. 8—iii. 5. The Bride's first dream.
(*c*) iii. 6—v. 1. The royal Espousals.

Second Canto. The Bride seeks and finds the King and brings him to her home ("I am my Beloved's," vi. 3, vii. 10).

(*a*) v. 2—vi. 9. The Bride's second dream.
(*b*) vi. 10—viii. 4. Homeward thoughts.
(*c*) viii. 5-14. The Return home.

For the higher meaning of the whole poem, see p. 89.

Proverbs rises ever and anon into lofty flights of song, but, as a whole, it consists of gnomic and didactic rather than pure poetry. As the wisest sayings of Israel's wisest men, this book represents the mature experience of Solomon's prosperous middle life; and to its selection from the 3000 proverbs uttered by Israel's chief sage are added other terse apophthegms from the school which he founded. Chaps. xxx., xxxi. are probably much later than his reign, but as we cannot fix their date they are best read here. The Hebrew name of the book includes both "proverb" and "parable" in its meaning, and was applied to any pointed saying, especially if it conveyed its thought through a figure. Its root idea is that of comparison, putting this and that together, and noting their likeness and unlikeness that they may illustrate each other. Such forms of instruction date from an early stage of civilisation. The Greek name of the book is frequently used of the parables of Christ, which find their Old Testament counterpart here. Proverbs is ethical rather than theological, guiding to action as the Psalms guide to devotion. Even when religious, it deals with the moral aspect of religion common to all creeds, and exhorts to a faithful performance of duty in all relations of life, though it speaks throughout of our conduct as it is in the sight of God. Hence in later days it appealed more directly to the Gentile mind than any other Hebrew book. Moreover, as its wisdom bears far more on conduct than on speculation, it is practical rather than philosophical. Its keynote is *Justice and judgment are more acceptable than sacrifice*, xxi. 3 (Matt. ix. 13, xxiii. 23; Mark xii. 32-4). The thought that the fear of God, which is the beginning of wisdom, is something grander and wider than conformity to any outward rites, is a remarkable one for a book produced in an age which saw the noblest outcome of the Ceremonial Law in the Temple. Its sections are:—

(*a*) i. 1-6. Introduction stating that the aim of the whole is to answer the question "What is wisdom?"

(*b*) i. 7—ix. 18. First exhortation concerning wisdom.

(*c*) x. 1—xxii. 16. First collection of 400 proverbs.

(*d*) xxii. 17—xxiv. 22. Second exhortation concerning wisdom.

(*e*) xxiv. 23-34. Some sayings of the wise.

(*f*) xxv. 1—xxix. 27. Second collection of proverbs made under Hezekiah.

(*g*) xxx. Prophecy of Agur, son of Jakeh.

(*h*) xxxi. Prophecy of Lemuel's mother.

In *Ecclesiastes* the lyric outburst which began with the Psalms of Israel's foremost poet dies down into prose, yet prose of a highly poetical cast. A period of literary stagnancy succeeds. The reasons given for assigning the book to a later age than Solomon's do not amount to convincing proofs, so we act upon the time-honoured view that it represents the repentance of his sorrowful old age. "Many go through David's sins without his repentance, and Solomon's experiences without his conclusions, and these are the men who rail at both" (*Ker*). This saddest book of the Bible is often misunderstood by those who fail to perceive in it the utterances of two voices in a single soul. The lower voice is that of the man of the world, who tries every form of earthly pleasure, base and noble, and finds that none can satisfy the heart of man; who goes the whole round of human speculation seeking to read the riddle of the world before he has been chastened by submission and elevated by trust in God. It is a voice of doubt, sinking into despair, and we have its keynote in the phrase *Under the sun*, which occurs here 29 times and nowhere else. The higher voice is that of a divinely taught man, who desires to teach others through his own painful experience. He cannot solve all the perplexities of life, but he can point out the path of true blessedness. Its keynote is *God is in heaven, ruling the whole earth and rewarding those who serve Him*. (1 Cor. xv. 58). The sections of Ecclesiastes are :—

(*a*) i., ii. The search after Happiness and its failure.

(*b*) iii. 1—vi. 9. Nature's harmony and man's discord.

(*c*) vi. 10—viii. 15. Life as a whole is unsatisfying, yet it shall be well with the godly.

(*d*) viii. 16—xii. 14. The highest good attainable is being what God means us to be.

Observe that in Proverbs "wisdom" means "piety"; in Ecclesiastes "sagacity" and "knowledge."

III. PERIODS AND DATES.

The dates for these 103 years are those given in "Oxford Helps." Some good authorities make them one year later throughout. Henceforth a table of Reigns, which form most convenient landmarks, will be given each term for constant reference.

Observe that the reign of David fills 93 chapters, that of Solomon 89 chapters; also that the reigns of Saul (1096—1056), David (1056—1016), and Solomon (1016—976) each occupy 40 years; and that Asa was contemporary with all the first seven Kings of Israel.

(1) B.C. 1018—1004 (14 years). From the choice of a site for the Temple to its Dedication. *The House of God that Solomon built.*

    (*a*) 1018—1016. David's Preparation. Psalms xxxvi., xxxvii., cxxxiii.; 2 Sam. xxiv.; 1 Chron. xxi.—xxix. 22; Psalms xxvi., xxviii., xxx., cxxxix., cxxxi., lxxxvi., cxlv.; 2 Sam. xxiii. 1-7.

    (*b*) 1016—1012. Solomon's Preparation. 1 Kings i.—v.; 1 Chron. xxix. 23-30; 2 Chron. i., ii.; Psalms lxxii., xlv.

    (*c*) The Building and Dedication (1012—1004), 1 Kings vi.—ix. 9; 2 Chron. iii.—vii.; Psalms cxxxii., i., cxxvii., cxxviii., l., lxxxi., lxxvii., lxxxii., xlii., xliii., lxxxiv.

(2) B.C. 1004—976 (28 years). From the dedication of the Temple to the revolt of the Ten Tribes. *The Glory and Declension of Solomon.* 1 Kings ix. 10—x.; 2 Chron. viii.—ix. 28; Song of Songs; Proverbs; 1 Kings xi.; 2 Chron. ix. 29-31; Ecclesiastes; Psalms lxxxviii., xlix., lxxiii., cxi., cxii., xci.; 1 Kings xii. 1-19; 2 Chron. x.

(3) B.C. 976—955 (21 years). From the revolt of the Ten Tribes to the death of Jeroboam. *The religious Schism and political Disruption.* 1 Kings xii. 20—

xiv.; 2 Chron. xi., xii.; Psalm lxxxix.; 1 Kings xv. 1-8; 2 Chron. xiii.

(4) B.C. 955—915 (40 years). From the death of Jeroboam to the accessions of Jehoshaphat and Ahab. *The Strife between Israel and Judah.* 1 Kings xv. 9-24; 2 Chron. xiv.—xvi.; 1 Kings xv. 25—xvi. 28.

Three Kings of Judah.

Rehoboam, 976—959.
Abijah, 959—956.
Asa, 956—915.

Six Kings of Israel.

Jeroboam I., 976—955.
Nadab, 955—953.
Baasha, 953—931.
Elah, 931—929.
Zimri, seven days.
Omri, 929—917.

IV. GEOGRAPHY.

(See " Oxford Helps," Maps VI., VII., and IX., and § xxxiii.)

About the middle of the mountain ridge, or rather, high uneven plateau, which traverses Palestine from the Plain of Jezreel to the Desert of Paran, rise two hills, Zion on the west (2540 ft. above the sea), with the lower height of Acra or Millo to its north, and Moriah on the east (2435 ft.), with the lower height of Bezetha to its north. The Tyropæan Valley divides them. They form an almost impregnable natural fortress (2 Sam. v. 6, 7, R.V. margin; Psalm cxxv. 1), round three sides of which the deep ravines of Hinnom and Jehoshaphat or Kidron wind like a continuous natural fosse. Other mountains surround them, of which the chief is Olivet (2724 ft.), " the mount before Jerusalem " (1 Kings xi. 7). The climate of this high region is more healthy, equable, and temperate than that of any other part of Palestine. Upon these twin hills, the "rock of the plain or table land" (Jer. xxi. 13), clusters the city of *Jerusalem*, " beautiful in elevation " (Psalm xlviii.), which God chose for His abode. They mark its twofold character as a political centre from the time when David set up his throne on " Zion " (which means " the sunny mount "), and as a religious centre from the day the Temple rose on " Moriah " (which means "the mount provided by Jehovah"). After the Disruption, and still more after the Babylonian Captivity, when little was left of corporate national life, it was Moriah rather than Zion that formed Israel's focus.

Jerusalem at its largest in the days of Agrippa was rather more than four miles in circumference. If we set aside the probable but not certain identification of it with the Salem of Gen. xiv. 18, and the Moriah of Gen. xxii. 2, we find first mention of it in Josh. xv. 8, and the first incident in its history was, like the last, a destructive siege (Judg. i. 8 ; Luke xix. 43, 44). In the sixteen centuries between its capture by Judah and its capture by Hadrian, it was besieged at least 25 times and twice razed to the ground. No other city has had such a fate. David chose it for his seat of government, as strong, central (Ezek. v. 5), brilliantly captured, and common property of Judah and Benjamin. Judah's capital henceforth, like Judah's dynasty, was unchanged. It surpassed every other city both in its glory and its humiliation. For ere human sin and Divine love found their lowest and highest exemplifications there (Rev. xi. 8) it had been at once the Holy City, Ariel ("the hearth of God," Isa. xxix. 1, R.V.), and the unholy city, shrine of foul and horrid idols. The old Jebusite worships clung to its soil, and were never thoroughly rooted up. So at the base of Mount Zion, which has given a name to heaven (Heb. xii. 22), lay Gi-hinnom (in Greek, Gehenna), that defiled valley where ever-burning fires consumed the refuse of the city (Isa. xxx. 33, R.V. margin), whose name the Jews borrowed for hell (Mark ix. 43, R.V.).

V. HEROES.

Keynote, *Solomon*, 1 Cor. i. 19, 20.

A number of men of unusual power and influence for good or evil had made David's age, and he was greatest among the great. The calm prosperity of his latter days and of his son's reign moulded no such grand characters as those which had made the building of the Temple possible. Of the men who first worshipped in it, *Solomon* only stands out in bold relief during an age notable for its works rather than its heroes. No one occupies so large a space in sacred history of whom we have so few personal details. He seems to have inherited the beauty and fascination of both his parents, and some of his rare sagacity may be traced to Ahithophel (2 Sam. xii. 24, xi. 3, xxiii. 34). His great intellectual powers were strenuously cultivated with a view to his filling the post of heir (1 Kings i. 30) left vacant by Absalom's death when he was about ten years old. David had united the genius of a poet and the insight of a prophet with the prudence of a man of action. In Solomon we see a new intellectual type (1 Kings ii. 6, 9, v. 7). He was the first of "the wise" of whom we often read hereafter (Prov. i. 6; Isa. xxix. 14; Jer. xviii. 18). The wisdom he sought and obtained of God was that of Ecclesiastes rather than of Proverbs, and was displayed in the administration of justice (1 Kings iii. 28; Prov. xxix. 4, 14, xxv. 5), and in ardent pursuit of knowledge (1 Kings iv. 29-34). Finally, God was with him (1 Kings i. 37, iii. 28; 1 Chron. xxii. 11, 16, xxviii. 20; 2 Chron. i. 1), took him for His own son (2 Sam. vii. 14; 1 Chron. xvii. 13, xxii. 10, xxviii. 6), and gave him a great work to do.

Such were the gifts and privileges of Solomon. Never had earthly glory and human wisdom a greater opportunity, never was their insufficiency for man's goodness and happiness more strikingly shown. He and his people instead of influencing their heathen neighbours were influenced by them. Like that other brilliant young man for whom Christ longed (Mark x. 21), Solomon loved the world more than he loved God. He knew the good, and chose the evil. He expounded a father's duties, and apparently spoiled his own son; he painted ideal marriage (Prov. v. 18, 19), and crowded his harem with foreign women against whose wiles his wisdom was as powerless as Samson's strength (Neh. xiii. 26). He preached justice, yet practised oppression (1 Kings xii. 4). He was sagacious and equitable, yet he actually thought to thwart God's purposes by slaying his appointed successor. With one hand he reared the Temple of the God of Israel; with the other, pursuing an unlawful, short-sighted, and disastrous policy of toleration, he raised long-enduring altars (2 Kings xxiii. 13) for the shameful worship of the Phœnician Ashtoreth, the cruel worship of the Ammonite Molech, and even for that worship of the Moabite Chemosh or Baalpeor whose terrible punishment in the wilderness (Num. xxv.) ought to have made its revival impossible (2 Cor. vi. 16). We will not add one to the divers speculations as to the final destiny of this man who sinned against so much light, but we note that the utterances of his God-given wisdom are not shut out from the Book of God because his crime was as great as his genius, nor was his dynasty supplanted because he had done his best to throw away a rare heritage of loyalty. Heir to a kingdom whose strength depended upon its unity, and whose unity depended upon its faith, he had made shipwreck of both. We speak of the trial of adversity. It was prosperity which led even a David astray and which destroyed a Solomon (see Ecclus. xlvii. 12-23).

VI. THE COMING MESSIAH.

"One greater than the Temple is here. . . . A greater than Solomon is here."—Matt. xii. 6, 42.

As the militant kingdom of Christ in the present is typified by the reign of David, so the triumphant kingdom of Christ in the future is typified by the reign of Solomon (Isa. xi., xxxii. ; Rev. xix. 16), the peaceful *king* whom God called His son, who ruled Israel, and extended his dominion over the heathen ; the wise *prophet*, who taught the fear of the Lord ; the *priestly* prince who offered prayer for his people, who entered the Temple Court with sacrifices (2 Chron. viii. 12, 13), and even burned incense in the Holy Place (1 Kings ix. 25) ; who also performed the highest sacerdotal act in solemnly blessing the people (2 Chron. vi. 3). The Psalms which celebrate his glory are only entirely true of the one Son of David who fulfilled all the conditions of God's covenant with him (Luke i. 32), and so realised the ideal not realised by Solomon, and obtained God's infallible (Num. xxiii. 19) promises to David and his seed, which Psalm lxxxix. reiterates, in order to point the mournful contrast between what might have been and what was.

Of direct Prediction our period contains little. Under the secularising spell of Solomon's reign, Israel's great

Hope was in abeyance. The Jewish Talmud regarded the Song of Songs as an allegory of the dealings of Jehovah with Israel, and Christian theology has from very early times found a key to it in Eph. v. 25-32, and expounded it of Christ as the Bridegroom of the Church (not of the individual soul, that is only the unscriptural fancy of unwise mystics). While we learn from it what His love is, and what our devotion to Him should be, we must beware of fantastic application of details, for the colouring is local and Oriental throughout. Canto I. typifies His First Coming to dwell with us (Psalm cxxxvi. 23 ; 2 Chron. vi. 18 ; John i. 14); Canto II. typifies His Second Coming to take us to Himself when He has made our earth His (Heb. ix. 28 ; 1 Thess. iv. 17).

The Rabbis referred Prov. x. 25 to the Messiah (Isa. xxviii. 16), and it is impossible not to see ultimate reference to truths yet to be revealed in Prov. xxx. 4 (Col. i. 13-19 ; 1 Cor. i. 24 ; John i. 1-4), and in Prov. viii., which anticipates the doctrine of the Incarnation by teaching that the Wisdom of God dwelt with men (1 Cor. i. 30 ; Col. ii. 3).

VII. God's Revelation of Himself to Man.

Jehovah, El Shaddai, and Jehovah Sabaoth had expressed God's Eternity, God's Omnipotence, and "the Majesty of His Glory." Solomon's Dedicatory Prayer is far in advance of its age in its intensely spiritual apprehension of His Infinitude and in placing Prayer above Sacrifice. The profounder thought of this period, ever looking within, recognising that the external things of life are not its most important things, and uttering itself in the Sapiental Books of Proverbs, Ecclesiastes, and perhaps Job, found rest in apprehending God's Wisdom (Prov. viii.) and God's Holiness. He is first spoken of as the Holy One in Job vi. 10 ; Prov. ix. 10 (R.V.), xxx. 3 (R.V.) ; Psalm lxxviii. 41, lxxxix. 18 (the word used in Deut. xxxiii. 8 and Psalm xvi. 10 is different). This name, occurring very often in the prophets of later times, reminds us of that threefold assertion three times over of God's holiness, which may be directly connected with the doctrine of the Three in One (Psalm xcix. 3, 5, 9, R.V.; Isa. vi. 3 ; Rev. iv. 8).

VIII. Man's Relation to God in Worship.

At Solomon's accession, Zion and Gibeon were both centres of national worship. This dual system ended when Solomon had spent $7\frac{1}{2}$ years in carrying out the plan David received (as Moses received the plan of the Tabernacle) from God Himself. His Temple only existed 34 years in its original splendour, but Israel's history ramifies from it as a centre henceforth. The boundary between Judah and Benjamin passed through it. So it belonged to no one tribe, but was for the whole nation forum, fortress, sanctuary, and university.

Imagine a massive stone building about 45 ft. high, cased in cedar without, so that it resembled a log house, and overlaid with gold within, so that it shone like the sun, in three divisions. (*a*) *The Porch*, 15 ft. deep and 180 ft. high, supported upon two pillars of richly ornamented capitals, and hung with shields (2 Chron. xxiii. 9). In every view of the Holy City, this must have been the most conspicuous object. (*b*) *The Holy Place* (60 ft. by 30 ft.), where the priests ministered. It contained the Table and Altar of Incense, and was lighted by ten lamps. Round it clustered 30 small chambers in three stories, forming three terraces, and, seen from without, not unlike the side aisles of a church. (*c*) *The Holy of Holies* (30 ft. square), where only the high priest ministered. It contained the Ark with its guardian Cherubim, and was dark save for the Shechinah. Outside this structure was the Court (612 ft. square), where the people worshipped round the great Brazen Altar, which stood on the natural surface of the rock, once Araunah's threshing floor. The irregular mass of that rock may still be seen beneath the Kubbet es Sakhra (miscalled "the Mosque of Omar"), together with some of the mighty and highly finished masonry of Solomon's outer wall.

Solomon's Temple differed (*a*) from the Tabernacle, for it exactly doubled all its dimensions, and was far more permanent and splendid ; (*b*) from Herod's Temple, whose area was 1000 ft. square, in being smaller and more primitive, and in having no separate courts for Gentiles and for women ; (*c*) from Pagan Temples, in that it contained no statue or sacred animal to represent the indwelling divinity; (*d*) from Christian sanctuaries, in that it was smaller than many parish churches, in that its holiest place was at the west end, and in that it was intended only for the priests, and surrounded, not by a quiet cloister, but by a court crowded with sacrificing priests, worshipping people, sheep, and oxen.

Observe that when the externals of public worship were most sumptuous and imposing, the most flagrant example of apostasy in high places was given.

The national unity so recently achieved has been broken up for ever. That portion which has Ephraim for its leader (Hosea xiii. 1, R.V.) and Samaria for its capital has already departed from the true worship, and is ready to depart from the true faith. Its history will be our chief subject next term, while Judah, its more faithful and longer-lived rival, will occupy us wholly during our Sixth Term. How the Ten Tribes differed from the Two in character, position, and destiny must be our first consideration.

IX. QUESTIONS.

(See pp. 13, 18.)

[Questions I., V., XV., XVII., XXI., XXIV., XXVII., and XXX. may be answered with the help of any books.]

I. How did David sin in numbering the people? (10.)

II. Show that David and his people endured each of the calamities specified in 1 Chron. xxi. 12. (6.)

III. (*a*) God loved Solomon; (*b*) Solomon loved God; (*c*) God loved Solomon's people; (*d*) Solomon's people served God. Give *one* reference for each of these assertions. (4.)

IV. Name the two tribes that furnished architects for the Tabernacle and the Temple. What allusions to the Tabernacle are there in the history of Solomon? (6.)

V. Draw a ground plan of Solomon's Temple. (15.)

VI. Consider Solomon's Prayer of Dedication as a prophecy of Israel's future history. (10.)

VII. What was the only recorded conquest of Solomon's reign? What three incidents of Bathsheba's life are recorded in this term's reading? (4.)

VIII. Describe the condition of the original inhabitants of Palestine during Solomon's reign. (6.)

IX. Give a brief account of the three occasions on which God spoke to Solomon. (6.)

X. Consider Solomon as a type of Christ. (15.)

XI. Does the name of God occur in the Song of Songs? Give *four* New Testament references to justify the Christian allegorical interpretation of the Song of Songs. (6.)

XII. Illustrate by *two* examples from Scripture history the truth of each of the following sayings:—Prov. i. 7, i. 32, iii. 6, v. 22, ix. 8, x. 24, xi. 2, xi. 10, xi. 21, xii. 19, xiv. 32, xv. 1. (24.)

XIII. What may we learn from Proverbs as to the right and as to wrong use of the lips? Give *twelve* references on each subject. (12.)

XIV. Prove that the teaching of the Incarnate Wisdom of God was anticipated by the teaching of Wisdom in the Book of Proverbs, by writing out short Gospel parallels to as many passages as you can in Prov. i.—ix. (30.)

XV. Show that "Under the sun" is a key to Ecclesiastes, by proving from other passages of Scripture that the following statements are not absolutely true in themselves, but only relatively true from the speaker's point of view:—Eccles. i. 4, i. 8, i. 9, 10, i. 15, ii. 11, ii. 16, iii. 19, vi. 8, viii. 15, ix. 5. (20.)

XVI. Find *nine* allusions to a life beyond the grave in Proverbs, Ecclesiastes, and the Psalms read this term. (9.)

XVII. Briefly explain the allusions or metaphors in the following passages:—1 Kings i. 5; Cant. i. 5, ii. 5; Prov. iii. 20, xxv. 11, 23; Eccles. xii. 6; Psalm xlii. 1. (24.)

XVIII. For each of the following Psalms give *two* references to Proverbs, Job, or Ecclesiastes, tracing the resemblance between the Psalter and the Sapiental Books:—i., xxxvii., xlix., l., lxxiii., lxxxviii., xci., cxi., cxii., cxxxix. (20.)

XIX. How often does "vexation of spirit" occur in Ecclesiastes? How does R.V. render it? (4.)

XX. What allusion can you find in the Psalter to the office of the Korahites described in 1 Chron. xxvi. 12-19? (2.)

XXI. Point out the probable allusions to contemporary

or earlier history in Psalm lxxii. 8, xlv. 12, cxxxii. 6, lxxxi. 5, 7. Describe the probable occasion of Psalm lxxxix. (10.)

XXII. What relation was Rehoboam's favourite wife to him? What do you know about her? (5.)

XXIII. What historical associations guided Jeroboam in choosing Bethel and Dan for religious centres? (10.)

XXIV. Show clearly what constituted "the sin of Jeroboam, the son of Nebat." (9.)

XXV. What king was named as a reformer 300 years before he lived? Mention another monarch named in prophecy long before he was born. (2.)

XXVI. Where, when, by whom, and with what result were the battles of Zemaraim and Mareshah fought? (8.)

XXVII. What do you know of the following places?— Cabul, Ezion-geber, Gezer, Gibbethon, Ophir, Sheba, Tadmor, Tarshish, Tirzah. (27.)

XXVIII. What do you know of the following people? —Adoram, Asaph, Ethan, Hadad, Jonathan son of Abiathar, Lemuel, Rezon, Tibni. (16.)

XXIX. Make a complete list of the prophets who were sent to Israel and Judah during this period. (14.)

XXX. What allusion can you find in the prophetical books to (*a*) David, (*b*) Solomon's molten sea, (*c*) the schismatic worship at Bethel, (*d*) the enmity between Ephraim and Judah, (*e*) Omri? (10.)

XXXI. Make a list of the names of God in the Psalms of this period. (30.)

XXXII. Give references for the following:—(*a*) "A bag of gems in a heap of stones." (*b*) "The dance of Mahanaim." (*c*) "Rest on every side." (*d*) "The lamp of the wicked is sin." (*e*) "They walk to and fro in darkness." (*f*) "Extortion maketh a wise man foolish." (*g*) "He that uttereth a slander is a fool." (*h*) "He abhorreth not evil." (*i*) "The way of him that is laden with guilt is exceeding crooked." (*j*) "Death shall be their shepherd." (*k*) "Weary not thyself to be rich." (*l*) "Follow after faithfulness." (*m*) "Let thy garments be always white." (*n*) "Of thine own have we given Thee." (*o*) "In all labour there is profit." (*p*) "Your work shall be rewarded." (*q*) "I was by Him as a master workman." (*r*) "He shall have pity on the poor and needy." (*s*) "Then they will be thy servants for ever." (*t*) "A man is tried by his praise." (*u*) "It was brought about of God." (*v*) "The early rain covereth it with blessings." (*w*) "God seeketh again that which is driven away." (*x*) "Whoso offereth the sacrifice of thanksgiving glorifieth Me." (*y*) "She laugheth at the time to come." (*z*) "God hath set eternity in their heart." (26.)

For *Second Series* of Questions, see p. 309.

FIFTH TERM.

THE DAYS OF THE PROPHETS. DECLINE AND FALL OF THE KINGDOM OF THE TEN TRIBES.

B.C. 915–697.

1 Kings XVI. 29—XXII., 2 Kings I.—XX., 2 Chron. XVII.—XXXII. Psalms XXXIII., XLVI., XLVII., XLVIII., LXV., LXVI., LXVII., LXXV., LXXVI., LXXX., LXXXIII., LXXXVII. Jonah. Amos. Hosea. Joel. Isaiah I.—XXXIX. Micah. Nahum. (133 *chapters*.)

"Should not a people seek unto their God? ... To the law and to the testimony!"—ISA. viii. 19, 20.

17th MONTH (34).

1 Kings XVI. 29—XXII. 49. 2 Chron. XVII.—XX. Psalms XXXIII., LXXXIII., XLVI., XLVII., XLVIII. 1 Kings XXII. 50-53. 2 Kings I.—VIII. 24. 2 Chron. XXI. 2 Kings VIII. 25—IX. 2 Chron. XXII. 1-9. 2 Kings X., XI., 2 Chron. XXII. 10—XXIII. 2 Kings XII.—XIII. 9. 2 Chron. XXIV. 2 Kings XIII. 10—XIV. 2 Chron. XXV.

18th MONTH (33).

Jonah. Amos. Hosea I.—IV. 2 Kings XV 1-12. 2 Chron. XXVI. Joel. Isa. VI. 2 Kings XV. 13-38. 2 Chron. XXVII. Isa. II.—V. 2 Kings XVI. 2 Chron. XXVIII. Micah I., II. Isa. I.

19th MONTH (33).

Isa. VII.—X. 4, XIV. 28-32. XXVIII. 2 Kings XVII., XVIII. 9-12. Hosea V.—XIV. Psalm LXXX. 2 Kings XVIII. 1-8. 2 Chron. XXIX.—XXXI. Micah III.—VII. 2 Kings XVIII. 13. 2 Chron. XXXII. 1. Isa. XXXVI. 1, X. 5—XII. 2 Kings XX. 1-11. 2 Chron. XXXII. 24. Isa. XXXVIII. 2 Kings XX. 12-19. 2 Chron. XXXII. 23, 25-31. Isa. XXXIX. Psalm LXXXVII. Isa. XIII.—XIV. 27.

20th MONTH (33).

Isa. XV.—XXVII. Nahum. 2 Kings XVIII. 14—XIX., XX. 20, 21. 2 Chron. XXXII. 2-22, 32, 33. Isa. XXXVI. 2-22, XXXVII., XXIX.—XXXV. Psalms LXXV., LXXVI., LXV., LXVI., LXVII.

I. GENERAL SUMMARY.

LOOKING at the extent and fertility of its territory and its material resources, the kingdom of the Ten Tribes promised to be greater and more prosperous than that of the Two, which had only half its population. Looking at guarantees for political endurance and religious welfare, Judah had the capital chosen for God's abode (Psalm lxxxvii. 1-3), the Temple with the visible sign of His presence (1 Kings viii. 11), the Priests and Levites (2 Chron. xi. 13, 14), the accumulated treasure of Solomon, and sovereigns reigning by Divine right.

Nineteen kings, of nine different families, ruled Israel during 255 years. Nineteen kings, all of the House of David, ruled Judah during 388 years. The turbulent usurpers who seized Israel's crown never gained that stable power which came naturally to the monarchs of a long hereditary line, associated with Divine promises of permanence and glory. The very smallness of Judah's kingdom strengthened it by concentrating its interests about one dynasty and one city.

Not one of the kings who received Israel's allegiance did right in the eyes of the Lord; and since no worthy people is ever ruled for centuries by unworthy kings, this was an effect quite as much as a cause of the estrangement from God which proved that nation's destruction (Hos. xiii. 9, R.V.). Seven of Judah's kings could be commended for piety, and though their people in her last evil days sinned as deeply against the First Commandment as Israel had done, throughout her history they kept the Second Commandment better (see p. 55).

We must sometimes follow the common usage of calling the Northern Kingdom " Israel " (1 Kings xii. 20), which strictly includes too much; as " Ephraim," a frequent name for it in later prophets, strictly includes too little. The popular use of the term " Jews," *i.e.*, men of Judah (a term which first occurs in 2 Kings xvi. 6), for the whole nation before the Captivity, is misleading.

The first half-century of Israel's history was occupied by a desultory war with Judah, in which Judah not only gained the day, but weakened her neighbour until their powers were about equal (Prov. xviii. 19). This struggle was followed by an alliance as fatal to Judah as the war had been to Israel, and by a century of peace till Amaziah's rash vanity provoked fresh strife, in which Judah was worsted. The Syrian wars, with their varied fortune, form a background to the history of the 40 years of Omri's dynasty, Israel's king being practically Benhadad's vassal at one time (1 Kings xx. 2, 3, 34). The vigorous rule of Jehu's house for 100 years raised Israel to her greatest prosperity. Then during her last half-century a rapid succession of fierce soldiers possessed themselves of the throne (Hosea viii. 4, x. 3), while her enemies closed about her. Palestine lay between the great rival powers, Egypt and Assyria. Had Israel and Judah been united and faithful to God they might have withstood both. Instead, we see the miserable spectacle of Israel combining with Syria for a third and last conflict with Judah, in presence of their two common foes. Twenty years later, Israel's futile struggle against Assyria and equally futile attempts at friendship with Egypt ended in her downfall.

Assyria's first direct attack was in 771 (2 Kings xv. 19). God's mercy rather than Israel's merit had averted an earlier one (2 Kings xiv. 25-7), and deferred her fall for a century; but in 771 evidently Israel, and possibly Judah also, was already tributary to that all-absorbing power. The story of Israel's Captivity is (like that of Judah's) in three chapters. (Compare the prediction uttered by Isaiah in 742, Isa. vii. 8.)

(*a*) 740. Captivity of the Trans-Jordanic Tribes and of Galilee, under Tiglath-pileser.

(*b*) 721. Fall and captivity of Samaria and its neighbours, under Shalmaneser IV. and Sargon.

(*c*) 677. Colonisation of Samaria with Gentiles, under Esar-haddon.

Judah's Chronicles we have, but not the corresponding volume for Israel (1 Kings xxii. 39). So all her history is but partially known to us, and her ultimate fate is wrapped in still deeper obscurity. Judah was restored and re-established after her fall, but Samaria was left to bear her guilt (Hos. xiii. 16, R.V.), and her national existence has never been renewed. From the Chosen Race, God has made a further choice of Two Tribes only. What became of the Ten? Archæology has now cast such a broad light on the lands of their captivity, that it smiles at the popular notion of them as "lost," and at all the extravagant speculations born of that notion. How far they remained in the lands they had been deported to, were merged in the neighbouring Gentiles (Hosea ix. 17), and may be recognised now among the gallant Afghans who bear Hebrew names and cherish Hebrew traditions; and among the Nestorians by Lake Oroomiah, who also bear Hebrew names and have Hebrew faces, speak a Syriac dialect, retain many Mosaic observances, and reckon themselves Israelites: how far they returned with their Jewish brethren who are spoken of as "Israel" (Ezek. xiv. 1; Ezra x. 1; Zech. xii. 1), and as representing the Twelve Tribes (Ezra vi. 17; Acts xxvi. 7) after the Restoration (see also Ezek. xxxvii. 16, 17): how far they can be identified with the Samaritans and other peoples of Northern Palestine who spoke their language, reproduced their customs, claimed to be Israelites and faithful adherents of the Mosaic Law, and fostered abiding enmity with Judah, and who in the New Testament are accounted strangers rather than Gentiles, are matters on which those who have thought most are least ready with positive assertions. (See Wilkinson's "Israel My Glory.") We know that there are promises of blessing to Ephraim as distinct from Judah still unfulfilled. We know that the Messiah, who was born and who died in Judah, chiefly lived and taught in what had been the Northern Kingdom, among "the lost sheep of Israel's house," and that the witnesses of His Resurrection and builders of His Church were "men of Galilee" (Acts i. 11, ii. 7).

This lesson at any rate stands out for all time in the prophets of Ephraim. Heartless luxury, grasping dishonesty, violence and oppression, careless disregard of Divine laws, and self-willed impiety ruin not only individual lives, but the corporate life of the state whose welfare is entrusted to each of its citizens (Num. xxxii. 15).

Reserving special consideration of Judah for next term, we notice her prosperity under Jehoshaphat; her depression after his death; that most striking and fully told episode of her history when the dynasty was barely saved from extinction; a century of recovery and renewed vigour under three able sovereigns, followed by the disastrous reign of her worst king; and finally how faithful Hezekiah and Isaiah saved her from the false friendship of Egypt, and how when the people's own utmost effort had been made, God saved her from the determined enmity of Assyria (2 Chron. xxxii. 1, 7, 8, R.V.).

We have reached an age when there are frequent points of contact between sacred and secular history, and many recently discovered monuments confirm the Biblical narrative. See Prof. Sayce's "Fresh Light from Ancient Monuments" (Religious Tract Society, 3s.), Dr. Kinns' "Graven in the Rock" (Cassell, 12s. 6d.), and the Bishop of Ossory's "Echoes of Bible History" (Sunday School Institute, 4s.).

Rehoboam's defeat by Shishak is pictured in the great Egyptian Temple of Karnak. Ahab is named as an ally of Benhadad on a monolith from Nimrud commemorating Shalmaneser I.'s victories. Mesha describes his successful revolt from Israel on the Moabite stone now in the Louvre, Paris. Jehu appears among the tributaries of Shalmaneser II. of Assyria on the famous obelisk of black basalt from Nimrud. Uzziah and Ahaz are mentioned more than once on some fragments of Assyrian tablets recording the reign of Tiglath-pileser II. The monolith and black obelisk may be seen in the British Museum; so also may the bas-reliefs of Sennacherib seated on his throne before besieged Lachish, his countenance defaced (doubtless by the sons who slew him); and a cylinder whereon he, telling half a story whose other half he must have wished for ever untold, relates how he shut up Hezekiah the Jew in Jerusalem as a bird is shut up in a cage.

Of the three offices associated with Israel's national and religious life to which men were set apart by a solemn anointing (Lev viii; 1 Sam. xvi.; 1 Kings xix. 16; 1 Chron. xvi. 22), which all foreshadowed the Christ (John i. 41, R.V.), we considered the Priestly in the Second, and the Kingly in our Third Term. This term the Prophetic claims our chief attention. Enoch was the first (Jude 14) and S. John the last (Rev. x. 11) who "prophesied." The Seventy whom Moses the Prophet chose anticipated that prophetic order (Num. xi.), which actually dates from Samuel (Acts iii. 24) and ends with Malachi; and prophets first take a leading part in Israel, a kingdom built up by two prophets, Ahijah and Shemaiah, rather than in Judah which still had the regular priesthood.

Etymologically, the Greek work whence "prophet" comes has this threefold significance : (*a*) Telling forth, teaching and preaching, announcing God's will (2 Chron. xxxvi. 15, 16); (*b*) Telling for, interpreting and expounding God's will (Exod. vii. 1); (*c*) Fore-telling, predicting future events, revealing God's will (1 Peter i. 10, 11).

All this the Hebrew Prophets did, and they were at once the national poets, historians, evangelists, pastors, teachers, censors of morals, physicians, patriots, and statesmen ; often living together and wearing a distinctive garb (Zech. xiii. 4). From every part of the country, and every station in life, sometimes honoured, sometimes insulted and persecuted, they came before men with their great commission, "Thus saith Jehovah" (Deut. xviii. 18 ; Jer. i. 9) ; and their simultaneous rise in this age was a first fulfilment of Joel ii. 28, 29. The nations of whom they wrote have passed away, but the same types of national character still exist ; and if we read their threatenings and warnings aright, we learn from them the great lessons which all history has to teach (Prov. xiv. 34), and see how the whole course of this world carries out the purposes of God (Isa. xiv. 24-7).

II. BOOKS TO BE READ.

(See "Oxford Helps," § v.)

This term two-thirds of our reading is from the prophetic books, with which we now make our first acquaintance. These seven books form the first of the three groups into which the sixteen prophets whose works are preserved fall. An interval of silence for half a century during the evil reign of Manasseh succeeds them. They are all written in highly poetical prose, varied by occasional bursts of actual poetry. After each prophet's name and country, etc., is given the approximate date of his prophecy, the name of the people to whom he was sent, and of the king then reigning. For the twelve *Psalms* of this period, see p. 200.

Jonah, son of Amittai, of Gath-hepher in Zebulon, Elisha's successor, and also Elijah's servant, if we may believe the ancient Jewish tradition which finds him in 1 Kings xvii. 17, xviii. 43, and 2 Kings ix. 4. (823—782.

Concerning Nineveh. In the reign of Jeroboam II.) His keynote is *Judgment averted by repentance*, which has a threefold illustration in the Phœnician crew, the Hebrew prophet, and the men of Nineveh (Jer. xviii. 7, 8; Acts x. 35; 2 Peter iii. 9). He was the first apostle of the Gentiles, the first missionary, and he shows forth God's dealings with the vast Gentile world. We have through him a majestic revelation of God's wrath and pity, each bestowed where most deserved and least expected, anticipating Matt. xx. 16; Luke xv. 31, 32, xviii. 14. National rather than personal feeling made him grudge God's mercy to Nineveh, and his narrowness was divinely rebuked. For what the Ninevites were called upon to abandon was probably a scheme for attacking Israel (2 Kings xiv. 25-7). The message to them resembled that to Pharaoh (Exod. v. 1; Psalm cv. 15), and their conduct and its issue may be contrasted with his. There is no finer illustration of the moral grandeur of true religion than this solitary prophet of a petty state in the midst of the greatest city in the world. Observe also that Jonah, writing the story of his own typical life, forms the link between Elijah and Elisha, uttering unwritten prophecy, and the later authors of written prophecy.

Amos, a herdsman of Tekoa, in Judah. (808—782. Concerning Israel. In the reign of Jeroboam II.) While Jonah was pleading Israel's cause abroad, Amos was in direct conflict with her sins at home. No prophet describes and denounces them with more vigour, and *Special punishments for special sins* is his keynote (Heb. ii. 2; James iv. 17). He also foretells judgments on Israel's immediate neighbours, including Judah. Unlike his contemporary Joel, he is orator rather than poet, and he takes many illustrations from his calling.

Hosea, son of Beeri, and, according to tradition, of the tribe of Issachar. (782—721. Concerning Israel and Judah. In the reigns of Jeroboam II., Jotham, and Ahaz.) *God's knowledge of us, the knowledge that we may have and that Israel refused to have of Him* is the keynote (Luke xix. 44; John xvii. 3) of "the Jeremiah of Israel," contemporary of her last seven kings, through whom God uttered His last gracious, pitiful, and urgent pleadings with the incorrigible nation. He is the first, but not the last, prophet whose personal history is made a symbol to his countrymen (Hos. xii. 10), and he and Amos together enable us to expand the historian's brief statement that "Israel did evil." Through them also we can picture the gathering calamities of her last days: drought and failing harvests (Hos. ii. 9; Amos iv. 7-9, i. 2), plague (Amos iv. 10), earthquake (Amos iii. 14, 15, ix. 1), eclipse (Amos viii. 9), and the gradual approach of the Assyrian host (Amos i. 2-15, vi. 14, vii. 17, ix. 7-10; Hos. v. 13, x. 6; Isa. v. 26-30). There are nine brief allusions to Judah, and no predictions concerning the Gentiles. The close of this sorrowful book is lighted by a promise of future restoration.

Joel, son of Pethuel, according to an uncertain tradition a Reubenite. (808—790. Concerning Judah. In the reign of Uzziah.) Conjecture as to his date ranges from Jehoshaphat to Josiah, but most probably he lived in the reign of Uzziah, and was the earliest prophet of Judah. His abrupt and direct address, whose vigorous diction and impassioned fervour place it high in Hebrew literature, marks the transition from the earlier prophets, whose deeds and sayings only are recorded, to the later writers of elaborate predictions and revelations. *The cry of repentance followed by deliverance* is his keynote (Acts iii. 19). His book contains what is probably the first dim prophecy of the Assyrian invasion, and the first mention of the Greeks who were destined to play a part only second to that of the Jews in moulding the world's future history.

Isaiah, son of Amoz, of the house of David, (756—697. Concerning Judah. In the reigns of Uzziah, Jotham, Ahaz, and Hezekiah.) This greatest Old Testament prophecy falls into two portions, separated by four chapters of history.

Part I., chaps. i.—xxxix. Predictions directly referring to the times in which they were written.

Part II., chaps. xl.—lxvi. Predictions from the standpoint of the Babylonian Captivity, which we reserve therefore for next term. *Salvation of Jehovah* is the meaning of the prophet's name (which, like those of his sons, was symbolical, Isa. viii. 18), and the keynote of his book (Titus ii. 11; Heb. v. 9). He utters the first clear prediction of the Babylonian Captivity (xxxix. 6, 7) 112 years before it took place, and 20 years after Ephraim's captivity (see also Micah iv. 10). He is the chief, as Jonah was the first, messenger of good tidings to the Gentiles (Rom. x. 20), and there are nearly 80 quotations from him in the New Testament, where he is named 21 times.

Micah, of Moresheth Gath, or of Mareshah in Judah. (756–697. Concerning Israel and Judah. In the reigns of Jotham, Ahaz, and Hezekiah.) His threefold prophecy, calling upon (*a*) all men, (*b*) Israel and Judah, and (*c*) the mountains, to hearken, was uttered during Israel's destruction, and Judah's devastation under Ahaz and restoration under Hezekiah. *Man sinful and justly punished; God righteous and yet merciful* is his keynote (Rom. iii. 26), and he looks beyond the impending destruction of Israel into the far future of Judah. Like Amos, he makes many rural allusions. He is mentioned by Jeremiah (Jer. xxvi. 18, 19), and quoted by Zephaniah and Isaiah.

Nahum, of Elkosh in Galilee, or possibly born in captivity at Alkush on the Tigris. (726—697. Concerning Nineveh. In the reign of Hezekiah.) Conjecture as to his date ranges from 850 to the Restoration, but most probably he wrote shortly before Sennacherib's invasion. He was the last, as Ahijah of Shiloh was the first, prophet of Israel, and his prophecy is one sustained shout of wild exultation over the fall of his nation's great conqueror. Its awful keynote is *I am against thee* (James iv. 4; Rev. ii. 16). 220 years after the judgment foretold by Jonah had been averted, 100 years after the circumstances of its capture and desolation had been exactly described by Nahum, *i.e.*, in 606, Nineveh was taken by Cyaxares.

III. PERIODS AND DATES.

We divide these 218 years into four periods, of which the last two overlap by five years that we may have a complete view of Hezekiah's reign. Isa. xxxviii. 6, and 2 Kings xx. 13, compared with 2 Kings xviii. 15, are among several proofs that the true order of its events is given below. Observe that Chronicles emphasizes (*a*), Isaiah (*c*) and (*d*), and Kings (*e*).

Assyrian records show that the first of the two Assyrian

invasions, that in 713, took place in the reign of Sargon (Isa. xx. 1). Sennacherib may have acted as his lieutenant in it. Our information about the Kings of Assyria is still fragmentary, and all their dates as given below are more or less uncertain. All in italics are named in Scripture. The table of reigns should be before the student throughout.

(1) B.C. 915—883 (32 years). From the accessions of Jehoshaphat and Ahab to those of Athaliah and Jehu. *The Mission of Elijah and Elisha. First conflict with Baalism.* 1 Kings xvi. 29—xxii. 49; 2 Chron. xvii.—xx.; Psalms xxxiii., lxxxiii., xlvi., xlvii., xlviii.; 1 Kings xxii. 50-53; 2 Kings i.—viii. 24; 2 Chron. xxi.; 2 Kings viii. 25—ix.; 2 Chron. xxii. 1-9.

(2) B.C. 883—770 (113 years). From the accessions of Athaliah and Jehu to the death of Zechariah. (The readings carry us to 756 in the history of Judah.) *Ephraim's best days under Jehu's House. Second conflict with Baalism.* 2 Kings x., xi.; 2 Chron. xxii. 10—xxiii.; 2 Kings xii.—xiii. 9; 2 Chron. xxiv.; 2 Kings xiii. 10—xiv.; 2 Chron. xxv.; Jonah; Amos; Hosea i.—iv.; 2 Kings xv. 1-12; 2 Chron. xxvi.; Joel; Isa. vi.

(3) 770—721 (49 years). From the death of Zechariah to the Fall of Samaria. *Ephraim's Decline and Destruction.* 2 Kings xv. 13-38; 2 Chron. xxvii.; Isa. ii.—v.; 2 Kings xvi.; 2 Chron. xxviii.; Micah i., ii.; Isa. i., vii.—x. 4, xiv. 28-32, xxviii.; 2 Kings xvii., xviii. 9-12; Hosea v.—xiv.; Psalm lxxx.

(4) B.C. 726—697 (29 years). From the accession to the death of Hezekiah. *Judah's Reformation and Deliverance under her greatest King.*

    (*a*) The great Passover (726—713). 2 Kings xviii. 1-8; 2 Chron. xxix., xxx., xxxi.; Micah iii.—viii.

    (*b*) The Invasion of Sargon (713). 2 Kings xviii. 13; 2 Chron. xxxii. 1; Isa. xxxvi. 1, x. 5—xii.

    (*c*) Hezekiah's sickness (712). 2 Kings xx. 1-11; 2 Chron. xxxii. 24; Isa. xxxviii.

(d) The Babylonian Embassy (712—701). **2 Kings xx. 12-19; 2 Chron. xxxii. 23, 25-31; Isa. xxxix.; Psalm lxxxvii.; Isa. xiii.—xiv. 27, xv.—xxiii.** (Oracles concerning ten of Judah's neighbours.) **Isa. xxiv.—xxvii.** (Prophecy concerning the whole earth.) **Nahum.**

(e) The Invasion of Sennacherib (701—697). **2 Kings xviii. 14—xix., xx. 20, 21; 2 Chron. xxxii. 2-22, 32, 33; Isa. xxxvi. 2-22, xxxvii., xxix.— xxxv.** (Prophecies during Invasion.) **Psalms lxxv., lxxvi., lxv., lxvi., lxvii.**

Ten Sovereigns of Judah.		*Thirteen Kings of Israel.*	
Jehoshaphat	915—889.	Ahab	917—898.
Jehoram	893—885.	Ahaziah	898—897.
Ahaziah	885—883.	Joram	897—883.
Athaliah	883—877.	Jehu	883—855.
Joash	877—838.	Jehoahaz	855—838.
Amaziah	838—808.	Jehoash	838—823.
Uzziah	808—756.	Jeroboam II.	823—782.
Jotham	756—742.	*Interregnum.*	
Ahaz	742—726.		
Hezekiah	726—697.	Zechariah	771—770.
		Shallum	One month.
		Menahem	770—761.
		Pekahiah	761—759.
		Pekah	759—739.
		Interregnum.	
		Hoshea	730—721.

The last nine Kings of Assyria.

Pul	...	770—?
Tiglath-Pileser II.	...	745—727
Shalmaneser IV.	...	727—722
Sargon	...	722—705
Sennacherib	...	705—681
Esarhaddon I.	...	681—668
Assur-bani-pal	...	670—630?
Assur-etil-ilani-ukinni.		
Sin-sarra-iskun (or Saracus).		

IV. Geography.

(See "Oxford Helps," Maps VII., VIII., and IX.)

The kingdom of Israel was 9375 square miles in extent, or a little less than Yorkshire, Lancashire, and Cumberland. Jeroboam II. extended it from Hamath on the north to the Valley of Willows, between Moab and Edom, on the south. When it broke up, large portions to the east and south-east of Jordan fell to Uzziah (2 Chron. xxvi. 10). The kingdom of Judah was 3435 square miles in extent, or a little less than Northumberland, Durham, and Westmoreland. Besides Benjamin, South Dan and Simeon were reckoned in it, but early sank into insignificance. *Samaria* was the only city in Palestine created, like Alexandria and Constantinople, by a monarch for his capital. It clustered on the side of a long flat-topped hill, rising in the centre of a wide basin-shaped valley, encircled by the mountains of Ephraim. Rather more than 20 miles to the north-east, on a hill gently swelling from the plain of Esdraelon (the Greek form of "Jezreel"), beautiful with trees and springs, stood *Jezreel*, "the Versailles of Israel's Paris."

With Jonah we embark for the first time in sacred history on the Mediterranean, and cross the desert to the banks of the Tigris. *Assyria* was the oldest of those great empires of history of which the British Empire is the youngest. At its largest, its sway stretched from Ethiopia to India, and it extended from the Halys and Mediterranean on the west to the Caspian Sea and the great Salt Desert on the east, from Armenia on the north to the Persian Gulf and Arabian Desert on the south. It included peoples as diverse as those in the modern Turkish Empire, and the Assyrians themselves were an amalgam of three races, yellow-skinned Shemites, dark-skinned Cushites, and fair-skinned Chaldeans of Mongolian origin. *Nineveh*, once the chief centre of commerce, and the largest and richest city in the world, was so utterly destroyed that only shapeless mounds of earth and rubbish marked its site until Botta, Layard, and others lifted its shroud of sand between 40 and 50 years ago. Since then Sir Henry Rawlinson and other archaeologists, unriddling the secret of the cuneiform character, have read on countless clay tablets the story of its remote past.

V. HEROES.

Keynotes
{ *Elijah*, Acts xxvii. 23.
Elisha, Gal. vi. 10.
Jehoshaphat, 1 Peter ii. 13, 14.
Jehoiada, Mal. ii. 7.
Hezekiah, Psalm cxlvi. 3-5.
Isaiah, Gal. i. 11, 12. }

The Kingdom of the Ten Tribes produced the grandest character of this age, the greatest prophet since Moses. *Elijah*, like Melchizedek, is "without father, without mother, without genealogy." The Rabbis said that in him the uncompromising Phinehas returned to earth, and for centuries the Jews believed that he would come again to restore and relieve (John i. 21). Improbable conjecture makes him a native of Thisbe in Naphtali. He was a sojourner among the brave but rude shepherds of Gilead, which was to Jerusalem and Samaria what the Scottish Highlands were to the Lowlands a century ago. Some five or six times he appeared among men, disappearing as suddenly. Bold and swift as David's Gadite allies (1 Chron. xii. 8), stern and lofty, of fiery zeal and unflinching courage, he stood forth as a witness (*a*) For the disestablished worship of Jehovah; his name means "Jehovah is my God." (*b*) For the national unity, apparently shattered for ever (1 Kings xviii. 31). (*c*) For the moral law (1 Kings xxi. 20) trampled under foot by the weak apostate Ahab, who, not wholly without conscience but wholly without resolution, became a tool in the hands of that most relentless and unscrupulous of women who was the very embodiment of lawless paganism and the first persecutor of the Church. The characteristic words afterwards adopted by his successor (1 Kings xvii. 1, xviii. 15; 2 Kings iii. 14, v. 16; Luke xxi. 36) give us the secret of his power; and his short, urgent petitions afford glimpses into a life of unbroken communion with God. Lest, however, we should feel only the distant awe with which he inspired his contemporaries when he came among them

in the all-constraining influence of a divinely guided life
(1 Kings xviii. 7), we are allowed to hear that one unanswered prayer for death, wrung from him when, after facing Ahab and 850 false prophets, he fled from Jezebel, mind and body alike over-wrought (1 Kings xix. 3, R.V. margin). Round him the prophets rallied as they had not rallied since Samuel; and our next hero is his successor, a contrast to him at every point. Elijah, the prophet of the desert, living with God apart from men, the solitary champion of truth (1 Kings xviii. 22, xix. 10, 14) "ordained for reproofs, whose word burned like a lamp" (Ecclus. xlviii. 1-11), who came to denounce and destroy, to challenge the world's standards of thought and action, to rebuke boldly and directly vain-glorious luxury and popular sin, was the type of Christ's Forerunner, the predecessor of the hermit, the monk, the ascetic, and the Puritan. *Elisha*, son of Shaphat of Abel-meholah in Manasseh, giving up considerable wealth to be the servant of God (1 Kings xix. 19), dwelling in cities among men, the life and soul of the patriotic party (as Isaiah and Micah were later), the friend and counsellor and father (2 Kings vi. 21, xiii. 14) of all men, ever ready to comfort the sorrowful and succour the poor, is the type of Christ Himself (Matt. xi. 18, 19; Acts x. 38), and thus, though less in personal grandeur, he is greater because more Christ-like in spirit than Elijah. He was the first Hebrew prophet who became an oracle and monitor of other nations. His whole ministry covers 65 years, and of its last 50 years there is little record. Miracles, mainly of mercy, are more prominent in it than in that of Elijah. No express teaching of either is handed down, but their successor Jonah begins the line of literary prophets.

Judah's heroes this term are two kings, one priest, and one prophet. *Jehoshaphat* is the most like David in character of all her kings (2 Chron. xvii. 3-5; 1 Kings xxii. 43). His zeal for God's law, his personal piety, his righteous administration and vigorous foreign policy raised his kingdom to the highest point reached since the Disruption. *Jehoiada*, who was born in the reign of Solomon and lived to see eight sovereigns of Judah and eleven sovereigns of Israel, reared again the stem of

David, when it had been cut down to the very roots. In his person the priesthood took a more important place than it had ever done before, so he is reckoned its second as Aaron was its first founder. The power thus gained it never wholly lost afterwards. Public-spirited integrity was the most noteworthy characteristic of this faithful guardian of Church and State. *Hezekiah*, whose character is thrown into strong relief by those of his father and his son, is more unreservedly commended than any other king of Judah, and no king had a more lofty sense of his mission. His reign and its literature fills 77 chapters of the Bible. Possibly grandson of one prophet (2 Chron. xxvi. 5; Isa. viii. 2; 2 Kings xviii. 2), and son-in-law of another (tradition makes Hephzibah Isaiah's daughter, 2 Kings xxi. 1; Isa. lxii. 4), he reigned during a period of the strongest prophetic influence since Elijah. No sickness is so pathetically recorded in Scripture as that which threatened to leave Judah without an heir to the throne and defenceless before the fell swoop of the Assyrian. In Hezekiah's great reformation he cared equally for the restoration of true worship and the preservation of true doctrine (2 Chron. xxix. 25; Prov. xxv. 1), and sought, like David, to gather all Israel about him in the bond of a common faith (2 Chron. xxx. 1). With one hand he cultivated the arts of peace, and was, like David, a poet; with the other he strengthened Judah for war, and, like David, defeated on their own ground the Philistines, who in the days of Ahaz had again become formidable foes (2 Chron. xxviii. 18; 2 Kings xviii. 8). God delivered him from the power which defied all human might, and since he guided the Jews through that great crisis of their history which determined whether they would trust in God or in man, to him Judah owed in no small degree the continuance of her existence for another century. But by his side throughout there stood his trusted kinsman *Isaiah*, the first Jewish prophet of whom we have personal details. Save the facts named in 2 Chron. xxvi. 22, xxxii. 20, 32, and the tradition that he was sawn asunder under Manasseh (suffering martyrdom for an alleged contradiction between Exod. xxxiii. 20 and Isa. vi. 1; see Heb. xi. 37), all we know about him is from his own book.

The turning-point of his life was the vision described in Isa. vi. Henceforth the great powers of intellect, imagination, enthusiasm, and will of the young descendant of David were consecrated to the service of God and his country. For 60 years he guided the affairs of the nation, and he has since influenced Christendom more than any other Old Testament author with the possible exception of David. The abrupt and impassioned utterances of his predecessors gave place to his magnificent rhythm and sustained grandeur of expression, while at the same time his inspired genius uttered loftiest thoughts with a directness and simplicity that provoked the satire of the inflated rhetoricians of the age (Isa. xxviii. 9-13), but won then as now many an ear and heart to attend to the things of God.

VI. THE COMING MESSIAH.

"This is of a truth the Prophet." "Isaiah . . . saw His glory and spake of Him." —John vi. 14, xii. 41.

Three successive prophets present to us one complete Type of Christ. The two greatest Old Testament miracles are the raising of the poor Gentile's son by Elijah, and the raising of the rich Israelite's son by Elisha. The story of *Elijah's* Assumption is the grandest Old Testament assertion that for the righteous departure from this life is gain, and though *Elisha* died like other men, "after his death (to quote the Apocrypha) his body prophesied" (Ecclus. xlviii. 13). These miracles were typical of that moral resurrection from Israel's darkest days which made her prosperity under Jeroboam II. possible. But also, together with the story of *Jonah*, whose meaning Christ Himself expounded, they foreshadow the *ascension, resurrection,* and *death* of Him who is the Life (1 Cor. xv. 22).

Types we have often met with already, but (always excepting the Psalms) Predictions have been few, brief, and isolated hitherto. Now in the Days of the Prophets, when the hopes first raised by the Hebrew monarchy are fast waning, we discern, according to the fine metaphor of Delitzsch, one star of promise describing a path from above downwards—"Jehovah will come to save His people and reign for ever"; and another describing a path from below upwards—"The anointed Son of David, greater than David himself, will reign over a regenerate Israel." The first promise found a preliminary fulfilment in the Restoration as we shall see, the second in Hezekiah. But we cannot examine them carefully without perceiving that they ultimately involve a more personal coming and a more extended reign of the Lord, and that the kingdom of David's Son would be more than earthly and human. The kingship no less than the priesthood of the Old Covenant made nothing perfect. It is when these two stars merge in one light that the twilight of the Old Testament vanishes before the glorious day of the Gospel.

There are two more allusions to the Promise to David in the historical books, 2 Kings viii. 19; 2 Chron. xxi. 7.

Nahum is the only one of the 16 prophetical books that contains no clear Messianic reference. The following summary of those in this term's Prophets are explained (like those in the Psalms) by New Testament references.

(1) Joel ii. 28-32; Acts ii. 16-21; Rom. x. 12, 13.
(2) Joel iii. 2; Matt. xxv. 31-46.
(3) Amos viii. 9, 10; Luke xxiii. 44, 45, 48.
(4) Amos ix. 11-15; Acts xv. 15-18.
(5) Hosea iii. 5; Matt. xxi. 9; John i. 49.
(6) Hosea vi. 2; 1 Cor. xv. 4; Matt. xx. 17-19.
(7) Hosea xi. 1; Matt. ii. 15, 20.
(8) Hosea xiii. 14; Heb. ii. 14; 1 Cor. xv. 54.
(9) Micah iv. 1-7; Luke i. 33; xxiv. 47; Rev. xxi. 24.
(10) Micah v. 1; Matt. xxvii. 30.
(11) Micah v. 2-5; Matt. ii. 1, 5, 6; Eph. ii. 14.
(12) Micah vii. 20; Luke i. 68-75.

Isaiah has been called "the Gospel Prophet" and "the Fifth Evangelist." Six of the 16 prophecies in chapters i.—xxxix. are directly quoted in the New Testament.

(13) Isa. ii. 2-4; Rev. xi. 15.
(14) Isa. iv. 2-6; Matt. xi. 28; Rev. vii 15 (R.V.).
(15) Isa. vi. 13; Gal. iii. 16.
(16) Isa. vii. 14-16; Matt. i. 22, 23; John iv. 34.
(17) Isa. viii. 14; Matt. xxi. 42-4; 1 Peter ii. 8.
(18) Isa. ix. 1-7; Matt. iv. 14-16; Luke ii. 11, 32; Heb. i. 8.

(19) Isa. x. 27 ; Acts x. 38.
(20) Isa. xi., xii. ; Acts xiii. 22, 23 ; Rom. xv. 12.
(21) Isa. xiii. 12 ; 1 Peter ii. 7.
(22) Isa. xvi. 5 ; Luke i. 32.
(23) Isa. xxiv. 23 ; Matt. xix. 28.
(24) Isa. xxv. 6-8 ; 1 Cor. xv. 54-7 ; Rev. xxi. 4.
(25) Isa. xxviii. 16 ; Matt. xxi. 42 ; Rom. ix. 32, x. 11.
(26) Isa. xxix. 18-24 ; Luke vii. 22 ; John. iii. 2.
(27) Isa. xxxii. ; Rom. xiv. 17 ; Acts ii.
(28) Isa. xxxv. ; Matt. xi. 5 ; John xiv. 6.

VII. God's Revelation of Himself to Man.

On the spot where Moses had been taught "the Old Testament Creed" (Exod. xxxiv. 5-7) Elijah received a still higher revelation of God. More than in the wind which drove the Red Sea before it; more than in the earthquake which shattered the walls of Jericho ; more than in the answering fire on Mount Carmel, God is to be heard in the voice of His Word (John i. 14, 18), and "declares His almighty power most chiefly in showing mercy and pity." Elijah was also taught then to discriminate from that Israel of the Called who had apostatised, an Israel of the Chosen (Matt. xxii. 16), who held and preserved invincible truth. This doctrine of a Remnant (Rom. xi. 1-5), of an Invisible Church, first enunciated to him, was further developed by Isaiah (Isa. vi. 13, x. 20, 21, xi. 11, 16, xxviii. 5, lxv. 8, 9), and so passed into the New Testament. Isaiah also was privileged to hear (as S. John heard 850 years later) echoes of the adoration offered by the unfallen company of heaven to the Holy, Blessed, and Glorious Trinity. (With Isa. vi. 1, 3, 8, compare John xii. 36, 41 ; Acts xxviii. 25, 26 ; Rev. iv.).

Each of the Prophets conveys some characteristic revelation. "God of Heaven," which became common when the Restoration brought Jew and Gentile into a new relation, is anticipated once in *Jonah*. "Jehovah," the special name under which God made a covenant with Israel, occurs 33 times in *Joel's* brief exhortation to return to Him. "God of Hosts" occurs nine times in *Amos*, and only once elsewhere, *i.e.*, in the contemporary Psalm lxxx. In *Hosea* (the

Old Testament exemplification of the wondrous Divine yearning over man which culminates in Luke xix. 41) the Lord not only declares Himself the Saviour and invites Israel to call Him "my God," but in the term "Ishi" uses a yet tenderer metaphor, occurring again in Jeremiah's last pleadings with Judah (Hos. ii. 16; Jer. iii. 14). The God of Vengeance, described in *Micah* i. 2-4, and *Nahum* i. 2-6, may be contrasted with the God of Nature, described in Amos iv. 13, v. 8, 9, ix. 6. *Isaiah* contains at least 40 names of God, some peculiar to himself, some having striking New Testament parallels. He speaks of "the Holy One" about 30 times, and of the "Lord of Hosts" about twice as often.

VIII. MAN'S RELATION TO GOD IN WORSHIP.

From the earliest times there had been High Places all over the land of Israel: that is, altars on which oil, honey, flour, incense, and sometimes animals were offered to God. They were sanctioned by the Patriarchs, by Samuel and Elijah, and by some of the most pious kings, notwithstanding Lev. xvii. 8, 9, and Deut. xii. 10-27; but at last Hezekiah removed them, for exactly the same reason that our Reformers swept away many mediæval usages, originally devout in intention, but inseparably connected at length with error and superstition. Two of these High Places became centres of idolatrous and schismatic worship of the True God under Jeroboam I., who led Ephraim at its worst, as Joshua had led it at its best. His great sin led to the far greater sin of Ahab, who disestablished the worship of Jehovah in favour of the worship of Baal and Ashtoreth or Astarte, Phœnician gods whose counterparts are easily recognised in every other heathen system. Solomon had already reared altars to them, and their worship is named among the sins of Israel's last days 2 King xvii. 16. (Asherah denotes Ashtoreth's wooden symbol.) But only for one evil period of 34 years (917—883) did Ephraim offend in Baal (Hos. xiii. 1) to the extent of constituting Baalism the state religion. Jehu, who combined the furious zeal of the fanatic with the cold-hearted remorselessness of the scheming politician, made a partial reformation, but there was no one to re-construct the true worship when he had destroyed the false, and neither he nor any one of the son of Nebat's successors was free from his sin of idolatry. Not arbitrary favour for Judah, but Israel's persistent sin accounts for the different fates of the two kingdoms (Hos. xi. 12).

In Judah we read of seven Apostasies of king and people, and of four Reformations, the full consideration of which we reserve for next term. Israel's day of grace is gone, her vine is "burned with fire and cut down." Will Judah, newly reformed and delivered, learn once for all the lessons of her sister's fall?

IX. QUESTIONS.

(See pp. 13, 18.)

[Questions XV., XXII., XXIII., XXIV., and XXV. may be answered with the help of any books.]

I. Name the successive capitals of Northern Palestine from 1426 to 721. How many capitals had Judah? (8.)

II. Mention the exact duration of the drought foretold in 1 Kings xvii. 1. (2.)

III. Illustrate 1 Kings xviii. 24 by quoting 12 previous occasions on which God "answered by fire." (12.)

IV. Can you name any of the 7000 spoken of in 1 Kings xix. 18? (4.)

V. Had Elijah any message for the House of David? (2.)

VI. Briefly discuss the character of Elijah, and point out some striking parallels between his life and those of Moses and our Lord. (15.)

VII. To how many kings living in her own lifetime was Jezebel nearly related? Was Ahab's marriage to her sinful? (6.)

VIII. "The Syrian prophet said to the King of Israel, 'Is thy servant a dog that he should do this thing?'" Criticise the historical accuracy of this illustration in the speech of an English Cabinet Minister. (3.)

IX. Make a list of Elisha's miracles, naming for each a parallel or a contrast among the miracles wrought by our Lord. Explain 2 Kings ii. 9. (16.)

X. What noted preacher of "total abstinence" assisted a royal reformer? (2.)

XI. Name the only subject buried in the royal sepulchre at Jerusalem, giving the reason for this special honour. (2.)

XII. Two calamities not alluded to in Kings or Chronicles took place in Uzziah's reign. One is described in a contemporary prophet, the other is mentioned by two contemporary prophets, and by a prophet 250 years later. What were they? (4.)

XIII. When and how did the King of Israel try to put a usurper on the throne of David? (2.)

XIV. (a) How many kings of Israel were there? (b) Which had the longest and which had the shortest reign? (c) Which founded the longest-lived dynasty? (d) Which took Jerusalem? (e) Of which only is the expression "all his might" used? (f) Which were wounded by Syrian bowmen? (g) Which died violent deaths? (h) Name the best, the worst, and the greatest of them all. (16.)

XV. Explain the following allusions in Hosea :—(a) "The blood of Jezreel"; (b) "The valley of Achor"; (c) "Their staff declareth"; (d) "The new moon shall devour them"; (e) "A cake not turned"; (f) "The wickedness of Samaria"; (g) "The calves of Bethaven"; (h) "The calves of our lips"; (i) "Memphis shall bury them." (18.)

XVI. What allusions are there in the prophets to the fall of Samaria? (6.)

XVII. Make a complete list of the prophets sent to Israel and Judah between 915 and 697. (12.)

XVIII. Point out the probable allusions to contemporary or earlier history in Psalms xlviii. 7, lxvi. 6, lxxvi. 5, 11, lxxxiii. 5, 9, 11, lxxxvii. 2. What occasioned Psalms xlvi., xlvii., and xlviii.? Explain by Pentateuch references Psalm lxxx. 1, 2, 8. (14.)

XIX. Draw out a genealogical table of the Kings of Judah down to Hezekiah, showing their descent from Solomon and relation to one another. (12.)

XX. Make a list of the chief names of God in the prophets of this period. (32.)

XXI. What allusions do they contain to (a) the Garden of Eden, (b) Adam, (c) Abraham, (d) the destruction of the Cities of the Plain, (e) Jacob, (f) Moses, (g) Miriam, (h) Israel's sin at Shittim, (i) Israel's idolatry in the wilderness, (*j*) Edom's conduct to Israel, (*k*) the battle of Bethhoron, (*l*) Gideon's victories? (15.)

XXII. What does Isaiah mean by (*a*) "the crown of pride," (*b*) "the valley of vision," (*c*) "the rod of God's anger," (*d*) "the land of the rustling of wings," (*e*) "the wilderness of the sea," (*f*) "the isles of the sea"? (6.)

XXIII. Explain briefly the following passages in Isaiah: —(*a*) vi. 13, (*b*) vii. 16, (*c*) xiv. 12, (*d*) xvi. 1, (*e*) xxii. 22, (*f*) xxx. 7, (*g*) xxx. 33, (*h*) xxxiii. 14, (*i*) xxxiv. 16, (*j*) xxxviii. 12. (30.)

XXIV. Explain fully Nahum's reference to "populous No." (4.)

XXV. Give as many instances as you can of worship being offered at High Places. (15.)

XXVI. Under what names and how often is the Pentateuch referred to in Chronicles? What was the first instance after the days of Moses of God's commands being committed to writing and regularly taught? (12.)

XXVII. What took place at Jerusalem on the first Sabbath day of which we have a detailed account? (2.)

XXVIII. What do you know of the following?— Amaziah the priest, Azariah the priest, Bidkar, Gomer, Jehosheba, Mattan, Shear-jashub, Shebna, Zedekiah son of Chenaanah, Zichri. (20.)

XXIX. Where, when, by whom, and with what results were the following battles of this period fought?—Aphek, Ramoth-Gilead, Tekoa, Desert of Edom, Zair, Valley of Salt, Beth-shemesh, Gaza. (32.)

XXX. How many New Testament allusions can you find to Elijah, Elisha, Jezebel, Uzziah, Zechariah son of Jehoiada, Jonah, and Joel? How many New Testament quotations are there from Amos, Hosea, Micah, and Isaiah i.—xxxix.? (40.)

XXXI. Illustrate the following passages from the history of this period:—James v. 10; 2 Cor. vii. 10; 2 Cor. vi. 14-16; Phil. iv. 17; Matt. x. 41. (10.)

XXXII. Give references for the following :—(*a*) "The grievousness of war." (*b*) "That sing idle songs." (*c*) "Swift to do righteousness." (*d*) "Sudden destruction upon the strong." (*e*) "The twilight that I desired." (*f*) "The king's son shall reign." (*g*) "Reproaches shall not depart."

(*h*) "There shall be no gloom to her that was in anguish."
(*i*) "Her rulers dearly love shame." (*j*) "Her pillars shall be broken in pieces." (*k*) "The man of God wept."
(*l*) "Take your pleasure and be blind." (*m*) "His sin is laid up in store." (*n*) "Hast thou found me, O mine enemy?" (*o*) "Let the feasts come round." (*p*) "Answer him not." (*q*) "I fear the Lord from my youth." (*r*) "Be Thou my surety." (*s*) Our eyes are upon Thee." (*t*) "I write My law in ten thousand precepts." (*u*) "The word of the Lord is with him." (*v*) "Every work that he began he did with all his heart." (*w*) "Thy worthies are at rest." (*x*) "He departed without being desired." (*y*) "They became abominable like that which they loved." (*z*) "When he was strong his heart was lifted up." (26.)

For *Second Series* of Questions, see p. 309

SIXTH TERM.

THE DAYS OF JEREMIAH.
DECLINE AND FALL OF THE KINGDOM OF JUDAH.

B.C. 697—588.

2 *Kings XXI.—XXV.*, 2 *Chron. XXXIII.—XXXVI.* 21. *Psalms XLIV., LXXI., LXXIV., LXXIX., CXXIX., CXXX. Isaiah XL.— LXVI., Zephaniah, Habakkuk, Jeremiah, Ezekiel I.—XXIV. Lamentations, Obadiah.* (130 *chapters.*)

"All My words ... receive in thine heart and hear with thine ears."— EZEK. iii. 10.

21st MONTH (33).
  2 Kings XXI. 2 Chron. XXXIII. 2 Kings XXII.— XXIII. 30. 2 Chron. XXXIV., XXXV. Zephaniah. Jer. I.— VI. 2 Kings XXIII. 31-7. 2 Chron. XXXVI. 1-5. Psalm XLIV. Habakkuk. Jer. XXVI. 1-7, VII.—X., XXVI. 8-24, XI., XII., XIV.—XX.

22nd MONTH (32).
  Jer. XXII., XXIII. 2 Kings XXIV. 1-17. 2 Chron. XXXVI. 6-10. Psalm LXXI. Jer. XLVI.—XLIX. 33, XXXV., XXV., XXXVI., XLV., XIII. 2 Kings XXIV. 18-20. 2 Chron. XXXVI. 11-16. Jer. XXIV., XXIX., XLIX. 34-9, XXVII., XXVIII., L., LI. Ezek. I.— XII.

23rd MONTH (33).
  Ezek. XIII.—XXIII. 2 Kings XXV. 2 Chron. XXXVI. 17-21. Jer. XXI. Ezek. XXIV. Jer. XXXIV., XXXVII., XXXII., XXX., XXXI., XXXIII., XXXVIII., XXXIX. 15-18. 1-14. LII. Psalms LXXIV., LXXIX. Lamentations. Obadiah. Jer. XL., XLI.

24th MONTH (32).
  Jer. XLII.—XLIV. Psalms CXXX., CXXIX. Isaiah XL. —LXVI.

I. GENERAL SUMMARY.

OUR story of the newly delivered Jewish Kingdom during its last century is one of unfulfilled promise and lost opportunity, similar to the story of ancient Israel in

Psalm cvi. 12, 13. It is among those deep disappointments of history that demand most thoughtful consideration. The fifteen years of life for which Hezekiah prayed gave him an heir to whom the throne of David owed its destruction. Of the incidents of Manasseh's long reign we know little; though the Prophets supply many details about its idolatries. But its terrible result is plainly stated in Jer. xv. 4, and Jewish tradition places Manasseh beside Jeroboam and Ahab as having no part in the life to come. "Too late" was written on all Josiah's gallant efforts; and the four weak and wicked kings (Isa. iii. 4, R.V.) who followed him were mere puppets (three of them actual nominees) of the two powers who acted like two huge beasts of prey, seeking to devour each other, but turning aside from time to time to snatch at the frightened creature who crosses their path. Foolish Judah clung still to the friendship of Egypt. In vain her later prophets denounced this treacherous alliance as Isaiah had done. His words (Isa. xxx. 7, R.V.) were justified when Pharaoh's feint of raising the siege of Jerusalem ended in retirement, without a battle, leaving it to its fate (Jer. xxxvii.). Yet, when all was over, they fled from their own ruin to Egypt, in spite of the warning that in so doing they would only share her ruin (Jer. xlvi. 17). For Egypt had now a mightier rival than even Assyria, and Judah, after defying Sennacherib, could only quail before Nebuchadnezzar. Nineveh had been taken in 606 (625 according to some authorities), and on its downfall rose the Babylonian Empire which overthrew, and the Persian Empire which restored the Jewish State. Isaiah had strenuously preached resistance to Assyria. Jeremiah as strenuously, but less successfully, advocated submission to Babylon as the foreordained conqueror of Judah.

Now, as Israel represents the Church, Dr. Arnold takes Egypt to represent in its milder, and Babylon in its darker aspect, that world in which the Church has to bear her witness and do her work. If it is so, we may find this lesson here. Dallying with the world's better side ends in destruction by its worse side. They will never win it for God who give it the trust and affection due to Him alone (James iv. 4). Jeremiah's policy may symbolise the teaching of Christ, and His practice in refusing to head a nation of insurgents (Matt. v. 39, xxvi. 52; John vi. 15, xviii. 36; 2 Cor. x. 4).

Observe how the Prophets fill in the historian's brief outline. They show us Jehoiakim alarmed for once and proclaiming a fast before the Lord. But when God's gracious response is brought to him, sitting in that luxurious palace whose builders are wrongfully left unpaid, he defies and destroys the written Word, and, in vain dependence on his Egyptian suzerain, meets with sceptical effrontery the predictions about the Babylonian host that was actually approaching his gates; and so we understand why he is omitted from S. Matthew's genealogy of Christ (Rev. xxii. 19), together with the wicked son of Jezebel's daughter (Psalm cix. 14), and Joash and Amaziah, who began well but ended ill (Ezek. xviii. 24). The prophets show us also the crooked intrigues of Zedekiah, and his treacherous folly in making compacts on all sides only to break them.

Such were the last of that grand line of kings whose crown for four and a half centuries had passed, in a way unparalleled in any other dynasty, from father to son in regular succession (1 Chron. iii. 10-16), without one civil war or one interregnum, save Athaliah's brief usurpation (1 Kings xv. 4). Moreover, for 250 out of 388 years Judah had been ruled by pious sovereigns, and had enjoyed unusual peace and prosperity. Ere we leave these kings of long ago I may help the reader to think of them as more than mere names, by suggesting, from the most familiar pages of modern history, one or two monarchs whom they resembled. Compare for instance, David with Robert Bruce, Solomon with Henry VIII., Rehoboam with Ethelred the Unready (that is, "deaf to good advice"), Asa with Edward III., Jehoshaphat with David I., Joash with Richard II., Amaziah with James IV., Hezekiah with Alfred the Great, Josiah with Edward VI., and Jehoiakim with Charles II.

From the three sieges of Jerusalem, which Nebuchadnezzar took three times, date three periods of seventy years or ten Sabbatical years, which it is helpful to discriminate.

(*a*) 606 536. The Servitude. In 605 King Jehoiakim seems to have been released and suffered to remain on his throne as a tributary prince, but much of the treasure of the Temple, several members of the royal family, and perhaps others, were carried off.

(*b*) 599—529. The Exile. In 599 King Jeconiah, with the royal family, the princes, nobles, artificers, and warriors, and much Temple and palace treasure, followed them to Babylon.

(*c*) 588—518. The Desolations. In 588 Judah's Captivity was completed by the deportation of King Zedekiah, the rest of his people, and the remaining spoil of the Temple. A wretched handful was left in Palestine, who might, however, have become the nucleus for a regathering of Israel without break on their own soil. For they were taught by Jeremiah, and ruled by the able and generous Gedaliah. The reckless violence of a scheming Jewish prince broke up this little community, and the Jews rightly regarded Gedaliah's assassination as a calamity great enough to be annually commemorated by a fast (Zech. vii. 5, viii. 19).

And now the House of God has been sacked; the City of God has been burned; His "Anointed" is a mutilated prisoner in a foreign land; prince and priest have fallen by the sword, and Judah is numbered among the nations no longer. Successive troops of captives have been driven by weary marches into the Eastern land, whence their father Abraham was called out. Others have found their way as fugitives to the Western land, whence God brought out their ancestors. A yet greater catastrophe calls forth their loudest lamentations, one which involves all the rest. Jehovah, who once chose them and crowned them with blessings, has now, after long provocation, cast them out from His Presence (2 Kings xxiv. 20, xiii. 23; Jer. xxiii. 39). That they can ever be a nation again is contrary to all probability and all analogy. Against it is the might of the vastest empire the world has ever seen, ruled by its greatest conqueror. Against it is the fact that their own wilfulness has rendered their destruction even more complete than he meant it to be; and that their moral and spiritual degradation seems past hope. But for it there is the promise of a faithful God.

II. Books to be Read.

(See "Oxford Helps," § v.)

This term more than half our period is represented by only two chapters. For the Prophets supply $1\frac{3}{5}$ths of our reading, and they were silent during the reigns of Manasseh and Amon. Of the six prophets who form the second group, we read all save Daniel, whose book stands midway between the second and third group, as it stands midway between history and prophecy.

For the six *Psalms* of this period, see p. 203.

Isaiah, Part I., is a mixture of narrative and prediction: its pulses throb with all the hopes and fears, the terror and defiance and exultation of the changeful age in which it was written. *Isaiah, Part II.*, is one majestic and symmetrical poem in three cantos—viz.,

(*a*) xl.—xlviii. Concerning Cyrus and the restoration of Israel as a nation.

(*b*) xlix.—lvii. Concerning the Servant of Jehovah and the salvation of many nations through Him.

(*c*) lviii.—lxvi. Concerning Zion's Light, through which all nations shall see God's glory and worship Him.

Ruined Judah and desolate Jerusalem form the foreground of its picture, though Isaiah cannot long have survived the able and prosperous King who reconstituted the state and fortified the capital. All the 66 chapters of Isaiah were universally ascribed to one author until some recent critics, observing this difference in their points of view, put forth the theory that while the son of Amoz wrote the first Book of Denunciation and Woe, the second Book of Consolation was penned 160 years later, by a member of the school of prophets which Isaiah founded (Isa. viii. 16), the whole being called after his name, as the whole Psalter is called after David. Were this proved, we might still receive Isa. xl.—lxvi. as part of the Canon. But it is not proved. The literary argument from alleged differences of vocabulary and style is far from conclusive, and though prophets generally speak of the future revealed to them from the standpoint of the present, there is no insuperable difficulty in conceiving that Isaiah may have been inspired vividly to imagine and depict the Captivity he had already foretold. Eleven New Testament quotations from chaps. xl.—lxvi. are directly referred to Isaiah, and no other prophet capable of penning thoughts so high and deep has ever been heard of. Their author was an incomparably greater man than any man of the Post-Exilian age; and had he been contemporary with Ezra, it is inconceivable that his name and personality should have been wholly forgotten. Minute study of Jeremiah also indicates that Isa. xl.—lxvi. had been already written. But we recognise it as a legacy to posterity rather than a gift to contemporaries (Isa. xlviii. 4-7), and therefore read it in connexion with the later age for which it was no longer a sealed book (Dan. xii. 9). Observe its frequent reference to "all nations," and these recurring notes in its glorious song, "Hearken," "Listen," "Keep silence," "Cry," "Awake," "Remember," "Fear not."

Zephaniah, son of Cushi, and perhaps great-great-grandson of King Hezekiah. (630—610. Concerning Judah. In the reign of Josiah.) His keynote is *The pure worship required by God* (Matt. iv. 10; Phil. iii. 3), and he predicts judgments and blessings for Gentiles as well as Jews.

Habakkuk, probably a Levite if not a priest, and one of the Temple choir. (609—599? Concerning Judah. In the reign of Jehoiakim?) His keynote is *Life by faith* (Gal. ii. 20; Heb. xi. 6), and the perplexities which he faces and solves are those of the individual soul rather than of the nation. His Prayer, which recalls the finest lyrics of earlier times and expands Isa. l. 10, is considered by Bishop Lowth "one of the most perfect specimens of the Hebrew ode." It is preceded by a dialogue between the Prophet (i. 2-4, i. 12—ii. 1) and the Lord (i. 5-11, ii. 2-20), concerning the approaching Chaldean invasion. That is blended here with the Scythian invasion about the middle of the seventh century B.C., which was the earliest recorded movement behind their mountain barrier in Asia of those Northern nomadic tribes who ultimately swept away the Roman Empire and built up modern Europe on its ruins. (See p. 140, and comp. Zeph. ii. 4-6; Jer. i. 13-15, vi. 3-5; Col. iii. 11.)

Jeremiah, son of Hilkiah (perhaps the high priest of 2 Chron. xxxiv.), a priest of Anathoth. (627—588. Concerning Judah. In the reigns of Josiah, Jehoiakim, Jeconiah, and

Zedekiah.) *Continue in sin, and it will prove its own punishment; Confess, and ye shall find mercy* is his keynote (Rom. vi. 21 ; 1 John i. 9). Like Nehemiah's history, his prophecy is interspersed with short and urgent prayers, and characteristic expressions recur again and again, such as, " Lord, Thou knowest " (xxix. 23, R.V.), " I swear by Myself," " The days come," " Not a full end." Twice (xxv. 11, xxix. 10) he clearly foretells the exact duration of the Captivity which Isaiah first announced (Dan. ix. 2). Isaiah soars like an eagle to behold with undimmed eye the source of light. Jeremiah sits in shadow like a dove to mourn over his fallen people with infinite pathos and tenderness. " Jeremiah is my favourite book now. It has taught me more than tongue can tell," writes Kingsley in 1850.

Obadiah. (588. Concerning Edom. In the reign of Zedekiah.) Its resemblance to Jer. xlix. 7-22 ; Lam. iv. 21 ; Ezek. xxxv. ; and Psalm cxxxvii. 7 suggests that it is of the same period, and most probably it was written shortly before Nebuchadnezzar's conquest of Edom in 583. *Judgment without mercy to the merciless* is its keynote (James ii. 13). " It expresses," says Stanley, " the Divine malediction on the sin most difficult to be forgiven, the desertion of kinsmen by kinsmen, of friends by friends, the readiness to take advantage of the weaker side, hounding on the victorious party, and standing on the other side in the day of the sorest need." (Comp. Isa. xxxiv. 5.)

Ezekiel, son of Buzi, a priest carried captive in 599, who prophesied by the banks of the Chebar in Northern Mesopotamia, 200 miles from Babylon, and who is not mentioned outside his own book. (594—574. Concerning Judah. In the reign of Zedekiah.) Tradition says that he was put to death by his fellow-exiles for rebuking their idolatry. His differs from former prophetical books in being chronological throughout, for in him the author preponderates over the seer, the poet, and the statesman. His prose is, however, always poetical, and the Dirge of the Kings (xix.), the Lay of the Sword (xxi. 8-17), the Dirge of Tyre (xxvii., xxviii.), and the Dirge of Egypt (xxxi., xxxii.) are actual poetry. His keynote is *Knowledge of God (a) by Israel* (Hos. ii. 20 ; John iv. 22), *(b) by the Gentiles* (Isa. xxvi. 9 ; Acts xi. 18 ;

Matt. viii. 11); and he develops more fully the doctrine, found in germ in Jeremiah, of the responsibility of the individual soul as separate from the collective nation. The independence of man from man is brought out by such a calamity as the fall of Jerusalem, and no prophet teaches this great moral lesson so simply. Observe these recurring phrases: "A rebellious house," "I, the Lord, have spoken and will do it," "I will recompense the sinner's way on his own head." Of the three parts into which Ezekiel's book falls, we read this term only Part I. (chaps. i.—xxiv.), Exhortations to Repentance before the Fall of Jerusalem. Ezekiel has been called "the Old Testament Apocalypse," and the parallels between it and Revelation are very close and numerous. Miss E. S. Elliott's "Prophecies of Jeremiah and Ezekiel" (Morgan & Scott, 6d.) is a helpful analysis of both books.

The Lamentations of Jeremiah, sixth and latest poetical book of the Old Testament, was written, perhaps at Mizpah immediately after the Fall of Jerusalem. It consists of four independent acrostics (see p. 176), and a concluding poem, not acrostic, and may be thus divided:—

   I. (*a*) The Prophet's Lament. (i. 1-11.)
      (*b*) The Lament of Jerusalem. (i. 11-22.)
  II. (*a*) The Prophet's Lament. (ii. 1-19.)
      (*b*) The Lament of Jerusalem. (ii. 20-22.)
 III.   The Prophet's Personal Sorrow. (iii.)
 IV. (*a*) The Prophet's Lament. (iv. 1-16.)
      (*b*) The People's Lament. (iv. 17-21.)
      (*c*) The Prophet's Consolation. (iv. 22.)
  V.   The People's Prayer. (v.)

Its keynote is *God chastens unwillingly and only for our good* (2 Cor. vii. 10; Heb. xii. 5-11). In Jewish synagogues it is still recited every year on the anniversary of the Temple's destruction. "Never did city suffer a more miserable fate, never was ruined city lamented in language so exquisitely pathetic" (*Milman*). It is probable that Jeremiah also wrote several of those Psalms of the Captivity which succeed, at the interval of a century, the jubilant Psalms of Hezekiah's reign. Their long wail best expresses the woe of Judah's fall.

III. PERIODS AND DATES.

I follow the common chronology as usual, but some good authorities extend this period of 109 years to 112 years by placing Manasseh's accession in 698 and the Fall of Jerusalem in 586.

(1) B.C. 697—640 (57 years). From the death of Hezekiah to the accession of Josiah. *Judah's Undoing through Manasseh.* 2 Kings xxi.; 2 Chron. xxxiii.

(2) B.C. 640—606 (34 years). From Josiah's accession to the First Siege of Jerusalem by Nebuchadnezzar. *Judah's last true King, and First Subjection, to Egypt.* 2 Kings xxii.—xxiii. 30; 2 Chron. xxxiv., xxxv.; Zephaniah; Jer. i.—vi. (Commission, Expostulation, and Vision of coming invasion). **2 Kings xxiii. 31-7; 2 Chron. xxxvi. 1-5; Psalm xliv.; Habakkuk; Jer. xxvi. 1-7, vii.—x., xxvi. 8-24** (Denunciation in the Temple Court). **Jer. xi., xii.** (Prophetic Tour and Conspiracy against Jeremiah). **Jer. xiv.—xvii.** (the Drought; approaching Fall and Restoration; the Sabbath). **Jer. xviii.—xx.** (the Potter's House and Valley of Hinnom). **Jer. xxii., xxiii.** (the Three Kings, the Rulers, and Prophets).

(3) B.C. 606—599 (7 years). From the First Siege to the Second Capture of Jerusalem by Nebuchadnezzar. *Judah's Second Subjection, to Babylon.* **2 Kings xxiv. 1-17; 2 Chron. xxxvi. 6-10; Psalm lxxi.; Jer. xlvi.—xlix. 33** (concerning the Nations). **Jer. xxxv.** (the Rechabites). **Jer. xxv.** (the Cup of God's fury). **Jer. xxxvi., xlv.** (Jeremiah's Roll). **Jer. xiii.** (the Journey to Euphrates).

(4) B.C. 599—588 (11 years). From the Second Capture of Jerusalem to its Third Capture and the Flight into Egypt. *Judah's Destruction and Dispersion.* 2 Kings xxiv. 18-20; 2 Chron. xxxvi. 11-16.

598. Jer. xxiv., xxix., xlix. 34-9 (Those taken and those left. Elam).

595. **Jer. xxvii., xxviii.** (the Yokes. Hananiah). l., li. (Babylon).

594. **Ezek. i.—vii.** (opening Visions and Signs).

593. **Ezek. viii.—xix.** (Judah's Apostasy and its result).
592. **Ezek. xx.—xxiii.** (against the Elders, the Land, the Princes, the King, and the Capital).
590. **2 Kings xxv.; 2 Chron. xxxvi. 17-21; Jer. xxi.** (Zedekiah's Inquiry just before the siege began). **Ezek. xxiv.** (Prediction of Jerusalem's Fall). **Jer. xxxiv., xxxvii.** (last Offer of Mercy during a pause in the siege).
589. **Jer. xxxii., xxx., xxxi., xxxiii.** (Promise of Restoration).
588. **Jer. xxxviii., xxxix. 15-18** (Imprisonment and Rescue of Jeremiah). **Jer. xxxix. 1-14** (the Fall of Jerusalem). **Jer. lii.** (Supplement to Jeremiah, by another hand probably). **Psalms lxxiv., lxxix; Lamentations; Obadiah; Jer. xl.—xliv.** (the Flight to Egypt).
Psalms cxxx., cxxix. (the Sorrow).
Isa. xl.—lxvi. (the Hope).

Seven Kings of Judah.

Manasseh	697—642.
Amon	642—640.
Josiah	640—609.
Jehoahaz	Three months.
Jehoiakim	609—599.
Jeconiah	Three months.
Zedekiah	599—588.

IV. GEOGRAPHY.

(See "Oxford Helps," Maps IV., VII., VIII., and IX.)

Next term we shall follow Judah into the land of her captivity. We now leave her disobedient remnant, in defiance of a very ancient command (Deut. xvii. 16), and fulfilment of as ancient a prophecy (Deut. xxviii. 68), forcing one of Israel's last great prophets back into the Egypt from which their first great prophet had brought them out (Jer. xliii. 7). We infer from Ezekiel, Jeremiah, and Josephus that most of these fugitives perished there, or were carried to Babylon later; but from that day to this, a Jewish colony has existed in Egypt. 250 years afterwards Alexandria became a centre of Judaism only second in importance to Jerusalem (Acts ii. 10, xviii. 24). The site of *Tahpanhes*, clearly an important frontier town (Jer. ii. 16, xliii., xlvi. 14; Ezek. xxx. 18), whither the fugitives went, long baffled inquirers. Within the last year or two, Dr. Flinders Petrie has found, in the lonely desert sands near the mud swamp of Pelusium, below a lofty mound long known in the Arab speech as "The Castle of the Jew's daughter," the palace of Pharaoh Hophra, and the courtyard where Jeremiah hid "in mortar in the brickwork" the symbols of Nebuchadnezzar's capture of this building. Its newly uncovered ruins tell plainly that the fiery destruction predicted for it by the prophet came to pass.

V. HEROES.

Keynotes {*Josiah*, Acts xx. 27.
{*Jeremiah*, 2 Cor. xii. 9.

Josiah was the only one of Judah's last seven kings who served the Lord. We blame Joash and Manasseh the more because they were impious in spite of their circumstances. We admire Josiah the more because amid utterly corrupt princes, priests, prophets, and people, he resolved to serve God himself, and to do all he could to recall the nation to His service also. He reformed with little support and little hope, and therefore he reformed fiercely and vehemently. The sunset light of Judah's history plays round him, and no death in her annals is so lamentable as that of her last royal hero.

Hezekiah had Isaiah beside him; Josiah had *Jeremiah*, not only able as a prophet to proclaim, in season, out of season, in palace and street, in venerated Temple and abhorred Gi-hinnom, the most unwelcome and unpalatable truths; but also able as a poet to pour out the mournfullest of dirges over imprisoned king, captive people, ruined sanctuary, and desolate city, when all had been said in vain More than half our reading this term is from Jeremiah's pen (for he was in all probability editor of the earlier, and author of the later parts of I., II. Kings), and he is "the one grand immovable figure which alone redeems the miserable downfall of his country from triviality and shame." He was the last seer who was also a statesman and counsellor of kings. He was the first who uttered his inspired counsel in that epistolary form afterwards made so illustrious by S. Paul. Like S. Paul also, we find him the centre and life of a group of devoted friends and faithful adherents, who were direct inheritors of the traditions of Josiah's reign; such as his brother Gemariah; his uncle and aunt Shallum and Huldah, with their son Hanamel; Delaiah and Urijah, the sons of Shemaiah; Hanan the son of Igdaliah; Zephaniah the son, and Seraiah and Baruch the grandsons of Maaseiah. Baruch was his Timothy and his Tertius, and as the first notable Scribe who committed God's word to writing, may be regarded as the predecessor of Ezra. And Jeremiah, forbidden to seek the love of wife and child, needed the sympathy and affection of friends not a little. At once priest and prophet (a rare combination), he could not, like Hosea, fall back upon Judah, though despairing of Israel; he could not, like Isaiah and Amos, fall back upon her prophets, though despairing of her priests; he saw that priest and prophet were alike corrupt, and he was called upon to declare it (Jer. xxiii. 11). Hence the rancorous hostility of both orders to their noblest representative. Jeremiah the priest was excluded from the Temple (Jer. xxxvi. 5). Jeremiah the prophet was persistently traduced and persecuted as a liar and traitor by the smooth-tongued utterers of popular predictions. And his was one of those gentle, sensitive, and highly strung souls for which the trust and love of others is the very breath of life. No prophet reveals himself so clearly in his writings. By nature shy, timid, shrinking, hesitating, and desponding, suffering deepest sorrow of heart at seeing things as they are, and called to the hard task of proving that all Judah most relied upon would avail her nothing, and of preaching submission and repentance to a self-willed and hardened people bent on resistance; by God's grace and his own manful resolve, he was bold, fearless, unflinching, determined, and even hopeful, through that faith tried in the fire which enabled him to read in the bright possibilities of the future a balance for the difficulties and distresses of the present. After forty years of courageous testimony, he refused the favour of the greatest of monarchs, and "gladly clung" (says Josephus) "to the ruins of his country, and to the hope of living out the rest of his life with its surviving relics." Here history leaves him (2 Chron. xxxv. 25, xxxvi. 12, 21, are the only

Biblical mentions of him outside his own book), and conflicting traditions speak of a peaceful end in Babylon, and a death by stoning in Egypt at the hands of his reprobate countrymen. Afterwards they reckoned him not a whit behind the very chiefest prophets, and daily expected that he, like Elijah, would return as the restorer of Israel (Matt. xvi. 14; John i. 21).

VI. THE COMING MESSIAH.

"*Lord, dost thou at this time restore the kingdom to Israel?*"
Acts i. 6.

Isa. xl.—lxvi., which may have been penned during the first persecution of the true faith in Jerusalem, contains the greatest Messianic Predictions of the Old Testament. A Messiah winning through much tribulation a kingdom not of this world, is a promise as appropriate to the age of Judah's Fall as the promise of a triumphant and glorious Messiah was to the age of David and Solomon. Isaiah's prophecies were fulfilled by Jews whose eyes were blinded to this aspect of the Coming One. The predictions about Cyrus in xli. 2, 25-7, have an ultimate fulfilment in Him who was to all mankind spiritually what Cyrus was to captive Judah politically. There are also nine great and detailed predictions, eight of which are quoted in the New Testament. Notice that the section about "the Servant of the Lord" is followed by one that speaks often of "the servants of the Lord" (Rom. v. 15-19).

(1) Isa. xl. 1-11 ; Matt. iii. ; John x.
(2) Isa. xlii. ; Matt. xii. 17-21 ; Luke ii. 32.
(3) Isa. xlix. ; Acts iv. 27 (R.V.), xiii. 47 ; Phil. ii. 7.
(4) Isa. l. 4-7 ; Heb. v. 8 ; Matt. xxvi. 67 ; John xvi. 32.
(5) Isa. lii. 13—liii. 12 ; Acts viii. 27-35.
(6) Isa. lix. 20, 21 ; Rom. xi. 26 ; Matt. i. 21.
(7) Isa. lx. 1-3 ; Matt. ii. ; John viii. 12 ; Eph. v. 14.
(8) Isa. lxi. 1-3 ; Luke iv. 17-21, iii. 22 ; John xii. 28.
(9) Isa. lxii. 10—lxiii. 6; Matt. xxv. 19, xxi. 5 ; 2 Thess. ii.
(10) Zeph. ii. 7 ; Luke i. 68.
(11) Zeph. iii. 8-20 ; John. i. 49, iv. 24 ; Acts viii. 27-38.
(12) Hab. ii. 3 ; Heb. x. 37.
(13) Hab. ii. 14 ; 1 John ii. 13, iv. 16, v. 20.

(14) Hab. iii. 13 ; 2 Cor. v. 19 (but see R.V.).
(15) Jer. xxiii. 5, 6 ; Rom. i. 3 ; 1 Cor. i. 30.
(16) Jer. xxx. 8, 9, 21, 22 ; Acts ii. 29-32 ; Heb. ii. 14-17.
(17) Jer. xxxi. 22 ; Luke i. 26-35.
(18) Jer. xxxiii. 15-17, 21, 22 ; Acts xiii. 22, 23; 2 Tim. ii. 8.
(19) Obad. 17-21 ; Rev. xi. 15-17.
(20) Ezek. xvii. 22-4 ; Rev. xxii. 16 ; Matt. xiii. 31, 32.
(21) Ezek. xxi. 27 ; John xviii. 36, 37 ; Matt. xxviii. 18.

Lamentations is read both in the English and the Latin Church during the week in which we commemorate the sufferings of our Lord (Lam. i. 12).

Compared with Isaiah's, Jeremiah's Messianic predictions are few. But through him we hear, for the first time, that the Old Covenant or Testament, which forms the theme of the first part of the Bible and gives it a name, was to be superseded. Nebuchadnezzar had just re-formed his siege for a final assault upon the famine-stricken city, when Jeremiah's sorrowful pleadings and warnings gave place to a joyous message of blessing for Israel's latter end (xxxi. 31-6). After a dim presage of the Incarnation (ver. 22) he passes to a clear announcement of a New Covenant, looking more than 500 years beyond the Restoration (contrast Jer. xxxi. 32 and Hag. ii. 5) to that Upper Room (Luke xxii. 11, 12 ; Acts i. 13, R.V., ii. 1), which became the birthplace of the Church of Christ, and in which each of the four clauses of this Royal Charter was reiterated and ratified. The promise is fourfold (see Heb. viii. 6-13, x. 9-18) :—

(*a*) Remission of Sins (Matt. xxvi. 27, 28, R.V.).
(*b*) A New Law (John xiii. 34, xiv. 23, 26, xv. 13, 14).
(*c*) A New Relationship (John xv. 15, 16, xvii. 6, 9, 11).
(*d*) A New Fellowship with Father, Son, and Holy Spirit (John xiv. 7, 9, 17 ; 1 John i. 3, ii. 20). See Miss Elliott's "Jeremiah and Ezekiel."

VII. GOD'S REVELATION OF HIMSELF TO MAN.

Again we note characteristic revelations in the Prophets of our period. Twice over from *Isaiah* we learn (Isa. xlii. 8, xlviii. 11) that the glory of God can be shared by no other being. Yet in Isa. ix. 6, 7 (as in Micah v. 2, 4 ; Psalm xlv. 6, 7, cx. ; and Jer. xxiii. 5, 6), two Divine and

Eternal Beings are spoken of ; and in Isa. xlviii. 16, lxi. 1-3 we have still plainer pre-Christian enumeration of the Co-eternal Three who ever live and reign One God. *Zephaniah*, the earliest of the group of prophets whose great theme will be God's judgment, seen in the convulsion and overthrow of all the kingdoms of that age, proclaims that He is righteous (iii. 5). *Habakkuk* humbly adores Him as the mysterious and awful Holy One (i. 12, 13, ii. 20). *Jeremiah* delivers the terrible message recalling the Name by which He had made Himself known to Israel (xliv. 26). He is henceforth "God of all flesh," "God in the Heavens" (cp. 2 Chron. xxxvi. 23), "King of the Nations," and, 65 times, "Lord of Hosts." Yet He has been in Jeremiah also "Jacob's Portion," "Israel's God and Hope and Holy One," and the "God of all Israel's families." *Obadiah's* message is from Adonai Jehovah, recalling Amos and Micah. *Ezekiel*, worldwide rather than national in his outlook, revives the ancient patriarchal name of El Shaddai (x. 5), which we met with last in Exodus. "God of Israel" occurs once, and in striking contrast to Isaiah and Jeremiah, Ezekiel contains no other name save "Jehovah."

VIII. Man's Relation to God in Worship.

Eight of Judah's kings led their people into seven Apostasies. Save Rehoboam, who repented in time, each was visited with a personal punishment in addition to the national punishment that followed the national sin.

(1) *Rehoboam :* hence Egyptian Invasion (2 Chron. xii. 1 ; 1 Kings xiv. 21-6).

(2) *Jehoram :* hence Philistine and Arabian Invasion (2 Chron. xxi. ; 2 Kings xi. 18).

(3) *Joash :* hence Syrian Invasion (2 Chron. xxiv. 18-23).

(4) *Amaziah :* hence Israelite Invasion (2 Chron. xxv. 14, 20-22).

(5) *Ahaz :* hence Invasion by Israelites, Syrians, Philistines, Edomites, and Assyrians (2 Chron. xxviii. 2, 19, 25 ; 2 Kings xvi. 2-4).

(6) *Manasseh :* hence Assyrian Invasion (2 Chron. xxxiii. 3-11 ; 2 Kings xxi. 1-16).

(7) *Jehoiakim* and *Zedekiah :* hence Babylonian Invasion (2 Chron. xxxvi. 8, 14 ; Jer. xi. 13, xvii. 2, xix. 5).

(1) and (2) may both be traced to the influence of a queen of foreign extraction. (4) is the only one of which we are not told that worship of Ashtoreth was set up. In (2), (5), (6), and (7) special mention is made of the worship of Baal. In (6) the worship of Jehovah was actually disestablished, and the true faith, for the first time in Judah, persecuted. Amaziah, Manasseh, Jehoiakim, and Zedekiah were taken captive, Jehoram and Joash were smitten with sickness, and Ahaz was ruined with his people. (1), (2), (5), and (6) were followed by Reformations, (3) and (4) being less flagrant, and (7) past reforming, save by the stern discipline of the Captivity. These Reformations, by which evil was for the time overcome of good, and ruin averted, were through

(*a*) *Asa*, completed by *Jehoshaphat*.
(*b*) *Jehoiada* in the reign of Joash.
(*c*) *Hezekiah*.
(*d*) *Josiah*.

Students would do well to work out fully this brief summary of Judah's religious history, for it has many lessons to teach us, as a nation, as a church, and as individuals.

We leave the Chosen People ruined, as Moses had warned them they might be ruined (Deut. xxix.), by serving false gods. Our next two terms will show them purged from this gross idolatry and restored, only to fall into a subtler idolatry which, under the outward forms of the true religion, will lead to another rejection of God and a yet more terrible fall. But before we resume their story we shall glance round at Nebuchadnezzar's work elsewhere as pictured by the Hebrew prophets.

IX. QUESTIONS.

(See pp. 13, 18.)

[Questions III., XIII., XVII., XVIII., XIX., XX., and XXVI. may be answered with help of any books.]

I. Where, when, by whom, and with what results were the battles of Megiddo and Carchemish fought? (8.)

II. Complete the genealogical table of the Kings of Judah from Hezekiah onwards. (7.)

III. Reconcile Jer. xxxii. 4, 5 and xxxiv. 2, 3 with Ezek. xii. 13 ; also Jer. xxii. 28, 30 with Matt. i. 12. (6.)

IV. (*a*) How many sovereigns of Judah were there? (*b*) Which had the longest and which had the shortest reign? (*c*) Which attained the greatest age? (*d*) Which of them made war with Israel? (*e*) Of which of them is it said that the Lord was with them? (*f*) Which of them were taken captive by their enemies? (*g*) Which died violent deaths? (*h*) Name the four best, the four worst, and the four greatest of them all. (*i*) Which of them is called King of Israel? (*j*) Which of them were buried in the royal sepulchres? (24.)

V. Make a complete list of the prophets sent to Judah between 697 and 588, and name three false prophets of the period. (8.)

VI. What do you know of Shaphan the scribe, and of four sons and two grandsons of his mentioned in the Bible? (7.)

VII. What do you know of the following?—Elnathan, Irijah, Ishmael son of Nethaniah, Jaazaniah son of Azur, Jehudi, Nehushta. (12.)

VIII. "We will not ride upon horses." Explain this vow by quotations from Isaiah and Ezekiel. (3.)

IX. What circumstances recorded by Jeremiah and Ezekiel account for Nebuchadnezzar's relentless policy to Jerusalem the third time he took it, though he had spared it twice before? (5.)

X. Show that Jerusalem was captured and the Temple pillaged at least eight times between 976 and 588. (12.)

XI. Give a brief summary of the chief incidents in Jeremiah's life. (10.)

XII. Quote ten prayers in the Book of Jeremiah, giving references only. (10.)

XIII. What does Jeremiah mean by (*a*) "The throne of God's glory," (*b*) "God's footstool," (*c*) "The mountain in the field," (*d*) "The joy of the whole earth," (*e*) "The King of Sheshach," (*f*) "The king . . . my servant," (*g*) "God's battle axe," (*h*) "The hammer of the whole earth," (*i*) "The iron furnace," (*j*) "The sword of the wilderness," (*k*) "The queen of heaven," (*l*) "The breath of our nostrils"? (12.)

XIV. Point out 20 coincidences of thought and expression between the Psalms read this term and Jeremiah's writings. (10.)

XV. To whom was the promise made that their life should be given them for a prey? (3.)

XVI. Consider Jeremiah and Ezekiel as types of Christ. (15.)

XVII. Enumerate four *signs* (or prophecies through symbolic acts done by the prophet) shown by Jeremiah to Israel, indicating what each signified. (8.)

XVIII. Enumerate six *signs* shown by Ezekiel, indicating what each signified. (12.)

XIX. Give short historical explanations of the vision of Ezek. viii., ix., and the parables of Ezek. xvii., xix. (8.)

XX. What may be gathered by comparison of Ezekiel with Genesis, Exodus, Isaiah, and Revelation as to the appearance and nature of the Cherubim and Seraphim? (10.)

XXI. Find 20 allusions to the Holy Spirit in Ezek. i.—xxiv., and Isa. xl.—lxvi. (10.)

XXII. Prove by quotations that Isa. xl.—lxvi. speaks of Judah's Captivity as past and not future, and account for this. (10.)

XXIII. Illustrate Acts viii. 28-38 by finding 20 New Testament quotations or references for Isa. lii. 13—liii. 12. (10.)

XXIV. Find 25 other New Testament quotations from Isa. xl.—lxvi., 6 from Jeremiah, and 5 from Habakkuk. (18.)

XXV. "The word *peace* runs as a golden thread through the tissue of the whole Book of Isaiah." Illustrate this. (10.)

XXVI. Explain briefly the following passages:—Zeph. i. 4, 5, 11; Hab. ii. 11; Jer. ii. 30, xii. 5, xxii. 10; Ezek. xviii. 4; Isa. lxv. 3, 4, 11. (16.)

XXVII. How often is God spoken of as King in the literature of this period? Give some of the other chief names of God in Jeremiah and Isa. xl.—lxvi. (24.)

XXVIII. What may we learn from the prophets of this period as to (*a*) the wages of sin, (*b*) the forgiveness of sins, (*c*) God's desire to save, (*d*) God's power to save, (*e*) guidance by God, (*f*) rest in God? Do not give more than 36 references altogether. (36.)

XXIX. What allusions do they contain to (*a*) the Creation, (*b*) the Garden of Eden, (*c*) Noah, (*d*) Job, (*e*) Abraham, (*f*) the destruction of Sodom, (*g*) Rachel, (*h*) Moses, (*i*) the Plagues of Egypt, (*j*) the Exodus, (*k*) Israel in the Wilderness, (*l*) Samuel? (14.)

XXX. Illustrate the following passages from the history of this period. Psalm cxix. 71; James v. 1-6; Heb. xiii. 3; Luke ix. 24; 1 John ii. 11; 1 Cor. vii. 29-31. (12.)

XXXI. Indicate briefly the contexts of the following:—

(1) "I am against them," "I am with thee."
(2) "I have made thee despised," "I will glorify them."
(3) "There is no healing for thee," "I will heal him."
(4) "I will make this city a curse," "A blessing is in it."
(5) "They shall be weary," "They shall not be weary."
(6) "The nations weary themselves for vanity," "Thy work shall be rewarded."
(7) "Take ye no rest," "Ye shall find rest."
(8) "Wilt Thou be angry for ever?" "I will not keep anger for ever."
(9) "Remember not former iniquities," "I will not remember thy sins."
(10) "We walk in darkness," "I will make darkness light."
(11) "We are called by Thy name," "I have called thee by thy name."
(12) "Come ye," "We come unto Thee." (24.)

XXXII. Give references for the following:—(*a*) "O deadly wounded wicked one!" (*b*) "The false pen of the scribes." (*c*) "O nation that hath no shame!" (*d*) "Neither could they blush." (*e*) "He whose might is his god." (*f*) "His boastings have wrought nothing." (*g*) "New every morning." (*h*) "Satisfied with My goodness." (*i*) "At peace with Me." (*j*) "A nation before Me for ever." (*k*) "Mighty to save." (*l*) "Plenteous redemption." (*m*) "Abundance of peace and truth." (*n*) "Why will ye die?" (*o*) "Seek meekness." (*p*) "Eat ye that which is good." (*q*) "Keep not back a word." (*r*) "Begin at My sanctuary." (*s*) "I said, Behold Me." (*t*) "I made him many." (*u*) "Because thine heart was tender, I have heard." (*v*) "He knoweth the secrets of the heart." (*w*) "Foolish prophets that follow their own spirit." (*x*) "They turned in fear one toward another." (*y*) "He shall come as a rushing stream." (*z*) "My sleep was sweet." (26.)

For *Second Series* of Questions, see p. 309.

SEVENTH TERM.

THE DAYS OF EZRA.
THE RESTORATION AND THE SECOND TEMPLE.

B.C. 606—397.

2 *Chron. XXXVI., 22, 23. Psalms LXXXV., XCII.—C., CII.—CVII., CXIII.—CXXVI., CXXXIV.—CXXXVII., CXLIV., CXLVI.—CL. Ezekiel XXV.—XLVIII. Daniel. Ezra. Esther. Nehemiah. Haggai. Zechariah. Malachi.* (129 *chapters.*)

"All the people went their way . . . to make great mirth, because they had understood the words that were declared unto them."—NEH. viii. 12.

25th MONTH (32).
  Ezek. XXV.—XLVIII. Dan. I.—IV., VII., V., VIII., IX.

26th MONTH (32).
  Dan. VI. 2 Chron. XXXVI. 22, 23. Ezra I.—III. 7. Psalms CII.—CVII.,CXXXVII. CXX.—CXXII., LXXXV. Ezra III. 8-13. Ezra IV. 1-5. Dan. X.—XII. Ezra IV. 6—VI. 13. Haggai. Zech. I.—VIII.

27th MONTH (33).
  Ezra VI. 14-22. Esther. Ezra VII.—X. Zech. IX.—XIV. Neh. I.—VII. Psalm CXXIII.—CXXVI. Neh. VIII., IX.

28th MONTH (32).
  Neh. X. Psalms XCIV., CXLIV., CXXXIV.—CXXXVI. Neh. XI.—XII. 26. Psalms XCII., XCIII., XCV.—C., CXIII.—CXVIII. Neh. XII. 27—XIII. 3. Psalm CXLVI.—CL. Neh. XIII. 4-31. Malachi. Psalm CXIX.

I. GENERAL SUMMARY.

THAT God is the God of Gentiles as well as of Jews is the first note of this term's reading. The world's history has been divided into three great epochs.

(1) *Primæval History*, from the dawn of civilisation in Egypt to the Fall of Babylon, the first capital of the world, in B.C. 538. Here the Semitic races predominate, but Israel is the only one of which we have more than a fragmentary account. (2) *Classical History*, from B.C. 538 to the Fall

of Rome, the second capital of the world, in A.D. 476. Here the Aryan races predominate. (3) *Mediæval and Modern History*, from A.D. 476 onward. Here history deals with all mankind.

We now approach the end of the first epoch, and sacred and secular history, hitherto quite distinct, begin to mingle. Israel influences and is influenced by Gentile powers, and thus the way is prepared for the mystery revealed to S. Paul (Eph. iii.), the subject of our Ninth Term's work.

In the first epoch the ruling power is physical, in the second intellectual, in the third spiritual. Of physical power, Nebuchadnezzar, the last of the Primæval conquerors, was the greatest representative. He was used to bring about the new historical epoch, and the Hebrew prophets were used to point out the significance of his work. "Like the great tragic chorus to the awful drama which was unfolding itself in the Eastern world," they uttered their sublime funeral anthems over the falling Primæval monarchies, and summed up the everlasting lesson of "the ruins of time" (see Isa. xl. 6-8). Joel, Amos, Micah, Isaiah, Zephaniah, Habakkuk, Jeremiah, Obadiah, and Ezekiel picture the falls of *Israel* and *Judah*, descendants of Jacob; the *Edomites*, descendants of Esau; the *Arabians*, descendants of Ishmael; *Moab* and *Ammon*, descendants of Lot; the *Syrians* and *Elamites*, descendants of Shem; the *Philistines*, *Tyrians*, *Sidonians*, and *Ethiopians*, descendants of Ham; also of the *Egyptians*, and finally of the *Chaldeans*, when Babylon drank of the cup she mingled for others (Jer. xxv. 17-26). (They are named above according to the nearness of their relation to Israel. Students are advised to look them out on the map, to read about them in § xxx. of "Oxford Helps," to find the references in the Prophets, and to observe that for Israel, Judah, Moab, Ammon, Elam, and Egypt, mercy as well as judgment was predicted.)

The political reconstruction of the world was then the Prophets' theme, surely a grand enough one to claim our attention. Yet they looked beyond that. Daniel completed their predictions with an announcement of the spiritual kingdom which would supersede and transcend for ever all the kingdoms founded on force.

A recently discovered inscription of Nebuchadnezzar's

runs thus: "I have made completely strong the defences of Babylon. May it last for ever." But on the north side of the mountain barrier that crosses the world from the Himalayas to the Pyrenees, lived fierce races who have more than once swept down upon the fertile south side, and dispossessed its less hardy inhabitants. Such a descent thence of a great Aryan tribe the Hebrew prophets had long foretold. History calls it the Medo-Persian conquest of Babylon. Its leader was Cyrus, the first of the ancient conquerors who was more than a despot and a destroyer, the first great man in Scripture who spoke a language akin to our own; referred to more honourably in Hebrew prophecy by Isaiah than any other Gentile; and in Greek literature by Xenophon than any other "barbarian" prince. His people went on and prospered till they met a still stronger Aryan race in Greece, and then the conquering Ahasuerus of the Hebrew Book of Esther became the conquered Xerxes of Greek history.

And now "the set time to have pity on Zion" had come (Psalm cii. 13; Dan. ix. 2). Her Captivity in Babylon was not, like that in Egypt, the personal bondage of individuals, but the political subjection of a nation. In Greek it is described by a word meaning "transportation" or "migration." The exiles were allowed to dwell together in considerable bodies, and to acquire property (Jer. xxix. 4-7). Yet we see the anguish of their exile not only through its Hebrew name which means "stripped bare," but through Isaiah, Lamentations, Ezekiel, and the Psalms. Its literature has a permanent interest, because it expounds "the sweet uses of adversity," and the power of the consolation that comes from God. The highest comfort offered to them, through Isaiah, was a picture of that supreme suffering of supreme Love, which was to ennoble suffering for ever, and console our sorrowful hearts again and again (see Isa. liii.).

Their Restoration, an event without parallel in history, was regarded as a second birth, a second Exodus. But from Egypt there came out, by the extraordinary interposition of God's power and in spite of an earthly sovereign, an entire people, bound together by common descent and common suffering, to take possession of a promised kingdom and assert their national independence. From Babylon there came out, by the ordinary working of God's providence, and through the action of an earthly sovereign, some 50,000 out of a whole nation, to form the central part of a scattered church, to hear the last words of prophecy, and to recognise in the writings of the past the abiding lessons of God.

For the mass of the exiles had accumulated property to the amount of £4,000,000 (Esth. iii. 9) in their new homes, and preferred to retain their faith, but sacrifice their patriotism; types of those who, ceasing to watch against sin, leave a higher for a lower religious life, and though distressed at first by the change, learn by degrees to find more pleasure in the world and less pleasure in the things of God. These Jews (known as "the Dispersion": see John vii. 35, R.V.) gradually spread far and wide, until, according to Josephus, there was scarcely a corner of the Roman Empire where they might not be found. The Greek conquest opened the way for this, and Greek rule neutralised many of the evils by which it was attended. In A.D. 1 there were three great sections of the Dispersion, the Babylonian, Syrian, and Egyptian. They still prided themselves on the purity of their descent, and a spiritual bond still united them. Jerusalem, no longer the centre of a nation and the capital of a royal race, became the holy city of a church and the capital of a creed, whose monotheism and Messianic hope had a far-reaching influence. Never again was the race to be confined within the borders of Palestine, and its name of *Hebrew* or *Israelite* henceforth gives place to the name of *Jew*, " born," says Josephus, " on the day they came out of Babylon." But all alike looked to the Temple as their religious centre, and contributed largely to its funds. No rival sanctuary disputed its place henceforth, though everywhere it was supplemented by synagogues.

Other results of the Captivity may be summed up thus:—

(1) Hitherto Israel had been constantly led away into the old idolatries that still clung to their soil. Henceforth, after close contact with heathenism in its fullest development at Babylon, they hated idolatry with a fanatical hatred. (See Psalm cxv.)

(2) Hitherto they had stumbled through too frank an

intercourse with other nations. Henceforth their religion became intensely national and exclusive, and they held that a man who read foreign books risked his hopes of eternal life. Yet their dispersion among other peoples made them perforce more cosmopolitan in their ideas, and this dispersion, with the accompanying stern purification from heathenism, fitted their faith to become the seedplot of the one truly universal religion of the world.

(3) Hitherto they had been ruled by kings. Henceforth they were ruled by priests.

(4) Hitherto they had paid little heed to the written word of God. Henceforth they regarded it with a well-nigh exaggerated reverence. Contrast Elijah, who was almost exclusively a preacher, with Ezekiel, who was almost exclusively an author.

(5) Hitherto the external ceremonies of religion had been all important, and their religious life mainly corporate. Henceforth reading the Scriptures, preaching, and above all prayer, became the essential things in public worship, and there was a new sense of individual responsibility, and of the grandeur of being true to one's convictions in the face of the whole world.

(6) Hitherto the Hebrew in which the Old Testament is penned had been a living tongue, written in the old Phœnician characters. Henceforth it gradually became a dead tongue, and at some unknown date before B.C. 300 the square characters now used were adopted. At the Restoration the Jews were bilingual. The last of their prophets still wrote in Hebrew, but the language of daily life and of all their subsequent literature was Aramaic or Chaldean (2 Kings xviii. 26, R.V.), the kindred tongue of the land of exile. Jer. x. 11, Dan. ii. 4—vii. 28, and parts of Ezra (see R.V.), all of which refer to the Gentiles, are in Aramaic, and it is called "Hebrew" in Acts xxii. 2.

(7) Hitherto they had been an agricultural people. Henceforth they became what they are now, a trading people, their commercial enterprise finding a first outlet at Alexandria.

The nation had returned, but not to be what it had been. The opportunity for proving a leader among the peoples as God's People, once lost, did not recur. Its humbler career henceforth teaches the sad lesson that in this life an evil past can never be entirely retrieved. The moral of the whole Captivity, which Jeremiah had foretold, is given by Ezekiel where he points to a restoration and renewal, not of national glory, but of individual goodness through the operation of the Holy Spirit of God.

II. BOOKS TO BE READ.
(See "Oxford Helps," § v.)

This term history, psalmody, and prophecy are represented in almost equal proportions. The three historical books cover only one of the six centuries between Judah's Fall and the Birth of Christ. Of the first seventy years we glean particulars from psalms and prophecies; of the last 393 from the Apocrypha. For the forty *Psalms* of this period, see p. 204. The life of Daniel, the last prophet of the second group, bridges the age of the Captivity. The three Post-Exilian prophets forming the third group close the Canon. They give us the result of former teaching rather than new doctrines.

Part I. of *Ezekiel* has already been uttered as a final message to Judah before her fall. Part II. (xxv.—xxxii.) proclaims God's Judgments upon seven foreign nations, and was written between the besieging and the capture of Jerusalem (with the exception of xxix. 17—xxx. 19, the date of which is 572). Part III. (xxxiii.—xlviii.), all written immediately after the capture, is a glorious Promise of Restoration, culminating in a vision of the Temple re-built and the land re-peopled.

Daniel, of the royal house of David (603—534). Chaps. i.—vi. are history mingled with prophecy. Chaps. vii.—xii. are prophecy written with the detail of history. There is no other book in the Bible with which this unique book can be classed. The Jews put it among the "Scriptures," not among the "Prophets." (See "Oxford Helps," § v.) Its Hebrew is strikingly like that of Ezekiel; there are many traces of its literary influence upon each of the Post-Exilian prophets, and many close parallels between it and Revelation. The narrative is interspersed, like Nehemiah's, with characteristic utterances of personal devotion. That its history is authentic is proved by contemporary and later references to its incidents. That its prophecies are inspired communications from God is attested by our Lord's reference to Daniel. That it may have taken its present form after Daniel's death is possible, and according to some authorities probable. Its keynote is *God's supreme and everlasting kingdom* (Mark i. 15; Rev. xi. 15), and it forms the first philosophy of history, "the first recognition of the continuous succession of ages, of the instructive fact that the story of humanity is that of a regular development of epochs, one growing out of another, cause leading to effect, race following race, and empire following empire, in a majestic plan in which the Divine economy is as deeply concerned as in the fate of the Chosen People" (*Stanley*).

Ezra and *Nehemiah*, which in many ancient MSS. form one book, are probably a compilation by various authors in continuation of Chronicles, which they closely resemble in style. Ezra i. (whose chronological place is between Dan. ix. and x.) is probably by Daniel; and Ezra ii.—iii. 1, and Neh. i.—vii. and xii. 27—xiii. 31, by Nehemiah. Ezra iii. 2—iv. 5 and iv. 24—vi. may be by Haggai. Certainly Ezra vii.—x., and probably Neh. viii.—x. are by Ezra. Ezra iv. 6-23 is probably a later addition by Ezra, and the statistics in Neh. xi. 1—xii. 26, which are brought down to B.C. 330, were probably prepared under Nehemiah's direction and added to after his death.

Esther is probably from the pen of Mordecai, and may have formed part of those Persian official records to which it alludes more than once. The story of how Haman gives to Mordecai what he had chosen for himself, while what he had chosen for Mordecai is given to him, fills the most secular book in the Bible, and the one which the Christian Church has hesitated most about receiving into the Canon. But the Jews said it would outlast all the rest of the Old Testament save the Pentateuch. And rightly. For not only is it a picture of the Dispersion, without which their history would not be complete; it also teaches once for all that what we falsely call "chance" works out God's purposes even when His hand is hidden (Matt. x. 29, 30; Rom. viii. 28). As Herodotus, Xenophon, and Berosus fill in the brief statement of Dan. v. 30 with details exactly corroborating the predictions of Isaiah, Jeremiah, and Habakkuk concerning the Fall of Babylon, so the historians of Greece paint the same wilfully imperious monarch that appears in Esther, and account for the fact that two foreigners were apparently rivals for the office of Grand Vizier by describing the great destruction of Persian nobles in the war with Greece that took place between Vashti's repudiation and Esther's marriage. This same war also explains the willingness of Xerxes' successor to have Jerusalem fortified as an important post on the line of communication with Egypt.

Haggai (520). His keynote is *Do your appointed work at the appointed time, zealously and steadily* (Mark xiii. 34; Heb. vi. 10). He dwells on hindrances from within, as the contemporary historians dwell on those from without. Both have in all ages to be overcome. With little of the poetic fire of his great predecessors, he utters vigorous and practical exhortation to men to consider their ways, and see themselves as they really are. No prophet ever appeared at a more critical juncture, and no prophet was more immediately successful.

Zechariah, son of Berachiah, priest as well as prophet, like Jeremiah and Ezekiel, and probably young since he returned with his grandfather Iddo, as Haggai was probably aged (520—518). His keynote is *The holy people with whom God dwells* (John xiv. 23; Eph. iii. 17). Part I. (i.—viii.) is dated, continuous, full of clear allusions to the events and circumstances of the time, and evidently all from the same hand. Part II. (ix.—xi.) and Part III. (xii.—xiv.) are very dissimilar in their subject-matter and style, undated, and disconnected. The contemporary allusions they contain are vague, and seem to point to a different, perhaps to a much earlier, state of affairs. Nor are they elsewhere attributed to the son of Berachiah. Hence some critics regard chs. ix.—xiv. as an anonymous prophecy, accidentally incorporated with Zechariah. The question does not at all affect its right to a place in the Bible (it is more than once quoted in the New Testament); and opinions differ so widely as to its date, if it is not by Zechariah, that I merely separate it from Part I., without placing it in a different period. See Dr. Marcus Dods' "Post-Exilian Prophets" for fuller discussion of the subject (T. & T. Clark, 1s. 6d.).

Malachi (397?). We are not even certain of this prophet's name. He is never mentioned elsewhere, and his designation means "messenger." Its use in Hag. i. 13, and Mal. ii. 7, iii. 1, has suggested that this book, which the Jews called "the seal of the prophets," is anonymous. (See Mal. i. 1, R.V. margin.) Its author was to Ezra and Nehemiah what Haggai and Zechariah had been to Joshua and Zerubbabel. In its rebuke of the demoralisation of the priesthood, the insolence of wealth, and the loosening of family ties, there are three leading thoughts. The Lord's Messenger, as contrasted with the Lord's Anointed of earlier prophecy; the ideal priest, as contrasted with the actual priest; the faithful few, as contrasted with the faithless many; all leading up to the keynote of *Pure and spiritual religion* (James i. 27; John iv. 23, 24). Malachi points to no new prophet, but to Elijah himself as the herald of the last and greatest crisis of Israel's history, and as the Old Testament closes we see the way opened by the great for the Greatest, and the Sun of Righteousness appears "with Moses and Elias" (see Luke ix. 30). "The age of Ezra was the last pure glow of the long days of the Old Testament seers, and Malachi closes the prophetic writings in a manner not unworthy of such lofty predecessors" (*Ewald*).

III. PERIODS AND DATES.

Of the 584 years which elapsed between the Fall of Jerusalem and the Birth of Christ, 191 bring us to the end of the Old Testament. But we deal with 209 years altogether this term, going back 18 years first of all, in order to trace the whole history of the captives from the First Deportation, since we did not follow any of the Jews to Babylon last term. The reigns of the Babylonian and Persian Kings form landmarks as convenient as those of the sovereigns of Palestine have hitherto been. Note these four Decrees:—

(*a*) 536. *First Decree* of Cyrus to the Jews generally, authorising their Return and the re-building of the Temple.

(*b*) 520. *Second Decree* of Darius to their opponents, to give effect to the First Decree.

(*c*) 458. *Third Decree* of Artaxerxes to Ezra, authorising the restoration of the Temple worship.

(d) 445. *Fourth Decree* of Artaxerxes to Nehemiah, authorising the building of Jerusalem.
  (1) B.C. 606—536 (70 years). From the First Siege of Jerusalem by Nebuchadnezzar to the First Decree. *The Captivity of Judah.* 590—572. Ezek. xxv.—xlviii. 606. Dan. i. 603—561. Dan. ii.—iv. 540. Dan. vii. 538. Dan. v., viii., ix. 537. Dan. vi.
  (2) B.C. 536—516 (20 years). From the First Decree to the Dedication of the Second Temple. *The Jews under Joshua and Zerubbabel.*
    536. 2 Chron. xxxvi. 22, 23 ; Ezra i.—iii. 7 ; Psalms cii.—cvii., cxxxvii., cxx.—cxxii., lxxxv.
    535. Ezra iii. 8-13.   534. Ezra iv. 1-5 ; Dan. x.—xii.
    529. Ezra iv. 6.   522. Ezra iv. 7-24.
    520. Ezra v.—vi. 13 ; Haggai ; Zech. i.—viii.
    516. Ezra vi. 14-22.
  (3) B.C. 516—458 (58 years). From the Dedication of the Second Temple to the Third Decree. *The Jews of the Dispersion.*
    483. Esth. i.   479. Esth ii.
    474—473. Esth. iii.—x.
  (4) B.C. 458—397 (61 years). From the Third Decree to the close of the Old Testament Canon. *The Jews under Ezra and Nehemiah.*   458. Ezra. vii.—x. 15.
    457. Ezra x. 16-44 ; Zech. ix.—xiv.
    445—433. Neh. i.—vii. ; Psalms cxxiii.—cxxvi. ; Neh. viii.—x. ; Psalms xciv., cxliv., cxxxiv.—cxxxvi. ; Neh. xi. 1—xii. 26 ; Psalms xcii., xciii., xcv.—c., cxiii.—cxviii. ; Neh. xii. 27—xiii. 3 ; Psalms cxlvi.—cl.
    432 ? (or 428 ? or 423 ?).   Neh. xiii. 4-31.
    397 (?).   Malachi ; Psalm cxix.

Six Kings of Babylon.

1. Nabopolassar. 625—604.
2. *Nebuchadnezzar.* 604—561.
3. *Evil Merodach.* 561—559.
4. Neriglassar (*Nergal-sharezer*, Jer. xxxix. 3). 559—556.
5. Laborosoarchod. 556—555.
6. Nabonadius. 555—538.

Nabopolassar was the founder of the empire, and Nebuchadnezzar was his son; *Evil Merodach* and Nabonadius were son and grandson of Nebuchadnezzar (see Jer. xxvii. 6, 7); Neriglassar and Laborosoarchod his son were usurpers. At the end of his reign Nabonadius made his son *Belshazzar* his associate in the kingdom and governor of Babylon. Those mentioned in the Bible are in italics.

Two Kings of Media.

1. Cyaxares (*Ahasuerus*, Dan. ix. 1). 634—595.
2. Astyages (*Darius*, Dan. v. 31). 594—536.

Six Kings of Persia.

1. *Cyrus*, founder of the empire. 558—529.
2. Cambyses (*Ahasuerus*, Ezra iv. 6). 529—522.
3. Gomates (*Artaxerxes*, Ezra iv. 7). 522—521.
4. Darius Hystaspes (*Darius*, Ezra iv. 5, 24, v., vi.). 521—486.
5. Xerxes (*Ahasuerus*, Esther). 486—465.
6. *Artaxerxes* Longimanus (Ezra vii.; Neh.). 465—423.

The mother of Cyrus was the daughter of Astyages, Cambyses was the son, and Xerxes' mother the daughter of Cyrus. Xerxes was son of Hystaspes and father of Longimanus. Gomates was a usurper. Cambyses, Gomates, Darius Hystaspes, and Xerxes are mentioned in Dan. xi. 2. The Bible name of each is given in italics. Many of the identifications are among the most recent discoveries of Biblical scholarship. Ahasuerus (like Pharaoh, Sultan, or Czar) is a title, not a name, and is applied to three different sovereigns in Scripture.

Of the five kings who followed Artaxerxes only the last, Darius Codomannus (336—331), is named in Scripture (Neh. xii. 22).

IV. GEOGRAPHY.

(See "Oxford Helps," Maps VIII., IX., X.)

From their mountain fastnesses and land of varied scenery and diverse products, from the hurrying, unnavigable torrent of Jordan, from their simple pastoral and agricultural life, the Jews, who since the Exodus had been isolated from the rest of mankind, were taken to the vast alluvial plains of Babylon, unbroken save by the works of their teeming population, nourished by broad and majestic willow-fringed rivers, where ships laden with merchandise (Isa. xliii. 14) thronged, and whence straight tributary canals irrigated the whole country (Psalm cxxxvii. 1, 2), to the largest walled city ever built, the capital of the world, the seat of empire of the greatest primæval conqueror. Its present desolation exactly fulfils Isa. xiii., but in the Hebrew prophets we catch glimpses of its ancient wealth and splendour, of its learning and its pride, of the glitter of its arms and the clash of its music. Secular historians have fully described its broad streets at right angles to each other, its four-storied houses, its parks and gardens and colossal public buildings, and its aged sanctuary, the grandest place of worship ever raised. Its influence on the captive race was permanent; and henceforth Babylon, Queen of the East and destroyer of Jerusalem, becomes in Scripture the type of the World, reappearing thus in S. John's vision of Imperial Rome, Queen of the West and destroyer likewise of Jerusalem, the only other seat of worldwide empire that can be named beside it (Rev. xviii.).

The Jewish caravans who, after the four months' march across the desert so joyously predicted in Isa. li. 11, regained their own land, found its state very different from that of the Palestine they had left. What was henceforth known as "Galilee of the Gentiles," was occupied by a half heathen people; in the centre were the Samaritans, whom they branded as Cuthites, *i.e.*, Assyrians, and as "proselytes of the lion" (2 Kings xvii. 26, 27), their determined antagonists ever after; beyond Jordan, Moab and Ammon had returned to a fearfully devastated land; on the west coast their ancient foes, the Philistines, were reasserting their independence; and on the south, hostile and vindictive Edom claimed all Judæa. The whole country west of the Euphrates was ruled by a Persian Satrap. Under him Zerubbabel (Ezra ii. 63) and Nehemiah (Neh. viii. 9) were successively Tirshathas or Pashas of Palestine.

V. HEROES.

Keynotes
- *Zerubbabel*, 1 Cor. i. 27.
- *Daniel*, 1 Peter iii. 14-16.
- *Ezra*, Matt. xiii. 52.
- *Nehemiah*, Luke xviii. 1.

Two princes of David's house, a statesman of the tribe of Judah, and a priest are the chief makers of this period of history. Of these one was a prophet and three were authors. *Zerubbabel*, or Sheshbazzar (both Chaldæan names, possibly indicating service to the King of Babylon, comp. Dan. i. 7), was the representative of David at the time of the Return, and the direct ancestor of Christ. He seems to have been the descendant of David's son Nathan, the son of Pedaiah, and the adopted son of Pedaiah's brother Shealtiel; his father and uncle both being sons of Neri, and adopted sons of the childless (Jer. xxii. 30) King Jeconiah, in whom Solomon's line died out (1 Chron. iii. 17-19; Luke iii. 27, 28, 31). The promise to Solomon was conditional (1 Kings ix. 4, 5), while the promise to David was absolute (2 Sam. vii. 12). Judah's royal line had been mown down relentlessly by Jehoram, the Arabians, Jehu, and Athaliah (2 Chron. xxi., xxii.; 2 Kings x.). Zedekiah had left daughters only, of whom we hear no more; Ishmael's violence had proved his unworthiness; and Daniel and his companions held office at the court of Babylon as Isaiah had foretold (Isa. xxxix. 7). Hence Zerubbabel's claim to be leader of his countrymen. Like Solomon, he built the Temple; like David, he regulated the courses of priests and Levites; like Hezekiah, he celebrated a great Passover. His life illustrates the sure success of a lofty and strenuous purpose. Of his death there are vague traditions only, and his children were without authority. But the hope of a renewal in him of the royal line found glorious fulfilment in the Son of Mary 500 years later. Since then there has been no undoubted representative of David.

Daniel's personality is far clearer than that of Zerubbabel. Tradition even tells us that "he had a spare, dry, tall figure, with a beautiful expression." Like Moses before, and S. Paul after, he acquired the wisdom and learning of the Gentiles to fit him for wide influence and great achievements, and became Rab-Mag, head of the wise men, or chief astrologer at the court of Babylon. Like Joseph in earlier, and other Jews in later times, he rose by sheer force of personal ascendency to the highest place among the Gentiles, as the mighty Nebuchadnezzar's Grand Vizier, and vindicated his royal descent by showing himself a born king of men. An incorruptible statesman, who risked his head to give advice wholesome both for prince and people; a devout servant of God, "wearing the white flower of a blameless life" at the headquarters of Vanity Fair; he showed that greater than the material power of Babylon was the moral power of one man doing his duty "with God to friend," cost what it might. And to him was given the eagle vision of the prophet, or rather of the seer, with extraordinary knowledge of the counsels of God, and he only of all the Old Testament saints received assurance from God Himself of his personal salvation. "He was one" (I quote Bishop Ken), "that kept his station in the greatest of revolutions, reconciling policy and religion, business and devotion, magnanimity and humility, authority and affability, conversation and retirement, interest and integrity, Heaven and the Court, the favour of God and the favour of the king."

We turn from Daniel to *Ezra*, from the prince born in David's palace to the priest born in exile, from the large-minded statesman to the stern reformer, from one of the last of the seers to the first of the editors and compilers whose scholarship and research shape the literature of that age of criticism and reflection (when, according to the Talmud, "the crown of learning was nobler than that of empire") which followed the great creative age of soaring poesy and inspired prophecy. We see him firing his countrymen's enthusiasm for God's law by precept and example, and inexorably putting down abuses, like his ancestor Hilkiah, in the strength of "the good hand of God upon him." And while he, the aged theologian and scribe, helped forward the political revival, *Nehemiah*, the young layman, half warrior, half statesman, architect, engineer, and earliest of archæologists, helped forward the moral reformation. The learned son of Aaron cannot be separated from the firm and upright but quick-tempered pasha. He, too, was a man of prayer as well as a man of action, and he left a splendid monument of his prudence and fidelity, of his devotion to duty and self-denying liberality, in making Jerusalem a strong fortress once more. We can easily understand why in early traditions his renown eclipses that of Zerubbabel or Ezra. But in calling our whole period after Ezra we act in the spirit of those later traditions which place Nehemiah's colleague on a level with Moses and Elijah. For what Nehemiah had done for the Holy City, Ezra did for the Holy Book (see Ezra vii. 14), whose influence has been yet more extensive and enduring. The "Moses of the Second Exodus," he is said also to have lived 120 years, to have written I. and II. Chronicles, to have formed the Old Testament Canon, and the council afterwards known as the Great Synagogue, to have introduced the character in which Hebrew has been written ever since, and to have established synagogues. These traditions may not be exactly true, but their existence proves Ezra's importance. For ourselves, we learn the same great lesson from all these four heroes of a crushed nationality: that we are impotent; that God is infinitely potent; that by living in fellowship with Him through prayer we may be endowed with a power not our own (Zech. iv. 6, 7; Dan. vi. 10; Ezra vii. 28, viii. 22; Neh. ii. 4).

VI. THE COMING MESSIAH.

"*They brought Jesus up to Jerusalem . . . into the Temple.*"
"*Jesus entered into the Temple of God, and cast out all them that sold and bought.*"—Luke ii. 22, 27; Matt. xxi. 12.

The cycle of Old Testament prophecy closes by telling both the time and the place of Messiah's coming.

(1) Ezek. xxxiv. 23, 24; John x.; Acts v. 31.
(2) Ezek. xxxiv. 29; John vi. 35.
(3) Ezek. xxxvii. 22-4; John i. 49; Rev. xxi. 3-5.
(4) Dan. ii. 34-45; Matt. xxi. 44; Rev. ii. 26, 27, xix. 15, 16.
(5) Dan. vii. 13, 14; Matt. xxiv. 30, xxv. 31, 32, xxvi. 64.
(6) Dan. ix. 24-7; Heb. ix. 26-8; Acts x. 38.

(7) Hag. ii. 7-9; Luke ii. 26, 27, 46; John xiv. 27.
(8) Zech. iii. 8; Rev. xxii. 16.
(9) Zech. vi. 12-15; Heb. iii. 3, viii. 1; Acts ii. 30.
(10) Zech. ix. 9-11; Matt. xxi. 4, 5, xxvi. 28; Heb. xii. 24, xiii. 20.
(11) Zech. xi. 12, 13; Matt. xxvi. 15, xxvii. 3-10.
(12) Zech. xii. 10; Luke xxiii. 48; John xix. 34, 37; Rev. i. 7.
(13) Zech. xiii. 7; Matt. xxvi. 31, 56; John xvi. 32.
(14) Zech. xiv.; Acts i. 11, 12; John iv. 10.
(15) Mal. iii. 1-3; Luke vii. 27, ii. 27; John ii. 13-16.
(16) Mal. iv. 2-6; Luke i. 17, 78; Matt. xi. 14, xvii. 10-13.

The Rabbis referred to Messiah the passages in Ezek. xliv.—xlviii. about the Prince, but looking at Ezek. xlvi. 16-18, etc., it seems more probable that they mainly refer to Zerubbabel.

Dan. ix. 24-7 is one of the most remarkable and also most difficult of Messianic prophecies. It sets forth the time and the purpose of Christ's death, and upon it was based an universal expectation of His approach at the Christian era. Clearly 70 weeks means 490 years, or 70 cycles of Sabbatic years, or an enlarged jubilee, or seven times the period of the Captivity. A similar period had already elapsed between Abraham's call and Joshua's conquest of Palestine (B.C. 1921—1431), and between Saul's accession and the Captivity (1096—606), and reckoning in lunar years, we find a similar period from the Persian era of Jewish restoration to the Roman era of Christ's coming (B.C. 538—62). Concerning the exact application of this prophecy there have been since the days of Jerome many conflicting opinions. Had the prediction been absolutely explicit, it must have compelled recognition of the true Messiah when He came, and thus thwarted its own fulfilment. Hence it was dim, but not too dim for the spiritually enlightened. (See Dan. xii. 10.) We do not know (a) which of the four Decrees (see p. 146) the commandment" of v. 25 refers to; (b) whether the Messiah's death occurs at the end of the 70 weeks (490 years) or the 69 weeks (483 years); (c) whether the years are solar years of 365 days or luni-solar years of 360 days; (d) what was the exact date of the Crucifixion. Out of many, varying slightly, I give two calculations, both of which place the Crucifixion in A.D. 32. (*a*) Taking the Third Decree, 70 weeks, and solar years, 458 B.C. to 32 A.D. is 490 years. (*b*) Taking the Fourth Decree, 69 weeks and lunar years, March 14th, B.C. 445 to April 6th, A.D. 32, is 483 years. April 6th is calculated as the day (see Luke xix. 42) of Christ's Entry into Jerusalem. The first seven weeks (v. 25) are also shown to bring us in lunar years to the close of the Canon, B.C. 445 to 397 being 49 lunar years. There is probably a threefold reference to (*a*) the profanation of the Temple in B.C. 168 and its restoration three years later, (*b*) the death of Christ, (*c*) the Last Days; and a corresponding explanation of "the prince that shall come" as Antiochus Epiphanes, Titus, and Antichrist.

Haggai foretells the place of Christ's coming. In the R.V., ii. 7 refers to the rich gifts brought by Gentiles to the House of God.

Next to Isaiah, Zechariah has the most numerous and detailed prophecies of Christ, especially of Christ suffering. To us they seem particularly easy of interpretation, but they must have been particularly hard to those who first heard them, while what was plainest to them probably seems hardest to us. *Tsemach* (shoot or sprout) is a title which occurs five times (sometimes without article, as if it had become a proper name) of the Messiah as

(*a*) Son of David, Jer. xxiii. 5, xxxiii. 15 (comp. S. Matthew).

(*b*) God's Servant, Zech. iii. 8 (comp. S. Mark).

(*c*) Son of Man, Zech. vi. 12 (comp. S. Luke).

(*d*) Son of God, Isa. iv. 2 (comp. S. John).

The title has special reference to the house of David, and therefore refers primarily to Zerubbabel. Further, its root idea is that Messiah was the grand result God looked for from Israel, the fruit-bearing Branch which would compensate for the barrenness of the rest of His vine. A different word (*netser*) is used in Isa. xi. 1 and Psalm lxxx. 15.

The Old Testament ends with the hopeful word, "He will come." The New Testament opens with the triumphant word, "He has come." In the Apocrypha there are no Messianic allusions beyond vague reference to the glory of the Chosen People. But in other literature of this later age, such as the Book of Enoch, the Psalms of Solomon, and the Fourth Book of Esdras, there are visions of a coming Deliverer, unlike the Old Testament prophecies in their extravagant fancies and frequent trivialities; unlike them also in not acknowledging His essentially Divine Nature, or the true import of His Human Nature. Yet these books speak of the Messiah as "Son of God"; and from the time of Daniel, "Son of Man" was universally regarded as a Messianic title. Hence the import of John i. 34; Matt. xvi. 13, xxvi. 63, 64.

VII. God's Revelation of Himself to Man.

That enlarged conception of God which taught the later prophets of the second group to dwell on His dealings with all mankind, appears in such titles as "Most High," "Lord and King of Heaven" (Dan.), "God of Gods" (Dan., Psalms), "God of Heaven" (Ezra, Neh., Dan., Psalms), "Lord of all the Earth" (Zech.). "Lord of Hosts" occurs 87 times in the three Post-Exilian prophets. The Court now for the first time set apart for Gentiles in the Temple was a symbol of the truth so grandly proclaimed in Mal. i. 11. "God of Jerusalem" occurs first in 2 Chron. xxxii. 19, and also in Ezra, marking the fact that only a part of the Chosen People had remained faithful (comp. Ezek xlviii. 35).

The thought that their God was no mere national deity such as other peoples acknowledged, and that He was no longer in direct communication with them, led to a deeper awe of Him, which showed itself in two ways. (*a*) By a "seasonable development" (to quote Westcott) of that doctrine of angels as agents and messengers between God and man, of which there are much earlier hints. (*b*) By a false reverence which, at some unknown date, replaced "Jehovah" by "Adonai" in Old Testament MSS., and then translated that by a Greek word which in its turn was literally translated "Dominus" in the Vulgate and "LORD" in our English Bible (see p. 34). At last the Name itself was only uttered in a whisper by the High Priest on the Day of Atonement, and came to be regarded as altogether mystical if not magical. This reticence was a sad symbol of the fresh joy of spiritual life sinking under the pressure of superstition. In the same spirit the Samaritans replaced "Jehovah" by "Shemeh," which means "the Name."

Esther is the only book in the Bible where the Name of God does not occur. But in the Hebrew text the four letters of the name Jehovah are found four times (Esth. i. 20, v. 4, 13, vii. 7), and the five letters of the name Ehyeh (Exod. iii. 14, R.V. margin) once (Esth. vii. 5), in an acrostic form. These sentences are the pivots of the whole story, the arrangement of letters is in each case too ingenious to be accidental, and three ancient MSS. emphasize these letters in all the five passages. All this goes to prove that the sacred Name was thus buried designedly in a book, which is remarkable throughout for "that undercurrent of faith which refers all to the Providence of Him whose name is never mentioned." The nearest literary parallel I know of is the signature Cynewulf, Bishop of Lindisfarne, put to his "Elena."

VIII. Man's Relation to God in Worship.

When in 538 the Persians became masters of Jerusalem, they ordered the re-building of the Temple in such generous terms that the descendants of those who had reared the Tabernacle with the spoils of Egypt enriched the Second Temple with the free-will offerings of Assyria. When in 480 the Persians became masters of Athens, they wrecked its national sanctuary, the Parthenon, and, as recent excavations on the Acropolis have proved, smashed all its exquisite statuary into ten thousand fragments. These two different effects were produced by the same cause, the Persian religion, which took its name from Zoroaster or Zarathustra, round whom the mists of ages have now gathered so thickly that scholars are not agreed as to whether he was an enlightened human teacher (some have ventured to fancy him Daniel's pupil) who was ultimately regarded as a god, or a mythical god whom time transformed into a man. (See Darmesteter's Zend-avesta). His followers worshipped without idolatry one supreme God, all good and all knowing, Ahura Mazda. The Evil

One, they said, is at war with Him, and men must range themselves on one side or other in the conflict, which will end in the triumph of good. (Both the creed and the race who professed it are now represented by the Parsis who 1100 years ago took refuge from religious persecution in India, whence their creed had originally sprung 1400 years before.) That God is a Spirit, and that He is One, had been far more fully revealed to the Jews ages before, yet they had worshipped Him idolatrously and gone after false gods. They never repeated these sins after the Captivity, and the extinction of them may be attributed not only to the wholesome discipline of sorrow, to the substitution of priestly for kingly rule, and to the new zeal of the teachers of God's law ; but also to the influence of Zoroastrianism, which Judaism probably influenced in its turn, and to the impressive sight of the destruction of Babylon's imposing idolatries by the Persian iconoclasts, as Isaiah had foretold in days when they seemed invincible (Isa. xxi. 9, xlvi. 1, 2).

So while the corrupted religion of the Ten Tribes does not seem to have survived their transportation, the faith of the Two, cherished by faithful Kings, Priests, and Prophets, preserved their inextinguishable nationality, while its own preservation became henceforth the great end of the restored nation. Those three great historic offices were no longer what they had been. Zerubbabel's kingship was a mere shadow of the old royal rule. Zechariah's last vision (Zech. vi.) had shown how in Maccabaean days it was to be merged in the priesthood. The crown is set on Joshua, not on Zerubbabel. "That would have been confusing ; a seeming restoration of the kingdom when it was not to be restored ; an encouragement of the temporal hopes which were the bane of Israel" (*Pusey*). The prophetic order had done its work of expunging from God's worship the popular heathenism. Habakkuk, Jeremiah, Ezekiel, and Zechariah had blended its ideal (Micah vi. 8) with the priestly ideal (Lev. xix. 2), and now the prophets and the condition described in Amos iii. 7 had passed away, and the first effect was an increased power of the priests, who must have been almost as numerous in proportion to the population in Judæa as the ecclesiastics in Papal Rome, and whose persons were almost as sacred to the multitude as those of the

Brahmins to the Hindus now. But three causes combined to lesson this importance ultimately.

(*a*) The diminished glory of the Temple. If the decree recorded in Ezra vi. was carried out, the Second Temple must have been larger than Solomon's, and its worship was more elaborate. It is characteristic of the age that, through the Psalms we know more about its worship than about its walls, more of its liturgy than of its structure. But the Holy of Holies was empty. The Ark, for which the restored sacred vessels were but a poor substitute, and round which their religion had centred for nine centuries, had been carried up to heaven (Rev. xi. 19), swallowed up by the earth, taken by an angel to some secret place, hidden on Gerizim to be found there at Messiah's coming (according to the Samaritans), buried on Mount Nebo by Jeremiah in a place that should not be known until God gathered His people again together (2 Macc. ii.), or laid up in the mysterious caverns of the Temple rock, once Araunah's granary (1 Chron. xxi. 20), where the wood was stored, by Josiah (a curious inference from 2 Chron. xxxv. 3) or by Jeremiah. Such were the six various traditions about it, and as no one has entered the Temple caverns for ages it may be there still.

(*b*) The dispersion of the Jews, through which Jehovah's worship was no longer associated only with the soil of Palestine as it had once been (1 Sam. xxvi. 19). When a compact state had given place to a scattered church, Synagogues, originating probably in the religious meetings of the captives in Babylon, became numerous, and were "the inspiring soul and abiding nurture of Judaism" (*Geikie*). Finding out the inevitable results of withdrawal from all ordinary religious privileges (which are too often illustrated in our remote colonies now), the exiles, whose two saving influences at first had been the personal teaching of Ezekiel and the literary teaching of the Psalms, determined that wherever ten Jews settled a congregation must be formed, if only in a little river-side oratory (Acts xvi. 13). So the synagogue gradually grew up, though we find few mentions of it until after the Maccabæan war. To a great extent its ritual reproduced that of the Temple, but it had neither sacrifices nor priests. The public worship which was now the chief witness to God's Presence among them was conducted by laymen learned in the Law, and consisted chiefly of prayer, a short sermon, and, above all, that stated reading of the Law which had been inaugurated by Moses and firmly established by Ezra. When the Syrian persecution made copies of the Law scarce, a second lesson from the Prophets was added to the daily service (Luke iv. 16, 17).

(c) The supplanting of the hierarchy of caste by the hierarchy of education. The Scribes originally were registrars or clerks (Jer. lii. 25) and royal secretaries (2 Kings xii. 10). Hezekiah seems to have employed them first in transcribing and preserving ancient writings (Prov. xxv. 1), and from the times of Baruch and Ezra their main work was handing down, expounding and enforcing the words of God, no longer a living voice through His prophets, but fixed in a Book whose growing value to the Jew may best be estimated from Psalm cxix., "the golden alphabet of Hebrew faithfulness." To these scribes (or "lawyers" to call them by their less official name) the ancient authority of priest and prophet was transmitted; and our modern clergy as "messengers, watchmen, and stewards of the Lord" (*Ordering of Priests*) go back rather to Ezra's pulpit than to Samuel's college or to Aaron's altar.

All Christians are spoken of as kings and priests, God still makes known His truth to them by the Holy Spirit as He did to the prophets of old; the princes of Christendom "rule all states and degrees committed to their charge by God" (Article XXXVII.), and "from the Apostles' time there have been orders of ministers in Christ's Church" for its regulation as an organised society. But the Church owns no earthly supreme head, offers no daily sacrifice for sins, and acknowledges no new prophetic messages from God. Christ only is our King, Priest, and Prophet in the full sense of these words now. The modification of those three ancient offices after 536 already foreshadows "the more excellent ministry" and "the better covenant" yet to come (Heb. viii. 6).

From the Post-Exilian Jews we may learn much concerning zeal for God's honour and love for God's word. But while every error in religion is the distortion of a truth, there is no religious truth that has not at some time been distorted into an error. The intensely national character of their religion degenerated into a haughty spirit of exclusiveness and an arrogant assumption of superiority to all other men. They doubted that a Jew could be lost or a Gentile saved, and the Book of Sifri in the Talmud maintains that "a single Israelite is of more worth in God's sight than all the nations of the world." Their zeal for the law of Moses, which had never been so rigidly observed, degenerated into a hardening of living principles to dead rules. Their three favourite maxims were: Be discreet in judging, Train up many scholars, Make a hedge around the Law. That hedge of elaborate tradition not only emphasized and fixed the Law, but gradually choked it with formulas and mere external observances. "It is a well-known principle in history that when the ceremonial is elevated to the same rank with the moral, the latter will soon be lost sight of" (*Stalker*), and so "duty had ceased to be infinite." All these types of degeneracy illustrate and are abundantly illustrated by the New Testament.

IX. QUESTIONS.

(See p. 13, 18.)

[Questions II., V., VII., IX., XI., XII., XVI., XVIII., XXIII., XXVIII., and XXXI., may be answered with help of any books.]

I. Find three lists of precious stones in the Bible. (3.)

II. Illustrate Ezek. xxxiv. by quoting 20 other passages from the Old and New Testament in which God's relation to man is spoken of under the same metaphor. (15.)

III. Without referring to Daniel's book, prove that its author was a prophet and a man of faith, very wise and very righteous. What passages in Daniel are quoted or referred to in the New Testament? (12.)

IV. Consider Daniel as a type of Christ. Do you agree with the statement that he is "the most perfect of all Scripture characters"? (15.)

V. What may we learn from the writings of this period as to the nature and ministry of angels? Of how many archangels do we hear in Scripture? (12.)

VI. Give a very concise history of what occurred between

B.C. 1921 and B.C. 1490 in quotations from (*not* references to) the Psalms of this period. (15.)

VII. Did those who returned from the Captivity represent twelve tribes or two? (9.)

VIII. The Second Temple was built "according to the command of God and the decree of Cyrus," both issued before the Return. Which prophet pictured its establishment, and where do we find the decree completely quoted? (2.)

IX. Briefly enumerate the particulars in which the Second Temple differed from the First Temple. (8.)

X. Give six New Testament references showing what constitutes the Temple of the Christian Dispensation. (6.)

XI. Of how many Passovers and of what notable events occurring at the Feast of Tabernacles is there record in the Old Testament? (9.)

XII. Mention under descriptive titles the eight visions of Zech. i.-vi., very shortly indicating the significance of each. (24.)

XIII. From what opposed monarchs of earlier times were Mordecai and Haman respectively descended? How is the group of captives to which Mordecai belonged characterised by Jeremiah? (4.)

XIV. Explain why intermarriage with aliens was prohibited to Israel. (5.)

XV. Name a good man falsely accused of wishing to make himself a king, and find a New Testament parallel. (2.)

XVI. How far was the solemn national compact described in Neh. x. 28-39 observed afterwards? (5.)

XVII. Chronologically, who is the latest person mentioned by name in the Old Testament? (2.)

XVIII. Illustrate Heb. xi. 33-8 from the history of the period from B.C. 606 to A.D. 1. (16.)

XIX. Where is common prayer first mentioned as part of the public worship of God? Show that prayer became more and ritual less important after the Captivity. (6.)

XX. Where do these expressions first occur: "the Jews," "the Holy Land," "the Holy City"? (6.)

XXI. Eight rebellious questions are asked by the Jews in answer to God's pleadings through Malachi. Quote in each case the pleading and the question. (4.)

XXII. Find eight New Testament quotations from Haggai, Zechariah, and Malachi. (8.)

XXIII. Explain briefly the following passages:— Ezek. xxviii. 14; Dan. iii. 25; Neh. viii. 8; Hag. i. 2; Zech. i. 21, viii. 19, ix. 13, xii. 11, xiii. 6; Mal. iv. 6. (30.)

XXIV. What allusions are there in the prophets of this period to (*a*) the Garden of Eden, (*b*) the institution of marriage, (*c*) Abraham, (*d*) Esau, (*e*) the Exodus, (*f*) the Law given on Horeb, (*g*) David, (*h*) Alexander the Great, (*i*) the Maccabees. (14.)

XXV. Make a list of the chief names of God in the writings of this period. (30.)

XXVI. Quote ten sentences from Psalm cxix. (R.V.) in which the Scriptures are called by ten different names. (5.)

XXVII. Name the only historical Old Testament book in which Palestine is not referred to, and the only prophetic book that contains no clear Messianic allusion. (2.)

XXVIII. Find the earliest Biblical allusions to (*a*) the King of Assyria, (*b*) Nineveh, (*c*) the Chaldeans, (*d*) Babylon, (*e*) Persia, (*f*) the Grecians, (*g*) the *Romans*, (*h*) *Cyprus*, (*i*) *Spain*, (*j*) India, (*k*) *China*, (*l*) *The ancestors of the present nations of Europe*. (Those in italics are mentioned under other names.) (12.)

XXIX. From the Old Testament prophets generally quote passages enforcing the fourth commandment. (7.)

XXX. From the Old Testament prophets generally quote passages anticipating the "mystery" spoken of in Eph. iii. 3-6, and give six Old Testament instances of Gentiles spiritually blest by contact with the Chosen People. (16.)

XXXI. From the direct prophecies (not general allusions) in the Old Testament construct a description of the Messiah's character, offices, and life on earth. (70.)

XXXII. Give references for the following:—(*a*) "The light dwelleth with Him." (*b*) "Light is sown for the righteous." (*c*) "I will curse your blessings." (*d*) "God turned the curse into a blessing." (*e*) "There shall be no more curse." (*f*) "I will make them a blessing." (*g*) "Thou hast made me glad through Thy work." (*h*) "The Lord hath made them joyful." (*i*) "The joy of the Lord is your strength." (*j*) "The day that I do make." (*k*) "Who maketh winds His messengers." (*l*) " Boys and girls playing in the streets." (*m*) " A people near unto Him." (*n*) " Satisfied with good." (*o*) " Every one unto his work." (*p*) " Be strong and work." (*q*) " Show the house." (*r*) Love truth and peace." (*s*) " Teach ye him that knoweth not." (*t*) " O that ye would hear His voice." (*u*) " In their security shall he destroy many." (*v*) " We are His." (*w*) " Because they wrought for Me." (*x*) " In his hand shall be destruction." (*y*) " I shall not die, but live." (*z*) " Righteousness shall make His footsteps a way to walk in." (26.)

For *Second Series* of Questions, see p. 309.

The Six Centuries from Judah's Fall to the Birth of Christ.

(1) B.C. 606—536 (70 years).   *The Subjection to Babylon*
(2) B.C. 536—332 (204 years).   *The Domination of Persia.*
(3) B.C. 332—301 (31 years).   *The Domination of Macedon.*
(4) B.C. 301—198 (103 years).   *The Domination of Egypt.*
(5) B.C. 198—168 (30 years).   *The Domination of Syria.*
(6) B.C. 168—63 (105 years).   *Independence under the Asmoneans.*

(7) B.C. 63—4 (59 years).   *The Domination of Rome.*

"The great epochs of revelation are widely separated by ages which serve at once for seed-time and harvest" (*Westcott*). Such were the periods of silence before Abraham's Call and the missions of Moses, Samuel, and the Baptist, when God no longer spoke directly to men, but left them to themselves to live out the law He had already given. We must acquire some knowledge of the four centuries of Divine silence which form the last of these periods, if we would understand the state of affairs when our Lord came. Four centuries never brought about a greater change in any country than they brought about then in Palestine. The literature of this age, which we call the Apocrypha, is far less familiar than the Old Testament and the New Testament, for it was not placed in the Canon by the Jews or by the Church, in accordance with the well-established principle "no living Prophet, no further Scripture." The character and names of its various books are given in the Sixth Article, each is described in § vi. of "Oxford Helps," and the books themselves are bound up with many old Bibles. External and internal evidence both place it on a lower level than the Canon, but it forms a valuable link between the Old and New Testament, so we do well to make some acquaintance with it. Its most noteworthy books are, from the historical point of view, 1 and 2 *Maccabees*; and from the literary point of view, *Ecclesiasticus*, representing the Hebraic Judaism of Palestine, and full of practical piety and wise humanity; and *Wisdom*, representing the

Hellenistic Judaism of Alexandria, and full of earnest thought and high philosophy, the last and fairest growth of Judaism. There is no certain reference to an Apocryphal book in the recorded words of Christ, but S. James in his short Epistle refers five times to Wisdom and 15 times to Ecclesiasticus, and there are other traces of the Apocrypha in the New Testament.

We will now look at this period of history, taking for our guide Dan. xi., whose circumstantial details of the first 240 years make it unlike any other Old Testament prophecy. Its picture of Judah's suzerains passes by a transition hard to mark into a far-reaching vision of the end of the world. This outline should be compared with § xiii. of "Oxford Helps," and also, if possible, with some such account of the period as those in Smith's "New Testament History," Angus's "Handbook," Milman's "History of the Jews," Westcott's "Introduction to the Study of the Gospels," or Stanley's "Jewish Church," vol. iii.

Perfect religious liberty and sympathy with their rulers, born of a common monotheism and hatred of idolatry, made the Persian Domination one of the happiest periods of Jewish history. Of the century following Nehemiah's rule we know almost nothing. Then the young Greek conqueror of the world, whose career is vividly pictured in Daniel, and who believed himself to be the Heaven-sent reconciler and pacificator of all mankind, spared and favoured Judæa, and linked East and West in a bond which has never since been broken, thus preparing the way for Christianity with its Eastern cradle and its Western throne. His work was perpetuated in Alexandria, the city he founded to bear his name, a second capital of the Jewish faith henceforth, and the common portal of the East and West to this day. The spiritual gains of the Persian period were followed by the intellectual gains of the Greek period, and on the banks of the Nile a new Israel, trained in all the wisdom of a new Egypt, arose. After Alexander's death in 323, the maritime regions of Palestine were for some 20 years buffeted in the strife between his successors. Then followed a peaceful century under five Macedonian Kings of Egypt, whose capital was Alexandria. All are mentioned as "Kings of the South" in Dan. xi. They were,—

(1) Ptolemy Soter, 320—283 (Dan. xi. 5).
(2) Ptolemy Philadelphus, 285—247 (v. 6).
(3) Ptolemy Euergetes, 247—222 (v. 7, 9).
(4) Ptolemy Philopater, 222—205 (v. 11).
(5) Ptolemy Epiphanes, 205—181 (v. 14).

Under Ptolemy Soter lived Simon the Just, the greatest High Priest between Joshua the son of Jehozadak and Jonathan the Asmonean. He is said to have finished Ezra's work by completing the Old Testament Canon and Nehemiah's work by fortifying the Temple. Under Ptolemy Philadelphus was produced the Septuagint. The Greek tongue had already proved itself the most perfect expression of human thought by becoming practically universal, and now God's Word appeared in what was hereafter to be the language of the New Testament. The Septuagint has been well called "The first Apostle of the Gentiles." Ptolemy Philopater alienated the Jews by forcing his way into the Holy of Holies, and cruelly persecuting them when a supernatural terror drove him forth. He was then at war with the Syrian king who had just taken "the well-fenced city" of Sidon. Him the Jews rashly welcomed as a deliverer, and thus passed under the sway of three Macedonian Kings of Syria, whose capital was Antioch, and who are mentioned in Dan. xi. as "Kings of the North." They were,—

(1) Antiochus the Great, 223—187 (Dan. xi. 10, 15).
(2) Seleucus IV., 187—175 (v. 20).
(3) Antiochus Epiphanes, 175—164 (v. 21, etc.).

Hitherto Israel's foreign suzerains, while exacting tribute, had respected their customs and left the conduct of their affairs to their own princes and priests. To the Ptolemies their relations had been almost wholly friendly, and they were yielding more and more to the spell of Greek art and culture. But between them and the Syrian Kings there was antagonism from the beginning, ending in the wanton attempt of Antiochus Epiphanes (a half-mad despot whose character reappears in great measure in Nero 200 years later) to Hellenise Judæa completely, to substitute the heathen "god of fortresses" for the God of Israel, and to extinguish their ancient religion by a ruthless persecution, which proved in the end its truest safeguard. The determined effort to destroy or deface every copy of the Law increased love for God's Word and zeal for its multiplication; the determined effort to trample out their nation roused an indomitable spirit of patriotism, which gave unity and complete independence to a race that had been a subject race for nearly 4½ centuries. It was for this crisis, which settled whether the true faith would perish or prevail, that the wonderful Book of Daniel had been "sealed up" (Dan. xii. 4). "Its sword-edge utterance, its piercing exhortation to endure in face of the despot, and its promise full of Divine joy of near and sure salvation" (*Ewald*) quickened their courage, and its earliest glorification of the martyr spirit spoke to the hearts of the first martyrs of whom history gives us any details. The story of this great struggle for civil and religious liberty is the finest episode of the whole period.

Mattathias, a descendant of Eleazar, son of Aaron, had five heroic sons, who achieved Judah's deliverance and founded a family which ruled for more than a century. From its ancestor Chashmon it was called Asmonean, or Maccabæan from a word meaning "hammer" (comp. Jer. l. 23, and Charles *Martel*), or from the initials of the first sentence of Exod. xv. 11. These priestly rulers were,—

(1) Judas, 166—161
(2) Jonathan, 161—143 } Sons of Mattathias.
(3) Simon, 143—135
(4) John Hyrcanus I., 135—106. Son of Simon.
(5) Aristobulus I., 106—105 } Sons of Hyr-
(6) Alexander Jannæus, 105—78 } canus I.
(7) Alexandra, 78—69. Widow of Jannæus.
(8) Hyrcanus II., 3 months } Sons of Jannæus
(9) Aristobulus II., 69—63 } and Alexandra.
(8) Hyrcanus II., 63—40
(10) Antigonus, 40—37. Son of Aristobulus II.

Judas is the Wallace of Hebrew history. No one ever united more generous valour with a better cause, and of all military chiefs he accomplished the largest ends with the smallest means. As Israel's preserver in its extremity, he has a place beside Moses, Samuel, and David. In 168 the standard was raised. In 167 he won decisive victories at Samaria,

Bethhoron and Emmaus in Philistia, and at Bethzur in 166, thus regaining the Temple. The crowning conflict of Adasa or Bethhoron, the Marathon of Jewish history, took place in 161, on the scene of Joshua's greatest triumph in 1450, traditionally also the scene of Sennacherib's destruction in 701. The army of Judas "advanced to victory," says the historian, "fighting with their hands and praying with their hearts." In the same year, the great "Hammer of the Gentiles" fell at Eleasa, the Hebrew Thermopylæ, dying, as all his brothers did, a violent death.

The last undoubted representative of the High Priest Joshua fled in 167 from the desecrated Temple to Egypt, and at Leontopolis founded a secondary rather than a rival Temple, to form a religious centre for the Hellenistic Jews of the Dispersion, thus professing to fulfil Isa. xix. 18, 19. This lasted for three centuries. Great was the degradation of the high priesthood, when in 162 the Syrians gave it to Alcimus, who had placed himself at the head of the Hellenising party. In *Jonathan*, however, a new and noble line of high priests was instituted. But alteration of a succession which had remained unbroken for nearly 900 years paved the way for further changes, and one Rabbi finds an explanation of Prov. x. 27 in the fact that during 410 years the First Temple had 18 high priests, while the Second Temple, during 426 years, had more than 300.

Simon snapped the last Syrian fetter when in 142 he took the citadel that over-awed God's sanctuary, and his successor saw the issue of a 40 years' strife in the formal recognition of Judah's independence in 128. *Hyrcanus I.* also conquered her two nearest relatives and bitterest enemies, Edom and Samaria, and in 109 razed the rival temple of Gerizim to the ground, thus triumphantly closing the 60 years of ecclesiastical commonwealth which form the first and best half of the Maccabæan age.

Seventy years of ecclesiastical monarchy (the last 37 merely nominal) followed. For the last six Maccabæan rulers assumed the title, not of "King of Israel," but of "King of the Jews" (contrast John i. 49 and Matt. xxvii. 37), the new phrase marking the new character of the monarchy. Their Greek names indicate the growing strength of Hellenism. Already in the reign of Hyrcanus the party strife between the two opposed sects of Pharisees and Sadducees, henceforth to play so large a part in Jewish history, had begun. The self-seeking ambition of the later Asmoneans led to family discord and political confusion, till *Alexander*, grandson of the Simon whose wisdom and valour "had made his honourable name renowned unto the end of the world," was a detested tyrant, and six years of civil war between his two sons ended in appeal to the arbitration of Rome. That ever encroaching and irresistible power restored *Hyrcanus II.* to nominal rule, and from B.C. 37 to A.D. 6 an Edomite dependant of Rome and his son held imposing sovereignty over Jacob's descendants. But practically from B.C. 63 to the awful close of their history as a nation, the Jews had no king but Cæsar. Aristobulus III., grandson of both Aristobulus II. and Hyrcanus II., was the last Asmonean high priest, and his beautiful and ill-fated sister Mariamne, wife to the Herod of Matt. ii. 1, and grandmother of the Herod of Acts xii. 1, and of Herodias, was the last of her race. See "Oxford Helps," § xxii.

During these six centuries Judaism had gained elasticity of shape without losing distinctness of principle. But its hierarchy had degenerated into a mere sect, its kingdom had ended in foreign usurpation. It had been weighed and found wanting, yet "a missionary nation was waiting to be charged with a heavenly commission, and a world had been unconsciously prepared to welcome it."

To sum up. We have seen the nation which was chosen to represent the whole race, created in God's image (First Term), trained to His likeness (Second Term), made to have dominion (Third and Fourth Terms), falling and thwarting His designs (Fifth and Sixth Terms), and restored by His grace (Seventh Term). 215 years of wandering for its ancestors; 215 years of bondage in Egypt; 450 years of struggle for mastery in Palestine; 450 years of national independence; 300 years' domination of the East, *i.e.*, of Babylon and Persia; 300 years' domination of the West, *i.e.*, of Greece and Rome; such was the historical preparation of the Chosen People for the greatest event in human history.

THE PSALMS.

ARRANGED IN THEIR HISTORICAL SEQUENCE.

I. History and Purpose of the Psalms.

AMID manifold differences of opinion and usage, all who worship God agree that their devotion may best be uttered in the words of an ancient volume of poems which we call the Psalms, from a Greek word meaning songs having a musical accompaniment, which its Hebrew authors called by the less comprehensive name of Tehillim, that is, Praises (see Psalm cv. 2, R.V. and A.V.). Sung or said ; in prose translation or metrical paraphrase ; in the vulgar tongue, or in Hebrew, Greek, or Latin ; within the stately Anglican cathedral, enriched by the heritage of many ages, yet ever adapting itself to the times ; in the sternly simple Scottish kirk ; in the Nonconformist chapel, bared of all that does not commend itself to a particular body of Christians ; in the Roman church, crowded with signs of traditional observance ; in the Greek or Oriental church, which recalls to us a yet dimmer past ; and in the Jewish synagogue, from whose ceremonial that of all Christendom sprang, Psalms are sung fervently, constantly, sometimes as the only, always as the chief form of spiritual song.

We open our Bibles to find a Bible within the Bible, "an epitome of the Bible" (to quote the phrase of Athanasius). Elsewhere we have God's words to us, here are our words to God, our answer to His revelation given in the rest of the Scriptures. Hence to every age and church, and to each pious heart, this is the best known and best loved part of Holy Writ. Its naturalness and simplicity, its fresh joyousness and tender pathos, its diversity and breadth, its fervour of feeling and depth of thought, its sympathy with every mode of human life and every phase of nature, above all its spirituality, make it worth more and more to the individual with advancing years, and to the race with further evolution of the ages. "What sadness and melancholy comes over me at times, and I find myself shedding tears like a child! Then those wonderfully consoling Psalms of David and Asaph send a thrill of joy into my whole being." So wrote in his Journal, Alexander Mackay, pioneer missionary to Uganda, when persecution was raging against the church there in March 1887. The Psalms cannot lose their value while man longs for a personal relation to God, and feels that such a relation is possible. Therefore they have ever been an inspired manual of devotion in its sevenfold form: (1) Confession of sin; (2) Supplication for spiritual gifts; (3) Petition for temporal blessings; (4) Praise and thanksgiving; (5) Self-dedication; (6) Intercession; (7) Meditation upon God's words and works. Nor are they a manual of devotion only. "What is there necessary for man to know which the Psalms are not able to teach?" says Richard Hooker. "The choice and flower of all things profitable in other books, the Psalms do both more briefly contain and more movingly also express, by reason of that poetical form wherewith they are written" ("Ecclesiastical Polity," Book V., ch. xxxviii.).

The Psalms were at once the national ballads and national liturgy of Israel. They form an accompaniment of sweetest music to her whole history, from the plaintive Prayer of Moses to the last burst of praise in the restored Temple, or rather from her birthday pæan by the Red Sea (Exod. xv.) to the calm thanksgiving 1500 years later in the presence of the Lord's Christ, when the purpose of her national existence was fulfilled (Luke ii. 29-32). This music was not continuous, but specially enriched particular periods. Its chief age was the age of David, and the fact that he is the greatest lyric poet of the world may account for the fact that Hebrew poetry throughout is lyric rather than epic or dramatic. His rare genius mapped out the path of all its later achievements.

What use the Jews made of this their Prayer Book, and

how God's prophets not only sanctioned, but commanded use of music, vocal and instrumental, in public worship, we may gather from 2 Chron. v. 13, vii. 3, xx. 19-22, xxix. 25-30; Ezra iii. 10, 11; Neh. xi. 17, xii. 40-47. We read how in the daily service of the Second Temple, after the prayers and the burnt offering, the meat offering, and the offering of incense, and the priestly benediction, the silver trumpets sounded and the white-robed choir of Levites, standing on the fifteen steps between the Court of Israel and the Court of the Women, closed the service by singing with instrumental accompaniment the Psalm for the day, *i.e.*, one of these seven : xxiv., xlviii., lxxxii., xciv., lxxxi., xciii., xcii.

Such was the worship which the first Christians so regularly attended (Acts ii. 42, R.V.) and upon it the worship of the Church was shaped. The first example of Christian Common Prayer we have is based upon a Psalm (Acts iv. 24-30). Use of the Psalms in apostolic times is shown in 1 Cor. xiv. 26; Eph. v. 19; Col. iii. 16; James v. 13. In very early days they were sung by two choirs antiphonally, as they are sung in cathedrals now, and for 1500 years the *Gloria Patri* has been added to them to express the idea that Christians can enter more fully into the meaning of these inspired songs than those who first wrote and sang them. Luther, for instance, called his four favourite Psalms (xxxii., li., cxxx., and cxliii.) Pauline, saying they anticipated the great apostle's doctrine that our trust is in God's forgiving mercy, not in our own merits. In the Middle Ages, when our countrymen had only a Latin Bible, they had the Psalms in English, and these must have formed the best spiritual sustenance of many a devout soul in the ages we call "dark." Our Prayer Book version is more than 350 years old, being from Cranmer's Bible (1539), or more exactly Coverdale's (1535).

II. AUTHORS OF THE PSALMS.

(1) MOSES, who wrote Psalm xc.

(2) DAVID; 73 Psalms are ascribed to him in the headings, ii. is also called his in the New Testament, and x. is evidently his. Of these 75, five are probably of later

date, viz., lxv., ciii., cxxii., cxxiv., and cxliv. Hence we may regard 70 as really his.

(3) SOLOMON; two Psalms are ascribed to him in the headings, and i., cxxviii., cxxxii. are probably his also, making five in all.

(4) ASAPH; twelve Psalms are ascribed to him, of which l., lxxiii., and lxxvii. are almost certainly his, and also most probably lxxviii., lxxxi., and lxxxii. The other six seem to be of later date, of his school rather than his.

(5) HEMAN; lxxxviii. is ascribed to him, and eleven are of his school, viz., Korahite.

(6) ETHAN; to him lxxxix. is ascribed. On the last three authors a few notes may be added. When David first organised a full choral service for Divine worship, he set apart for its maintenance the following three families of prophets and singers, one from each of the Levite tribes. They were like the "colleges" of bards in other nations.

(a) Of the tribe of Gershon, the sons of Asaph. 1 Chron. xxv. 1-6; 2 Chron. v. 12, xx. 14, xxix. 13, 14, xxxv. 15; Ezra ii. 41, iii. 10; Neh. vii. 44, xi. 17, 22, xii. 35. At their head was Asaph, the son of Berachiah, a prophet (Matt. xiii. 35) and musical composer, who is placed on a par with David himself. Joah, Hezekiah's chronicler, seems to have been his descendant. 1 Chron. vi. 39, xv. 17, 19, xvi. 4-7, 37-42; 2 Chron. xxix. 30, xxxv. 15; Neh. xii. 46; 2 Kings xviii. 18, 37; Isa. xxxvi. 3, 22. (b) Of the tribe of Kohath, the Korahites, or Korathites, descendants of Korah, Kohath's grandson (Num. xvi. 1), also called sons of Heman 1 Chron. ix. 19, xii. 6. At their head was Heman, son of Joel, and grandson of Samuel, king's seer in the words of God, and singer. He is probably to be identified with Heman the Ezrahite (i.e., descendant of Zerah, son of Judah), who was famed for his wisdom. His Levite ancestor may have married a Judæan heiress, when he would be reckoned in both tribes. 1 Kings iv. 31; 1 Chron. ii. 6, vi. 33, xxv. 5, 6. (c) Of the tribe of Merari, the sons of Jeduthun. At their head was Ethan, or Jeduthun, son of Kishi, king's seer and singer, probably to be identified with the wise Ethan the Ezrahite. 1 Chron. vi. 44 (References in which more than one of these psalmists or schools are named are given once only.)

Of the 101 Psalms with headings we have now assigned 96 to their authors, and we have attributed five of the 49 anonymous Psalms to David or Solomon. This leaves five doubtfully headed, and 44 anonymous, of whose authorship no definite account can be given.

III. THE DIVISION OF THE PSALTER INTO FIVE BOOKS.

This division may have been suggested by the five books of Moses, and of the Prophets. (The Jews reckoned the twelve minor prophets as one book.) The five books of Psalms are roughly chronological, and were probably formed in succession. Each closes with a doxology. They are discriminated in the R.V.

BOOK 1 (Psalm i.—xli.) is the original Psalter, and was probably formed by Solomon. Jehovah occurs 272 times, and Elohim 15 times in it. It contains 39 Psalms by David, one by Solomon (?), and one anonymous.

BOOK 2 (Psalm xlii.—lxxii.) may have been compiled later by Solomon; others refer its formation to Hezekiah. Elohim occurs five times as often as Jehovah in it. It contains 17 Psalms by David, one by Solomon, one by Asaph, eight Korahite, and four anonymous.

BOOK 3 (Psalm lxxiii.—lxxxix.) may have been compiled by Hezekiah or perhaps by Josiah. Elohim and Jehovah occur equally often. It is liturgical in character, and contains one Psalm by David, one by Ethan, eleven Asaphite, and four Korahite.

BOOK 4 (Psalm xc.—cvi.) was probably compiled after the Captivity. Jehovah is the dominant name. It contains one Psalm by Moses, one by David, and fifteen anonymous.

BOOK 5 (Psalm cvii.—cl.) may have been compiled by Ezra. It is mainly liturgical, and uses Jehovah chiefly It contains twelve Psalms by David, three by Solomon (?), and 29 anonymous.

IV. PSALMS NOT IN THE PSALTER.

Of these there are about 25 in the Old Testament and three in the New Testament: viz., four by Moses (Exod. xv.; Num. xxi. 14, 15, and 17, 18; and Deut. xxxii.), one by Deborah (Judg. v.), one by Hannah (1 Sam ii.), four by

David (2 Sam. i., xxii., xxiii.; 1 Chron. xvi.), two by Isaiah (Isa. xii. and xxvi.), ten short prayers by Jeremiah, one by Jonah, one by Habakkuk, and one by Hezekiah (Isa. xxxviii.), one by the Virgin Mary, one by Zacharias, and one by Simeon (Luke i., ii.). Nearly all these are easily discriminated in the R.V. The five other poetical Books of the Old Testament may each be regarded as the expansion of a Psalm, cp. Job and Psalm xxxix.; the Song of Songs and Psalm xlv.; Proverbs and Psalm i.; Ecclesiastes and Psalm xc.; Lamentations and Psalm lxxix.

V. THE HEADINGS TO THE PSALMS.

The authors of the Septuagint (the Greek translation of the Old Testament made in B.C. 285, and often referred to as the LXX.), evidently did not understand all the headings to the Psalms, which must therefore be older than the LXX. Some were probably affixed by the authors, others later from conjecture or tradition. The most thorough and cautious scholars hesitate about setting them aside, save in a few cases where internal evidence is clearly against them. Four insufficient reasons for rejecting a larger number have been given. (1) That these Psalms contain words and grammatical forms of later date than that assigned to them. Our knowledge of the stages of Hebrew, and of the possible modernisations of copyists, is too slender to warrant the sweeping conclusions sometimes based on considerations of this kind. (2) That the word "temple" must refer to Solomon's building. But see 1 Sam. iii. 3. (3) That definite hope for the future life is later than the time of David. This is pure assumption. See 2 Sam. xii. 23. (4) That all acrostic forms are late. Of this there is no clear proof, and at least two acrostics contain strong indications of David's authorship.

The Hebrew headings are explained in so many books that I need only say here that *Nehiloth*, *Neginoth*, and *Gittith* refer to musical instruments. *Sheminith*, *Alamoth*, *Higgaion*, *Shiggaion*, and *Selah* are musical directions. *Muth-labben*, *Aijeleth Shahar*, *Shoshannim*, *Shushan-Eduth*, *Mahalath*, *Leannoth*, *Al-tashheth*, and perhaps *Jonath elem rehokim*, are names of well-known tunes to which the Psalms in question were to be sung.

Six Psalms (xvi., lvi.-lx.) are called *Michtam*, which means either "a golden song," one of special richness and beauty; or "a mystery," one of deep import. Thirteen (xxxii., xlii., xliv., xlv. lii.-lv., lxxiv., lxxviii., lxxxviii., lxxxix., cxlii.) are called *Maschil*, meaning didactic, for the purpose of giving instruction. Fifty-five are addressed *to the Chief Musician*, that is, the choirmaster or precentor. These are liturgical adaptations of the psalmist's personal experience to the congregation. Fifteen short Psalms (cxx.-cxxxiv.) of singular tenderness and beauty form a Psalter within the Psalter, and are called *Songs of Ascents* or *Pilgrim Songs*, either because they were sung by the people going up to the great feasts (Isa. xxx. 29), or by the captives returning to the Holy City, or by the Levites on the fifteen steps in the Temple. Fifteen begin or end with *Hallelujah* (civ.-cvi., cxi.-cxiii., cxv.-cxvii., cxxxv., cxlvi.-cl.). Four begin with *Hodu* (which means "give thanks"), and may be termed *Eucharistic* Psalms (cv., cvii., cxviii., cxxxvi.).

Six are characterised as *New Songs* (xxxiii., xl., xcvi., xcviii., cxliv., cxlix. See Isa. xlii. 10; Rev. v. 9, xiv. 3). Six are *Morning Hymns* (iii., v., xix., lvii., lxiii., cviii.), and three are *Evening Hymns* (iv., viii., cxliii.). These nine are all David's. Five are called *Prayers*, viz., three of David's (xvii., lxxxvi., cxlii.); also xc. and cii. Two (xxxviii., lxx.) are entitled *"To bring to remembrance or record"* (1 Chron. xvi. 4), which may mean "to remind God of man." See Psalm cvi. 4; Rev. viii. 4; Acts x. 4; Lev. ii. 2.

Seven from early times have been reckoned *Penitential* (cii., cxxx., and five by David, vi., xxxii., xxxviii., li., and cxliii.). Three are *Imprecatory*, that is, they call down Divine judgment upon the wicked (xxxv., lxix., cix.). As the language of God's servant about *sin* they are absolutely right; as the language of God's anointed King upholding justice against wrong they are relatively right; as the language of personal desire for vengeance on particular *sinners* they express the imperfect enlightenment of the most enlightened ere Christ's new law was uttered, and differ widely from His sternest denunciations (Matt. v. 44; Luke ix. 55. Contrast 2 Chron. xxiv. 22 and Acts vii. 60).

Nine Psalms and five other Bible poems are *Acrostic*,

that is, each verse begins with a different letter of the Hebrew alphabet (Psalms ix., x., xxv., xxxiv., xxxvii., cxi.,* cxii.,* cxix., cxlv. ; Lam. i., ii., iii.,* iv. ; Prov. xxx. 10-31. Only those marked * are perfectly regular in structure). They are chiefly of a didactic character, and their form seems to have been adopted as an aid to memory for private devotion or public recitation.

A number of the Psalms are, more or less completely, *Historical*. These not only supplement and confirm other records, but are an illustration of how all the events of the past contain lessons for the present. Unlike any other national poems, they are thoroughly patriotic without in any way feeding national vanity. They show that all Israel's glory came from God, and all her misfortunes were due to herself. Observe lastly that many of the later Psalms are made up of quotations from earlier ones. Three are complete reproductions, viz., liii., lxx., and cviii.

VI. THE TWELVE MESSIANIC PSALMS.

Seven Psalms refer to the Suffering, Risen, Ascended Christ of the First Advent (xxii., xl., lxix., xvi., cxviii., xxiv, lxviii.) ; five to the Glorified Christ of the Second Advent (ii., xlv., lxxii., xcvii., cx.). In saying this we do not assert that every word of these is Messianic. They contain acknowledgments of sin, etc., which are inapplicable. Nor do we deny that the whole Psalter may be regarded as Messianic. The directly *prophetic* Psalms, such as ii., xlv., cx., are few. Even these describe a promise of good things to come connected in the first instance with David and Solomon, but only finding complete fulfilment in their greater Son. Nearly all the Psalms are, however, *typical*. "Thoughts beyond their thought to those high bards were given" (*Keble*); so when the Psalmist protests against scorn and abuse, enmity and treachery, which sought to ensnare and destroy a blameless man ; when he pictures suffering innocence and vindicated rightcousness ; when he utters his delight in the word and will of God, we know that unconsciously he is speaking in the name of Another, that the Psalter is the Prayer Book not only of Israel and of the Church, but also of Christ. Two lines of thought, traceable throughout, converge in Christ, (*a*) God drawing near to man, (*b*) Humanity in the person of its noblest Representative exalted to God. Before they rejected our Lord the Jews freely acknowledged the Messianic application of the most remarkable prophetic and typical psalms. Just as their whole religion was ultimately resolvable into a Messianic hope, so their whole method of Scripture study was Messianic application. They have since tried to explain these Psalms away. Our best guide to their interpretation is the use made of them by Christ and His Apostles. New Testament references will therefore suggest their interpretation here. Two-thirds of the Old Testament quotations in the New Testament are from the Psalms.

VII. Plan of this Scheme for the Psalter.

The Psalms are arranged in chronological order so far as that can be done, and we connect those whose dates and authors cannot be discovered with periods which may have produced them and which are certainly illustrated by them. We have no room for learned arguments and long lists of authorities; but in weighing the external evidence of the headings and the internal evidence of language, style, and allusions, I have availed myself of the works of not a few good scholars who have given special attention to the Psalms. For a clear, simple, and comprehensive account of them, I know none better than that in the later editions of Bishop Barry's "Teacher's Prayer Book," now issued in a separate volume. For a fuller exposition see Dr. Perowne's "Psalms" (Murray 10*s*. 6*d*.).

Our plan of dealing with each Psalm is this. After pointing out by whom, when, and under what circumstances it was written, with a reference for those circumstances, I give its number in the Psalter, a name indicating its character and theme, a summary of its leading thought, New Testament quotations or parallels, and one or two explanatory notes if needed. Finally, mention is made of its use in the Anglican Church, in the Jewish Synagogue, and elsewhere, and its special associations with the faithful of the past. Throughout I use the Revised Version, which is particularly helpful for the Psalms, as it clears up many difficult passages by its renderings, and enables us to follow their poetical structure by its method of printing them.

Students of the Psalms as a whole would do well to make out (*a*) A chronological table of all the allusions to past history, from the Creation to the accession of Saul, noting which made the deepest impression on the national mind. (*b*) A collection of the Psalter's testimonies concerning the state of man immediately after death, and the duration and character of the life beyond the grave. (*c*) A summary of the references to Jerusalem, as the holy city, the abode of God; as the royal city, the abode of the King; and as the centre of national life. Reference to the following pages will be aided, if the arabic numeral they assign to each of the Psalms be written beside its roman numeral in the student's own Bible.

It is to the *devotional* rather than to the *intellectual* or *practical* aspect of Christian life that the Psalms direct our attention, and this is the aspect most likely to be overlooked in the hurry and pressure of our daily life now. Much of the restlessness and spiritual hunger so common in these days is due to neglect of that communion with God which is as necessary for our spiritual welfare as the pure breath of heaven is for our physical welfare. Great will be our gain if fresh knowledge of "the Prayers of the son of Jesse" teaches us to pray as we have never prayed before.

SECOND TERM — THE THEOCRACY.

(1.) *One Psalm by Moses on the Plains of Moab about* B.C. 1451 (Num. xxvii. 12-14; Deut. xxxiv.).

XC. A PRAYER CONCERNING TIME AND ETERNITY. "How may man, whose true Home is the Everlasting God, best use this mortal life?" Quoted (ver. 4), 2 Peter iii. 8. Compare Deut. xxxiii. 15, 27 with vv. 1, 2; Gen. iii. 17-19, Num. xxvi. 64, 65, and Rom. vi. 23 with vv. 7, 8; Heb. xii. 5-11 with ver. 15. This archaic Psalm, which bears throughout the stamp of high antiquity, has been called the most sublime of human compositions. Moses evidently meant it to be his own funeral hymn, and it has since become the funeral hymn of the world. Burial Service and New Year's Eve Service. At Jewish burials in New Testament times, it was chanted during a slow sevenfold circuit round the bier.

Third Term. The Reign of Saul.

Twenty Psalms by David between 1064 and 1056. Compared with his later Psalms, David's early ones contain more exuberant and vigorous poetry, less profound thought and spirituality; show less self-knowledge, and make more vehement protestations of innocence. Reference to Acts. xxiii. 1 proves, however, that this is not always inconsistent with humility. They are marked by freshness of tone and style, and unclouded trust in God.

(2—5.) *Four during his youth at Bethlehem* (1 Sam. xvii. 15).

VIII. THE SHEPHERD'S EVENING HYMN. "Before the God of Nature, man is little; before the God of Grace, man is great." Quoted (ver. 2), Matt. xxi. 16 ; (ver. 4), Heb. ii. 6-9 ; (ver. 6), 1 Cor. xv. 27. Compare Job vii. 17. The antithesis brought out in this meditation on Gen. i. under the brilliant glory of an Oriental heaven is strengthened for us by larger knowledge of Nature's vastness, through modern science ; and of God's grace, through the Incarnation of our Lord. Ascension Day.

XIX. THE SHEPHERD'S MORNING HYMN. "Great is the majesty of God's starry heavens above, greater the majesty of His pure law within the heart of man." Quoted (ver. 4), Rom. x. 18 ; with ver. 12 cp. Rom. vii. 13. What Nature can and cannot teach, and what the Word of God is to His servants, could not be more accurately expressed. "Line" (ver. 4) means "string" or "music"; the allusion is to Nature's song without words. Christmas Day (for the Incarnation was the third and crowning revelation of God).

XXIII. THE SHEPHERD'S WATCH IN THE WILDERNESS. "My Divine Shepherd leads, restores, and comforts me, and I fear no evil." Compare Luke xv. 4-6 ; John x. 1-16 ; Heb. xiii. 20 ; 1 Peter ii. 25. With "thy rod and staff" (ver. 4), one to lead, the other to defend, cp. Zech. xi. 7. In some old liturgies, this Psalm took the place of the "Comfortable Words" in our present Communion Service.

XXIX. THE PSALM OF THE SEVEN THUNDERS. "Mighty is the voice of the Lord our King." With ver. 4 cp. John v. 25. This Psalm describes a storm sweeping over the whole land from Lebanon to Kadesh. The Jews use it on the first day of Pentecost to commemorate the thunders of Sinai; also on the evening of New Year's Day.

NOTE.—Some refer viii. and xix. to the mature experience of David the King. xxiii. 4, 5 suggests the circumstances of his flight from Absalom, and no more beautiful sequel to xxii. could be found (cp. xxii. 15 and xxiii. 4). The LXX. refers xxix. to the removal of the Ark to Zion. If not, however, products of his shepherd days, they are certainly reminiscences of them, and show how his religious life and his poetic power developed in the lonely watches of his youth.

(6, 7.) *Two on Saul's attempt on his life at Gibeah* (1 Sam. xviii. 11).

CXL. A PRAYER AGAINST THE VIOLENT MAN. "Save me from foes without, O Strength of my salvation." Quoted (ver. 3), Rom. iii. 13. With vv. 5, 7 cp. 1 Sam. xviii. 21-7; with ver. 13 cp. Heb. xii. 14. "When Saul cast the javelin at him" is the Syriac heading of this Psalm. Some, however, apply it to Doeg.

CXLI. A PRAYER FOR AID AGAINST ALL PERILS. "Save me from foes within, and from the snares of the wicked." With ver. 2 cp. Luke i. 9, 10. This Psalm is evidently connected with the preceding, and utters the shepherd-hero's sense of new peril in his new life at court. Used at the Daily Evensong of the Greek Church from very early times.

(8.) *One on his escape from Saul's assassins* (1 Sam. xix. 11, 12).

LIX. A GOLDEN PSALM ON GOD'S DEFENCE. "Save me from them that lie in wait." With ver. 3 cp. John viii. 40, 46; with ver. 7 cp. Mark xv. 29. "Heathen" (ver. 5) may refer to Doeg.

(9, 10.) *Two on his flight to Ramah or Nob* (1 Sam. xix. 18, xx.).

XIII. FEAR'S QUESTION. "How long wilt Thou forget me? Lighten my eyes, lest the enemy prevail." With ver. 1 cp. Rev. vi. 10. Third Collect for Evensong. Usque quo Domine? (How long, Lord?) was Calvin's motto. Princess Anne, daughter of Charles I., aged four, died with ver. 3 on her lips.

XI. FAITH'S ANSWER. "Why bid me flee? The Lord rules and judges men, and I trust in Him." With ver. 2 cp. 1 Sam. xx. 36; with ver. 7 (R.V.) cp. Matt. v. 8

and Psalm cxl. 13. Written perhaps after the encouragement of Jonathan's visit. Others refer it to Absalom's Rebellion.

(11, 12.) *Two when the Philistines seized him at Gath* (1 Sam. xxi. 10-15), *an incident only recorded in the heading to* lvi.

LVI. A GOLDEN PSALM OF THE SILENT DOVE AMONG ALIENS. "My foes are many, wily, and full of hatred. But God is for me and will deliver me." With ver. 9 cp. Rom. viii. 31; with ver. 13 cp. Jude 24.

XXV. AN ACROSTIC PRAYER FOR FORGIVENESS AND DELIVERANCE. "Put not Thy servant to shame in the presence of the enemy." With ver. 20 cp. Rom. ix. 33, and final verse of Te Deum, which formed the last words of S. Francis Xavier. Both the substance and structure of this Psalm indicate that it was written at the same time as xxxiv. But some refer it to Absalom's Rebellion, pointing to ver. 7, which does not, however, prove the author was no longer young; ver. 11, which may refer to circumstances not recorded (see xxxiv. 18); and ver. 22, which is probably a liturgical addition of later times, like xxxiv. 22 and xiv. 7. Petrarch concludes his autobiography by quoting the first clause of ver. 7, "than which," he says, "no words could sound sweeter."

(13.) *One on his escape from Gath by feigning madness* (1 Sam. xxii. 1).

XXXIV. AN ACROSTIC THANKSGIVING FOR FORGIVENESS AND DELIVERANCE. "Let others learn from my experience that God saves those who trust Him." Quoted (vv. 12-15), 1 Peter iii. 10-12; (ver. 20), John xix. 33-6. With ver. 8 cp. 1 Peter ii. 3; with ver. 13 cp. James i. 26. "Abimelech" was the title of the Philistine kings: see Gen xx. and xxvi., and cp. "Pharaoh" and "Cæsar." In 597 the dying S. Columba laid aside his pen for ever when he had transcribed ver. 9, leaving Baithune to write out the rest. The Dutch admiral Joost de Moor celebrated with this Psalm a victory over the Spaniards on May 25th, 1603.

(14, 15.) *Two in the Cave of Adullam* (1 Sam. xxii. 1, 2).

CXLII. A DIDACTIC PRAYER FOR RESCUE. "Forsaken of all men and brought very low, I cry to Thee, my Refuge." With ver. 3 cp. Mark xiv. 1. Ver. 7 (first clause) was S. Francis of Assisi's last quotation on his death-bed.

LVII. A Golden Psalm of Thanksgiving for Rescue. A Morning Hymn. "Thou wilt send from heaven to save me, and I will sing Thy praise among the nations." With vv. 3-5 cp. Acts ii. 31-3. Written perhaps when his family and friends had come to him. Easter Day.

(16.) *One in the Forest of Hareth on hearing of the massacre at Nob* (1 Sam. xxii. 21).

LII. A Didactic Psalm on Doeg the Edomite. "Boast not thyself, false-tongued deviser of wickedness, for God shall destroy thee." With vv. 2-4 cp. James iii. 5-8, and see description of the Edomite character in Obad. 3, 10; ver. 5 probably alludes to the Tabernacle, and ver. 8 to the trees on the north slope of Olivet where Nob was.

(17.) *One on hearing in the Wilderness of Ziph of Keilah's treachery* (1 Sam. xxiii. 11, 12).

LVIII. A Golden Psalm concerning the Recompenses of God. "Let those who are hardened in sin learn that there is a God who judges in the earth." With ver. 11 cp. Rom. xii. 19 and Rev. xxii. 12. Its connexion with Keilah is a conjecture, but the characteristics of this Psalm are those of David's early ones, and it closely resembles lii. The metaphor in ver. 9 is from a fire kindled for cooking in the wilderness.

(18.) *One in the Wilderness of Ziph on Saul's pursuit* (1 Sam. xxiii. 14, xxiv. 11, 14, 15, xxvi. 20).

XXXV. An Imprecatory Psalm concerning the Enemies of the Righteous Man. "Strive with my foes, judge my accusers, and save me from those who are too strong for me." Quoted (ver. 19), John xv. 25. With ver. 11 cp. Matt. xxvi. 60; with ver. 12 (R.V.) cp. John xvi. 32; with ver. 13 cp. Luke xiii. 34. The metrical structure is peculiar and artistic. David evidently alludes to the base enmity of Saul's jealous courtiers. Vv. 1, 2 formed the prayer of Thanew, mother of S. Kentigern, when in 518 she was cast adrift upon the Firth of Forth.

(19.) *One in the Wilderness of Maon on the Ziphites' treachery* (1 Sam. xxiii. 19-28).

LIV. A Didactic Psalm on the Enmity of the Godless and the Help of God. "Save me, and destroy my foes. Thou hast delivered, and I will give thanks."

With ver. 4 cp. Acts xxvi. 22. Ver. 7 may be explained by 1 Sam. xxiii. 27, 28. Good Friday.

(20.) *One on sparing Saul in the Wilderness of Engedi* (1 Sam. xxiv.).

VII. AN ODE CONCERNING CUSH THE BENJAMITE. " Save me from the foe who causeless hated me, and whom I spared, for I am righteous." Quoted (ver. 9), Rev. ii. 23. With ver. 8 cp. John viii. 46 ; with ver. 11 cp. Gen. xviii. 25. Cush, one of Saul's adherents of whom nothing is known, had slandered David to his master. Shiggaion means a poem of free and erratic structure.

(21.) *One on sparing Nabal* (1 Sam. xxv. 39).

XVII. A PRAYER COMPARING THE WORLD'S GIFTS WITH THE GIFTS OF GOD. " Hear me, uphold me, and keep me from my deadly enemies." With ver. 14 cp. Matt. vi. 2, Luke vi. 24, xvi. 8, 25, John xiv. 27 ; with ver. 15 cp. 1 John iii. 1, 2, Rev. xxii. 4. The connexion with Nabal is a mere inference from probability.

THE REIGN OF DAVID.

(A.) *One Psalm by Asaph and fourteen by David (all probably written at Jerusalem) during his glory and prosperity.* (1049—1036.)

This group of Psalms is noted for kingly dignity, perfection and maturity of style, profound thought, and intense devotion.

(22.) *One by Asaph on David's Accession* (2 Sam. v. 1-9).

LXXVIII. A DIDACTIC PSALM ON ISRAEL'S HISTORY FROM THE EXODUS TO DAVID'S CAPTURE OF JERUSALEM. " Trust God who hath done such great things for you, and follow not your fathers' rebellion." Quoted (ver. 2), Matt. xiii. 34, 35 ; (vv. 24, 25), John vi. 31. The date of this first and greatest Historical Psalm, the longest next to cxix., is fixed by the abruptness of its conclusion. It describes and vindicates the transfer of the spiritual and temporal headship from Shiloh and Ephraim to Jerusalem and Judah.

(23.) *One on the establishment of David's Throne* (2 Sam. v. 10).

XVI. A GOLDEN PSALM CONCERNING GOD'S HOLY

One. "Preserve me. Thou wilt take me out of Sheol and show me the path of life." Quoted (vv. 8-11), Acts ii. 25-32, xiii. 35-7. With ver. 4 cp. Lev. vii. 20, Zech. ix. 7; with ver. 5 cp. Num. xviii. 20. The priestly character of the Lord's Anointed may be referred to. With ver. 10 cp. John xx. 9.

(24.) *One when he desired yet feared to bring up the Ark* (2 Sam. vi. 9).

CI. THE GODLY RESOLVES OF THE LORD'S ANOINTED. (*A Speculum Regis or Mirror for Magistrates.*) "I will put away evil and follow good with a perfect heart." With ver. 1 cp. Matt. xxiii. 23; with ver. 2 cp. Matt. v. 48; with ver. 6 cp. 1 John iii. 3; with ver. 8 cp. Rev. xxi. 8. Here David limits for himself the usual despotic power of Eastern kings. Queen's Accession.

(25, 26.) *Two on bringing up the Ark.* (2 Sam. vi. 12-15).

XXIV. THE ANTHEM OF THE KING OF GLORY. "Only the pure shall ascend God's hill. Let the King of Glory enter His chosen abode." Quoted (ver. 1), 1 Cor. x 26; cp. Exod. ix. 29. With vv. 3, 4 cp. Heb. xii. 14; with ver. 8 cp. James ii. 1, 1 Cor. ii. 8. This Psalm, describing the true God and the true worshipper, was written by David on the greatest day of his life, to be sung antiphonally or alternately. The Levite choir who bore the Ark to Zion's summit are answered by another choir who receive it there. Ascension Day (see Mark xvi. 19). The Jews used it on the First Day of the week, though unaware of its fitness for what was to be the Day of Resurrection.

XV. EPILOGUE SETTING FORTH THE RIGHT WORSHIP OF THE KING OF GLORY. "He who would become God's guest must be pure and true, kind and honourable, unselfish and generous." Quoted (ver. 5), 2 Peter i. 10. Compare Psalm l.; Isa. xxxiii. 13-17; Mic. vi. 6-8; John iv. 24; 1 Cor. xiii.; 1 John iv. 20, 21. Ancient *usury* differed in several respects from modern *interest*. Ascension Day.

(27, 28.) *Two on the Promise given through Nathan* (2 Sam. vii.).

CX. AN ORACLE CONCERNING THE KINGLY PRIEST WHO LIVETH FOR EVER. "Jehovah promised to my Lord wide dominion and everlasting priesthood." Quoted oftener than any other portion of the Old Testament in the New

Testament—viz., in Matt. xxii. 44; Mark xii. 36; Luke xx. 42, 43; John xii. 34; Acts ii. 34, 35; 1 Cor. xv. 25; Heb. i. 13, v. 6, vi. 20, vii. 28, x. 13; 1 Peter iii. 22. Compare Dan. vii. 13, 14; Isa. ix. 6, 7. "Saith" in ver. 1 is a word used specially of Divine utterances. With ver. 3 cp. Rom. xii. 1; with ver. 4 cp. Zech. vi. 13 and Heb. vii.; with ver. 7 cp. John iv. 6, xix. 28. The Rabbis referred nearly every word of this Psalm to the Messiah, and the Targum of Jonathan renders ver. 1, " The Lord said to His Word." Christmas Day.

CXXXVIII. A PSALM OF PRAISE CONCERNING THE WORD OF THE LORD. "I and all the kings of the earth will thank Thee for Thy gracious words." With ver. 2 cp. John i. 1; with ver. 4 cp. Rev. xxi. 24; with ver. 8 cp. Phil. i. 6. Ver. 8 was Bishop Andrewes' favourite ejaculatory prayer.

(29, 30.) *Two on the Wars with Ammon and Syria, according to the Syriac heading* (2 Sam. x., xi., xii. 26-31).

XX. THE PEOPLE'S PRAYER FOR THE KING ON THE EVE OF WAR. "God grant thy desire, for we trust in Him. God save the King." With ver. 2 cp. 1 Kings viii. 44, 45; with ver. 3 (A.V. margin) cp. Lev. vi. 10, 11; with ver. 6 cp. John xi. 42. This verse is the King's uttered response to the people's supplication for him while he was in silent prayer. Queen's Accession, 2nd versicle before the Collect for the Day, 2nd versicle in Marriage Service, and Visitation of the Sick.

XXI. THE PEOPLE'S PRAISE FOR THE KING'S VICTORY. "God has granted his desire, and saved him with great glory." With ver. 3 cp. 2 Sam. xii. 30; with ver. 9 cp. 2 Sam. xii. 31; with vv. 4, 5 cp. 2 Sam. vii. 13, and Heb. vii. 15, 16. Ascension Day. Queen's Accession.

(31, 32.) *Two on the Wars with Edom* (2 Sam. viii. 13, 14, R.V. margin, x. 7-19; 1 Chron. xviii. 12, 13, xix. 6-19; 1 Kings xi. 15, 16).

LX. A GOLDEN PSALM OF TRIUMPH OVER EDOM. "Restore and save, O God." "All Israel shall submit to thee, My anointed; Moab, Edom, and Philistia are utterly humbled." With ver. 8 cp. James iv. 6, Isa. xvi. 6, Obad. 1, 3; with ver. 12 cp. 2 Cor. iii. 5. Ver. 9 refers either to Rabbah or Zobah, or possibly to Selah (2 Kings xiv. 7). This Psalm shows more clearly than the history that David fought against Syria of the Two Rivers (or Mesopotamia) and Syria of Zobah, and after suffering a critical reverse, won victory which brought him to the zenith of his power. During the campaign the Edomites took advantage of his absence in the north to revolt, and Joab was sent to quell their rebellion. Lot's children are pictured as washing the dust from Israel's feet (cp. 1 Sam. xxv. 41), Esau's are imaged by the slave to whom was thrown the shoe taken off for this washing; the Philistines, who had so long been Israel's mighty oppressors, cry aloud at last in forced homage or terror.

CVIII. A MORNING SONG OF PRAISE. This adaptation of lx. and lvii. 7-11 was probably made to celebrate some similar victory in later times. Ascension Day.

(33—36.) *Four on triumphing over all foreign enemies and establishing lordship over the surrounding heathen* (1 Chron. xviii. 6, xx. 3).

IX. AN ACROSTIC PSALM OF TRIUMPH OVER FOREIGN FOES. "Righteous Judge of the world, I will praise Thee. Thou hast destroyed the heathen and remembered the poor." With ver. 8 cp. Acts xvii. 31; with ver. 12 cp. Num. xxxv. 10-28; with ver. 13 cp. Acts ii. 31, 32.

II. THE CONQUERING KINGDOM OF THE LORD'S ANOINTED. "The heathen rage, but the Lord shall laugh them to scorn, and His Son shall be King over the whole earth." Quoted, Matt. xxvi. 63; Acts iv. 25-8, xiii. 33; Heb. i. 5, v. 5; Rev. ii. 27. Compare Rom. i. 4; Col. i. 18. Ancient Jewish interpreters ascribe the Psalm to David, and refer it to the Messiah. The New Testament not only ascribes it to David, but founds an argument on his authorship. Its date is fixed by the allusion to the great Promise, and to triumph over the heathen (ver. 12). Homage to the sovereign is still expressed by a kiss. Easter Day.

XVIII. THE HEBREW TE DEUM, DAVID'S LITURGICAL SONG OF VICTORY. (Repeated in 2 Sam. xxii.) "I love and praise and give thanks to the Lord, my Strength and Rock. He has delivered me from all my foes at home and abroad, and will show lovingkindness to me and my seed for ever." Quoted (ver. 49), Rom. xv. 9. With ver. 11 cp. 1 Tim. vi. 16; with ver. 28 cp. Matt. vi. 22, 23; with vv. 37-42 cp. 2 Sam. xii. 31; with ver. 48 cp.

Psalm cxl. Ver. 50 is David's only mention of his own name. The Theophany so magnificently described in vv. 6-15 may be a reminiscence of some great storm that fought for David. Compare Judg. v. 20, 21.

LXVIII. A NATIONAL THANKSGIVING FOR THE KINGDOM ESTABLISHED ON MOUNT ZION. "The God who went before us in the wilderness is gone up in triumph to dwell for ever in His holy place on Zion." Quoted, Eph. iv. 8-12; cp. Col. ii. 15. With ver. 1 cp. Num. x. 35; with ver. 4 cp. Exod. vi. 3; with ver. 11 (R.V.) cp. Exod. xv. 20, Judg. v., 1 Sam. xviii. 6; with ver. 12 cp. 1 Sam. xxx. 24; with ver. 18 cp. 2 Cor. vi. 16; with ver. 27 cp. Judg. v. 18; with ver. 29 cp. 2 Chron. ii.; with ver. 31 cp. Acts viii. 27-39. Ver. 22 speaks of enemies; ver. 30 alludes to the crocodile, emblem of Egypt. The Psalm was probably written for the festal procession which brought back the Ark from David's crowning campaign (2 Sam. xi. 11). Whitsunday. Used by the Jews on the Feast of Pentecost.

(B.) *Twenty-six Psalms by David during the sufferings that followed his great sin.* (1036—1024.)

The sorrowful Psalms of this period show that prosperity is more trying to spiritual life than adversity. The explanation of David's fall may possibly be seen in the state of heart depicted in Psalm xviii. 20-24.

(37, 38.) *Two after Nathan's rebuke* (2 Sam. xii. 13).

LI. THE SINNER'S CONFESSION (*Miserere Mei*). "Have mercy, O God; pardon, cleanse, and restore me, for I acknowledge my sin." Quoted (ver. 4), Rom. iii. 4. With ver. 3 contrast Gen. iii. 12, 13, 1 Sam. xv. 15, and cp. 2 Cor. vii. 9-11; with ver. 7 cp. Exod. xxiv. 5-8, Lev. xiv., Heb. ix. 18-23; with ver. 11 cp. 1 Sam. xvi. 14, 2 Kings xxiv. 20, Jer. xxiii. 39; with ver. 18 cp. 2 Sam. v. 9. Commination Service. A Penitential Psalm. It has guided the expression of repentance for centuries, and formed the dying prayer of the Chevalier Bayard, Dr. Arnold of Rugby, and many another saint. Vv. 3, 9, 17 are opening sentences at Morning and Evening Prayer; ver. 15 is one of the versicles before the Venite.

XXXII. THE PENITENT'S ABSOLUTION. A DIDACTIC PSALM. "At last I confessed, God forgave, and He will guide. Rejoice in Him, ye godly." Quoted, Rom. iv. 6-8; cp. Prov. xxviii. 13, 1 John i. 8, 9. Ash Wednesday. A Penitential Psalm. The Jews used it on the Day of Atonement. S. Augustine had it written on the wall over against his bed in his last illness, that he might win comfort from it.

(39—45). *Seven during a grievous sickness unrecorded in 2 Samuel. The seclusion it involved may account for the success of Absalom's intrigues* (2. Sam. xv. 6).

VI. PRAYER IN PAIN AND WEAKNESS. "Have mercy, I am wasted with sickness." Quoted (ver. 8), Matt. vii. 23. With ver. 1 cp. Jer. x. 24 and Rev. iii. 19. Ash Wednesday. A Penitential Psalm. Opening sentence of Morning and Evening Services.

XXXVIII. A PSALM IN SICKNESS TO BRING TO REMEMBRANCE. "I am full of pain, laden with iniquity, forsaken by my friends, and beset by enemies. I hope in Thee, make haste to help me." With ver. 9 cp. 2 Sam. xxiii. 5; with ver. 11 cp. Matt. xxvi. 56, Luke xxiii. 49; with ver. 13 cp. Matt. xxvii. 12, 14. Ver. 20 means that his cause is still the cause of right. Ash Wednesday. A Penitential Psalm. Used on the Day of Atonement.

XXXIX. A PRAYERFUL MEDITATION ON THE FRAILTY OF HUMAN LIFE. "Man is but a breath. My hope is in Thee. Deliver, hear, spare." With ver. 2 cp. xxxviii. 13, 14; with ver. 3 cp. Jer. xx. 9; with ver. 6 cp. Luke xii. 16-21; with ver. 11 (margin) cp. James iv. 14; with ver. 12 cp. 1 Peter ii. 11, Heb. xi. 13. This is the most beautiful elegy in the Psalter. Burial Service.

XLI. A PRAYER WHEN NIGH UNTO DEATH. "Heal me, for my enemies whisper against me, expecting me to rise no more. They triumph not, and Thou upholdest me for ever." Quoted (ver. 9), John xiii. 18, with a significant omission (see John ii. 24, 25). Ver. 1 refers to sickness, not poverty; "King's friend" (in ver. 9) means "privy councillor," 2 Sam. xv. 37, xvi. 16, 1 Kings iv. 5; ver. 13 is the doxology added by the compiler of Book I. (see p. 174). This Psalm evidently represents the crisis which settled the question of life or death for David. Offertory sentence (ver. 1).

XL. A NEW SONG OF PRAISE ON RECOVERY. "God has delivered me, and shown in what sacrifices He delights. Confound my enemies, and let those that seek Thee rejoice." Quoted (vv. 6-8), Heb. x. 5-10. With ver. 6 cp. Isa. xlviii. 8 and Exod. xxi. 5, 6; with ver. 7 cp. Psalm cxxxix. 16; with ver. 10 cp. Psalm li. 13. Good Friday.

LXX. A Psalm on Recovery to bring to Remembrance. Detached from xl. for liturgical use. Ver. 1, versicles before Venite. S. Vincent de Paul asked to have this Psalm read to him again and again on his death-bed.

V. A Morning Prayer on returning to Public Worship. "Lead me, because of my enemies. Thrust out the rebels, and let them that love Thee rejoice." Quoted (ver. 9), Rom. iii. 13. Ver. 3 (R.V.) shows that we should look out for the answers to our prayers; ver. 6 refers to Ahithophel; with ver. 11 cp. Psalm xl. 16 and Phil. iv. 4.

(46—51.) *Six during growing public disorder and disaffection to the throne* (2 Sam. xv. 1-12).

X. An Acrostic Prayer pleading against Lawlessness at Home. "Arise, O Lord, for the wicked oppress the poor, and say, God hath forgotten. But Thou art King for ever." Quoted (ver. 7), Rom. iii. 14. With ver. 4 cp. Psalm xiv. 1, John iii. 19. The LXX. regards ix. and x. as one Psalm. Their parallel structure and coincidences of language and style show their connexion; x. is a mournful supplement to ix. The brigandage and injustice which followed upon political tumult and foreign invasion are also pictured in Prov. i. 10-14.

XII. Man's Words and the Words of the Lord. "Help, for the faithful fail and the wicked walk on every side." With vv. 3, 4 cp. Jude 16, 2 Peter ii. 9-12, and Micah vii. 2-4; with ver. 6 cp. 1 Peter i. 23.

XIV. The Divine Vision of Godlessness. "The Lord beheld that all the children of men had turned aside, and had forgotten and denied Him." Quoted, Rom. iii. 10-12. (By a curious accident, St. Paul's further Old Testament quotations there were in most MSS. of the LXX. incorporated into this Psalm, whence they found their way into the Prayer Book Version.) With vv. 2-4 cp. Gen. vi. 12, Luke xviii. 2, Rom. i. 19, 20, 28; with ver. 3 cp. Eccles. vii. 29. Ver. 7 may be a later liturgical addition, copied possibly from liii. The atheism described is that of the *life* rather than the *lips*, moral depravity rather than intellectual doubt.

LIII. A Didactic Psalm. This reproduction, with slight variations, of xiv., was probably used for some signal defeat of Israel's enemies. (See ver. 5.)

LXII. IF GOD IS FOR US, WHO IS AGAINST US? "How long will ye set upon a man, treacherous liars? I wait on God, to whom power belongeth." With ver. 4 cp. John xi. 53; with ver. 12 cp. Rom. ii. 6, Gal. vi. 7, 1 Peter i. 17, cp. Psalm xlix. throughout. The word rendered "surely" in ver. 9 and "only" elsewhere occurs six times. Vv. 5, 6, 7 were inscribed outside the cavern where Captain Allen Gardiner and his heroic comrades, pioneer missionaries in Tierra del Fuego, lay down to die, as their last message home.

LXIV. GOD WILL REPAY. "Hear, preserve, and hide me from the secret council of evil-doers. Suddenly God shall wound them, all shall fear, and the righteous shall rejoice." Compare Matt. xxvi. 3, 4, 14-16, xxvii. 3-5. With ver. 3 cp. 2 Sam. xv. 3; with ver. 9 cp. Isa. xxvi. 9.

(52—54.) *Three in the Wilderness, fleeing from Absalom and exiled from God's house* (2 Sam. xv. 13-30).

CXLIII. THE FUGITIVE'S EVENING HYMN IN DARK PLACES. "The enemy hath smitten me down. Hear, guide, save, and quicken me, for I am Thy servant." With ver. 1 cp. 1 John i. 9; with ver. 10 cp. John xvi. 13; cp. Psalms lxiii. and xxvii. throughout. The LXX. heads it, "When he fled from Absalom his son." Delitzsch says, if not actually David's, it is an extract of the most precious balsam from the old Davidic psalms. Ash Wednesday. A Penitential Psalm. Ver. 2, opening sentence in Morning Prayer.

LXIII. THE FUGITIVE'S MORNING HYMN IN A DRY AND WEARY LAND. "My God, I thirst for Thee. I will praise Thee, for Thou hast been my help." With ver. 1 cp. John vii. 37 and 2 Sam. xvi. 14, xvii. 2, 29; it may be called "the keynote of personal religion." Donne says the spirit and soul of the whole Psalter is concentrated in this Psalm. A Daily Morning Psalm in the Eastern Church in very early times.

XXVII. THE FUGITIVE'S SURE CONFIDENCE. "Forsaken of all and cruelly maligned, I fear nothing, for the Lord is my Light and Salvation, and I shall yet praise Him in His Tabernacle." Quoted (ver. 6, LXX. version), Eph. v. 19. With ver. 1 cp. Micah vii. 8, John viii. 12, 1 John i. 5. Its first three words are the motto of the University of Oxford. With ver. 14 cp. Hab. ii. 3. In ver. 10 "father and mother" are used proverbially of the nearest and dearest.

(55—57.) *Three at Bahurim on the taunts of Shimei and treachery of Ahithophel* (2 Sam. xv. 31, xvi. 5-13, xvii. 23).

LV. A DIDACTIC PSALM OF THE CURSED AND BETRAYED SUFFERER. "With sore pain and terror of death within, and the enemy's reproaches without, O that I could flee altogether from the unholy city and treacherous friend, and be at rest! Destroy them, for I trust Thee." Quoted (ver. 22), 1 Peter v. 7. With v. 21 cp. John xii. 5, 6, Matt. xxvi. 25, 49; with ver. 23 cp. Eccles. vii. 17, 2 Sam. xviii. 12-14.

CIX. AN IMPRECATORY PSALM CONCERNING THE SON OF PERDITION. "My deceitful adversary has overwhelmed me with curses. Let them recoil upon his own head." Quoted (ver. 3), John xv. 25; (ver. 8), Acts i. 20. With ver. 7 cp. John xvii. 12 and Matt. xxvi. 24; with ver. 13 cp. Matt. xxiii. 38 and xxiv.; with ver. 31 cp. Zech. iii. 1, 2, 1 John ii. 1, 1 Tim. ii. 5. The attitude is that of either accuser or advocate. It seems best to take vv. 6-19 as the adversary's words, and vv. 20—31 as David's application of them. S. Chrysostom calls this awful Psalm a prophecy under the form of imprecation. But our Lord's words about Judas, who was self-condemned and self-destroyed, contain no trace of personal vengeance, nothing inconsistent with John iii. 17 and Luke ix. 56.

LXIX. AN IMPRECATORY PSALM CONCERNING MANY REPROACHFUL ADVERSARIES. "For Thy sake I have borne reproach, derision, desolation, and shame. Let my persecutors be blotted out of the book of life, and save me." Quoted (ver. 4), John xv. 25; (ver. 9), John ii. 17, Rom. xv. 3; (ver. 21), Matt. xxvii. 34, John xix. 28, 29; (vv. 22, 23), Rom. xi. 9, 10; (ver. 25), Acts i. 20. With ver. 8 cp. John i. 11, vii. 5; with ver. 12 cp. Matt. xxvii. 27-30. There is a good reason to believe that the physical cause of our Lord's death was a broken heart (see ver. 20). Vv. 35, 36 may be a liturgical addition. Internal evidence has led some to assign this Psalm to Jeremiah, whose circumstances it certainly describes; but our knowledge of David's sufferings is not complete enough to warrant us in setting aside the heading, and to David it is twice clearly ascribed in the New Testament. It looks beyond the type to the Antitype throughout. Good Friday.

(58—62.) *Five at the time of David's greatest anguish and danger, when he crossed Jordan, and battle was imminent* (2 Sam. xvii.).

XXII. THE PSALM OF THE PASSION. "God has forsaken me, all laugh me to scorn, and I am brought into the dust of death. Thou hast answered, and I will praise Thee. The whole earth shall turn to the Lord and worship Him." Quoted (ver. 1), Matt. xxvii. 46, Mark xv. 34, cp. 2 Cor. v. 21; (ver. 8), Matt. xxvii. 43, cp. Matt. iii. 17; (ver. 18), Matt. xxvii. 35, John xix. 24; (ver. 22), Heb. ii. 11, 12. With ver. 7 cp. Matt. xxvii. 39; with ver. 15 cp. John xix. 28; with ver. 16 cp. John xx. 25; with vv. 25, 26 cp. John vi. 53-8, Lev. vii. 11-21; with ver 27 cp. John xii. 32; with ver. 28 cp. 1 Cor. xv. 24, 25; with ver. 30 cp. 1 Peter ii. 9. No circumstances of David's life are on record to which this Psalm is altogether applicable, so some refer it to an exile in the Captivity. But it vividly depicts the sufferings peculiar to death by crucifixion, unknown to the Jews till the Romans conquered Judæa. One Sufferer alone realised its language, which He directly applied to Himself, and we can only account for its portrayal from within of what Isa. liii. portrays from without, by the foresight of supernatural revelation. The Jewish commentary on the Psalms explains its Hebrew title thus, "On him who leaps as a stag, and brightens the world in the time of darkness." Good Friday.

XXXI. THE PRAYER OF FAITH TRIED WITH FIRE. "I am defamed, forgotten, and wasted with grief. Deliver me. Great is Thy goodness. Take courage, ye godly." Quoted (ver. 5), Luke xxiii. 46, cp. Acts vii. 59. With ver. 11 cp. Matt. xxvi. 56; with vv. 22, 23 cp. 2 Cor. i. 4. Some with less probability refer this to David's flight from Saul, others attribute it to Jeremiah. Ver. 5 formed the last words of Polycarp, Bernard, Charlemagne, Anskar, Columbus, Tasso, Lady Jane Grey, Jerome of Prague, Nicholas Hottinger, Luther, Melanchthon, and many others.

LXI. A CRY FROM THE END OF THE EARTH. "Hear me, my Refuge. Let Thy lovingkindness and truth preserve me." With vv. 6, 7 cp. John vi. 58, Heb. vii. 14-16. Ver. 8, versicle in Marriage Service and Visitation of the Sick.

III. A MORNING HYMN IN THE MIDST OF MANY AND GREAT DANGERS. "My foes are many, but I will not fear.

Arise and save me, my Shield." With ver. 2 cp. 2 Sam.
xvi. 8; with ver. 4 cp. 2 Sam. xv. 25; with ver. 6 cp.
2 Sam. xv. 12, xvii. 11; with ver. 7 cp. Num. x. 35; with
ver. 8 cp. Jonah ii. 9, 2 Sam. xxiv. 17, Luke xxiii. 34.

IV. AN EVENING HYMN IN THE MIDST OF MANY AND
GREAT DANGERS. "How long will ye seek after falsehood? The Lord will hear and preserve me." Quoted
(ver. 4, R.V. margin), Eph. iv. 26. With ver. 3 cp. John ix.
31; with ver. 4 cp. 2 Sam. xviii. 5; with ver. 5 cp. Heb.
xiii. 15; with ver. 6 cp. Psalm lxxx. 1, 3; 2 Cor. iv. 6 and
Num. vi. 26. Ver. 7 contrasts his hungry followers with their
opponents. First Psalm at Compline in the old Service Books.

FOURTH TERM. THE REIGN OF DAVID.

(C.) *Ten Psalms by David of uncertain date, probably
written during the closing years of his reign.* (1024—1016.)
(63—65.) *Three concerning the ways of God and the ways
of men.*

XXXVI. THE WICKED LOVE DARKNESS THOUGH GOD
GIVES LIGHT. "The wicked heart utters its oracles against
God, but the children of men take refuge in Him who can
abundantly satisfy." Quoted (ver. 1), Rom. iii. 18. With
ver. 9 cp. John iv. 14; Rev. xxii. 1.

XXXVII. AN ACROSTIC ON THE LATTER END OF
THE UPRIGHT AND OF THE WICKED. "Fret not thyself,
but trust in the Lord. Delight in Him. Rest in Him.
Commit thy way to Him. Wait for Him. The wicked
shall be cut off; the righteous shall abide for ever." Quoted
(ver. 11), Matt. v. 5. With ver. 1 cp. Prov. xxiv. 19; with
ver. 4 cp. Job xxvii. 10; with ver. 16 cp. Prov. xv. 16;
with ver. 23 cp. Jer. x. 23; with ver. 32 cp. Luke xiv. 1.
This Psalm resembles Job, and solves the problem dealt
with in that book.

CXXXIII. A SONG OF ASCENTS CONCERNING UNITY.
"Brotherly love is good and pleasant as oil and dew."
Compare 1 Cor. xii.; 2 Cor. xiii. 11; Eph. iv. 3; Phil. ii. 2, 3;
Prov. xiii. 10. With ver. 3 cp. Lev. xxv. 21. This song,
which has, says Herder, the fragrance of a lovely rose, may
have been written on David's third anointing (1 Chron. xii.
38-40), or on the pacification of Sheba's revolt. Hermon and

Zion represent North and South Israel united under David.

(66—68.) *Three concerning the Sanctuary.*

XXVI. PRAYER ON ACCESS TO THE SANCTUARY. " Judge, examine, and redeem me, that I may fitly enter Thy habitation which I love." Compare 1 Cor. xi. 28, 31 and Psalms xv. and xxiv. With ver. 9 cp. Matt. xiii. 40.

XXVIII. PRAYER AND PRAISE ON ENTERING THE SANCTUARY. " Draw me not away with the wicked. Thou hast heard, my Strength. Bless Thy people." With ver. 2 cp. Dan. vi. 10 ; with ver. 5 cp. Rom. i. 20. Ver. 9, versicles before Collect for the Day, and ver. 22 of Te Deum.

XXX. A SONG OF PRAISE AT THE DEDICATION OF THE HOUSE OF THE LORD ON MOUNT MORIAH (2 Sam. xxiv.). " I will extol Thee, for Thou hast delivered and healed me, and turned my mourning into dancing." Compare James v. 15 ; 1 Chron. xxi. 16, 28, xxii. 1. David himself may have been smitten by the pestilence. Used on the Feast of Dedication (John x. 22). One of the closing entries in the Diary of the heroic Bishop Hannington speaks of the strength and comfort gained from this Psalm in his last hours.

(69—72.) *Four on Communion with God.*

CXXXIX. THE MYSTERY OF MAN'S BEING AND OF GOD'S PRESENCE. " Thou knowest me altogether, and I am ever in Thy presence. Search me, try me, and lead me." Compare Acts xvii. 28 ; Rom. xi. 33 ; Eccles. xi. 5. Aben Ezra calls this " the crown of all the Psalms." Note that its attempt to fathom the most profound subjects of human thought leads neither to abstract speculation nor to intellectual self-congratulation, but to humble prayer for salvation from sin.

CXXXI. A SONG OF ASCENTS CONCERNING UNQUESTIONING FAITH. " I do not exercise myself in things too wonderful for me." Compare Matt. xviii. 3, xix. 14 ; 2 Sam. vi. 22.

LXXXVI. A PRAYER FOR GUIDANCE AND STRENGTH. " Hear and save, most Mighty, most Merciful. Teach me Thy way, and show me a token for good." Quoted (vv. 8, 9), Rev. xv. 4. With ver. 11 cp. Matt. vi. 21-4. Some refer this to Saul's persecution. Others regard it as a late recast for liturgical use of one of David's Psalms. Ver. 2, versicles in Marriage Service and Visitation of the Sick.

CXLV. An Acrostic Hymn of Praise to God for what He is. "I will extol Thee, my King, for Thou art great and glorious, good and gracious, merciful and mighty. Thy kingdom and Thy praise shall be for ever." Compare Acts xvii. 24, 25; Psalm civ.; Dan. vii. 27. We find David's "last words" in 2 Sam. xxiii., but his half of the Psalter could not conclude more fitly than with this magnificent invitation to all God's creatures to laud and magnify His glorious Name. Whitsunday. In the ancient Church it was the grace at the mid-day meal.

The Reign of Solomon.

Five Psalms by Solomon, five by Asaph, five by the Sons of Korah, one by Heman, and three of unknown authorship. (1016—976.)

(73.) *One by Solomon on his Accession* (1 Kings ii. 12, iii. 28).

LXXII. The Peaceful Reign of the Righteous King. "Let the King's son and heir judge the poor, save the needy, and rule from the Red Sea to the Mediterranean, from the Euphrates to the Desert; and let all nations call him happy." With ver. 2 cp. Rev. xix. 2; with ver. 6 cp. 2 Sam. xxiii. 4; with ver. 8 cp. Exod. xxiii. 31. Tarshish and the isles represent Europe; Sheba in Arabia, Asia; and Seba or Meroe, Africa. The Jewish Targums most emphatically refer this Psalm to the Messiah (Matt. xii. 42). Vv. 18-20 are the doxology and note added by the compiler of Book II. "Prayers of David" is a general name for the Psalms.

(74.) *One by the Korahites on Solomon's marriage to Pharaoh's daughter* (1 Kings iii. 1).

XLV. A Didactic Song of Loves concerning the Bridegroom-King. "Ride on in triumph, O fair and mighty, O gracious and glorious King. Leave thy father's house, O king's daughter, for the King desires thee, and thy children shall be princes." Quoted (ver. 6), Heb. i. 8, 9; cp. Matt. xxv., 2 Cor. xi. 2, Eph. v. 25-32, Rev. xix. 6-9. The Jews regarded this Psalm as Messianic. With ver. 2 cp. Isa. xxxiii. 17, Luke iv. 22, 1 Peter ii. 22; with ver. 6 cp. 2 Sam. vii. 12, 13; with ver. 16 cp. Psalm xxii. 30, Rev. v. 10. Christmas Day.

(75—78.) *Four by Solomon on inaugurating the Temple worship* (1 Kings viii.).

CXXXII. A SONG OF ASCENTS CONCERNING THE LORD'S CHOICE OF ZION AND PROMISE TO DAVID. "Remember David's vow to find Thee an abode, and Thy promise to establish his throne. Arise into Thy resting place with the Ark of Thy strength." Compare Luke i. 32, 33 ; 2 Tim. ii. 8 ; Rev. xxii. 16. With ver. 8 cp. Num. x. 33-6, 2 Chron. vi. 41, 42. This grandest Song of Ascents was clearly written after David's days, but not long after. Christmas Day. Versicles before the Collect for the Day.

I. CONCERNING THE HAPPINESS OF WISDOM. "Blessed is the man who delights in God's law. His way shall prosper, but the way of the wicked shall perish." With ver. 3 cp. John xv. 1-8 ; with ver. 4 cp. Matt. iii. 12 ; with ver. 5 cp. Luke xxi. 36 ; with ver. 6 cp. 2 Tim. ii. 19. Its resemblance to Proverbs suggests that Solomon wrote this Psalm as a preface to the Psalter he compiled for the new Temple. Jer. xvii. 5-8 seems to be a paraphrase of it.

CXXVII. A SONG OF ASCENTS CONCERNING DOMESTIC BLESSINGS. "God only can give our labours their increase. Children are His reward." Compare 1 Cor. iii. 7 ; Matt. vi. 25-34. With ver. 2 cp. 2 Sam. xii. 25 (R.V. margin); with vv. 3, 4 cp. 1 Chron. xxvi. 2-5. This Psalm, an expansion of Prov. x. 22, refers to the rapid growth of population in the peace and prosperity that followed long years of war and tumult. Churching of Women. Used apparently at the presentation of the firstborn (Exod. xxii. 29; Luke ii. 22, 23).

CXXVIII. A SONG OF ASCENTS CONCERNING HOME HAPPINESS. (A sequel to cxxvii.) "Blessed shall the godly be, as breadwinner, husband, father, and citizen." Compare Titus ii. 4, 5. Solemnisation of Matrimony.

(79—82.) *Four by Asaph, of uncertain date, illustrating the Temple worship and Solomon's dominion.*

L. ACCEPTABLE SACRIFICE. "God hath shined out of Zion, and cometh to judge His people. He looks not for mere outward observances, but for thanksgiving, trustful prayer, and righteous conduct." Compare Psalm xl. 6-11, li. 16, 17 ; 1 Sam. xv. 22 ; Isa. i. 11-20 ; Jer. vi. 20, vii. 21-3 ; Amos v. 21-4 ; Micah vi. 6-8. With ver. 3 cp. Heb. i. 2, John iii. 32, xiv. 19, Rev. i. 7 ; with ver. 5 cp. 1 Thess. iv.

16, 17; with ver. 14 cp. Heb. xiii. 15, Rom. xii. 1. The opening name of God only occurs elsewhere in Josh. xxii. 22. This Psalm must have been written in the best age of Hebrew poetry.

LXXXI. A Festival Psalm on the Exodus. "Sing aloud to God who delivered Israel from bondage, and will feed them and subdue all their foes if they hearken to Him." With ver. 10 cp. John xv. 7, Isa. vii. 11 (A.V. margin). The Jews used it on the Fifth Day of the week, and probably on the Feast of Trumpets and the Feast of Tabernacles.

LXXVII. Ancient Mercies a Pledge of Present Help. "I cried in trouble, Hath God forgotten? Then I remembered Thy wonders of old." Compare Hab. iii.; 1 Cor. ix. 10; Heb. x. 36. With ver. 13 cp. 1 Kings viii. 30; with ver. 14 (R.V.) cp. 1 Kings viii. 60.

LXXXII. A Vision of Judgment. "God judges the judge, therefore let him be just. Human authority is sacred, yet limited and delegated." Quoted (ver. 6), John x. 34-6. With ver. 2 cp. Acts x. 34, James ii. 1-4; with vv. 3, 4 cp. Psalm lxxii.; with ver. 6 cp. Exod. xxi. 6 (R.V.), 1 Sam. ii. 25 (R.V.), and Psalm viii. 5 (R.V. margin); cp. 2 Chron. xix. 6, 7, Isa. iii. 13-15. The Jews used it on the Third Day of the week.

(83—85.) *Three by the Korahites of uncertain date, illustrating the Temple worship.*

XLII., XLIII. A Didactic Psalm by a Priest in Exile beyond Jordan. "My soul thirsts for God, and is cast down when I remember the worship of His house. Plead my cause against an ungodly nation, and bring me to Thy holy hill." With ver. 2 cp. Matt. v. 6; with ver. 7 cp. Jonah ii. 3. xliii. 3 seems to refer to the Urim and Thummim; "Tabernacles" alludes to the Holy Place and Holy of Holies; xliii. is virtually the conclusion of xlii. (See R.V.) "Cast down" in ver. 5 is represented in the LXX. by a word which our Lord uses in Matt. xxvi. 38, thus applying the Psalm to Himself. "The language of this exile is the language of the human heart, under the stress of the purest and deepest desire that man can know" (*Liddon*). In some old liturgies xlii. is used instead of the "Comfortable Words" of the Communion Service.

LXXXIV. The Devout Pilgrim's Joyous Song

ON APPROACHING THE SANCTUARY. "I long for the courts of the Lord, for they that dwell in Thy house are blessed." Compare Luke ii. 37. "The living God" only occurs elsewhere in the Psalter in xlii., which may be by the same author; ver. 9 is a prayer for the King. With ver. 10 cp. 1 Chron. ix. 19; with ver. 11 cp. Rev. xxi. 23, Eph. iii. 20. Used by those who journeyed up to Jerusalem for the three great Feasts (Deut. xvi. 16).

(86—91.) *Six closely resembling in style and tone the Sapiential Books of Solomon's period—i.e., Job, Proverbs, and Ecclesiastes. Their dates are unknown.*

LXXXVIII. A DIDACTIC PSALM BY HEMAN ON THE LAND OF FORGETFULNESS. "I am desolate and afflicted, and my life draweth nigh to unremembered Sheol, where all is forgotten." Compare Matt. xxvi. 38, 56, xxvii. 46; John xii. 27; 2 Tim. i. 10. This is the saddest of all the Psalms, but ver. 1 shows that its dark doubt is not absolute despair. Good Friday.

XLIX. A KORAHITE MEDITATION UPON MAN'S MORTALITY, THE OLD TESTAMENT VERSION OF DIVES AND LAZARUS. "Rich and wise die with poor and foolish. All are alike appointed as a flock for Sheol. But God will redeem my soul from its power." Quoted (ver. 17), 1 Tim. vi. 7; cp. Matt. xvi. 26, Luke xvi. 19-31. With ver. 14 cp. Rom. xiii. 12; with ver. 15 cp. John xiv. 3.

LXXIII. THE SURE AND CERTAIN HOPE. FAITH'S TRIUMPH OVER HONEST DOUBT. *By Asaph.* "The prosperity of the wicked troubled me till in God's sanctuary I considered their latter end, and knew that God is my Refuge and my Portion for ever." With vv. 25, 26 cp. Phil. iii. 8, 2 Cor. iv. 16-18, v. 1. The Syriac version says this Psalm was written on the death of Absalom. Perhaps the oppressions at the end of Solomon's reign are referred to (1 Kings xii. 4).

CXI. A HALLELUJAH ACROSTIC CONCERNING THE WORKS OF THE LORD. "I will give thanks, for God's works are great and eternal, gracious and just." With ver. 5 cp. Matt. vi. 33; with vv. 7, 8 cp. Luke xvi. 17; with ver. 10 cp. Prov. i. 7, ix. 10, John vii. 17. Easter Day, probably because of an ancient application of ver. 5 to the Passover.

CXII. A HALLELUJAH ACROSTIC CONCERNING THE

Fear of the Lord. "Blessed is the God-fearing. Wealth, riches, peace, and enduring remembrance are his." Quoted (ver. 9), 2 Cor. ix. 9. With ver. 5 cp. Luke vi. 35.

XCI. The Life Hid in God. "He that abideth in God shall be shielded from all fears and all adversities. God's angels shall guard thee, because thou hast set thy love upon Him." Quoted (vv. 11, 12), Matt. iv. 6; Luke iv. 10, 11. With ver. 13 cp. Rom. xvi. 20, and the Litany; with ver. 16 cp. Luke ii. 30; cp. Job v. 17-23, 1 John iv 16-18. This Psalm is in the form of a dialogue.

The Reign of Rehoboam.

(92.) *One Psalm by Ethan on Shishak's Invasion. About* 970 (1 Kings xiv. 25, 26).

LXXXIX. A Didactic Psalm on God's Covenant with David. "Our all-sovereign God chose David, and promised that his throne should endure. But now Thou hast cast it down to the ground. Where are Thy former mercies?" Quoted (ver. 20), Acts xiii. 22; (vv. 36, 37), John xii. 34. The Targums interpret this Psalm of the Messiah. With ver. 19 cp. Acts v. 31; with ver. 27 cp. Col. i. 15, 18. Ver. 52 is the doxology added by the compiler of Book III. Some refer this Psalm to the reign of Jehoiakim, while Ewald conjectures that it expresses loss of the hope that David's line would be restored through Zerubbabel. **Christmas Day.**

Fifth Term. The Reign of Jehoshaphat.

One anonymous Psalm, one Asaphite, and three Korahite (915--889.)

(93.) *One written perhaps during the famine in Israel, and the religious revival in Judah* (2 Chron. xvii. 9).

XXXIII. A New Liturgical Song of National Trust in God. "Praise the Lord who hath created heaven and earth, and whose eye is on them that fear Him." With ver. 6 cp. John i. 1-3, Job xxxiii. 4, Gen. i. 26; with ver. 9 cp. Heb. xi. 3; with vv. 10, 11 cp. 1 Cor. i. 19-31. Mention of horses suggests that the Psalm is later than those of David. It might have been written at

several different periods, but illustrates this one very well.
Ver. 22, closing versicles in the Litany.

(94.) *One Asaphite on the confederacy of Moab and Ammon against Israel, written perhaps by Jahaziel* (2 Chron. xx. 1-18).

LXXXIII. A SONG IN THE TEMPLE IMPLORING GOD'S AID. "The sons of Lot, Ishmael, and Esau, with Amalek, Philistia, Tyre, and Assyria, consult together against us. Destroy them as Thou didst destroy the Canaanite and Midianite confederacies of old." With vv. 15-18 cp. Phil. ii. 10, 11.

(95—97.) *A Triplet of Korahite Songs celebrating Israel's victory* (2 Chron. xx. 19-28).

XLVI. A SONG ON THE EVE OF BATTLE IN THE WILDERNESS OF TEKOA. "God, our Refuge and Strength, is with us, and will help us right early." With title cp. 1 Chron. xv. 20; with vv. 4, 5 cp. Rev. xxi., xxii. 1-5. This is the original of Luther's famous hymn, "Ein' feste Burg ist unser Gott."

XLVII. A SONG OF DELIVERANCE IN THE VALLEY OF BLESSING. "Shout unto God with triumph. He shall subdue the peoples under us, and we gather together to be His." (An expansion of xlvi. 10.) With ver. 5 cp. Exod. iii. 8, Acts i. 9; with "shields," in ver. 9, cp. Hos. iv. 18 (R.V. margin). Ascension Day.

XLVIII. A SONG OF THANKSGIVING IN THE TEMPLE. "The City of the Great King is beautiful, for there is God known for a Refuge. He will be our Guide for ever." Quoted (ver. 2), Matt. v. 35. Compare Lam. ii. 15. With ver. 7 cp. 2 Chron. xx. 36, 37. Jewish commentators refer this Psalm to the Messiah. Whitsunday. The Jews used it on the Second Day of the week.

These three Psalms are often referred to Sennacherib's defeat, and they contain several coincidences with Isaiah. They were doubtless used in 700, but suit the circumstances of the early deliverance even better.

THE DECLINE AND FALL OF ISRAEL.

(98.) *One Asaphite Psalm. About* 740? (Compare Hosea.)

LXXX. A MOURNFUL PRAYER FOR THE PERISHING

SONS OF JOSEPH. "Turn us again and save us, O Shepherd of Israel. For the vine Thou broughtest out of Egypt is ravaged." With vv. 1, 2 cp. Num. ii. 18-24, iii. 23, 25; with ver. 3 cp. Acts iii. 26; with ver. 8 cp. Isa. v., Jer. ii. 21, Ezek. xix., Hos. x. 1, and Gen. xlix. 22; with ver. 17 cp. Eph. i. 20, Rev. i. 13-16.

THE REIGN OF HEZEKIAH.

Two Asaphite Psalms, one Korahite, and three anonymous, written perhaps by Hezekiah. (Compare Isa. xxxviii.)

(99.) *One Korahite on the tribute brought to Hezekiah. About 711.* (2 Chron. xxxii. 23.)

LXXXVII. A SONG CONCERNING ZION, THE GLORIOUS MOTHER OF MANY NATIONS. "God loves Zion, and shall establish her, and count who was born there when He writeth up the peoples." Compare Eph. ii. 19, iii. 3-6; Col. iii. 11; John x. 16; and contemporary prophecies— *e.g.,* Isa. ii. 2-5, xix. 23-5, xl.-lxvi.; Micah iv. 1-4. In anticipating the mystery revealed to S. Paul of the brotherhood of all men in Christ, this striking Psalm stands alone in the Old Testament.

(100, 101.) *Two Asaphite on the invasion by the Assyrians, and the deliverance from them. About 700.* (2 Kings xix.)

LXXV. A SONG CONCERNING THE JUDGE OF THE WHOLE EARTH. "We thank Thee, for from Thee alone cometh the destruction of the wicked and the lifting up of the righteous." With ver. 2 cp. John v. 25-9; with ver. 4 cp. 2 Kings xviii. 35; with ver. 8 cp. Rev. xiv. 10; cp. 1 Sam. ii. 1-10 and Isaiah throughout. The reference to looking for human aid from all quarters save the North has suggested that they feared Northern enemies, of whom the chief were the Assyrians. This is, however, conjectural.

LXXVI. A SONG OF EXULTATION OVER THE DEATH SLEEP OF THE MIGHTY. "God is known in Judah as glorious and excellent. At His rebuke the stout-hearted are spoiled." With ver. 1 cp. 2 Chron. xxx. 1; with ver. 3 cp. Isa. xxxvii. 33; with ver. 10 cp. Acts iv. 27, 28. Internal evidence fixes the date.

(102-104.) *Three after signal deliverance and special harvest blessing. About 700.* (Isa. xxxvii. 30.)

LXV. A Song of Harvest Thanksgiving. "Blessed are Thy people, O Lord. Thou hast stilled the tumult, and all creation is enriched by Thy goodness." With ver. 7 cp. Matt. viii. 27 and Isa. xvii. 12-14. This Psalm may be adapted from one of David's by his descendant.

LXVI. A Passover Song of Deliverance after Sore Trial and Earnest Prayer. "Come and see the terrible works of God, who observes the nations, who has brought us out into a wealthy place." With ver. 10 cp. 2 Peter i. 7. Ver. 6 alludes to the two great Passover miracles (Exod. xiv.; Josh. iii.); ver. 12 may refer to the famous Assyrian cavalry. Both style and substance connect this Psalm with lxv., but its date cannot be certainly fixed. Thanksgiving after a storm at sea.

LXVII. A Liturgical Harvest Song of Benediction. (*Deus Misereatur.*) "Bless us, that all men may know Thy saving health, and praise Thee together." Compare Acts i. 7, 8; Psalm xxii. 27; Num. vi. 24-6. Solemnisation of Matrimony and second canticle at Evensong.

Sixth Term. The Decline and Fall of Judah.

One Korahite Psalm, two Asaphite, and three anonymous.
(105.) *One Korahite, probably occasioned by some unrecorded disaster in the later days of the monarchy.*
XLIV. A Didactic Psalm in Time of Great National Calamity. "We have heard what Thou didst for our fathers of old. But now Thou hast cast us off, yet we have not forgotten Thee. Rise up for our help, O Lord." Quoted (ver. 22), Rom. viii. 36. With ver. 17 cp. Hos. xi. 12; cp. also 1 Kings viii. 33-50. Conjectures as to its date range from the days of David to those of the Maccabees. Antiphon in Litany.

(106.) *One in time of fear and trouble.*
LXXI. A Psalm of Trustful Old Age concerning God's Righteousness. "From my youth I have trusted Thee. Forsake me not in my old age, for my enemies are many. My redeemed soul shall praise Thee." With ver. 17 cp. Phil i. 6. The LXX. gives this contradictory heading: "A Psalm of David, of the Sons of Jonadab, and of those who were first led captive." It may be a

Rechabite (Jer. xxxv.) adaptation of Psalms xxii., xxxi., xxxii., and xl.; others refer it to Jeremiah. Visitation of the Sick. Last verse of Te Deum.

(107, 108.) *Two Asaphite on the Fall of Jerusalem*, B.C. 588 (2 Kings xxv.).

LXXIV. A DIDACTIC PSALM ON THE PROFANATION AND DESTRUCTION OF THE TEMPLE. "The enemy has fired Thy sanctuary and burned up all Thy synagogues. Thou didst great things for us of old. Arise, plead Thine own cause." Compare Jude 5; Matt. xxi. 13, xxiii. 38. With ver. 9 cp. Lam. ii. 9.

LXXIX. A SORROWFUL PLEADING FOR THE SLAUGHTERED PEOPLE AND RUINED CITY. "Jerusalem is wasted, Thy servants lie unburied, and we are brought very low. Remember not our fathers' iniquities, but deliver us." Compare Luke xix. 41-4 and Lamentations; with vv. 6, 7 cp. Jer. x. 25; with vv. 4, 9 cp. Dan. ix. 16. Some attribute these two Psalms to Shishak's invasion, others to the time of the Maccabees. See 1 Macc. i. 44-64, iv. 38, vii. 16, 17, ix. 26, 27; 2 Macc. i. 8, v. 12-16, viii. 33. They may be by Jeremiah. Ver. 9, antiphon in Litany.

(109, 110.) *Two representing the darkest hour of the Captivity* (2 Chron. xxxvi. 17-20).

CXXX. A SONG OF ASCENTS CONCERNING GOD'S ABUNDANT FORGIVENESS. (*De profundis*.) "Out of the depths I cry. I wait on Thee, and hope in Thee." Compare Rom. iii. 24, 25; 2 Cor. iv. 8-10; Titus ii. 14. Ash Wednesday. A Penitential Psalm.

CXXIX. A SONG OF ASCENTS CONCERNING ISRAEL'S AFFLICTIONS. "Great have been my afflictions, yet the enemy hath not prevailed. Let all Zion's haters be ashamed." Compare John xvi. 33. With ver. 8 cp. Ruth ii. 4.

SEVENTH TERM. THE RESTORATION AND THE SECOND TEMPLE.

The Psalms of this period are only a softened echo of David's strains; not experimental, autobiographical heart-searchings, but liturgical and national hymns for the ordinary Temple service. They lead us up from the deep sorrow of the Captivity, through the mingled music of the Songs of Ascents, to the four great groups of Thanksgiving Psalms which close the Psalter.

(111—117.) *A sequence of six Psalms and one detached Psalm, written towards the close of the Captivity as the prospect of return gradually brightened*, 538—536. (Ezra i. 1-6.)

CII. A PRAYER OF THE AFFLICTED WHEN HE IS OVERWHELMED. "In pain and loneliness and reproach, a weak and dying creature, I cry to God, who endureth for ever, for the time to have pity on Zion is come." Quoted (vv. 25-7), Heb. i. 10-12. With ver. 26 cp. 2 Peter iii. 10; with ver. 13 cp. Jer. xxv. 11, xxix. 10, Dan. ix. 2. The heading of this Psalm, which contains many thoughts and words from earlier psalms, stands alone in appointing it for *private* devotion. Ash Wednesday. A Penitential Psalm. Ver. 1, versicles in Confirmation and Marriage Services, and Visitation of the Sick.

CIII. A THANKSGIVING FOR INDIVIDUAL AND NATIONAL SALVATION. "Bless the Lord who forgives, heals, redeems, and satisfies, and pities like a father. Brief is His wrath and everlasting His mercy." Quoted (vv. 15, 16), James i. 10; 1 Peter i. 24. With ver. 8 cp. Exod. xxxiv. 6, 7, 2 Peter iii. 15; with ver. 13 cp. Luke xv. 11-32; with ver. 20 cp. Matt. vi. 10. The evidence of language and style as well as the connexion with cii. is against the ascription to David. Ver. 10, versicles after the Lord's Prayer in the Litany.

CIV. A HALLELUJAH PSALM OF CREATION. "Bless the Lord who created the heavens and earth and sustains all His creatures." Quoted (ver. 4), Heb. i. 7. With ver. 2 cp. Matt. xvii. 2. The Psalm is an ode on Gen. i., whose order is followed throughout. Compare Job xxxviii., xxxix.; 1 Cor. viii. 6; Rev. iv. 11. Its landscape of mountain, springs, and cedars, bounded by distant sea covered with ships and swarming with a monster brood, may be found in Lebanon. Whitsunday.

CV. A EUCHARISTIC AND HALLELUJAH PSALM RECOUNTING GOD'S MARVELLOUS WORKS FROM ABRAHAM'S CALL TO THE EXODUS. "God promised Canaan to Abraham, preserved his descendants in their wanderings, and brought them out of Egypt with gladness." Compare Rom. xv. 4. Vv. 1-15 are taken from David's Song of Praise (1 Chron. xvi. 8-22 see p. 64). Whitsunday. Used by the Jews on the First Day of the week.

CVI. A HALLELUJAH PSALM RECOUNTING THE REBELLIONS OF ISRAEL FROM THE EXODUS TO THE DAYS OF THE JUDGES. "Our fathers sinned and God's wrath was kindled. We have sinned with them, yet gather us from among the heathen." Compare 1 Cor. x. 1-12; Dan. ix. With vv. 47, 48 cp. 1 Chron. xvi. 35, 36. Ver. 48 is the doxology added by the compiler of Book IV. The terse and simple style of cv., cvi. indicates that they may have been meant for instructing the young.

CVII. A EUCHARISTIC PSALM OF LIFE IN SIX STANZAS. "Thank the Lord for His goodness to the wanderers (cp. John viii. 12), the prisoners (cp. Luke iv. 18; Rom. vii. 24, 25), the sick (cp. Matt. iv. 23), the storm-tossed (cp. Matt. viii. 26), and the perishing (cp. John vi.)." Matt. vi. 25, 26 may be regarded as its keynote. Isaiah and Job are frequently quoted and referred to. With ver. 9 cp. Luke i. 53. Ver. 16 may refer to the capture of Babylon (Isa. xlv. 1, 2). With ver. 20 cp. John iv. 50, Luke vii. 7; with ver. 43 cp. Hos. xiv. 9. This Psalm was perhaps sung at the Feast of Tabernacles described in Ezra iii. Thanksgiving after a storm at sea.

CXXXVII. A REMINISCENCE OF SILENT SUFFERING IN BABYLON. "We wept in Babylon, thinking of the Zion we can never forget. O Lord, recompense Edom and Babylon." Compare Obadiah and Rev. xviii.

(118—121.) *A triplet of Songs on approaching and entering Jerusalem, with a Korahite thanksgiving as a sequel*, 536. (Ezra iii.)

CXX. A SONG OF ASCENTS CONCERNING DECEITFUL TONGUES AND HATERS OF PEACE. "Deliver me from lying lips, for I dwell among the turbulent, yet long for peace." Compare Ezra iv. 1, 4 and John iv. 9.

CXXI. A SONG OF ASCENTS CONCERNING ISRAEL'S KEEPER. "My help cometh from the Lord. He will keep thee from all evil." Compare Luke xii. 4-7. "Keep" occurs six times. See R.V.

CXXII. A SONG OF ASCENTS CONCERNING JOYOUS

Entrance into the Holy City. "We stand within thy gates, where are the thrones of David's house. Peace be within thee, Jerusalem." Compare Heb. xii. 22 ; Isa. xxx. 29 ; Exod. xxiii. 17. Internal evidence is against David's authorship, and his name is omitted in the LXX.

LXXXV. Praise for Restoration and Prayer for the Restored. "Lord, Thou hast forgiven, and turned our captivity. Our land shall yield her increase. Quicken us again." With vv. 10, 11 cp. Rom. iii. 25, 26, John i. 14. Christmas Day. Ver. 7, versicles before the Collect for the Day.

(122—125.) *Four Songs while the work was interrupted and opposed by their enemies*, 445—433. (Neh. iv.-vi.)

CXXIII. A Song of Ascents concerning the Eye of Hope. (*Oculus Sperans* was the old name of the Psalm.) "Filled with the foe's scorning and contempt, we look to Thee, our Master." Compare Col. iii. 23, 24, and Neh. ii. 19, iv. 4, ix. 36, 37.

CXXIV. A Song of Ascents concerning Hope not put to Shame. "Had not the Lord been for us, we had been overwhelmed. But He is our Help, and we are escaped." Compare Rom. viii. 31. David's name is omitted in the chief versions, and in some MSS. If originally from his hand, it may have been adapted to the experience of the restored Jews, as a sequel to cxxiii. Thanksgiving after Victory. Ver. 8, versicles in Confirmation Service.

CXXV. A Song of Ascents concerning Israel's Defence. "The Lord is round about His people as the mountains are round about Jerusalem." Compare Gal. vi. 16 ; Zech. ii. 5.

CXXVI. A Song of Ascents concerning the Turning of Zion's Captivity. "Our joy is like a dream, as we rejoice over the great things the Lord hath done for us." Compare Matt. v. 4; John xvi. 22; Gal. vi. 7-9 ; Luke viii. 39. Vv. 5, 6 were engraved on the walls of the Beauchamp Tower by Edmund Poole, imprisoned there in 1562.

(126, 127.) *Two Liturgical Prayers for the Second Temple* (Neh. xi. 22, 23).

XCIV. A Lyric Psalm for the Fourth Day of the Week. (LXX. heading.) "How long shall the arrogant wicked afflict Thine heritage? The Lord shall

cut them off in their own evil." Quoted (ver. 11), 1 Cor
iii. 20. With ver. 1 cp. Heb. x. 30, Deut. xxxii. 35; with
ver. 3 cp. Psalm xiii. 1; with ver. 12 cp. Heb. xii. 3-11,
James i. 12; with ver. 21 cp. Matt. xxvii. 1-4. The conjectures as to the date of this Psalm, which the LXX.
ascribes to David, are very numerous. It borrows from
many earlier ones. The Jews used it at the Feast of Tabernacles.

CXLIV. A NEW SONG PRAYING FOR ISRAEL'S PROS-
PERITY. "Rescue me from the hand of strangers. Happy
and prosperous are Thy people." With ver. 12 cp. 1 Peter
ii. 5. Vv. 1-11 is made up of extracts from David's Psalms.
To these a national prayer is added.

(128—130.) *Three Liturgical Thanksgivings for the Second Temple.*

CXXXIV. A CONCLUDING SONG OF ASCENTS CON-
CERNING THE PRIESTLY BENEDICTION. The pilgrims at
the close of their journey greet the priests and Levites
in the Temple (vv. 1, 2) keeping their night watch (see
1 Chron. ix. 33; Luke ii. 37; Rev. xvi. 15), who bless them
in return (Num. vi. 23-7); cp. 1 Tim. ii. 8.

The first seven Songs of Ascents were written after the
Captivity; of the next seven, two are by David, three (?)
by Solomon, and two were written during the Captivity.
The fifteenth was added after the Captivity as a doxology.

CXXXV. A HALLELUJAH PSALM ACKNOWLEDGING
ISRAEL'S GOD TO BE THE ONE TRUE GOD. "Praise the
great Creator, who chose and redeemed Israel and gave
them Canaan." Quoted (ver. 14), Heb. x. 30. With ver.
5 cp. Mark xii. 32, 1 Cor. viii. 6, Neh. ix. 5-38. This is
a mosaic from the earlier Psalms and prophets, and was
probably sung in alternate responses by priest and people.

CXXXVI. THE GREAT HALLEL. A EUCHARISTIC
PSALM (in alternate responses, with a burden sung in full
chorus). "Give thanks to God, whose mercy endureth for
ever, for our creation, redemption, preservation, and all the
blessings of this life." Compare 1 Tim. iv. 4. This "Jewish
national anthem" is also a mosaic of earlier Psalms, and
the three following groups may be regarded as expansions
of it. It was sung on the evening of the battle of Emmaus. B.C. 167.
See p. 168.

(131—138.) *Seven Royal Psalms, with a closing Doxology*

concerning the joyful coming of Jehovah the righteous King. A Missionary Hallel. The LXX. ascribes XCIII.—C. to David, and XCII. has been attributed to him also. Others refer all these Psalms to Isaiah at the time of Hezekiah's Reformation, and they closely resemble his later prophecies. Others make them post-Restoration Psalms. They are evidently liturgical and continuous.

XCII. A Song for the Sabbath Day to God the Creator. "Thou hast made me glad through Thy works. Thine enemies shall perish and the righteous shall flourish." With ver. 5 cp. Rom. xi. 33; with ver. 10 cp. 2 Cor. i. 21, 1 John ii. 20. Ver. 13 alludes to the trees in the Temple Courts. "Jehovah" occurs seven times in this Psalm, which was used at the early morning sacrifice. The Talmud explains its title by saying it is "a Psalm for the future age of the Messiah, the day which is wholly a Sabbath." Used by the Jews on the Seventh Day of the week (Num. xxviii. 9, 10), and on the Second Day of the Feast of Tabernacles.

XCIII. A Psalm of Praise to God the Ruler of all Creation. "Thy throne is established of old, and holiness becometh Thine house." Compare Rev. xix. 6 and Psalm xcii. 8. Used by the Jews on the Sixth Day of the week.

XCV. A Psalm of Praise to God the Shepherd of Israel. (*Venite.*) "Worship God joyfully, and harden not your hearts as your fathers did." Quoted, Heb. iii. 7—iv. 11; "in David" merely means "in the Psalms." With ver. 4 cp. 1 Kings xx. 28. Used by the Jews on Friday Evening. It has formed the Invitatory Psalm at Morning Prayer in both the Eastern and Western Church from very early times.

XCVI. A New Song to God the Righteous Judge. "Give God the glory due to Him, all peoples, and let the earth exult in His coming." With ver. 10 cp. Act xvii. 22-31. This Psalm is an adaptation of the second part of David's Song of Praise (1 Chron. xvi. 23-33).

XCVII. A Psalm of Praise to God Exalted far above all Gods. "Let earth rejoice and tremble, and ye that love the Lord hate evil." Quoted (ver. 7), Heb. i. 6. With ver. 1 cp. Psalm lxv. 5; with ver. 10 cp. 2 Tim. ii. 19; with ver. 11 cp. Mal. iv. 2.

XCVIII. A New Song to God who hath wrought Salvation. (*Cantate Domino.*) "Let the whole earth rejoice, for the Lord's salvation is known to all." With ver. 1 cp. 1 Cor. xv. 57; with vv. 8, 9 cp. Rom. viii. 21-3. First Canticle at Evensong.

XCIX. A Song of Praise to the Holy God who hears Prayer. "The Lord is great in Zion. He heard His servants of old, and they kept His statutes." With vv. 3, 5, 9 (R.V.) cp. Isa. vi. 3, Rev. iv. 8; with ver. 9 cp. Luke xxiv. 52, Acts i. 12, John xii. 41; cp. Rev. xi. 15-18.

C. A Psalm for the Thankoffering to the Good God whom all serve joyfully. (*Jubilate.*) "Let all lands know that Jehovah is God, and rejoice." Compare Acts ii. 46, 47. With ver. 5 cp. 2 Chron. v. 13. Second Canticle at Morning Prayer.

The wide recognition of God's wonderful interposition on behalf of His captive people is the original theme of these eight Psalms (Ezek. xxxvi. 21-4; Dan. iv. 17, 25, 35). Their complete fulfilment is to be found in the universal preaching of the gospel and the Advent in glory of Christ.

(139—144.) *Six Psalms forming the Egyptian Hallel for the Passover, very doubtfully attributed to David, more probably post-Restoration.*

CXIII. A Hallelujah Psalm on the God of Glory and Grace. "Praise the Lord. His glory is high above the heavens, yet He humbleth Himself to raise the poor." With vv. 5, 6 cp. Phil. ii. 5-8. Compare the songs of Hannah and of the Virgin Mary. Easter Day. Versicles in Confirmation Service.

CXIV. The Deliverance of God's Nation through the Red Sea and Jordan. "At the presence of Jacob's God, sea and flood were driven back, and the rock became a fountain of water." With ver. 7 cp. Matt. xxiv. 29, 30; with ver. 8 cp. 1 Cor. x. 2, 4. Easter Day.

CXV. A Hallelujah Psalm contrasting the God of Heaven with the Idols of Men. (*Non nobis, Domine.*) "Not unto us be glory. For God hath been mindful of us and will bless us." Vv. 1-8 and 16-18 are said by the congregation, vv. 9-11 by the Levites and choir, vv. 12-15 by the Priest. Compare 1 Cor. viii. 4; 1 John v. 21.

CXVI. A Hallelujah Psalm on the Deliverance of God's Servant. "I was brought low and God saved me. What shall I render unto Him?" Quoted (ver. 10), 2 Cor. iv. 13. With ver. 16 cp. Isa. lxv. 23, 1 Cor. vii. 14. It illustrates the depth of religious life in individuals at this time. Churching of Women.

CXVII. A HALLELUJAH PSALM. "Let all nations praise the Lord." Quoted, Rom. xv. 11. This shortest of the Psalms seems to have formed the usual doxology with which the congregation was dismissed.

CXVIII. THE GREAT HOSANNA. A EUCHARISTIC PSALM. "The Lord is on our side, and in His name will I cut off all the nations that compass me round. I shall not die, but live, and declare His works." Quoted (ver. 6), Heb. xiii. 6; (ver. 22), Matt. xxi. 42, Acts iv. 11, 1 Peter ii. 4-7; (vv. 25, 26), Matt. xxi. 9, xxiii. 39. The Psalm is in alternate responses, and seems designed for solemn entrance into the Temple on some great festival, perhaps that of Neh. viii. 13-18. Easter Day. Used by the Jews on the Feast of Tabernacles.

These six Psalms are termed the great Hallel by some Jewish authorities, others giving that name to cxxxvi.; cxi. and cxii. formed an introduction to them. They were used at the three great Feasts, at the New Moons, and at the Feast of Dedication. At the Passover, cxiii., cxiv. were sung before the second cup, and cxv.—cxviii. after the fourth cup, when supper was ended (Matt. xxvi. 30).

(145—149.) *Five Psalms, forming a Second Hallel for daily Morning Prayer. The LXX. attributes cxlvi.—cxlviii. to Haggai and Zechariah, and the group may have been written for the Dedication of the Wall of Jerusalem,* 433. (Neh. xii. 27-43.)

CXLVI. A HALLELUJAH PSALM. "Praise the Lord, who is thy Help and Hope, O my soul." Compare Rev. i. 4-6.

CXLVII. A HALLELUJAH PSALM. "Praise the Lord, who feedeth and upholdeth all, O Jerusalem." Compare Rev. iv. 10, 11.

CXLVIII. A HALLELUJAH PSALM. "Praise the Lord, all-sovereign Creator, ye children of men with all the company of heaven." Compare Rev. vii. 11, 12. The *Benedicite* is a paraphrase of this Psalm.

CXLIX. A NEW SONG AND HALLELUJAH PSALM.

"Praise the Lord, who is King of Israel, in the assembly of saints." Compare Rev. xix. 5.

CL. A HALLELUJAH PSALM. "Praise the Lord in His sanctuary and in the firmament, all that hath breath." Compare Rev. v. 8-14. This forms a doxology to the whole Psalter. Ver. 6 was chanted by Severinus, missionary to the tribes of the Upper Danube, when he lay dying (A.D. 462) and his brethren could not sing for sorrow.

(150.) *One Psalm probably written by Ezra, but also attributed to David and Daniel.*

CXIX. "THE GREAT ALPHABET" (*Masorah*), "THE GOLDEN A.B.C." (*Luther*), AN ACROSTIC PSALM OF THE LAW. Compare 1 Peter i. 23. All its verses, saving 122 and 132, refer to the Scriptures under one of these ten names (the Jews connect their number with the Decalogue), *word, ways, testimonies, judgments, law, statutes, ordinances, precepts, commandments, faithfulness.* This Psalm, which has been called "an epitome of all true religion," "the Biblical expression of the unchanging Law of Right," and "the Jewish Ode to Duty," illustrates the close of the Canon, and the new value and importance attached to the written Word by the restored Jews (Psalm cii. 18), the succession of whose prophets ended in Malachi; whose kings were no longer of the house of David; and whose priests no longer ministered before an Ark over-shadowed with the Divine Glory. From the days described in Neh. viii. 1-12, the Book which contained the record of their past and the promise of their future was regularly multiplied, and taught, and made the basis of an elaborate doctrine. When we meet the Jews again in the New Testament, their veneration for it has degenerated into a new form of superstition and idolatry.

EIGHTH TERM.

THE DAYS OF THE SON OF MAN.
THE GOSPEL PREACHED TO THE JEWS.

B.C. 6—A.D. 51.

S. *Matthew,* S. *Mark,* S. *Luke,* S. *John, Acts* I.—*XIV., James,*
1 *Peter, Jude,* 2 *Peter, Hebrews.* (130 *chapters.*)

"Then opened He their mind, that they might understand the Scriptures."
—LUKE xxiv. 45.

29th MONTH (32).
  Matt. I.—XI. 19, XII., XIII.
  Mark I.—VI. 13. Luke I.—IX.
  6, XI. 14—XII. 12. John I.—
  V.*

30th MONTH (33).
  Matt. XI. 20-30, XIV.—XXII.,
  XXVI. 6-13. Mark VI. 14—
  XII. 37, XIV. 3-9. Luke IX.
  7—XI. 13, XII. 13—XX. 44.
  John VI.—XII. 19.

31st MONTH (32).
  Matt. XXIII.—XXVII. Mark
  XII. 38—XVI. Luke XX.
  45—XXIV. John XII. 20—
  XXI. Acts I.—VIII.

32nd MONTH (33).
  Acts IX.—XII. James, 1 Peter,
  Jude, 2 Peter, Hebrews, Acts
  XIII., XIV.

I. GENERAL SUMMARY.

"THE Days of the Son of Man" (Luke xvii. 22) prefaced the last chapter in the history of Israel and the first chapter in the history of the Church. We consider them in the first aspect this term; in the second, next term.

Christ came 4000 years after the Creation; nearly 1500 years after the Exodus; 1000 years after the First Temple was built; and 500 years after the Second Temple; in an age when the fair promise of the Restoration had been blighted (see pp. 160, 169). Through the Roman conquerors of Palestine, detested Edom had given Israel

---

* For the Gospels see p. 244. They are read in about 85 days, and contain 3779 verses. Therefore, as their chapters are much broken up, it will be a good rule to read them at the rate of $\frac{3779}{85} = 44\frac{1}{2}$ verses a day.

a king in Herod, the low-born usurper, tyrant over an unwilling people, and more than suspected apostate (see p. 228). When Archelaus was deposed, the Jews sought the direct rule of a Roman procurator, thinking they would be freer to manage their own affairs thus. And so the sceptre finally departed even in name from Judah, for what Josephus calls "Agrippa's illegal assumption of the procurator's power" from A.D. 41—44 cannot be reckoned as a restoration of the monarchy. Agrippa II., the last descendant of the Asmoneans, sided with the Romans when war broke out in A.D. 66 The Roman had always shown an aptitude for assimilating conquered nations to himself. The Jew alone doggedly refused to be in friendly relation to him. Each utterly misunderstood, hated, and despised the other, and though Cæsar tolerated Judaism as he tolerated the religions of all his subjects, many insults and outrages were offered to it by his officials and soldiers.

As for the Jews, though the old demon of idolatry had been finally cast out (Luke xi. 24-6), their creed had shrunk into a dead formula, their religion into a network of elaborate rules, which nourished self-righteousness and fanaticism, but left out "the weightier matters of the law" (Matt. xxiii. 23). Murder in the name of orthodoxy they could justify; what they could not tolerate was teaching of truths new and old that opposed itself to their interests. And while the formalist is always harder to influence than the worldling who makes no religious profession, his pedantic scrupulosity is too often compatible with indifference or actual unbelief. Let us, then, take heed lest even in the midst of our religious observances the law of Christ lose its hold upon our hearts, lest we deceive ourselves, and substitute a routine use of the means of grace for a life hour by hour under the power of grace.

Again and again the Jews rose in small fruitless seditions, and, as Tacitus admits, their patience could endure no longer when Gessius Florus proved even more insolent and rapacious than his predecessors. Suddenly they made themselves masters of Jerusalem, and in November 66 inflicted a crushing defeat upon the Romans at Beth-horon. Vespasian and Titus, both afterwards Emperors, were sent to subdue the revolted province, the country was conquered, and in 70 Jerusalem was besieged. Her children were within her (Luke xix. 43, 44), for the blockade began at the Passover, just 40 years (always a significant period in sacred history) after the Lamb of God had been slain, and the city was crowded to suffocation. It seemed as if the nation had given itself a "rendezvous of extermination," and history tells no tale of such unspeakable horror and overwhelming misery as that of the awful fulfilment of their awful words to Pilate (Matt. xxiii. 35, xxvii. 25). Within, the distracted people devoured each other, until all were devoured by the irresistible foe without. Josephus, who was no Christian, says in his famous History that it was certainly God who had brought the Romans to punish His people; and that He had doomed this city to destruction as a polluted city, and was resolved to purge His sanctuary by fire. Even Titus felt himself to be the instrument of a calamity far crueller than he wished or intended, and said, as he looked at the city's defences: "God has been my helper! God it was that pulled down the Jews from these formidable walls, for what could the hands of men or their engines have availed against them?" With the obstinacy of despair they contested every inch; the Temple streamed with the blood of its priests; its altar slopes were piled with corpses (cp. 2 Kings xxiii. 16); and on the same day of the year that Nebuchadnezzar had burned it, the House of God was fired, and sank in ashes (Matt. xxiii. 38, xxiv. 2). Without the city gates (Heb. xiii. 12) Jews were crucified in such multitudes that "room was wanting for the crosses and crosses for the carcases"; they were sold for slaves in such multitudes that at last none would buy them. For the second time, Jerusalem was razed to the ground, and disappears from history for 60 years.

In A.D. 132 the crushed people made a final revolt under Bar-Cocheba, who claimed to be the Messiah. When this had been suppressed, their God-given land was legally appropriated by the Romans, and the plough passed over desolate and desecrated Moriah. A new city called Ælia Capitolina was reared on Zion, and peopled by a Roman colony. None but pagans or Christians were suffered to enter it, but the capitation tax the Jews had formerly paid for the Temple worship (Matt. xvii. 24) was still exacted from them and used to erect a temple to Jupiter Capitolinus on Mount Moriah (John xix. 15). For 200 years the name of Jerusalem was never heard, and Judaism henceforth was a religion deprived of its two most characteristic features, a temple and sacrifices.

"Thus fell and for ever" (says Dean Milman) "the metropolis of the Jewish State. It might almost seem to be a place under a peculiar curse; it has probably seen a far greater portion of human misery than any other spot upon the earth." In B.C. 588 it had already been taken ten times, and unsuccessfully besieged twice, and we read of twelve other captures or sieges between 588 and the Christian era. It had had many privileges and sinned many sins (all summed up in 1 Thess. ii. 15, 16). Its highest privilege was to receive the words of God from His own Son; its greatest sin was the deliberate rejection of both message and Messenger. Then it suffered the heaviest punishment history records (Luke xiii. 34, 35). Comparison of Matt. x. 23, xvi. 28, xxiv. 34, and John xxi. 22 shows that its Fall was a Coming, though not the final Coming of Christ. (See Alford, etc., etc.) He had five times predicted it and foretold many of its most striking features. The great prophecy of Matt. xxiv. blends, so that we cannot completely discriminate them until all has been fulfilled, the three catastrophes which close the three Dispensations of the world's history, both the former being types of the last, viz., the Flood in the past at the end of the Patriarchal Dispensation, the Fall of Jerusalem in the near future at the end of the Jewish Dispensation, and the final Judgment of the Son of Man in the distant future, at the end of the Christian Dispensation (see p. 25).

Dean Stanley notes only three other events of equal magnitude with the Fall of Jerusalem: the Fall of Babylon, which ended Primæval History; the Fall of Rome, which ended Classical History; and the Fall of Constantinople, which ended Mediæval History (see p. 138). But the Fall of Jerusalem has the peculiar interest of involving the dissolution of a religious dispensation with the agony of an expiring nation.

Or, looking only at Hebrew history, we may observe three Desolations of God's House: by the Philistines in

B.C. 1116; by the Chaldeans in B.C. 588; and by the Romans in A.D. 70; and two crowning catastrophes for Israel, viz., that of B.C. 588, which through Jeremiah's preaching became a new birth to the Chosen People; and that of A.D. 70, which through Christ's preaching led to the development of the Church. On both occasions the city might have been saved had it listened to the preacher (*Dr. Payne Smith*).

Again we observe that the Chosen People were three times expatriated: to Egypt B.C. 1706 to 1491; to Babylon B.C. 606 to 536; and to all lands from A.D. 70 onwards. In each case the expatriation and the return was foretold, and its period fixed, clearly in the second and vaguely in the other cases (Gen. xv. 13; Jer. xxv. 12; Dan. viii. 14; Luke xxi. 24). As they have twice literally returned, historical analogy points to a third literal return. See also Isa. xi. 11, 12; Amos ix. 15, passages not applicable to B.C. 536. Fifty years ago there were scarcely 8000 Jews in Palestine. Now (1892) 42,000 of the 58,000 inhabitants of Jerusalem are Jews, and there are at least 100,000 Jews in Palestine, whose number steadily increases (cp. p. 141). Other conquered and captive peoples have vanished utterly, this "inexhaustible race" has survived all the determined efforts of Pharaoh, Nebuchadnezzar, Titus, and others to abolish it; and the Prussian king who asked for the briefest and most convincing statement of the evidences of Christianity had it in the one word "Israel."

Israel's downfall began in B.C. 740, and was consummated in A.D. 70. Since then it has ceased to be the medium of God's dealings with mankind, and although represented in nearly all the states and kingdoms of the world, it has never been recognised as one of them. The legend of the Jew Ahasuerus who spurned Christ on His way to Calvary, and was doomed to roam the earth till He came again in glory, simply sums up the nation in the individual (Deut. xxviii. 25, R.V.). In Milman's "History of the Jews" (Routledge, 3*s*. 6*d*.) may be read the story of its wrongs and oppressions for the last eighteen centuries, wrongs such as no other race could have survived. Even as I write, Western Christendom having at last learned that there are better ways of serving Christ than by continuing to bring

His blood (Acts v. 28) upon every generation of His own guilty nation, is protesting against new outrages upon the Jews of Eastern Europe. Meanwhile we hear of this new and growing desire among them to return to their own land, and in Bessarabia there is the dim dawn of a national recognition of Him whom they once rejected (Zech. xii. 10). God has called Israel an everlasting nation (Jer. xxxi. 35-7; Isa. xliv. 21, liv. 10, lxvi. 22), and promised it a hopeful future (Jer. xxix. 11, xxxi. 17, R.V.). Our duty to it as Christians is plain (Psalm cxxii. 6; Isa. lxii. 7; Rom. xi. 25-32, R.V.).

II. BOOKS TO BE READ.

(See "Oxford Helps," § xv.)

We have often turned already for explanation of the Old Testament to the New Testament as its continuation and completion. We now find in our study of the last seven terms the best interpretation of the New Testament. It consists of four biographical sketches, one narrative concerning some missionaries, twenty-one letters, and one description of a heavenly vision (*Liddon*). It is commonly regarded as the work of eight writers, of whom six were apostles. There is, however, reason, as we shall see, to regard it as the work of nine authors, of whom four only were apostles, two were the Lord's brethren, and three wrote under the express guidance of S. Peter and S. Paul. Of these nine, we make acquaintance with all save S. Paul this term. Geographically, we may note, that S. Matthew, S. James, and S. Jude wrote in Palestine; S. John in Asia Minor; S. Luke, S. Paul, and perhaps S. Peter mainly in Europe; and the apparent connexion of S. Mark and the author of Hebrews with Alexandria makes them representatives of Africa. Chronologically, 1 Thessalonians (A.D. 52) is its earliest, and S. John's Gospel, written some 45 years afterwards, its latest book, and S. Paul's Epistles are most of them earlier than the five General Epistles and the Gospels. We, however, not only begin with the Gospels that we may begin with our Lord's life; we recognise that a true instinct placed the General before the Pauline Epistles in most of the ancient texts; and after studying through them the Gospel preached to the Jews, we turn next term to Gentile Christianity as shown in the life and writings of S. Paul, and to the consummation of the Divine revelation through S. John.

The Gospels. In Acts we see that the Apostles proclaimed not a code of morality, nor a philosophical theory, nor a body of abstract doctrine, but a series of facts to which they had been eye-witnesses, and for the reality of which they not only hazarded but laid down their lives, as the present sense of "martyr," which originally meant simply "witness" (see Rev. ii. 13, R.V. and A.V.) proves. The plain recital of the story of Christ's life was their "gospel." Passed from mouth to mouth, and diligently rehearsed to their converts (Luke i. 4, R.V. margin; 2 Thess. ii. 15), it lived on, not in writing, but in their memories. "Commit nothing to writing" had been a favourite Rabbinic precept, and as yet they shrank from placing it in the hands of unbelievers.

It soon acquired a settled form throughout the Church. Twenty years after the Crucifixion, *i.e.*, in A.D. 51, the form in which S. Paul taught it in Asia Minor was found to agree absolutely with the form in which it was taught in Jerusalem, as he tells us in an epistle whose date and authenticity none dispute (Gal. ii. 1-10). Of the countless acts and words of Christ (John xxi. 25) His apostles selected the most significant, and the general plan of their narrative was always the same; the same stories were related in the same way; and often, especially in recounting Christ's discourses, the same words were used. They dwelt chiefly upon the incidents of the Passion, and all was arranged with a view of being committed to memory.

Within 30 years of Christ's death, ere the living witnesses to the facts had passed away, and therefore ere there was any possibility of legendary embellishments to the story, various attempts were made to write it down in preparation for a new age and a fresh generation of Christians (Luke i. 1). Three transcripts (produced probably between A.D. 55 and A.D. 65) of the original oral Gospel have survived, and the fact that all others have passed away utterly proves that these, S. Matthew, S. Mark, and S. Luke, were its authorised and universally accepted record.

They were three because the life of Christ was too complex for a single history, and Christian truth too wide to be given in any one set of formulas. All heresy springs from inordinate desire to define, distinguish, and isolate its manifold elements; all error is but the exaggeration of some truth taken out of its relation to other truths. So various early heretics took one Gospel only, to the exclusion of the others, and perverted its characteristic teaching. Thus, then, "the pattern of sound words" (2 Tim. i. 13) which the Apostles, directly inspired by the Holy Spirit according to Christ's promise (John xiv. 26; Mark xiii. 11), had shaped, was condensed in the Apostles' Creed, and expanded in the Synoptical Gospels. The Gospels were the result, not the foundation, of the Apostles' teaching and their common oral basis (as I have already indicated in describing it) accounts for all their peculiarities. They agree less than if they had been written in direct relation to each other, and more than if they had been quite independent narratives by three different men. We accept them, not on the bare assertion that their individual authors were inspired, but on the proved fact that they represent the experience of the whole Christian Society that had known Christ in the flesh, and received the Holy Spirit to guide them into all truth (John xvi. 13). No history ever had such an authentication, and alongside the written record the unbroken chain of living witnesses to its truth has continued, as we shall see next term. For fuller exposition of the now generally accepted hypothesis of an original oral Gospel, see Archbishop Thomson's article in Smith's "Dictionary of the Bible."

Finally, together with this corporate testimony of the whole Church, we have the individual testimony of the disciple whom Jesus loved, and who was gifted with the deepest intuition into Divine truth. He evidently wrote with the Synoptical Gospels before him, designedly supplementing them. The evidence for the historical accuracy of the Gospels is well summed up in Dr. Wace's "Authenticity of the Gospels" (Religious Tract Society, 4d.).

That S. Matthew, in its first Aramaic form, of which only the record survives, may have been the earliest Gospel; that S. Mark was probably written after the allusion to its author in Col. iv. 10, A.D. 63; that S. Luke's Gospel shortly preceded his Acts, whose history is doubtless brought down to the time of writing it, *i.e.*, to 63; and that S. John's Gospel was written at the very close of the first century, are the most definite statements we can safely make as to their dates.

The following summary of the peculiarities of each as contrasted with the others should be worked out fully:—

S. Matthew, the earliest Gospel, was written in Judæa for the Jews, by one of the Twelve. It is $\frac{1}{4}$ narrative, and is notable for its many Old Testament quotations, and for dwelling on the discourses of Jesus, whom it presents to us as the Messiah and Son of David, and as the King coming to restore Israel's monarchy, the Priest fulfilling all the Old Testament types, and the Prophet teaching a new law of life in the Sermon on the Mount. It shows us Christianity as the end and perfection of Judaism, as a royal law of freedom; and looking at the Past in a didactic way, relies on the power of Tradition and Precedent, and expounds the relation of the Old and New Testament to each other. Its keynote is *Come to fulfil*, Matt. v. 17 (cp. Isa. xxxiii. 22, and Rom. i. 3), and James, Jude, and Hebrews are its best commentary. "Son of David" occurs seven times here and only thrice in S. Mark and S. Luke. "That it might be fulfilled" occurs eight times here and not in S. Mark or S. Luke. "Your heavenly Father" occurs 15 times, only twice in S. Mark, and only once in S. Luke.

S. Mark, the shortest Gospel, was written in Rome (?) for the Romans, by the cousin of S. Barnabas, who may or may not have been an eye-witness of what he relates, but who wrote under the direction of S. Peter. It is $\frac{1}{2}$ narrative, and is notable for its vivid and forcible style and graphic details, and for dwelling on the deeds of Jesus, whom it presents to us as the Servant of God and Minister of mercy to the world, and as the King ruling nature and man. It shows us Christianity as a great social force moulding men's outer lives anew; and looking at the Present in a practical way, relies on the power of Active Energy, and expounds Christian Practice, emphasizing works as the outcome of faith. Its keynote is *Come to minister*, Mark x. 45 (cp. Isa. xlii. 1-4 and Acts x. 38), and S. Peter's Epistles are its best commentary. Several Latin words occur here and not elsewhere, and it has most in common with the other Gospels.

S. *Luke*, the longest Gospel, was written in Greece (?) for the Greeks, by a Gentile physician and medical missionary, who had not been an eye-witness of what he relates, but who wrote under the direction of S. Paul. It is $\frac{1}{3}$ narrative, and is notable for its pathos and literary beauty, and for dwelling on the conversations of Jesus, whom it presents to us as the Son of Man and Saviour of sinners, and as the Priest offering Himself in sacrifice. It shows us Christianity as a new creation of the inner lives of men; and looking at the Future in a human and historical way, relies on the power of Thought, and expounds a doctrine concerning Man, emphasizing faith as the source of works. Its keynote is *Come to save*, Luke xix. 10 (cp. Isa. ix. 6, Rom. viii. 3), and S. Paul's Epistles are its best commentary. "Grace," which occurs but three times in John, and never in Mark or Matthew, occurs often in Luke as in S. Paul's writings.

S. *John*, the latest Gospel, was written in Asia Minor for the whole Church, by one of the three chosen Apostles, who was Christ's first cousin and His nearest and dearest follower. It is $\frac{1}{3}$ narrative, and is notable for its profound spiritual teaching and symmetrical structure, and for dwelling on the progressive manifestation of Jesus and on the growing unbelief of the Jews contrasted with the growing faith of the disciples. It presents Him to us as the Son of God and Incarnate Word, and as the Prophet revealing highest truths. It shows us Christianity in its infinite relations; and looking at Eternity in a philosophical and poetical way, relies on the supreme power of Love, and expounds a doctrine concerning God. Its keynote is *Come in My Father's Name*, John v. 43 (cp. Isa. liv. 13, 1 John v. 20), and S. John's Epistles and Apocalypse are its best commentary. It has least in common with the other Gospels, not using many of their most familiar words, and using at least 65 words not found in them. It is at once the simplest in manner and the most difficult in matter of all. For the Harmony of the Gospels, and the exact order in which they should be read, see p. 244.

Acts, probably written at Rome, forms S. Luke's sequel to his Gospel, and both are addressed to the same official of high rank. Its record, like that of the Gospels, covers a period of about 34 years. "Acts," not "The Acts," is the literal rendering of its title, for it is not a history of the Twelve (eight of whom it names in Acts i. 13 only), but of the organisation of the Church and of the progress of Christian truth among representative men of very different types. It may be regarded as "the Gospel of the Holy Ghost," as the first Church History and the first Missionary Report. Acts i.—xiv. has for its keynote *Witnesses to Christ's Resurrection* (Acts i. 8; cp. Luke xxiv. 47, 48).

The Epistles. The life of Christ comes to us through four writers, the doctrine concerning Christ through six, viz., two (Peter and John) who believed on Him when He was on earth (John vi. 67-9); two (James and Jude) who, though near Him throughout His earthly life, did not believe till He rose from the dead (John vii. 5 ; 1 Cor. xv. 7 ; Acts i. 14); and two (Paul and the author of Hebrews) who probably never knew Him on earth, but believed on Him ascended to Heaven, even as we may believe, though we have not had a miraculous vision or the spoken testimony of His companions (Acts ix. 5 ; Heb. ii. 3). This multiplied witness shows us: (*a*) That Divine Truth cannot be summed up in any one man's apprehension of it, however deeply he be taught of God. (*b*) That there was nothing mechanical in the inspiration under which the New Testament was written. We receive it, as we receive the Old Testament, in portions tinged with the individuality of different human minds, that it may be perfectly adapted to our complex nature. (*c*) That there may be real unity without absolute uniformity. The churches in Jerusalem, Asia Minor, Alexandria, and Europe each had their characteristic differences (not disagreements) according to the different types of teaching which they received from their founders, in whose writings these differences are reflected.

The General or Catholic Epistles differ from others in not being addressed to particular churches or individuals. James and 1 Peter address the Dispersion, Jude and 2 Peter address all Christians (but 2 Peter iii. 1 may imply that both S. Peter's Epistles address the Dispersion) Hebrews probably addresses all Jewish Christians, and is practically though not in name a General Epistle. The whole group has for its theme the Risen and Ascended Christ, is deeply influenced by the Old Testament, and alludes often to later apocryphal books and various Jewish traditions. It represents Judaic Christianity. The strong likeness between the pictures of declension in S. Paul's Pastoral Epistles and those in 1 and 2 Peter and Jude indicate that they were written at the same time. S. James was martyred in 62, and S. Peter (together with S. Paul) in 67. Both wrote soon before they died, and S. Jude's Epistle must have been written shortly before 2 Peter. Hebrews must have appeared before the Fall of Jerusalem, but cannot have been written long before. This is all we can affirm as to their dates, so no years are here mentioned lest dates should give an erroneous impression of exact information. Students are strongly recommended not only to study each Epistle in detail, but to read it through at a sitting as they would read a friend's letter.

James and Jude were the Lord's brethren (Mark vi. 3). Some identify them with His apostles and first cousins, the sons of Alphæus. In that case we should not be told within six months of His death, and just after the apostolic confession of faith, that His brethren did not believe in Him (John vi. 69, vii. 5; see also Jude 17). Nor is there any other instance of cousins being called "brethren." Some rashly assume that they were younger children of our Lord's Mother. In that case they would not have asserted the authority over Christ which they did assert on more than one occasion, nor would He then have commended her to S. John's care. In all probability they were the sons of Joseph by a former marriage. S. James, after the Twelve had dispersed far and wide according to Christ's command (Mark xvi. 15) for missionary work, presided over the Church in Jerusalem, having the position, if not actually the title, of its Bishop (Acts xii. 17, xv., xxi. 18; Gal. i., ii.). At the hands of the Sadducean party whom his Epistle so pointedly rebukes, he was martyred, boldly witnessing that Jesus is the Christ. To this death, which filled up the cup of Jerusalem's iniquity, there may be an allusion in Heb. xiii. 7, and his own words (James v. 6) are prophetic of it. We know nothing certain about S. Jude's life, labours, and death, and history mentions S. Peter for the last time in Acts xv. Concerning his latter years, besides his Epistles and 1 Cor. ix. 5 and Gal. ii., there are only uncertified traditions and legends that cannot be true.

The Epistle of *S. James* is addressed to Jews, many of whom were Christians, while the other four Epistles are addressed to Christians, many of whom were Jews. It contains more allusions to Christ's discourses than all the other Epistles put together, but fewer allusions to Christian doctrine, which it assumes rather than expounds. There is little in it which a pious and enlightened Jew could not accept, and to its author Christians are but ideal Jews. He has not only the new light of the Christian teacher, but the fervour, sternness, and pointed brevity of the Hebrew prophet. Through him Jerusalem received her last warning from God. His keynote is *Christian faithfulness must express itself in the energy of loving service.* "Temptation," "Riches," "Patience," "Wisdom" are its recurring thoughts, and "the worthlessness, religiously speaking, of unfruitful knowledge is its theme" (*Liddon*).

1 *Peter* bears throughout the traces of familiarity with the acts and words of Christ, and many minute similarities between S. Peter's sermons in Acts and his Epistles prove the genuineness of both. The many points in which they echo the utterances both of S. James and of S. Paul (2 Peter iii. 15, 16) show us that the teachings of those two great leaders, though in apparent opposition, are really in harmony. S. Peter reconciles them, standing as he does doctrinally just between them. Its keynote is *Endure, submit, for ye are the heirs of salvation.* "Resignation" and "Hope" are its recurring thoughts.

The picturesque Epistle of *S. Jude* is like a rough sketch of S. Peter's second Epistle; indeed, their likeness is too close to be accidental. It is remarkable for its threefold arrangement throughout. We note/11 triplets of word and idea. Its keynote is *Contend for the Faith.*

2 *Peter* alternates between passionate warning and earnest exhortation, and has more unity and coherence than 1 Peter. Its keynote is *Stand fast in the Faith.*

Of the canonicity, importance, and authority of *Hebrews* there is no doubt, but there is great doubt as to its author. It is the one absolutely anonymous Epistle, and we do not know exactly whence or whither it was sent. Early testimonies of the Eastern Church are vague and conflicting; in the Western Church it was attributed to S. Paul for the first time 300 years after it was written. Loose conjecture has always favoured his authorship, but scholarly criticism is generally against it. Many differences of literary style between it and S. Paul's writings are pointed out. They are evident to some extent in the English, but far more in the Greek. It teaches the same truths as S. Paul, but from quite a different point of view; and it is scarcely possible that Gal. i. 11, 12 and Heb. ii. 3 could have been penned by the same hand, as one asserts and the other disclaims for the writer the position of an apostle taught by Christ Himself. Luther's guess that it was written by Apollos has been adopted by Alford, Plumptre, and other eminent modern scholars. For this there is no positive evidence, but we cannot name any other New Testament Christian who is so likely to have written it. Without presuming to dogmatise where great authorities disagree, I separate it from S. Paul's Epistles that we may fitly conclude our study of Judaic Christianity by learning why Judaism " vanished away" when it had produced something higher than itself.

Hebrews deals with the relation of Judaism as a system of worship to Christianity. Its stately rhetoric is the finest Greek in the New Testament. Its keynote is *Christ our High Priest*, and its recurring thoughts, "A better covenant," "By how much more," "Living," "Eternal," "Perfect," "Draw near," "Consider," "Hold fast."

For all these Epistles see Archdeacon Farrar's "Early Days of Christianity" (Cassell, 6s.).

III. PERIODS AND DATES.

This term we overstep the 57 years marked out for it in order to close our epoch with the Fall of Jerusalem, A.D. 70. Next term we retrace our steps in order to take the story of Gentile Christianity as a whole. Our chronology is only approximately accurate, the dates given by different authorities for the Conference varying from 47 to 52; but it cannot be far wrong. For clear understanding of our story, we must note the dates of the Roman Emperors and of the rulers of Palestine.

(1) B.C. 6—A.D. 26 (32 years). From Gabriel's message to Zacharias to the Divine anointing of our Lord for His life. *The Coming of the Messiah.* **Matt. i., ii.; Luke i., ii., iii. 23-38; John i. 1-18.**

(2) A.D. 26—30 (3½ years). From the Divine anointing for His life to the human anointing for His death. *The Ministry of the Messiah.* **Matt. iii.—xx.; Mark i.—x.; Luke iii. 1-22, iv.—xix. 28; John i. 19—xi.**

(3) A.D. 30, March 31—May 17 (48 days). From the human anointing for His death to the Ascension. *The Death and Resurrection of the Messiah.* **Matt. xxi.—xxviii.; Mark xi.—xvi.; Luke xix. 29—xxiv.; John xii.—xxi.; Acts i. 1-12.**
(See p. 251 for the details of all these periods.)

(4) A.D. 30—35 (5 years). From the Ascension to the appointment of deacons. *The Hebrew Church.* **Acts i. 13—v.**

(5) A.D. 35—40 (5 years). From the appointment of deacons to the conversion of Cornelius. *The Hellenistic Church.* **Acts vi.—ix. 31.**

(6) A.D. 40—45 (5 years). From the conversion of Cornelius to the Mission from Antioch. *The Founding of the Gentile Church.* **Acts. ix. 32—xii., James, 1 Peter, Jude, 2 Peter, Hebrews.** (Two or three years probably separate Acts v. 42 from Acts vi. 1; and Acts ix. 31 from Acts ix. 32, and a period of one or two years separates Acts xi. 26 from Acts xi. 27.)

(7) A.D. 45—51 (6 years). From the Mission from Antioch to the Conference at Jerusalem. *S. Paul's First Journey.* **Acts xiii., xiv.**

Twelve Emperors of Rome.

Augustus B.C. 12—A.D. 14.
Tiberius A.D. 12—37.
Caligula 37—41.
Claudius 41—54.
Nero 54—68.
Galba 68—69.
Otho 69 (3 months).
Vitellius 69 (1 month).
Vespasian 69—79.
Titus 79—81.
Domitian 81—96.
Nerva 96—98.

Rulers of Palestine.

(See " Oxford Helps," § xxii.)

Herod, King of Judæa, etc., B.C. 37—4.
Archelaus, Ethnarch of Judæa, B.C. 4—A.D. 6.
Herod Antipas, Tetrarch of Peræa and Galilee, B.C. 4—A.D. 39.
Herod Philip, Tetrarch of Ituræa and Trachonitis, B.C. 4—A.D. 33.

Five Roman Procurators of Judæa, A.D. 6—26.
Pontius Pilate, Procurator, 26—36.
Four Roman Procurators, 38—51.
Antonius Felix, Procurator, 51—60.
Porcius Festus, Procurator, 60—62.
Albinus, Procurator, 62—64.
Gessius Florus, 14th and last Procurator, 64—70.

Agrippa I., King of Judæa and Samaria, 41—44.
Herod, King of Chalcis, 41—48.
Agrippa II., King of Chalcis, 49—70.

IV. Geography.

(See " Oxford Helps," Maps IX., X., XI.)

Not only did Christ begin His ministry on Jordan's banks, close to the spot where Israel entered Canaan under Joshua: He had previously gone down from Palestine into Egypt, and had been brought up thence by Divine command. If we may believe that the evidences for the Sinaitic Peninsula outweigh those for the traditional idea that Quarantania in Judæa was the scene of His Temptation, we see further that He had passed through 40 days of trial where Israel had been tried for 40 years. Farther west and farther south He had not been. He also went as far north as Phœnicia, as far east as Peræa. But His life as a whole was spent in a space represented by one or two English counties.

At His birth, Herod ruled all that had been divided among the Twelve Tribes and Idumea also, a larger kingdom in all than David's. During His ministry, Samaria and Judæa formed the Roman province of Judæa under a procurator, while Galilee (once the portion of Asher, Naphtali, Zebulun, and Issachar) and Peræa (once the portion of Reuben and Gad) were ruled by Antipas. What had once been Manasseh's eastern portion was under the sway of Philip (Luke iii. 1).

Six hundred years of Gentile domination had left many traces in new half-heathen cities with foreign names. The most famous New Testament names, such as Cæsarea (the Roman capital of Judæa), Capernaum (the Roman capital of Galilee), Tiberias, Julias, Cæsarea Philippi, Bethsaida, Cana, Chorazin, Nazareth, Gadara, Emmaus, and Bethany, are not mentioned at all in the Old Testament.

Reserving the geographical extension of the Church to be dealt with from the beginning next term, we now note the places most hallowed by the Lord's presence—viz., Bethlehem, His birthplace; Nazareth, His own city in youth; Capernaum, His own city in manhood (Matt. ix. 1); Bethsaida and Cana, each the home of five of the twelve Apostles; the Lake of Galilee, "the most sacred sheet of water which this earth contains" (*Stanley*), as significant of His teaching as the stern desert was of the Baptist's teaching; Bethany, His favourite retreat in Judæa; and Jerusalem, where His work was completed.

The ancient town of *Bethlehem* lies on the ridge of a long grey hill, only 300 feet lower than the top of Helvellyn, six miles to the south of Jerusalem. *Bethany* nestles on the eastern slope of Olivet, on the road to Jericho, one mile and three-quarters from Jerusalem (John xi. 18).

But though Christ began His public ministry in Judæa, and was born and died there, He began to proclaim His gospel in *Galilee*, which remained throughout the chief scene of His work. Its soil was the most fertile and its climate the finest in Palestine. Well-wooded, it yielded wine and wheat and olive oil abundantly. Its 240 towns and villages filled it with the hum of many-coloured life. Since the Captivity, it had been largely peopled by heathen, and was looked down upon therefore by the southern Jews (Matt. iv. 15). Many Syrians, Phœnicians, Arabs, and Greeks had settled there in Christ's day, but its Hebrew inhabitants, though less bigoted and narrow than the Judæans, were most faithful to the Law, and had more of its life if less of its form. Their mountain air made them patriots and heroes. Again and again they were the first to defy the Roman arms, and they were the last to defend the ruins of Jerusalem. "The Galilean loves honour, the Jew loves money," says the Talmud. The beautiful Lake, named Chinnereth, Gennesaret, or Tiberias, $12\frac{1}{4}$ miles long by nearly 7 miles wide at its widest (*i.e.*, about the length of Loch Maree, but wider), was called "the Eye of Galilee." Deserted now, its bright waves were then thronged not only with fishing boats, but with Roman war vessels, and gilded pinnaces from Herod's palace. They are fringed with gay oleanders and set in smiling pastures; their shore line is broken into exquisite little bays, and the hills slope up gently from the water. The Rabbis expressed their enthusiasm for its beauty in a proverb which had a deeper meaning than they knew, "God has created seven seas in the land of Canaan, but one only—the Sea of Galilee—has He chosen for Himself." On its shores, which Josephus calls "the crown of Palestine," and on the much-frequented high road from Damascus to Ptolemais (Isa. ix. 1), lay the thriving and busy little town of *Capernaum*, whose inhabitants had no leisure for the teaching of Christ (Matt. xi. 23). It is now too utterly destroyed for its site to be certainly determined.

Nazareth is a secluded mountain village 1200 feet above the sea, in an amphitheatre of hills, overlooking one of the little folds of the great plain seen as the hills open. The comely women and bright-eyed children who still gather about its clear and abundant fountain attest its pure air ; while the traces of terrace cultivation on its hills, and the many cemeteries, show how large its population once was. Amid the peaceful loveliness of its myriad flowers and gardens of fig and orange and olive and cypress, Jesus passed His youth of humble obedience and patient obscurity, and even as the Risen Lord who claimed Paul's allegiance called Himself by its name (Acts xxii. 8). In Mohammedan lands His followers are still known as Nazarenes.

V. HEROES.

Keynotes
{ *The Lord Jesus*, 1 Peter ii. 21.
John the Baptist, Ezek. ii. 4, 5.
S. Peter, Psalm li. 12, 13.
S. Stephen, Rev. xii. 11.
S. James, Psalm i. 1, 2. }

The instinct of hero-worship is an universal and ennobling one, and we have throughout recognised it by dwelling on the best and greatest men in Bible history. New Testament writers tell us little of the earliest Christian heroes and saints. For them the transcendant personality of *the Lord Jesus* completely filled eye and thought and heart. In Him we recognise the Almighty Creator of the world who deigned to be its Almighty Redeemer. The Word was God, and the Word became flesh (John i. 1, 14). We receive with adoring faith the crowning mystery of the Incarnation, anticipated dimly in the Old Testament and clearly recorded in the New Testament, as the one possible explanation of Christianity and the one solution of all the problems concerning man's relation to God. Strong and terrible as is the power of evil over human hearts, we dare to cherish the highest hopes for ourselves and for our fellow-men, because on this earth not only has a death of infinitely meritorious self-sacrifice been died, but one perfect human life has been lived, and the ideal of humanity has in Christ become real. "We cannot conceive what is implied in a nature of which omnipotence, omnipresence, and omniscience are attributes, far less present them adequately in words as united with human weakness and local limitation" (*Geikie*). As the uncreated and eternal Son "of the Substance of the Father," He is for ever incomprehensible. But since He lived on earth to be our Example, we may gaze reverently upon Him as "Man, of the Substance of His mother, born in the world" (*Athanasian Creed*), and behold in Him the highest perfection of all that human goodness of which our Heroes hitherto have been noble but partial types. The Son of Man, "in the truth of our nature made like unto us in all things sin only except" (Article XV.), was more faithful than Abraham; more blameless than Joseph; more patient than Job; more heedless of self than Moses; zealous with a purer zeal than that of Phinehas; more dauntless than Joshua; more disinterested than Gideon; more devout than Samuel; more desirous to fulfil God's will than David; wiser than Solomon; more earnest in the service of God than Elijah; more earnest in the service of men than Elisha; juster in judgment than Jehoshaphat; a greater restorer of Divine worship than Jehoiada; with stronger trust in God than Hezekiah, and clearer insight into the things of God than Isaiah; a more single-hearted reformer than Josiah; a more unswerving preacher of unwelcome truth than Jeremiah; holier than Daniel; a greater teacher of God's law than Ezra; more prayerful than Nehemiah; and the builder of a grander Temple than that of Zerubbabel. Pre-eminently meek and lowly in heart (Matt. xi. 29), He, unlike all these other saints, never hinted at a personal need of repentance; He advanced claims of absolute sinlessness, appealing to earth (John viii. 46), to Hell (John xiv. 30), and to Heaven (John viii. 29) in support of them, which, in any other, would be the very delirium of religious pride, but which are a greater reason for regarding Him as more than human than any of the wonders He wrought. His own character was more miraculous than any of His miracles. Men acknowledged Him to be perfect in thought (Heb. vii. 26), word (John vii. 46; Luke iv. 22), and deed (Mark vii. 37). Not only was every thought and emotion and desire holy, but none was in excess. With us any supreme pre-occupation leaves us apathetic to other things: Christ always had "a heart at leisure from itself." Hence that absolute unselfishness and ever ready sympathy, which were as prominent as any traits could be in such a perfectly balanced and altogether harmonious character. Seven times in all, once of a blind man, of a leper, of a childless widow, thrice of the multitude, and once in His own parable (Luke x.), we read that "He was moved with compassion." Consider how much you have accomplished in the last $3\frac{1}{2}$ years of your own life, and then try to realise the unity of purpose and intensity of effort that made Christ's ministry the turning-point of the world's whole history. Two other characteristics which no painter can depict must have struck those who saw Him on earth: insight, before which all the self-satisfied hypocrisies of a decadent religion shrank back, while the humble penitent drew near; and majesty, which tempered intense love for Him with overwhelming reverence. "Certainly a flame of fire and starry brightness flashed from His eyes (says Jerome), and the majesty of the Godhead shone in His face."

But we may not try to sum up His character as we have summed up those of others. The inspired singer who prophesied of Him checks our presumption, and reminds us of our true attitude before Him, "He is thy Lord, worship thou Him" (Psalm xlv. 11); and we bow down uttering the words of that most ancient Church hymn, "Thou only art holy, Thou only art the Lord, O Christ!" But

"Though He is so bright and we so dim,
We are made in His image to witness Him"
(*Robert Browning*),

to testify that He is no mere historical character in the past, but our living, loving Saviour in the present, who bids the sinful come to find pardon; the weak come to find strength; the perplexed come to find light; the sorrowful come to find joy; the weary come to find rest; the tempest-tossed come to find peace; the hungry and thirsty come to find satisfaction. Coming to Him in prayer, we may be as truly near to Him as were those whom He succoured and taught when on earth.

We can add nothing to Christ's own eulogy of His grandly heroic forerunner, *John the Baptist* (Matt. xi. 9-11), save the comment that he is almost the only great man who has been content to merge his own glory wholly in that of another (John iii. 30). To utter self-abnegation, he added that unfaltering steadfastness which enabled him to fulfil his course (Acts xiii. 25), although he was cut off in the prime of manhood. In him the voice of prophecy spoke again, after a silence of four centuries.

Of Christ's first twelve followers we hear much collectively, and note their growing faith culminating in S. Peter's confession, and their too frequent dulness of apprehension, which took the Master's figurative expressions literally and His literal expressions metaphorically. But S. *Peter* is the only one of whom there are many individual incidents in the Gospels. He stands out as the first (Matt. x. 2) in this first chapter of Christian history. His special work was opening the gates of the Church at Pentecost to the Jews and at the baptism of Cornelius to the Gentiles (Matt. xvi. 19). His priority was personal, not official; for afterwards it is S. James who presides over the Jewish and S. Paul who is chiefest Apostle in the Gentile Church. "Whatsoever thy hand findeth to do, do it with thy might" was always S. Peter's motto, says Professor Blunt; and throughout he is the same zealous, eager, impulsive disciple, wavering and falling, yet rising to a higher height. He shows us what we too often are, but also what we may be if we follow Christ with the same ardent loyalty and deep affection.

Lastly, let us name S. *Stephen*, the immediate predecessor of S. Paul, the protomartyr of the Church, of whose rare intellectual power and spiritual fervour we get but one glimpse; and *S. James*, the Lord's brother, whom we see first in S. John's account of the marriage in Cana, and last in the pages of Josephus and Hegesippus. They describe him as a Nazarite and uncompromising observer of the Mosaic Law, venerated for his extraordinary sanctity, and called the Just, and the Bulwark of the People.

VI. THE MANIFESTATION OF THE MESSIAH.

"*All this is come to pass, that the Scriptures of the prophets might be fulfilled.*"—Matt. xxvi. 56.

Of Christ, who is Himself in heaven, we have (as S. Ambrose beautifully says) not only the *image* in the Gospel, but the *shadow* in the Law. These two, with the living witness of the Holy Spirit through the Church, form a threefold testimony to Him. The answer to Question XXXI. on p. 162, surveyed the shadow as a whole. Its parts we have traced term after term in following "the Hope of the Promise which God made" to His people. We have seen how from the day Eve welcomed Cain to that in which their aspirations centred in Zerubbabel, the Messianic thought colours the whole Old Testament history, and in the subsequent national depression they threw themselves more and more on the future till the hateful reign of Herod stirred their desires to white heat. The Herodians, it is true, attenuated the Jewish faith in a coming Deliverer into a vague hope of general progress and prosperity, as some would attenuate the Christian faith in a coming Saviour now. Josephus never betrays any personal interest in the Messianic doctrine, yet he bears the strongest testimony to its powerful hold on the nation. At the Christian era there was universal doubt, uncertainty, and expectation. From Daniel's great prophecy three calculations were made, fixing B.C. 17, A.D. 67, and A.D. 135 as the date of the Messiah, and to these may be attributed their desperate challenge to the Romans in 66, and the success of Bar-Cocheba's pretensions in 132. That was the last public profession of the earlier creed. The utmost limit to which His coming could be delayed had been passed, and they shaped despairing legends—truer than they seemed—that the Shechinah had gone to the Mount of Olives and pleaded with the people in vain for three years before the city fell; and that the Messiah actually appeared at the destruction of the Temple, but was suddenly carried away to be revealed at His proper time.

And meanwhile, why had they not received Him when He came? There was abundant witness to Him. Five preliminary announcements, by Gabriel to Zacharias and the Virgin, by angels to the shepherds, by the Spirit to Simeon, and by a star to the Magi, were followed by the Baptist's three testimonies. Sixteen times before and once after His resurrection, Jesus declared Himself the One to whom the Prophets bore witness, using the word Messiah (i.e., Christ) six times; sixteen times also was He acknowledged as such by others, the word Messiah being used six times. And although no Jew could have pictured Him beforehand as He actually was, we cannot imagine any other Saviour who could have satisfied as He did all the wants which were felt in His days. Atonement, independence, restoration, dominion, union, in their highest sense, were what He offered and what they refused. (See p. 249.)

As a solemn warning to ourselves, let us note these three causes of their refusal:—

(a) *Prejudice.* "Pre-occupation of the mind by fixed opinions (says Dr. Geikie) leads to a wrong reading of any evidence. We unconsciously distort facts or invent them to support our favourite theories, and see everything through their medium. . . . The only way we can hope to see truth in its own white and unbroken light is, as Christ tells us, by our becoming little children." The rigid literalism and unchanging conservatism of the Rabbis shut out the light of the new and spiritual truths put before them by Christ.

(b) *Worldliness.* Their religious leaders were lovers of money (Luke xvi. 14, R.V.), and it was for their advantage that Jesus should die (John xi. 50). So they clung to gain till they lost all. The multitude loved the violence for which their prophets had so often reproved them, and they preferred the brigand (Luke xxiii. 18, 19). So they suffered every conceivable outrage from their conquerors. Pilate loved Cæsar's favour (John xix. 12-16), and condemned where he wished to acquit, in obedience to the clamour of a mob. And Cæsar sent him into ignominious exile.

(c) *Self-will.* They had shaped an easy religion of rigid outward observances, leading to exclusive pride and self-righteousness, while permitting many "pleasant sins." With the national conscience thus weakened and perverted, they spurned the hard religion of faith and love which led to unselfish humility.

And so the Messiah could only weep over the doomed city that He yearned to save. Yet He had come not to destroy the Past, but out of it to form the Future. That which concerns Him has complete fulfilment (Luke xxii. 37, R.V.) now that He has taught in the Past as a Prophet greater than Moses, now that He intercedes for us in the Present in virtue of His one sacrifice as a Priest greater than Aaron (Heb. ix. 24), now that His coming draweth near in the Future as a King greater than David.

VII. God's Revelation of Himself to Man.

Ever since Adam and Eve hid themselves from God (Gen. iii. 8), a cloud of sin (Isa. lix. 2) had shut out the undimmed glory of the true Light from man. The story of the Bible is the story of how God gradually dispersed that earth-born cloud, and with infinite patience and longsuffering revealed Himself to men as they were able to bear (John xvi. 12) the revelation. But never had they seemed more ignorant of God than in this day of dead Judaism and unutterably corrupt heathenism (Rom. i. 25, ii. 24; 1 Cor. i. 21), the day in which Christ, who as Son of God knew Him perfectly, came as Son of Man to reveal Him perfectly (Heb. i. 1-3; John i. 18). Only God can comprehend God, but He was made man that we might apprehend Him, might know Him (John xvii. 3; 1 John i. 2, 3, ii. 13, v. 20), and draw near to Him (1 Peter iii. 18; Heb. vii. 19, x. 19-22; Eph. ii. 18; Rom. v. 1, 2; John xiv. 6). The Incarnate Son revealed these three things:—

(*a*) God's Power (Matt. xix. 26).

(*b*) God's Glory (Isa. xl. 5; cp. Exod. xxxiii. 18). Both had been to some extent made known already, but both had been forgotten (Rom. i. 20, 23; Matt. xxii. 29).

(*c*) God's Goodness and Love, which men were farthest from finding out and yet most yearned after (1 John i. 5, iv. 8-10). It was of the Divine Character above all that the Son was "the express image." Even now men have but slowly learned to replace their human notion of a God of revenge, who is to be slavishly feared, by Christ's Divine portrayal, culminating in His death (1 John iii. 16; Tit. iii. 4), of a God of Love, who is to be humbly loved.

He made this revelation in three ways. (*a*) *By what He taught.* As at each previous stage of revelation, a new truth came in a new Name of God. Men had occasionally ventured to think of Him as FATHER already (Deut. xxxii. 6; 1 Chron. xxix. 10; Isa. lxiii. 16, lxiv. 8), and to find a Divine symbol in human fatherhood (Eph. iii. 15, R.V. margin). But He came in the Father's name, proclaiming it clearly and constantly (John v. 43, xvii. 6), and His witness to it, as Hausrath points out, was one of the strongest proofs of the absolute perfection of His human nature (see Westcott's "Revelation of the Father").

(*b*) *By what He was.* He enabled us to know and see the Father through knowing and seeing Him (John xiv. 7-9; Matt. i. 23). His life was an unveiling of God to the eye of man's sense, that the eye of man's spirit might understand Him (*Liddon*). His Incarnation is the foundation truth of our creed as a race and as individuals. "All past history, so far as it has any permanent significance, appears to be the preparation for that great mystery, and all subsequent history the gradual appropriation of its results" (*Westcott*). (*c*) *By giving the Holy Spirit* to reveal Him as He had revealed the Father (Acts xvi. 7, R.V.).

There is abundant proof in the Acts of the Apostles that the Church from the first regarded her Founder as Divine. For her members His words recorded in Matt. xxviii. 20 stated not an abstract doctrine, but a fact of daily experience. Accordingly they prayed to Him in heaven, as they had spoken to Him on earth, which being Jews they could not have done had they regarded Him as merely human. With Acts i. 24 cp. John vi. 70, ii. 24, 25; xxi. 17; with Acts ii. 21, vii. 59, 60 (R.V.), and ix. 14, cp. 1 Cor. i. 2; with the significant word "began" in Acts i. 1 cp. Mark xvi. 20, 2 Cor. vi. 1.

Lastly, observe how the doctrine of the Three in One underlies the whole of Christ's teaching, Matt. xxiii. 8-10, R.V. (cp. John xiv. 26); John iii. 5, 16, xiv., xv., xvi. His one explicit statement of it in Matt. xxviii. 19 is not, however, speculative, but practical. "The highest mystery of the Faith is conveyed in the words which are the passport into the Christian community" (*Westcott*). So indeed the whole wondrous revelation of "Divine Humanity renewing nature" (*E. B. Browning*) had a directly practical issue (1 John iii. 2; 2 Peter i. 4). In the grand words of Athanasius's famous treatise on the Incarnation, § liv., "He became human that we might be made divine."

VIII. MAN'S RELATION TO GOD IN WORSHIP.

Herod's Temple has been so often pictured and described that we need not dwell upon it. Edersheim's "Temple and its Services" (Religious Tract Society, 5*s.*) gives a scholarly and complete account of it. This grandest of all the three Temples reared at Jerusalem, the one honoured by our Lord's presence, was finally completed in A.D. 65, the year before the war with Rome broke out. Five years later not one stone was left on another (Matt. xxiv. 1, 2).

Henceforth, realising the teaching of Mal. i. 11 and John iv. 24, we turn to the living Temple of the future, which had Christ for its corner-stone, and for its foundation the Apostles (Eph. ii. 20), that first company of believers which has grown up into the great Christendom of to-day, and will, we trust, grow into the greater Christendom of to-morrow. Christ began to form His Church when He gathered five disciples about Him by Jordan (John i.). He first named it after Peter's confession of the central truth upon which it was to be founded (Matt. xvi.). Its birthday, and the day it first found itself face to face with the world, was the Day of Pentecost A.D. 30. That transformed a handful of dejected, faint-hearted, materialising Galilean peasants into the heroic preachers and confessors who enlightened the world. The transient gift of tongues was the symbol of a permanent and far greater gift of spiritual power on the day which began the last phase of God's dealings with men; the day when He followed up the promise to Abraham and the law of Moses, the Tabernacle and Temple where dwelt as visible emblem of His presence the Shechinah, and the tabernacling in a mortal body of His own Son *among* men, by sending His Spirit to dwell *in* men (John xiv. 17). "More than this God could not give; nearer than this He could not be" (*Farrar*).

And now the teaching of Christ, with its two new keynotes, correlatives of each other, the Fatherhood of God and the Brotherhood of Men, was to be practically illustrated. The political comprehension of mankind in one great empire would give way to a moral federation of mankind through a common faith.

The first two stages of the history of that Church which placed men in a new relation to each other were:—

(1) The Hebrew Period, when it consisted of Jews of Palestine speaking Aramaic, and probably reckoned as only one more synagogue in a city which already had 480.

(2) The Hellenistic Period, when it included Jews of the Dispersion speaking Greek. See "Oxford Helps," § xiii.

We begin next term by considering the steps that led to the formation of a Gentile Church.

Here it only remains for us to show that Christ placed men in a new relation, not merely to each other, but to God. He taught that religion does not depend upon external precepts, but upon surrender of the will to God; that good acts have no value apart from good motives; that hatred, not violence, is the essence of murder; that God looks at the sinful thought rather than the criminal deed. He did more than teach. Human sin, a far more heinous thing than men had hitherto thought it, is taken away once and for ever by the Sinless One (John i. 29), who laid down His life for men.

> "Yea, once Immanuel's orphaned cry His universe hath shaken,—
> It went up single, echoless, 'My God, I am forsaken!'
> It went up from the Holy's lips amid His lost creation,
> That, of the lost, no son should use those words of desolation."
> E. B. Browning.

IX. QUESTIONS.

(See pp. 13, 18.)

[For all the Questions pp. 244-277 may be consulted, and for Questions IV., VI., XVIII., XXIII., XXIX., and XXXI. any other books.]

I. What Old Testament allusions are there to the town and to the house in which Christ was born? (6.)

II. Draw out in tabular form a contrast in character and circumstances between Christ and His Forerunner. (12.)

III. Illustrate Luke iv. 13 and Heb. iv. 15, by showing that each of the three temptations in the wilderness was afterwards repeated in a somewhat different form. (3.)

IV. Ahaz was rebuked for not asking a sign (Isa. vii.). Christ rebuked the Jews for asking a sign. Explain this. (5.)

V. Which of Christ's miracles were wrought on the Sabbath? and how did He vindicate His action on each occasion? (14.)

VI. Which of His miracles were not to be proclaimed? Why was this silence enjoined? (8.)

VII. Show that among those who came to Christ there were representatives of (1) the Ten Tribes, (2) the Two Tribes, (3) Samaritans, (4) Greeks, (5) Romans, (6) Women, (7) Children, (8) Citizens, (9) Rustics, (10) Rich, (11) Poor,

(12) Honourable, (13) Degraded, (14) Wise, (15) Unlearned. (15.)

VIII. Quote our Lord's description of the Apostle Bartholomew, and mention two Canaanitish women commended for their faith in this term's reading. (3.)

IX. Illustrate Heb. ii. 17, by showing that our Lord suffered hunger, thirst, weariness, and poverty; that He wept, and passed through severe mental anguish. (9.)

X. On what occasions did He express (1) Joy, (2) Sorrow for human suffering, (3) Tender consideration for others, (4) Pity for the multitude, (5) Sympathy and affection for His friends, (6) Filial love, (6) Surprise, (8) Disappointment, (9) Indignation, (10) Anger, (11) Disdain, (12) Zeal for God's glory? (12.)

XI. How did He illustrate in His own life His teaching that men ought always to pray? Give references. (20.)

XII. Quote instances of (1) His patience and humility, (2) His courage, (3) His prudence, (4) His tenderness to and love of children, (5) His personal fulfilment of the Mosaic Law. (15.)

XIII. Show that He claimed Divine power to forgive sins, and assumed and accepted titles given to God in the Old Testament. (10.)

XIV. Give examples of that Divine knowledge of men's thoughts through which His disciples were persuaded that He came forth from God. John xvi. 30 (R.V.) (8.)

XV. Name seven occasions on which His look and bearing awed and confounded His foes. (7.)

XVI. Four times before the multitude and five times to the Apostles He alluded prophetically to His Resurrection. Quote the passages, and show that He also foretold the Pentecostal gift of the Spirit and His own Second Coming. (10.)

XVII. Once He called Himself "the King," and once He called His disciples "little children." Give references. Where is He called "Our Lord" for the first time? (3.)

XVIII. What do you understand by these expressions: *Miracle, Parable, Gospel, Repentance, Kingdom of Heaven?* (10.)

XIX. Illustrate the special characteristics of each Gospel by enumerating some incidents, etc., peculiar to it. (20)

XX. Which Evangelist makes most and which fewest quotations from the Old Testament? Name the only miracle recorded by all the Evangelists. (3.)

XXI. What evidence is there in the Synoptists of the ministry in Judæa and in S. John of that in Galilee? (8.)

XXII. Show that S. John recognises though he does not directly relate, (a) that Christ's birth was miraculous, (b) that He was reputed son of Joseph, (c) that in youth He was subject to His mother and Joseph, (d) that He dwelt at Nazareth, (e) that the Spirit came upon Him at His baptism, (f) that He was rejected at Nazareth, (g) that He appointed twelve Apostles, (h) that the Baptist was imprisoned, (i) that Christ ascended to heaven. Find in S. John the ground of the accusation in Matt. xxvi. 61. Is there any reference to the Sacraments in S. John? (12.)

XXIII. Briefly define the following New Testament terms: (a) Pharisees, (b) Sadducees, (c) Herodians, (d) Zealots, (e) Scribes, (f) Lawyers, (g) Chief Priests, (h) Rulers of the Synagogue, (i) Proselytes, (j) Publicans, (k) Libertines, (l) Greeks, (m) Grecians. (26.)

XXIV. Analyse shortly S. Peter's first sermon, indicating the thread of his argument, and show that the leading theme of all his teaching was Christ Risen. (8.)

XXV. Point out the causes, instigators, and immediate results of each of the four Persecutions of the Church recorded in Acts i.—xii. (8.)

XXVI. Discriminate in this term's period of history *three* persons named James (*i.e.*, Jacob); *four* named Philip; *five* named Joseph; *five* named John; *five* named Judas; *five* named Mary (*i.e.*, Miriam); and *eleven* named Simon or Simeon. (38.)

XXVII. Trace the influence of the Sermon on the Mount in the Epistle of S. James. (12.)

XXVIII. Trace the influence of words and incidents in the Gospels on S. Peter's Epistles. (15.)

XXIX. Consider the historical accuracy of the statements in John vii. 52, viii. 33; Heb. vii. 3, 27, ix. 3, 4. (10.)

XXX. Write out the fifteen practical inferences in Hebrews introduced by "wherefore," "therefore," or "then." (8.)

XXXI. Explain briefly the following passages: Matt.

viii. 22, xxiii. 5; Luke xii. 5, xvi. 9, xxiii. 31; Acts ii. 23; 1 Peter iii. 19; 2 Peter i. 20; Jude 19; Heb. vi. 3-6. (30.)

XXXII. Give references for the following (the first four occur more than once):—(*a*) "Thy faith hath saved thee." (*b*) "Follow Me." (*c*) "Weep not." (*d*) "He cannot be My disciple." (*e*) "Able to save to the uttermost." (*f*) "Able to guard you from stumbling." (*g*) "Out of death into life." (*h*) "To each one his work." (*i*) "That we may see and believe." (*j*) "Said I not, If thou believedst thou shouldst see?" (*k*) "Take heed what ye hear." (*l*) "Take heed how ye hear." (*m*) "Have ye not read?" (*n*) "Let him that readeth understand." (*o*) "Do good, despairing of no man." (*p*) "Make straight paths for your feet." (*q*) "Ye have need of patience." (*r*) "Your Father knoweth." (*s*) "A people for God's own possession." (*t*) "Good stewards of the manifold grace of God." (*u*) "Ye have taken your pleasure." (*v*) "Because he gave not God the glory." (*w*) "He is guilty of an eternal sin." (*x*) "Doth the spirit . . . long unto envying?" (*y*) "Men spake from God." (*z*) "This He said, making all meats clean." (32.)

For *Second Series* of Questions, see p. 309.

THE GOSPELS

ARRANGED IN THEIR HISTORICAL SEQUENCE.

I. Method and Purpose of the Gospels.

THE difficulties of Biblical chronology culminate when we come to the Life of our Lord. The one point on which all good authorities agree is that an exact HARMONY OF THE FOUR GOSPELS cannot be constructed. As memoirs containing infinitely beautiful pictures of the infinitely beautiful Life they are perfect. But as formal biographies they are confessedly fragmentary and obviously incomplete, more like lectures on the Life than annals of it. Dean Alford represents all the scholars when he points out that their authors wrote with no design of being pieced together into a complete history, and all attempt to do this must be merely conjectural. John xxi. 25 warns us that we have only a selection of events, and the notes of time throughout are few and vague.

S. Matthew's style has the most appearance of continuity, yet he diverges most widely from chronological methods. S. Luke professes to write "in order" (Luke i. 3), but that does not necessarily involve (says Dr. Westcott) order of time, but rather of logical or moral sequence. S. Mark's clear and precise story furnishes several accurate and valuable chronological data. S. John's narrative appears to be chronological throughout, but the points of contact between it and that of the other Evangelists are not always easy to fix. Moreover, there is not one absolutely certain date in the whole Gospel history. And when we look elsewhere for additional information, we only learn that outside our four Gospels traditions concerning Christ are very few, slight, and untrustworthy. Knowing the Gospels we know all that can now be known about His life.

For our spiritual instruction they are all-sufficient. Their purpose, as expressed in John xx. 30, 31, can be fulfilled without exhaustive information or an exact table of dates. As a whole, they may be fragmentary, but they are not fragments. Each has *unity* and *design*, a spiritual law binds together its several parts, and its selection of representative facts is grouped according to its own dominant idea and conveys its peculiar lesson (see p. 221). Their real harmony is essentially moral, not mechanical. It is not to be found in an ingenious mosaic of disjointed fragments, but in contemplation of each narrative at its proper point of sight. This brings out the manifoldness of the record of Christ's many-sided life, while the unbroken spiritual concord in four independent histories is a convincing proof of their inspiration.

When all this has been said, however, it is still possible to get a fifth and most instructive view of our Lord's sojourn on earth by combining these narratives, and so forming a general idea of the course of events. Nor need we ignore the special characteristics of each Gospel or fail to recognise throughout that while the substance of our Harmony deals with *facts*, its arrangement deals with *probabilities.*

The dates given below are agreed on by many good authorities. Some make the Crucifixion one year earlier, others two (or three) years later than A.D. 30. Here are the points from which all the dates must be calculated. Herod's Temple was begun in B.C. 19. The course of Abijah went out of office on October 9th, B.C. 6. Herod died April 1st, B.C. 4. Tiberius began his joint rule with Augustus A.D. 12. Pilate was deposed A.D. 36.

The plan we adopt with regard to all those incidents whose exact place in the narrative cannot be determined is to assume that the order is chronological wherever we have not proof to the contrary (a large assumption, looking at the many cases in which sequence of time can be shown to give place to sequence of thought), and to regard the unity of each Gospel by breaking it up as little as possible. Where the order of time is not evident, we shall follow the

Evangelists in grouping together incidents that illustrate each other. S. John's order we leave unchanged, and we only depart twice from that of S. Mark, and five times from that of S. Luke.

II. DIFFICULTIES.

Ours is the practical purpose of reading the Gospels together in the best way. Therefore we need not enter upon interminable discussions of problems that can never be solved. Their solution, had it been essential, could have been given in two or three words; but the silence of Scripture baffles speculation. Every disputed point has been determined in this Harmony after much consideration and fullest consultation of those whose scholarship gives them the right to an opinion. But lest probabilities be taken for certainties, I will briefly mention the chief questions that arise.

(1) What was the duration of our Lord's Ministry? Three Passovers are mentioned by S. John, so it could not have been less than two years. If John v. 1 also refers to a Passover (see R.V. margin) it must have been three years. Other excellent authorities explain John v. 1 of Pentecost or Tabernacles or Purim or the Feast of Trumpets in September. Even so, Luke vi. 1 implies a Passover other than those of John ii. and vi. (but see R.V.), and Luke xiii. 7, 32 suggests three years, *i.e.*, 3½ years from the Baptism. Moreover 3½ years is always a significant period in the prophetic writings.

(2) Do Mark vi. and Luke iv. refer to one or to two rejections at Nazareth? If to one, which gives it in the right order?

(3) Do Luke v. 1-11 and Matt. iv. 18-22 refer to the same event? If so, did it precede or follow the great Sabbath at Capernaum?

(4) Do Matt. v.—vii. and Luke vi. report the same sermon? If so, was it preached at the beginning or in the course of the ministry in Galilee?

(5) Did the conflict of Matt. xii. 22-45 take place in the order indicated by S. Mark or in that indicated by S. Luke?

(6) Do the incidents of John ix.—x. 21 belong to the Feast of Tabernacles or to the Feast of Dedication?

(7) What is the relation of the events of Luke ix. 52—xviii. 30 to each other, and to S. John's narrative? This great episode is an argument against the observance of an exact order of time in the Gospels, and an illustration of their real mode of sequence. Many of its sayings occur elsewhere in different contexts, but they may very naturally have been uttered more than once. Throughout its keynote is *To Jerusalem—to suffer*, and the burden of its teaching is the contrast between the spiritual and the literal Israel, between the true and the false people of God. We understand it best by reading it as a whole, though all its incidents may not have occurred in the six months to which we assign them.

(8) Did the Last Supper take place on Nisan 13 or Nisan 14, on or before the Passover day?

III. AUTHORITIES.

Erudite references to authorities are not characteristic of this simple and practical volume. But its readers may like to have the names of some of the books found helpful in preparing this Harmony:—Westcott's "S. John" (Speaker's Commentary) and "Introduction to the Study of the Gospels"; Farrar's "S. Luke" and "Life of Christ"; Geikie's "Life and Words of Christ"; Smith's "New Testament History" and "Dictionary of the Bible"; Conder's "Life of Christ"; Hanna's "Our Lord's Life on Earth"; Stalker's "Life of Christ"; Edersheim's "Ministry and Services of the Temple"; and Trench's "Miracles of our Lord."

IV. PLAN OF THIS HARMONY.

Each of the three years of the Ministry has its own distinguishing feature. Note also that there is positive evidence for our division of the third year, and circumstantial evidence for our division of the second year, but that the similar division of the first year is purely conjectural. To each of the ten Periods two mottoes are prefixed, one from Old Testament prophecy anticipating Christ's coming and fulfilled by Him, the other from those earliest Christian writings (some even earlier than the Gospels), which vouch for all the main facts of the Gospel story, and form its most important corroboration. The following matters are emphasized throughout, generally by use of italics.

(*a*) *Miracles*, which are most numerous in the Fourth Period. Thirty-five are described, but many others were wrought. Their distribution is significant, and the key to their meaning lies in the fact that they were not mere wonders of Christ's power, but redemptive acts of His grace and expressions of His character, each at once a work and a revelation. Christ was Himself the great miracle of which His particular miracles were merely sparks or emanations. They entered with Him, not to disturb but to repair the harmony of nature. See Liddon's "Elements of Religion," Lecture II.

(*b*) *Parables*, of which there are three chief groups: one in the Sixth Period (see Matthew) after the first great crisis of conflict with the Pharisees; one in the Eighth Period (see Luke) during the journey to Jerusalem; and one on the Day of Gainsayings (see Matthew). We reckon the recorded Parables as thirty-five in number, but they are less easily counted than the Miracles. Some make 50; others only 27. S. John represents the higher stage of teaching which had got beyond Parables.

Clearly the recorded Miracles and Parables are only specimens of Christ's works and words (see John xii. 37; Matt. xiii. 34). Observe that Miracles were most numerous at the beginning, to call attention to His teaching; and that not until He has been rejected by "the wise" does He systematically teach "the babes" by Parables, fixed first in the imagination and memory, and gradually enlightening the understanding afterwards. Never yet had been speaking so simple, yet so profound; so pictorial, yet so absolutely true.

(*c*) Only the leading truths of the chief *Discourses* of Christ can be indicated. Observe the progressive character of the teaching throughout, and the mode of addressing men as men, which makes Christ's words come with fresh force to each fresh generation; and note that *Authority*, *Boldness*, *Power*, and *Graciousness* are His most striking characteristics as a Preacher.

(d) *Seven Visits to Jerusalem* form useful landmarks. This, like all our enumerations, refers to *records*, not to *events*. From the silence of the Gospels we can never safely argue. Luke xiii. 34 implies more than the three visits during the Ministry recorded as having occurred before these words were uttered.

(e) *Our Lord's Manifestation of Himself as the Divine Messiah of Prophecy and Recognition as such* should be noted, with the time, circumstances, and extent of each successive manifestation. He made no sudden proclamation of His office, nor did He continually revert to it. For (1) He desired to shun popular excitement, that His words might have time to take root and bear fruit. (2) He could neither descend to their ideal, nor raise them to His. They looked forward to a political Messiah who would exalt their race, establish the Mosaic Law in its Rabbinic form for ever, and destroy the heathen. Their hope had degenerated into a standing conspiracy of the nation against its actual rulers. For this, the idea of the true suffering Messiah, establishing a kingdom on love not on force, ruling *in* not *over* men, could not be substituted at once, and even after the Resurrection the Apostles themselves had not entirely unlearned the notions of the past. (3) Instead of the human or angelic Messiah of their thoughts, He slowly revealed the Divine Messiah. Hence, though He never refused the title when given to Him, and habitually spoke of Himself as Son of Man (a recognised name of the Messiah, see p. 155), and implied Messiahship continually by His acts, He only assumed the title openly towards the end of His Ministry, and His public and official claim to be the Divine Messiah (Mark xiv. 61, 62) was reserved for a moment when all false expectations of political revolution were at an end, and swift sentence of death was its inevitable outcome (see p. 272).

(f) *The development of Opposition*, more and more noisy, persistent, and pitiless, is one of the most perplexing features of the history. Why was not He welcomed by the world He came to save? Why is not every knee bowed to Him now in grateful homage? This opposition was foretold from the first (Luke ii. 34), and expected by Christ Himself throughout. He set forth its cause and true character (John xv. 19, 24), and the latest Evangelist expounds it more fully than his predecessors in those "comments" which are peculiar to His Gospel. John i. 5, 11, iii. 19, 20, 32, xi. 51, 52, xii. 37-43. *Demanding a sign* was one significant form of this opposition, met each time in a noteworthy way.

(*g*) Rejected by the unbelief of the religious leaders of His own nation, and by His fellow-townsmen of Nazareth and Capernaum, He was received by the poor of Galilee, by the Samaritans, and by the *Gentiles*.

(*h*) First by vague allusion, then by direct prophecy, *Christ foretold His own Passion*; 22 of the 30 allusions to it were made after S. Peter's Confession (*i.e.*, almost within the last six months), and in five of them the Resurrection is named. This prophecy culminates in the command to commemorate for ever (1 Cor. xi. 25, 26), not His life, nor His teaching, nor His miracles, nor even His resurrection, but His shameful death, which seemed to all defeat. When His followers anticipated triumph, He calmly predicted His rejection. When His enemies were certain that they had secured the destruction of Himself and His doctrine, He looked forward with majestic confidence to His ultimate universal dominion. No more convincing proof that His power and wisdom were alike Divine could be given (Isa. xlvi. 10).

(*i*) Remembering that Christ was not only the greatest Teacher of God's Will, but also the greatest Example of conformity to it, we note lastly how His life was throughout a life of *Prayer*, and a perfect demonstration of the *duty*, *privilege*, and *power* of supplication to God.

Endeavour is made in the following pages to give the best possible Life of our Lord by neither superseding nor supplementing the Gospels, but by putting the student in a position to read their record with fresher and fuller appreciation of its meaning. Other noble lives stir us up to emulation, and rouse our admiration and affection for those who lived them. That is all. But in the case of this Life that cannot be all. All that Christ surrendered, all that He did, all that He taught, and all that He suffered, was for us men and for our salvation, and knowing *about*

Him as He lived then on earth, through the well-attested memoirs of His four disciples, cannot leave us where it found us. Before us, as before the Jews, more than 1860 years ago, is placed the alternative of accepting or rejecting Him; for God compels no man to believe against his will. May I say then to every reader of this volume, Ask yourself, as the familiar story of the Saviour is once more put before you, " What difference has His life and death made to me? Did He, or did He not, give Himself for me in vain?" If He is already all in all to you, thank Him afresh for what He has done. If you have never sought Him, seek Him now; trust yourself, your life here, your life hereafter, once for all to that freely given and fully proved love. Add one more to those myriads of His redeemed, who can testify that He blesses above all we ask or think those who through faith have learned to know *Him* as He lives now in Heaven.

FIRST PERIOD.

B.C. 6 to A.D. 26.

BIRTH, INFANCY, AND YOUTH OF CHRIST.

Matt. i., ii.; Luke i., ii., iii. 23-38; John i. 1-18.

"*Unto us a Child is born.*"—Isa. ix. 6.
" *Born of a woman, born under the law.*"—Gal. iv. 4.

S. Luke's Introduction. Character and purpose of the Gospels. Luke i. 1-4.

S. John's Prologue. The Divine and Eternal Word creating the world and manifesting Himself to man through His Incarnation. Christ the only begotten Son of God. John i. 1-18.

Legal Pedigree as Abraham's seed and Solomon's heir. Christ the greatest Son of David and King of Israel Matt. i. 1-17.

Natural Pedigree as David's descendant through Nathan. Christ the greatest Son of Adam and the Son of Man. Luke iii. 23-38.

B.C. 6. Early in October (?), in the Temple at Jerusalem, announcement to Zacharias the priest of the birth of John as forerunner of the Lord God. Luke i. 5-25.

B.C. 5. End of March (?), at Nazareth, first announcement to the Virgin Mary (type of the Church) of the birth of JESUS, God's Son and David's heir. Her visit to Elisabeth. *The first Christian hymn.* Luke i. 26-56.

B.C. 5. Early in July (?), at a city of Judah, birth of John, greatest son of Aaron. *The second Christian hymn.* Luke i. 57-80.

At Nazareth, second announcement to Joseph (type of Israel) of the birth of JESUS, the Divine Saviour from sin. Matt. i. 18-25.

B.C. 5. End of December (or B.C. 4, beginning of January), at Bethlehem, JESUS BORN, and made known to the shepherds (types of the poor who gladly receive the Gospel), by angels as a Saviour, Messiah the Lord. *First adoration.* Luke ii. 1-20. The latest research confirms the traditional date of mid-winter.

Eight days later, Jesus is circumcised and named, thus beginning to fulfil the Law as perfect Man. Luke ii. 21.

B.C. 4. February. *First visit to Jerusalem.* In the Temple, Jesus redeemed as a first-born son (Exod. xiii.; Num. iii. 13), presented to God the Father, enrolled in the register, and received by Simeon and Anna (types of the faithful remnant of Israel), to whom He is made known by God the Holy Spirit as Jehovah's Messiah. *The third Christian hymn.* Luke ii. 22-38.

At Bethlehem, the Magi, to whom He has been made known by a star as the King of the Jews, pay the *first formal homage* to Christ. His *first Manifestation to the Gentiles.* First persecution, by Herod. Flight into Egypt (tradition says to Memphis). Massacre of the Innocents. Death of Herod on April 1. Return to Nazareth. Matt. ii.; Luke ii. 39. The Magi were probably Persians, and represented the Zoroastrian system, the purest form of religion which man has devised without knowledge of the True God. See p. 156.

A.D. 8. PASSOVER. *Second visit to Jerusalem.* In the Temple, Jesus announces, in His *first recorded words,* His Divine parentage and life-work with its sacred law of self-sacrifice. His youth of sinless obedience and obscure toil as our Example. Luke ii. 40-52.

SECOND PERIOD.

Summer of A.D. 26 to Passover of A.D. 27.

THE PREPARATION FOR THE MINISTRY.

Matt. iii., iv. 1-11; Mark i. 1-13; Luke iii. 1-18, 21-3, iv. 1-13; John i. 19—ii. 12.

"*The Lord hath anointed Me to preach good tidings unto the meek.*"—Isa. lxi. 1.
"*He Himself hath suffered being tempted.*"—Heb. ii. 18.

In the wilderness of Judæa, John, aged 30 (1 Chron. xxiii. 3), begins to preach repentance, to baptize, and to give His *first testimony to Jesus* as the Coming One, and to the Kingdom of God as now at hand. Matt. iii. 1-12; Mark i. 1-8; Luke iii. 1-18.

In Jordan, Jesus (aged about 30, Num. iv. 3; 2 Sam. v. 4), is baptized by John, and, while praying, anointed by the Holy Spirit as Prophet, Priest, and King, and thus set apart for His work and made known as God's beloved Son by *the First Voice from Heaven*, heard probably by Jesus and the Baptist only. Matt. iii. 13-17; Mark i. 9-11; Luke iii. 21-3.

In the wilderness, He fasts 40 days, and as the Second Adam retrieves man's Fall by overcoming the threefold temptation for body, spirit, and soul; concerning sense God, and man; to lust of the flesh, vainglory of life, and lust of the eyes; or to reliance on self not on God, religious presumption, and earthly ambition; or in one word, to self-will. Thus His absolute sinlessness is tested and proved. Matt. iv. 1-11; Mark i. 12, 13; Luke iv. 1-13. S. Matthew evidently gives the temptations in the order in which they occurred, which is followed above.

At Bethany beyond Jordan, John gives His *second testimony to Jesus* as the Son of God and the Lamb of God, or divinely given atonement for sin. Jesus calls His first disciples, Andrew, John, Peter, James (?), Philip, and Nathanael, and thus begins to form His Church. They acknowledge Him as Messiah, and Nathanael calls Him Son of God and King of Israel. John i. 19-51.

At a marriage feast in Cana of Galilee, Christ works His 1*st miracle*, changing water into wine, at once a gracious leave-taking of His old home life, and a figure of the better covenant He would bring in. The disciples believe. His first visit to Capernaum. John ii. 1-12.

THIRD PERIOD.

Passover to Feast of Tabernacles, A.D. 27 (6 months).

CHRIST REVEALING HIMSELF TO THE WORLD IN JUDÆA.

John ii. 13—iv. 42.

" *The Lord shall suddenly come to His Temple.*"—Mal. iii. 1.
" *To the Jew first.*"—Rom. i. 16.

FIRST PASSOVER.—*Third visit to Jerusalem. First Cleansing of the Temple* by Christ, as a Reformer urging amendment, to prepare it for His first preaching there (comp. p. 269). In answer to the *first demand for a sign*, He gives the Temple as representing His body, and makes a *first mysterious allusion to His death and resurrection* (see Matt. xxvi. 61, xxvii. 40, 63). He works many miracles and many Jews believe. John ii. 13-25.

At Jerusalem, to a member of the Sanhedrin, the Rabbi Nicodemus, He utters His *First Discourse* about the Birth from Above, one of the clearest proclamations of His Divine nature and mission, containing the whole gospel in epitome, and including a *second mysterious allusion to His Passion.* John iii. 1-21.

In the land of Judæa, His disciples baptize, and large numbers come to Him. John's *third testimony to Jesus* as the Messiah, at Ænon. John iii. 22-36. Westcott regards vv. 16-21 and 31-36 as comments by the Evangelist.

At Sychar, to a Samaritan woman, Jesus utters His *Second Discourse* about the Living Water, and makes the *first distinct avowal that He is the Messiah.* Many Samaritans believe and acknowledge Him as the Saviour of the world. John iv. 1-42.

NOTE.—Taking John iv. 35 literally, Christ must have been eight or nine months in Judæa, and only three or four in Galilee. But John iv. 3, 45 suggests that the Passover of 27 was still recent when He left

Judæa, and the events in Galilee before the Passover of 28 must have occupied at least six months. It may therefore be merely a familiar proverb expressing the interval between seed-time and harvest. The inference from John vii. 11, that He was usually at Jerusalem for the Feast of Tabernacles, determines the date here given.

Fourth Period.

Tabernacles A.D. 27 to Passover A.D. 28 (6 months).

Christ Revealing Himself to the World in Galilee.

Matt. iv. 12-24, viii. 2-4, 14-17, ix. 2-34, xiv. 3-5 ; Mark i. 14—ii. 22, v. 22-43, vi. 17-20 ; Luke iii. 19, 20, iv. 14—v. ; viii. 41-56 ; John iv. 43-54.

"*In the latter time hath He made the land of Zebulun and the land of Naphtali glorious.*"—Isa. ix. 1 (R.V.).

"*Jesus, who went about doing good.*"—Acts x. 38.

Imprisonment of John the Baptist in Castle Machærus on the eastern shore of the Dead Sea. Matt. xiv. 3-5 ; Mark vi. 17-20 ; Luke iii. 19, 20.

At Cana, 2*nd miracle*, healing of fever the son of a nobleman (possibly Chuza). The first Christian household. Matt. iv. 12 ; John iv. 43-54. Westcott refers John iv. 44 to Judæa, not Galilee. Comp. John ii. 24, 25.

On a Sabbath in the synagogue at Nazareth, Jesus preaches, and for the *second time declares Himself the Messiah* in His First Sermon. *First open opposition* from His fellow-citizens, who seek to kill Him. Luke iv. 14-30.

He begins to dwell at Capernaum, and to preach the Gospel to the mixed race of Galileans, "the lost sheep of the house of Israel." Matt. iv. 13-17 ; Mark i. 14, 15.

By the Lake of Galilee, Peter, Andrew, James, and John receive their second and final call, and Peter prays to Christ as to God. First miraculous draught of fishes (3*rd miracle*). Matt. iv. 18-22 ; Mark i. 16-20 ; Luke v. 1-11.

A Great Sabbath at Capernaum, "a day of faith."— In the Synagogue, 4*th miracle*, a demonaic healed (overcoming passion), and 5*th miracle*, Peter's mother-in-law healed (overcoming disease). Many others healed. Demons acknowledge Jesus as Messiah, Son of God, and Holy One of God. Matt. viii. 14-17 ; Mark i. 21-34 ; Luke iv. 31-41.

FIRST CIRCUIT THROUGH GALILEE after solitary prayer.—Multitudes seek Him and come to Him, and great numbers are healed. Matt. iv. 23, 24 ; Mark i. 35-9; Luke iv. 42-4.

In a certain city, *6th miracle*, a leper cleansed (overcoming pollution). Multitudes come to hear and to be healed. Christ retires for solitary prayer. Matt. viii. 2-4 ; Mark i. 40-45 ; Luke v. 12-16.

At Capernaum, *7th miracle*, a paralytic healed (overcoming weakness). Christ's Divine claim to forgive sins leads to a *second opposition*, from the Scribes and Pharisees (comp. Luke vii. 49 ; Matt. xxvi. 65), and a *first accusation of blasphemy*. Matt. ix. 2-8 ; Mark ii. 1-12 ; Luke v. 17-26.

By the Lake, He teaches the multitude who resort to Him, and calls Matthew, who in Capernaum shortly after gives a farewell feast to his friends, at which Christ teaches the universality of the gospel, anticipates His teaching by parables in two vivid similitudes, and makes a *third allusion to His departure*. *Third and fourth oppositions* from the Pharisees (comp. Luke xv. 1 ; Matt. xi. 19), because He received sinners and did not enforce fasting. Matt. ix. 9-17 ; Mark ii. 14-22 ; Luke v. 27-39.

On the same day, *8th and 9th miracles*, a diseased woman healed and the only daughter of Jairus raised from the bed of death (overcoming death). Matt. ix. 18-26 ; Mark v. 22-43 ; Luke viii. 41-56.

10th and 11th miracles, two blind men who acknowledge Jesus as Son of David and a dumb demoniac healed (overcoming loss of faculties). *Fifth opposition* from the Pharisees (comp. Matt. xii. 24), and first suggestion of aid from Beelzebub. Matt. ix. 27-34.

NOTE.—All the typical miracles of healing wrought by our Lord are represented in this Period, and five forms of opposition, recurring hereafter more vehemently, are illustrated.

Fifth Period.

Passover to Feast of Tabernacles, A.D. 28 (6 months).

CHRIST IN CONFLICT WITH THE WORLD. FROM THE FIRST SABBATH CONTROVERSY WITH THE PHARISEES TO THEIR OPEN AND BLASPHEMOUS REJECTION OF HIM.

Matt. iv. 25—viii. 1, viii. 5-13, x. 2-4, xi. 2-19, xii.; Mark ii. 23—iii.; Luke vi. 1—viii. 3, 19-21, xi. 14—xii. 12; John v.

"*They that seek after my life lay snares for me.*"—Psalm xxxviii. 12.
"*Consider Him that hath endured such gainsaying of sinners.*"—Heb. xii. 3.

SECOND PASSOVER.—*Fourth visit to Jerusalem.* At the pool of Bethesda, 12*th miracle*, a man impotent for 38 years healed on the Sabbath. Brought, it seems, before the Sanhedrin, and accused of Sabbath-breaking and blasphemy, Jesus claims to be Son of God and Son of Man, and the Prophet whom Moses foretold; assumes God's highest attributes, lays bare their worldliness and blindness, and declares that not only the Baptist and His own works, but Moses, and the Scriptures, and God Himself, all that they most professed to honour, bear witness to Him. Henceforth the Pharisees *seek to kill Him*, this *first deliberate hostility* from them fixes His doom, and He leaves Jerusalem probably for 18 months. John v.

On a Sabbath shortly after the Passover, in the cornfields near Capernaum, Christ vindicates the Law from superstition, declaring Himself greater than the Temple; and on another Sabbath, in the synagogue at Capernaum, heals a man with a withered hand (13*th miracle*). Because He thus protests against the perversion of a divinely given benefit into a burden, the Nationalist party of the Pharisees and the Romanising party of the Herodians *consult together for His destruction.* Matt. xii. 1-14; Mark ii. 23—iii. 6; Luke vi. 1-11.

By the Lake, great multitudes follow Him, and many are healed. Demons again acknowledge Him the Son of God. Matt. xii. 15-21; Mark iii. 7-12.

After solitary prayer, He appoints twelve of His disciples

Apostles: viz., two sons of Jonah, *Simon* surnamed Cephas or Peter, and *Andrew*; two sons of Zebedee and Salome, *James* and *John*, both surnamed Boanerges (all four fishermen); and *Philip* (all five of Bethsaida); Nathanael, or *Bartholomew* (*i.e.*, son of Tolmai); three (or four?) sons of Alphæus and Mary, *Matthew* or Levi, the taxgather, *Thomas* or Didymus, *James*, and *Judas* surnamed Lebbæus or Thaddæus, son (or brother?) of James (all five of Cana); *Simon* the Canenæan or Zealot (*i.e.*, follower of Judas of Giscala, and therefore a Jew of the strictest and most patriotic type), and *Judas* son of Simon. The surname Iscariot (*i.e.*, of Kerioth in Judæa) may belong (John vi. 71, R.V.) to both these two last. Matt. x. 2-4; Mark iii. 13-19; Luke vi. 12-16.

Having thus laid the foundations of His Church, Christ utters on Kurn Hattin, the mountain by the Lake of Galilee, the SERMON ON THE MOUNT, its new Law, "the Magna Charta of our faith." Summary:—(*a*) The Citizens of the Kingdom. (1) Their character in *nine Beatitudes*; showing that true blessedness lies in what we *are*, not in what we *have* (Luke xii. 15); (2) Their influence, to preserve and to guide. (*b*) The New Law as a fulfilment of the Old Law, both generally and specially. (*c*) The New Life. (1) Its acts of devotion; (2) Its aims; (3) Its conduct; (4) Its dangers. (*d*) The Great Contrast described in the 1*st parable* of the *Two Foundations*, Matt. iv. 25 — viii. 1; Luke vi. 17-49.

In Capernaum, 14*th miracle*, Christ heals of paralysis the servant of a Roman centurion, already a proselyte to Judaism, who becomes the *first Gentile believer*, and whose faith Christ specially commends. Matt. viii. 5-13; Luke vii. 1-10.

At Nain, 15*th miracle*, He raises a widow's only son from the bier, and is recognised as a great Prophet. Luke vii. 11-16.

In answer to the Baptist's question, He appeals to His miracles as proofs that He is the Coming One of prophecy, and bears witness to His Forerunner. Matt. xi. 2-19; Luke vii. 17-35.

At Capernaum, in a Pharisee's house, a sinful woman bears witness to Jesus as the Messiah by solemnly anointing Him. His forgiveness of her rouses *fresh opposition* from the Pharisees, stimulated by the recent organisation of His followers, and the growing enthusiasm of the people. *2nd parable* of the *Two Debtors.* Luke vii. 36-50.

SECOND CIRCUIT THROUGH GALILEE.—The first Christian sisterhood. Luke viii. 1-3.

A GREAT DAY OF CONFLICT AT CAPERNAUM.—16*th miracle,* blind and dumb demoniac healed. The people are ready to acknowledge Jesus as Son of David, but the Pharisees and Scribes from Jerusalem affirm that He works miracles through Beelzebub, and choose darkness for their portion by this deliberate and conscious enmity. Hitherto Christ had avoided open collision with the religious leaders of the people. Now He passes from self-defence to rebuke, shows that His power is at once superior to and contrary to Satan, that the old demon of idolatry had only given place to new demons of self-righteous unbelief, and warns them that their wilful rejection of the revelation of His presence and power would be sin against the Holy Ghost (1 Cor. xii. 3), and therefore unpardonable. In answer to the *second demand for a sign* He gives Jonah, making a *fourth allusion to His death and resurrection,* and declaring Himself greater than Jonah or Solomon. Matt. xii. 22-45; Mark iii. 20-30; Luke ix. 14-36.

Interruption and interference from His mother and brethren (probably the children of Joseph's first marriage) leads Him to expound the difference between natural and spiritual kindred. Matt. xii. 46-50; Mark iii. 31-5; Luke viii. 19-21.

Dining afterwards with one of the Pharisees, He first calls them hypocrites, utters His *first great declaration of a triple woe* upon them, and referring to the national treatment of all God's messengers, makes *a fifth allusion to His departure.* The Pharisees vehemently seek to ensnare Him, and in presence of a great multitude He teaches His disciples to fear God only. Luke xi. 37—xii. 12.

NOTE.—Sowing began in October, when the early rains ended the long summer drought, and recalled the husbandman to the plough. Hence the multitude of Luke viii. 4, xii. 1, may have been pilgrims to the Feast of Tabernacles, and the Twelve were probably sent forth as soon as the people had returned home. These are the only indications of date to fix the limits of this Period.

THE GOSPELS.

SIXTH PERIOD.

Tabernacles, A.D. 28, to Passover, A.D. 29 (6 months).

CHRIST IN CONFLICT WITH THE WORLD. FROM THE FIRST TEACHING OF THE MULTITUDE BY PARABLES TO THE CULMINATION OF HIS POPULARITY AND LARGE DEFECTION OF HIS FOLLOWERS.

Matt. viii. 18—ix. 1, ix. 35—xi. 1, xiii. 1—xiv. 1, 2, 6-36; Mark iv. 1—v. 21, vi. 1-16, 21-55; Luke viii. 4-18, 22-40, ix. 1-17; John vi.

"*I will open my mouth in a parable.*"—Psalm lxxviii. 2.
"*A man approved of God unto you by mighty works and wonders and signs.*"—Acts ii. 22.

A GREAT DAY OF PARABLES.—From a boat on the Lake, Christ utters *five* and in the house afterwards *three parables* of the Kingdom of Heaven: viz., (*a*) *The Sower* (its origin from God). (*b*) *The Secret Growth* (its unperceived progress). (*c*) *The Tares* (its counterfeit by the devil). (*d*) *The Mustard Seed* (its progress in outward extent). (*e*) *The Leaven* (its progress in inward influence). (*f*) *The Hid Treasure* (the kingdom as a gift from Heaven to men). (*g*) *The Merchant seeking Pearls* (as a power in the individual). (*h*) *The Drag Net* (as a wide working instrument among men leading to the final separation between good and evil). Matt. xiii. 1-53; Mark iv. 1-34; Luke viii. 4-18.

Just as He is about to cross the Lake, He answers two aspirants to discipleship, suggesting what is involved in following Him. Matt. viii. 18-22.

On the Lake He calms a great storm (17*th miracle*). In the country of the Gerasenes on the eastern shore of the Lake, He heals a savage demoniac, who acknowledges Him the Son of God, and sends him as a missionary to his own people in Decapolis (18*th miracle*). The permission given to the legion of demons to enter some swine, stirs up *the first popular opposition* to Christ. Matt. viii. 23—ix. 1; Mark iv. 35—v. 21; Luke viii. 22—40.

Nazareth *rejects Christ for the second time*. Matt. xiii. 54-8; Mark vi. 1-6.

THIRD CIRCUIT THROUGH GALILEE.—He sends forth the *Twelve Apostles* to the Twelve Tribes of Israel to proclaim the kingdom of heaven as the *first Missionaries of His Gospel*, thus converting followers into fellow-workers; and gives them the *first Pastoral Charge* concerning the extent and character of their mission; their conduct and responsibility; and the inevitable persecution and unfailing reward of His messengers in all future ages. The reference to His coming again and the *first mysterious mention of the Cross* form a twofold *sixth allusion to His departure*. He then continues His own circuit. Matt. ix. 35—xi. 1; Mark vi. 6-13; Luke ix. 1-6.

At Machærus (or in the palace at Julias), Herod's Feast takes place, leading to the martyrdom (after at least 18 months' imprisonment) of the Baptist. Matt. xiv. 1, 2, 6-12; Mark vi. 14-16, 21-29; Luke ix. 7-9.

Shortly before the THIRD PASSOVER, at Bethsaida Julias on the east side of the Lake, whither He has retired with the Apostles newly returned from their mission, Christ feeds more than 5000 people (*19th miracle*, the only one recorded in all the Gospels). They acknowledge Him as the Prophet foretold by Moses, and attempt to make Him King by force. He retires for solitary prayer, and meets His disciples on their way to the western shore, walking on the sea (*20th miracle*). They acknowledge Him Son of God, and at Capernaum a great multitude gather round Him to be taught. Many are healed. Matt. xiv. 13-36; Mark vi. 30-55; Luke ix. 10-17; John vi. 1-24.

In the synagogue at Capernaum, Christ's Feast leads to His most profound teaching about spiritual life. Answering the *third demand for a sign*, in a twofold sermon to the multitude (v. 26-40) and to the Pharisees (v. 41-59), He declares Himself the true Bread of Life from Heaven, whose flesh would be given for the life of the world, *the first clear public allusion to His Passion*. He has thus made His most unreserved public declaration of His character and claims, calling on men to believe not merely in His words, but on Him; and this demonstration of the spiritual character of His Kingdom results in a great winnowing of His disciples, the first instance of the offence of the Cross. *Many depart from Him*, but Peter in the name of the Twelve confesses Him the Holy One of God. For the first time He refers to Iscariot's treachery. John vi. 25-71.

SEVENTH PERIOD.

Passover to Feast of Tabernacles, A.D. 29 (6 months).

CHRIST REVEALING HIMSELF TO HIS DISCIPLES IN OUTLYING HEATHEN REGIONS.

Matt. xv.—xviii.; Mark vi. 55—ix.; Luke ix. 18-50; John vii. 1.

"*I will also give thee for a light to the Gentiles.*"—Isa. xlix. 6.

"*We were eye-witnesses of His majesty . . . in the holy mount.*"—2 Peter i. 16, 18.

FOURTH AND FINAL CIRCUIT THROUGH GALILEE.—Mark vi. 55, 56; John vii. 1.

In answer to the Scribes and Pharisees who came *as spies from Jerusalem to discredit Him* with the Galileans, Christ shows how their tradition had perverted the Law, abolishes caste, and anticipates the abrogation of Mosaic ceremonialism. Matt. xv. 1-20; Mark vii. 1-23. (With Mark vii. 19, R.V., compare Acts x.)

Departing to Phœnicia, in consequence of their malignant hostility, He is acknowledged as Son of David by the *first believer from heathendom*, a Canaanite by birth, a Greek by language, and a Roman citizen by position, so representing the three most influential peoples of the Pagan world. He tests and then commends her rare faith (Gal. iii. 7, 9), and heals her demon-vexed daughter (21*st miracle*). Matt. xv. 21-28; Mark vii. 24-30.

In Decapolis, a half-heathen region between Damascus and Jabbok, He heals a deaf man (22*nd miracle*), and many others, and is followed by a great multitude (comp. Mark v. 20), 4000 of whom He feeds (23*rd miracle*). They glorify the God of Israel. Matt. xv. 29-38; Mark vii. 31—viii. 9.

On His return to the western shore of the Lake at Dalmanutha, the Pharisees, in ominous coalition with the *Sadducees who now oppose Him for the first time*, make a *fourth demand for a sign*. In His last public teaching in Galilee, He again gives them the sign of Jonah, *type of His death and resurrection (eighth allusion)*, and warns His disciples against their hypocrisy. Matt. xv. 39—xvi. 12; Mark viii. 10-21.

Crossing the Lake again, at Bethsaida Julias He heals a blind man (24*th miracle*). Mark viii. 22-6.

At Cæsarea Philippi, a great centre of heathen worship, after He has prayed, His teaching and the Apostles' faith culminate in *Peter's great Confession* of Him as Messiah, Son of the Living God. Solemnly ratifying it, Christ makes *first mention of His Church*, and lays the cornerstone of the New Society on this fundamental truth, promising Peter the privilege of being the first to proclaim it both to Jew and Gentile. (See Acts ii., x.) This is followed by the *first clear prophecy of His death and resurrection* at Jerusalem to the Twelve, and a *second mysterious mention of the Cross*. Matt. xvi. 13-28; Mark viii. 27—ix. 1; Luke ix. 18-27.

One night a week later on Mount Hermon, as He prays, *Christ's revelation of Himself culminates* in the vision of His Glory given to Peter, James, and John. The two greatest representatives of the Law and the Prophets are in converse with Him *concerning His death*, and a *Second Voice from Heaven*, heard by the three Apostles, proclaims Him God's beloved and chosen Son. *Second clear prophecy of His sufferings*. Identification of the Baptist with Elijah. At the foot of the Mount, He preaches faith as the only source of strength, and heals an epileptic boy (25*th miracle*) Matt. xvii. 1-21; Mark ix. 2-29; Luke ix. 28-43.

During a farewell secret journey through Galilee, He utters the *third clear prophecy of His betrayal, death, and resurrection*. Matt. xvii. 22, 23; Mark ix. 30-32; Luke ix. 43-5.

At Capernaum, He provides the half-shekel tribute (Exod. xxxviii. 26) for Himself and Peter, but while thus teaching obedience, shows Himself Lord of the Temple, Son of the King of Kings, and Ruler over creation (26*th miracle*). He teaches His disciples concerning humility, stumbling-blocks for others, and unselfishness, rebuking the selfish ambition and rivalry which the Twelve begin to display; fixes the extent and limit of toleration; and in the 11*th parable* of the *Merciless Servant* exacting a debt 1,250,000 times smaller than the one he had been forgiven, explains the Christian law of forgiveness. Incidentally, He again refers to Himself as the Messiah. Matt. xvii. 24—xviii. 35 ; Mark ix. 33-50 ; Luke ix. 46-50.

EIGHTH PERIOD.

Tabernacles, A.D. 29, to Passover, A.D. 30 (6 months).

CHRIST REVEALING HIMSELF TO HIS DISCIPLES JOURNEYING TOWARDS JERUSALEM. FINAL REJECTION BY JERUSALEM, SAMARIA, AND GALILEE.

Matt. xi. 20-30, xix., xx.; Mark x.; Luke ix. 51—xi. 13, xii. 13—xix. 28 ; John vii. 2—xi.

" *Who hath believed our report ?* "—Isa. liii. 1.

" *Preaching good tidings of peace by Jesus Christ (He is Lord of all).*"—Acts x. 36.

Christ refuses to go publicly to the Feast of Tabernacles, but secretly pays His *Fifth visit to Jerusalem,* and in the midst of their talk concerning Him in the Temple, vindicates His Sabbath miracles, and declares that He is sent by God. Much discussion as to whether He is the Messiah. At the close of the Feast, He utters His great promise of the Holy Spirit, with a 12*th allusion to His departure* whither they could not find Him. *Unsuccessful attempt to arrest Him,* and division among the people and in the Sanhedrin. John vii. 2-52.

Teaching in the Temple next morning, He defeats a base *plot by the Pharisees to ensnare Him,* and compels these self-righteous religionists to condemn themselves, while He exercises the Divine prerogative of forgiveness. In the Treasury, He declares Himself the Light of the World, and the great object of faith to the multitude, many of whom believe. Then He analyses the unbelief of the Jews, showing Himself the Son of God, and discriminating children of Abraham through faith from children of the devil through unbelief. After *the* 13*th and* 14*th allusions to His departure* whither they could not find Him, and *to the lifting up of the Son of Man,* He closes the discussion by claiming for Himself the absolute sinlessness which He elsewhere attributes to God only (Luke xviii. 19), and assuming the great name I AM. They violently oppose

Him, making a *first attempt to stone Him*. John vii. 53—viii. 59.

As He begins His last solemn progress towards Jerusalem (see p. 247), He is *rejected by a Samaritan village*, and shows how His mission differs from that of Elijah. Luke ix. 51-6.

At another Samaritan village, He heals ten lepers (27*th miracle*), and accepts the faith of one. Luke xvii. 11-19.

He crosses Jordan into Peræa, followed by multitudes. Matt. xix. 1, 2 ; Mark x. 1.

After giving three illustrations of the sacrifices of true discipleship, He sends forth the *Seventy Disciples*, whose number is typical of the seventy nations of the earth reckoned by the Jews, to preach the coming of God's kingdom, especially to the heathen of the outlying districts. He receives the tidings of their success with joy and thanksgiving, declaring Himself the Son of God, and uttering a terrible woe on the highly favoured scenes of His chief teaching which had now utterly rejected Him, followed by an invitation to the weary and heavy laden of the whole world. Luke ix. 57—x. 24 ; Matt. xi. 20-30.

A lawyer's tempting question leads to the 12*th parable* of the *Good Samaritan*, teaching the brotherhood of all men, and showing Christ as the minister of mercy when law and sacrifice had failed. At Bethany on Olivet, He visits Martha and Mary, and teaches concerning the one thing needful. After praying in a certain place, He teaches His disciples the LORD'S PRAYER as the model of all prayer, and in the 13*th parable* of the *Friend at Midnight* enforces prayer as the chief means of grace. Luke x. 25—xi. 13.

In answer to an ill-judged request, Christ shows the folly and sin of covetousness in the 14*th parable* of the *Rich Fool*; and discourses concerning God's providence, illustrates watchfulness by the 15*th parable* of the *Servants waiting for their Lord*, makes a 15*th allusion to the Passion* as His baptism of suffering, and closes with the 16*th parable* of the *Barren Fig-tree*, on the coming judgments of God. Luke xii. 13—xiii. 9.

In a synagogue on the Sabbath, He heals an infirm woman (28*th miracle*), rousing an utterly unreasonable *opposition*, but shaming all His adversaries. Discourse on the way to Jerusalem concerning the Narrow Door, and the universality and spirituality of the Kingdom of God. Message to Herod, *first prediction of the Fall of Jerusalem*, and 16*th allusion to His death* as taking place there. Luke xiii. 10-35.

In the house of a chief Pharisee on the Sabbath, He heals a dropsical man (29*th miracle*), and rebukes struggles for precedence in the 17*th parable* of the *Great Supper*, showing how the last are made first. Luke xiv. 1-24.

Surrounded by great multitudes, He bids them count the cost of discipleship, making *a third mention of the Cross, in the parables* of the *Unfinished Tower* and the *Prudent King*. *Parables*, in answer to *Pharisees murmuring*, of the *Lost Sheep* (the guileless wanderer from the Church), the *Lost Drachma* (the lost slumberer in the Church), and the *Prodigal Son* (the wilful apostate from the Church), testifying the free mercy to men of God the Son, God the Spirit working through the Church, and God the Father. *Parables* of the *Provident Steward* (reproof of worldliness and covetousness), of *Dives and Lazarus* (closing with an *allusion to His resurrection from the dead*), and of the *Unprofitable Servants*. General lessons of forbearance, forgiveness, faith, and humility. Luke xiv. 25—xvii. 10.

In answer to the Pharisees, He shows the character of the Kingdom of God, and utters to the disciples a *fourth clear prophecy of His sufferings and rejection*, speaking of His Second Coming. 26*th* and 27*th parables* of the *Importunate Widow* and of the *Pharisee and Publican*. Luke xvii. 20—xviii. 14.

In answer to an *ensnaring question by the Pharisees*, He shows the provisional character of the Mosaic legislation and enunciates the Christian law of marriage. Matt. xix. 3-12; Mark x. 2-12.

He welcomes and blesses little children, and shows the young ruler, a half-hearted rich man, that God claims us and ours wholly, making a *fourth mention of the Cross*. Further discourse with the disciples concerning riches leads to the 28*th parable* of the *Labourers in the Vineyard*, showing that in Heaven there are no struggles for precedence; and that God looks at the quality not the quantity of our services; not at what we *do*, but at what we *are*, neither to ourselves nor to the world, but in His own sight. Matt. xix. 13—xx. 16; Mark x. 13-31; Luke xviii. 15-30.

In December, Feast of Dedication, *Sixth visit to Jerusalem*. On the Sabbath day, after *a 21st allusion to the coming night when He could work no longer*, Christ heals a man born blind (30*th miracle*), who becomes the first confessor of Christ to his cost and the first conscious sufferer for His sake. To him Christ clearly reveals Himself as the Son of God. The new congregation and new spiritual Temple of which he is a type are described in the Parabolic Discourse of the Good Shepherd, wherein Christ *clearly and publicly foretells His voluntary death, in terms implying His Resurrection*. John ix.—x. 18.

In Solomon's Porch, answering an impetuous appeal from the divided people concerning His Messiahship, He appeals to His work as its proof and declares Himself one with God. *Second attempt to stone Him.* John x. 19-39.

He retires to Bethany beyond Jordan, and the many (probably former disciples of the Baptist) who there believe constitute His last large following. John x. 40-42.

At Bethany on Olivet, after prayer, He raises Lazarus, dead four days, from the grave (31*st miracle*), in this crowning miracle proclaiming His absolute power over death ere He submits to it. Martha confesses Him Messiah and Son of God. Thereupon the Sanhedrin, in which the Sadducæan party predominates, close the long controversy by *formally determining on His death*. He retires to Ephraim, near Bethel, with His disciples. John xi. 1-54.

On the final journey from Ephraim to Jerusalem, alone with the Twelve, Christ utters the *fifth clear prophecy of His suffering* (quoted Luke xxiv. 7), stating that in fulfilment of Old Testament prophecy He should be mocked, scourged, and crucified by Gentiles, and rise again the third day. Matt. xx. 17-19; Mark x. 32-4; Luke xviii. 31-4.

Salome's ambitious request for her sons is checked by the announcement that He had come *to give His life for a ransom* (24*th allusion*). Matt. xx. 20-28; Mark x. 35-45.

In Jericho, He heals two blind men, who acknowledge Him Son of David (32*nd miracle*). Matt. xx. 29-34; Mark x. 46-52; Luke xviii. 35-43.

In Jericho, He lodges, self-invited, with the tax-gatherer Zacchæus, a whole-hearted rich man, and in the 29*th parable* of the *Minæ* teaches *His departure* to receive a kingdom and return, to judge every man according to his *works* (comp. 34*th parable*). Luke xix. 1-28.

Discussion at Jerusalem as to whether Jesus will come for the Passover. John xi. 55-7.

NINTH PERIOD.

Nisan 9 to 16 A.D. 30 (one week).

THE PASSION OF CHRIST.

Matt. xxi.—xxvii.; Mark xi.—xv.; Luke xix. 29—xxiii.; John xii.—xix.

"*The Lord hath laid on Him the iniquity of us all.*"—Isa. liii. 6.

"*Who loved me, and gave Himself up for me.*"—Gal. ii. 20.

SATURDAY, MARCH 31.—At Bethany, in Simon's house, Christ accepts Mary's homage as an anointing to *prepare Him for burial* (26*th allusion*). Many believe through seeing Lazarus. Matt. xxvi. 6-13; Mark xiv. 3-9; John xii. 1-11.

SUNDAY, APRIL 1.—*Seventh visit to Jerusalem.* Triumphal entry to claim His heritage and give the Jews a final choice between accepting or rejecting their *King*. The enthusiastic crowd of provincials receive Him with acclamation as the Son of David, but amid their shouts He mourns over the obstinate unbelief of the city He came to deliver, and utters a *second prediction of its Fall.* (Note that on this day the paschal lamb was chosen: Exod. xii. 3.) Matt. xxi. 1-11, 15-17; Mark xi. 1-11; Luke xix. 29-44; John xii. 12-19.

MONDAY, APRIL 2.—On the road from Bethany to Jerusalem, He condemns the fig-tree whose unusually early show of leaves had no corresponding promise of fruit. By this 33*rd miracle*, the only miracle of destruction, He completes the 16th parable, symbolises the inevitable ruin of the impenitent Jews, warns against hypocrisy, and illustrates the power of faith. Matt. xxi. 18, 19; Mark xi. 12-14.

At Jerusalem, *Second Cleansing of the Temple* by Christ the *Priest*, as a Judge pronouncing condemnation, to prepare it for His final preaching there (comp. p. 254). Many are healed in the Temple. Matt. xxi. 12-14; Mark xi. 15-19; Luke xix. 45-8.

TUESDAY, APRIL 3.—On the way into Jerusalem the fig-tree is found withered. THE GREAT GAINSAYINGS IN THE TEMPLE, a *final combined attempt to ensnare Him*. He meets the demand of a formal deputation from the Sanhedrin "By what authority?" with an unanswerable preliminary question; and in the 30*th*, 31*st, and* 32*nd parables* of the *Two Sons*, the *Wicked Husbandmen*, and the *Wedding Garment at the Marriage of the King's Son*, claims to be God's last great Messenger to His people, and instructs concerning false profession, abused privileges, and lost opportunities, and the coming blessing for the Gentiles. The people still take Him for a *Prophet*. He answers the Pharisees' and Herodians' test by showing that they had themselves acknowledged Cæsar by accepting his coinage; the Sadducees' test by Mosaic proof of the future life; and the Lawyer's test by a perfect summary of the whole Law. He then puts them all to silence by His counter-question concerning David's Son; proving His double claim to the throne of David and of God. Matt. xxi. 20—xxii.; Mark xi. 20—xii. 37; Luke xx. 1-44.

Sevenfold woe foretold to the Scribes and Pharisees whose hypocrisy made void the Law they professed to honour. Christ refers to Himself as Messiah, and by mention of the one Father, the one Master, and the one Teacher (see R.V.), indicates the relation of the whole Trinity to man, and closes with a *third prediction of the Fall of Jerusalem*. Commendation of a widow, teaching that the essence of charity is self-denial. Matt. xxiii.; Mark xii. 38-44; Luke xx. 45—xxi. 4.

In response to the request of some *Greeks* (first fruits of Europe, the Christendom of the future), who come to His cross from the West, as the Magi came to His cradle from the East, Christ, after prayer, *completes His self-revelation to the World*, foretelling that *when lifted up* He will draw all men to Him. A *Third Voice from Heaven*, heard by the gathered crowd, confirms His words. On leaving the

Temple finally, He makes a last appeal to men in the Father's name, to which S. John prefixes a comment explaining His rejection, and referring to Christ Isaiah's vision of the Lord of Hosts. John xii. 20-50.

On Olivet, Christ discourses to the Twelve of the Last Things, dealing with their four questions as to the (*a*) *time* and (*b*) *sign of the Fall of Jerusalem* (*predicted for the fourth time*), and the (*c*) *time* and (*d*) *sign of His appearing and the end of the world.* He passes from judgment of the Rulers and of Jerusalem to judgment of the whole World, in the *three last parables*, 33rd, 34th and 35th, of the *Fig-tree and all Trees*, the *Ten Virgins* (the Church watching), and the *Talents* (the Church working; every man judged according to His *opportunities*: comp. 29th parable), and the Discourse on the Son of Man judging those who had not known the Law. He closes by a *28th allusion to His death by crucifixion* two days thence. Matt. xxiv., xxv., xxvi. 1, 2 ; Mark xiii. ; Luke xxi. 5-38.

Meanwhile the Sanhedrin, maddened by the public exposure of their hypocrisy, meet to arrange the manner of His arrest, and *bribe Judas to sell his Master* to them for the price of the meanest slave, one-third of the price of what Mary had lavished in loving homage. Matt. xxvi. 3-5, 14-16 ; Mark xiv. 1, 2, 10, 11 ; Luke xxii. 1-6.

WEDNESDAY, APRIL 4, an unrecorded day of solemn preparation for the Passion, spent at Bethany.

THURSDAY, APRIL 5 (Nisan or Abib 14). S. John's introductory words. John xiii. 1. Peter and John sent to Jerusalem to make preparation for the FOURTH PASSOVER. Matt. xxvi. 17-19 ; Mark xiv. 12-16 ; Luke xxii. 7-13. Christ with the Twelve enters the Upper Room in Jerusalem for the Paschal Feast. The first cup (of consecration) passed round and hands washed. Matt. xxvi. 20 ; Mark xiv. 17 ; Luke xxii. 14-18. He settles the dispute about precedence which arose when they were taking their places by washing their feet Himself. Luke xxii. 24-30 ; John xiii. 2-17. The Lamb, etc., is then set out, the bitter herbs eaten, the dishes removed, the second cup filled, and the inquiry concerning the Feast asked and answered (Exod. xii. 26, 27 ; Deut. xxvi. 5-9). After this, the first part of the great Hallel (Psalms cxiii, cxiv.) is sung, the second cup passed round, and the hands washed again. As the unleavened bread is dipped in the sauce which commemorated the mortar of their bondage, with another thanksgiving, Christ foretells His betrayal, indicates to Peter and John the traitor, utters his awful doom, and dismisses him to complete his treachery. Matt. xxvi. 21-5; Mark xiv. 18-21; Luke xxii. 21-3; John xiii. 18-35.

Then the lamb is eaten, and during the subsequent distribution of unleavened bread followed by the third cup (of blessing) Christ institutes *the Sacrament of the Lord's Supper* as a perpetual memory of *His precious Death* until His coming again. Matt. xxvi. 26-9; Mark xiv. 22-5; Luke xxii. 19, 20; 1 Cor. xi. 23-5. The fourth cup (of joy), the second part of the Hallel (Psalm cxv.—cxviii.), and a final prayer and thanksgiving conclude the last true Paschal Feast. Christ thrice foretells Peter's denial, and again speaks of His sufferings as fulfilling prophecy. John xiii. 36-8; Luke xxii. 31-8; Matt. xxvi. 30-35; Mark xiv. 26-31.

Christ *completes His self-revelation to His Apostles* by His *Last Discourse* concerning the Paraclete sent by the Father and the Son to testify of Him to men. He deals with His relation to the Father and to His disciples, with the law and progress of revelation, gives them a new commandment, and *for the 30th time refers to His departure.* After leaving the Upper Room, He utters the Parabolic Discourse of the Vine and its Branches, typifying their union with Him and love for one another in face of the world's hatred; and speaks of the Paraclete's testimony to the world and to the Church, of sorrow turned into joy and failure issuing in victory. Then our great High Priest offers Himself as Victim in His *Prayer of Consecration* for Himself (v. 1-5), His apostles (v. 6-19), and all believers (v. 20-26). Westcott suggests that this may have been uttered in the Temple Courts, which were thrown open at midnight during the Passover. John xiv.—xvii.

Crossing Kedron, Christ enters the Garden of Gethsemane on the slope of Olivet. His solitary prayer and mysterious Agony, as the Sinless One bearing our sins, "the sufferings of His soul forming the soul of all His sufferings," is witnessed by the Three who had seen His Glory. Matt. xxvi. 36-46; Mark xiv. 32-42; Luke xxii. 39-46; John xviii. 1, 2.

He is betrayed by Judas, and, after display of His power that proves Him a willing Victim (John x. 18), is arrested by the emissaries of the Sanhedrin, and heals Malchus' ear (34*th miracle*). After a futile resistance, the disciples all forsake Him. Matt. xxvi. 47-56; Mark xiv. 43-52; Luke xxii. 47-53; John xviii. 3-12.

FIRST TRIAL soon after midnight, in the High Priest's house at the north-east corner of Mount Zion, by Annas the legitimate, though deposed, High Priest. No witnesses are brought, but Jesus is *practically condemned to death*, and insulted by the servants. John xviii. 13, 14, 19-23; Luke xxii. 54.

SECOND TRIAL in the same house, by Caiaphas, the actual High Priest, and an informal gathering of part of the Sanhedrin. False witnesses accuse Him of speaking against the Temple, perverting His words. Questioned by the rulers of the nation, He confesses Himself Messiah and Son of God, and is *potentially condemned to death* for "blasphemy." *First Derision* as Messiah by the High Priest's servants. Matt. xxvi. 57-68; Mark xiv. 53-65; Luke xxii. 63-5; John xviii. 24. In the courtyard below, Peter, who has followed with John, being questioned by two or three servants, thrice denies his Lord. Matt. xxvi. 58, 69-75; Mark xiv. 54, 66-72; Luke xxii. 55-62; John xviii. 15-18, 25-7.

FRIDAY, APRIL 6 (First Day of Unleavened Bread).— THIRD TRIAL at dawn, in the Gazith or Hall of Polished Stones, or some other chamber adjoining the Temple on Mount Moriah, by a formal assembly of the Sanhedrin. Again He confesses Himself Messiah and Son of God, and is *formally condemned to death by the ecclesiastical authorities*. Matt. xxvii. 1, 2; Mark xv. 1; Luke xxii. 66-71.

The suicide of Judas. Matt. xxvii. 3-10; Acts i. 18-20.

FOURTH TRIAL in the Prætorium or official residence of the Roman governor in the castle of Antonia, north of the Temple on Mount Moriah, by Pontius Pilate, procurator of Judæa. *First accusation* of sedition against Rome, the pretext for demanding His death being that He threatened to use force to establish His Kingdom, while the real offence in their eyes was that He would not use force. He makes no reply, but in a first private interview with Pilate acknowledges Himself King of the Jews with a kingdom not of this world. First warning to Pilate in the awe-inspiring aspect of his Prisoner. *1st acquittal* by Pilate. *Second accusation* of insurrection. Pilate's *first expedient* of sending Him to Herod. Matt. xxvii. 2, 11-14; Mark xv. 1-5; Luke xxiii. 1-7; John xviii. 28-38.

FIFTH TRIAL in the old palace of the Asmonean princes on Zion, by Herod Antipas, tetrarch of Galilee. *Third accusation* met with unbroken silence. *Second Derision* as King by Herod and his soldiers. *2nd acquittal* by Herod. Return to the Prætorium. Luke xxiii. 8-12.

SIXTH TRIAL in the Prætorium by Pilate, who, after a *3rd declaration of His innocence*, proposes for a *second expedient* to release Him as an act of artificial grace, not plain justice, and receives in his wife Claudia Procula's message a second warning. But the Jews ask for Barabbas, the brigand and murderer. For the Holy and Righteous One they demand that most shameful and painful form of death which was reserved for felonious slaves. After a *4th acquittal* Pilate scourges Jesus, and He endures a *Third Derision* as King from the Roman soldiers. As his *third expedient*, Pilate brings Him before the people, saying, "Behold the Man," and pronouncing a *5th acquittal*. Mention of the Son of God awes him with a third warning, and in a second private interview Christ calmly judges His judge. Mounting his tribunal for the third time, Pilate makes a final attempt to release Christ, washing his hands with a *6th acquittal* of "this righteous man." The maddened people accept the guilt of His blood, loudly professing allegiance to their Roman conqueror only, and thus disclaiming all their Messianic hopes, and demanding *formal condemnation to death by the civil authorities* of their true King, which Pilate at last pronounces. Matt. xxvii. 15-31; Mark xv. 6-20; Luke xxiii. 13-25; John xviii. 39—xix. 16.

Rejected by the Pharisees, condemned by the Sadducees, denounced by the multitude, and forsaken by His own disciples, Jesus is led to death by the Romans. On the way He utters His last Sermon and *fifth prediction of the Fall of Jerusalem* to the pitiful women who bewail Him. Simon bears His cross. Matt. xxvii. 32; Mark xv. 21; Luke xxiii. 26-32; John xix. 17.

About nine o'clock, at Golgotha, He refuses the soporific offered to alleviate the anguish of crucifixion, and is nailed to the cross between two robbers with a superscription in the three languages of the civilised world over His head, just as the morning daily sacrifice is being offered. *First Word* of priestly Intercession for the impenitent. He is mocked by the members of the Sanhedrin as Saviour, Messiah, and King of Israel; by the soldiers as King of the Jews; and by the multitude as Son of God. Matt. xxvii. 33-44; Mark xv. 22-32; Luke xxiii. 33-8; John xix. 18-24. *Second Word* of royal Grace for the penitent and believing robber (the first Jew won by the Cross). Luke xxiii. 39-43. *Third Word* of tender Love and care for His Mother. John xix. 25-7.

Noon. Three hours of supernatural darkness and awful silence begin. Three o'clock. *Fourth Word* of spiritual Agony. *Fifth Word* of physical Agony. *Sixth Word* of Triumph. *Seventh Word* of calm Trust, and then our Saviour yields up His spirit just as the evening daily sacrifice is beginning, and the first Sabbath trumpet sounding. The *sign from heaven* so long clamoured for appears, the Rent Veil of the Temple proclaims the Law abrogated and man brought nigh to God, earth quakes, the rocks are rent, and the tombs are opened. The centurion confesses Him righteous Son of God (the first Gentile won by the Cross), and the multitude mourn and fear exceedingly. Matt. xxvii. 45-56; Mark xv. 33-41; Luke xxiii. 44-9; John xix. 28-30.

In the evening, Joseph of Arimathaea obtains Pilate's permission to take away the body of Jesus, and when His death has been proved by the soldier's spear thrust, Joseph and Nicodemus bury Him with all possible honour in a new tomb in a garden near Golgotha, just as the wave sheaf (comp. Lev. xxiii. 10, 11; 1 Cor. xv. 20), is carried across Kedron. Matt. xxvii. 57-61; Mark xv. 42-7; Luke xxiii. 50-56; John xix. 31-42.

SATURDAY, APRIL 7, the Sabbath.—The disciples rest. The priests secure a guard for the tomb. Luke xxiii. 56; Matt. xxvii. 62-6.

Tenth Period.

Between Passover and Pentecost, A.D. 30, Nisan 17 to Sivan 3 (40 days).

The Resurrection and Ascension of Christ.

Matt. xxviii. ; Mark xvi. ; Luke xxiv. ; John xx., xxi.

"*Thou hast ascended on high.*"—Psalm lxviii. 18.
"*Now hath Christ been raised from the dead.*"—1 Cor. xv. 20.

SUNDAY, APRIL 8 ("The first Lord's Day").—In Joseph's garden, before dawn, there is a great earthquake, and Christ is raised from the dead, being thus *for the fourth time declared* (Rom. i. 4) *the Son of God.* Matt. xxviii. 2-4.

In the morning twilight, Mary of Magdala visits the tomb, and departs with the news that the Lord is not there. Matt. xxviii. 1 ; John xx. 1, 2.

At daybreak, Mary wife of Alphæus, Salome wife of Zebedee, Joanna wife of Chuza, and other women visit the tomb, and hear of the Resurrection from an angel, who sends them to tell the Apostles. Matt. xxviii. 1, 5-8 ; Mark xvi. 1-8 ; Luke xxiv. 1-11.

Mary of Magdala returns to the tomb with Peter and John, who find it empty and depart. John believes. *First Appearance* of the Risen Lord to her at the tomb. Luke xxiv. 12 ; John xx. 3-18 ; Mark xvi. 9-11.

Second Appearance to the other women returning to Jerusalem. Matt. xxviii. 9, 10.

Third Appearance to Peter. Luke xxiv. 34 ; 1 Cor. xv. 5.

The Sanhedrin bribe the guard to promulgate an impotent fabrication. Matt. xxviii. 11-15.

Fourth Appearance in the evening, on the road to Emmaus, to Cleopas and another. The Lord discourses on His fulfilment of Old Testament prophecy, and is made known to them "in the breaking of the bread." Mark xvi. 12, 13 ; Luke xxiv. 13-32.

Fifth Appearance, later in the evening in the Upper Room at Jerusalem, to ten Apostles and other disciples.

The Lord's *first charge to His Church to evangelise the world*, and His Easter evening gifts to it: viz., peace (comp. John xiv. 27), assurance, understanding, spiritual authority, power to work miracles, and the Holy Spirit quickening them with new faith in anticipation of His endowing them with new power at Pentecost. Mark xvi. 14; Luke xxiv. 33-48; John xx. 19-23; 1 Cor. xv. 5.

SUNDAY, APRIL 15. *Sixth Appearance* in the evening in the same Upper Room to the Eleven Apostles. Thomas worships Him as Lord and God. John xx. 24-9.

Seventh Appearance by the Lake of Galilee to Peter, James, John, Thomas, Nathanael, and two others, probably Philip and Andrew (viz., the six first called and the convinced doubter). 35*th miracle*. Second miraculous draught of fishes, typical of the gathering in of a perfect Church in heaven, as the 3rd miracle had been typical of the gathering in of a militant Church on earth. The Lord again made known "in the breaking of the bread." Peter's threefold confession undoes his threefold denial. John xxi. 1-23.

Eighth Appearance on Kurn Hattin, in Galilee, to the Eleven and more than 500 disciples. He receives their homage as Lord of heaven and earth, and shows how the Chosen People of the past give place henceforth to the Universal Church of the future. He institutes *the Sacrament of Baptism* in the name of the Trinity as the rite of admission into it, and gives a *second charge to His Church to evangelise the world*, promising power to fulfil the command, and His abiding Presence till the consummation of the age. Matt. xxviii. 16-20; Mark xvi. 15-18; 1 Cor. xv. 6.

Ninth Appearance to James, "the brother of the Lord," 1 Cor. xv. 7. (There were but three to individuals in all. Acts i. 3 suggests other unrecorded Appearances.)

THURSDAY, MAY 17 (ten days before Pentecost).—*Tenth Appearance* in Jerusalem to the Eleven, whom He leads out to Bethany. After renewing His promise of the Spirit, and giving a *third charge to His Church to evangelise the world*, from Mount Olivet, while blessing them, He ascends to Heaven, where He ever liveth to make intercession for us, until He comes again in like manner as He went up. Mark xvi. 19, 20; Luke xxiv. 49-53; Acts i. 3-12; 1 Cor. xv. 7

S. John's Epilogue on the purpose of the Gospels, and a confirmation of his narrative, probably added by the Ephesian elders.   John xx. 30, 31 ; xxi. 24, 25.

" *By the mystery of Thy holy Incarnation ;*
By Thy holy Nativity and Circumcision ;
By Thy Baptism, Fasting, and Temptation ;
By Thine Agony and bloody Sweat ;
By Thy Cross and Passion ;
By Thy precious Death and Burial ;
By Thy glorious Resurrection and Ascension ;
And by the coming of the Holy Ghost,

GOOD LORD, DELIVER US."

NINTH TERM.

THE DAYS OF S. PAUL.
THE GOSPEL PREACHED TO THE GENTILES.

A.D. 51—97.

Acts XV.—XXVIII. 1 *Thessalonians.* 2 *Thessalonians.* 1 *Corinthians.* 2 *Corinthians. Galatians. Romans. Philippians. Colossians. Philemon. Ephesians.* 1 *Timothy. Titus.* 2 *Timothy.* 1, 2, *and* 3 *John. Revelation.* (130 *chapters.*)

"Thou hast known the sacred writings which are able to make thee wise unto salvation through faith."—2 TIM. iii. 15.

33rd MONTH (32).
  Acts XV.—XVIII. 17, 1 and 2 Thess. Acts XVIII. 18—XIX. 20. 1 Cor. Acts XIX. 21—XX. 1. 2 Cor. I.—III.

34th MONTH (32).
  2 Cor. IV.—XIII. Acts XX. 2. Gal. Rom.

35th MONTH (33).
  Acts XX. 3—XXVIII. Phil. Col. Philem. Eph. 1 Tim. Titus.

36th MONTH (33).
  2 Tim. 1, 2, 3 John. Rev.

I. GENERAL SUMMARY.

NO one chapter in the intertwined and unfinished history of mankind can be altogether isolated from its other chapters. Having rounded off the story of the literal Israel, the people who were chosen to be a kingdom of priests in the past (Exod. xix. 6), we must trace its connexion with the story of the spiritual Israel, chosen to be a kingdom of priests in the present (Rev. i. 6, R.V.: see p. 5). Israel was called out of the world; the Church is placed in the world, though not of it. Extraordinary privileges as regards God and extraordinary obligations as regards man characterise both. One nation only God knew and made

Himself known to (Amos iii. 2). Yet while Gentiles knowing only false gods were desiring the true God (Acts xvii. 23), Israel went after other gods whom they knew not (Jer. vii. 9), and so God removed them from their place among the nations, and "the times of the Gentiles" began.

From B.C. 606 to A.D. 45 they were prepared for the Gospel, just as Israel had been prepared for the Law from B.C. 1921 to 1490 (see p. 25). Individual Gentiles had already received blessing through contact with Israel (see p. 162, Question XXX.). And when the nations who had been scattered at Babel (Gen. xi.) were re-united under Nebuchadnezzar (Jer. xxvii. 4-7), Israel, hitherto kept apart, was placed in the midst of them to bear witness in the Gentile tongue to the true God (Jer. x. 11, R.V. margin; Dan. iii. 29); and the Psalms which we have called "the Missionary Hallel" (p. 209), anticipated blessing through Israel to all the world. Not only have Jew and Gentile lived in closest contact with each other since B.C. 606, but the history of the whole world may be grouped round that of the twelve tribes of Israel, whose names are on the gates of the City of the Future (Rev. xxi. 12; comp. Deut. xxxii. 8).

As we have seen, the Church in its infancy appeared to be only a sect of Jews who believed that the Messiah had come, and emphasized the Pharisaic doctrine of the Resurrection (Acts xxiii. 6). Christ's own fulfilment of the Law consisted in its spiritualisation, and once at least He had pointed to its abrogation (Mark vii. 19, R.V.). He sought Gentiles as well as Jews (John iii. 16, xii. 32), and strongly commended Gentile faith (Matt. viii. 10, xv. 28). But the first Christians seem to have had no clear conception of their faith as the one worldwide religion with whose expansion the ceremonial Mosaic Law would vanish away. The Greek in which the New Testament is written is symbolical of the universality of its revelation, and it was one of the greatest of Greek-speaking Jewish Christians, S. Stephen, who first enunciated two new truths as cardinal as the two uttered at Sinai (see p. 54). (*a*) All men, both Jews and Gentiles, are equally unacceptable to God in view of their fallen and sinful condition, and all are equally acceptable to God if they call upon Him through Christ (Rom. iii. 9, 22, 23, x. 12, 13). (*b*) The Mosaic Covenant is temporary and imperfect (Heb. viii. 13).

Let us now trace the application of these principles. S. Peter anticipates the first in Acts ii. 39, iii. 26; and it was acted on in the successive admissions to the Church of the Samaritans, somewhat heretical followers of Moses; of Candace's treasurer, a proselyte of the gate; and of Cornelius and his household, all of whom could hardly have been proselytes. But it was at Antioch that some Cyprian and African missionaries first preached to Gentiles as Gentiles (Acts xi. 20, R.V.). There the emergence of the Church from Judaism was further marked by the name "Christian," invented by the quick-witted Antiochenes and formed by adding a Latin suffix to the Greek translation of a Hebrew idea (comp. John xix. 20). That it was at first used by the world opprobriously, is clear from each recurrence of it in the New Testament (Acts xi. 26, xxvi. 28; 1 Peter iv. 16). Later on the Church adopted it and gloried in it (James ii. 7). It shows that our faith is not centred in a doctrine, but in a Person.

Meanwhile the Apostle through whom God "caused the light of the Gospel to shine throughout the world" had been called, and the mystery of a Gentile Church had been revealed to him (Eph. iii.; Acts xxvi. 16-18). Step by step he acted upon this revelation (Acts xiii. 46, xiv. 15, 27, xv., xviii. 6), and taught in accordance with it. (Rom. i. 16). And so we come to the most memorable journey on record (Acts xiii.), the first definite act of obedience to our Lord's last command (Mark xvi. 15). For in contrast to the Old Dispensation, where the *Proselyte* sought admission into Israel's congregation, in the New Dispensation the *Apostle* went out to seek converts whom he might lead into the Church. Divinely guided, S. Paul and his companions went westwards towards the scenes of the epoch-making events in the world's future history.

Three circumstances were in his favour, through which God had prepared men to receive the truth :—

(*a*) The intellectual conquest of the world by Greece had produced a unity of language, so that the Apostles speaking and writing in Greek were everywhere understood.

(*b*) The material conquest of the world by Rome had produced a political unity, which gave them free scope and fair protection everywhere.

(*c*) The dispersion of the Jews had carried some knowledge of the One True God and some purer notions of morality into many parts, and the heathen were often reached through the proselytes, of whom the larger number were women (Acts xiii. 50, xvii. 4, 12).

On the other hand, he had greater difficulties to contend with than any missionaries could have now in any part of the world. Disowned and cast out at Jerusalem, he carried a message to the Jews concerning the abrogation of their cherished exclusive privileges; despised and loathed as a Jew, he had to tell the Gentiles of a revelation that would supersede all their national beliefs and transcend all their proudest philosophies. But he went for Christ and with Christ, and God chose weak things that He might shame the things that were strong.

In A.D. 51 the Church contained these seven classes of Christians:—(*a*) Strict Hebraists, such as those in Acts xxi. 20. (*b*) Liberal Hebraists, such as S. Peter, Acts xi. 3. (*c*) Strict Hellenists, such as those in Acts ix. 29. (*d*) Liberal Hellenists, such as S. Paul. (*e*) Proselytes of Righteousness who were circumcised, such as Nicolas, Acts vi. 5. (*f*) Proselytes of the Gate who were uncircumcised, such as Cornelius. (*g*) Heathen converts, such as Trophimus, Acts xxi. 29. He is a type of nearly all the Christians of to-day, and he belongs chronologically to the last class brought into the Church (see Farrar's "Life of St. Paul." Cassell, 6*s*.).

What was to be the relation of this class to the Mosaic Law? Over that question arose the first controversy. It was settled, not without loss of velocity through friction meanwhile, but with ultimate gain, theoretically at the first synod of the Church, and in S. Paul's second group of Epistles; practically, just 40 years after the Resurrection, by the Fall of Jerusalem.

S. Paul recognises four stages in the world's history dating from four persons, of whom the first like the last stands at the head of a long line of representatives:—

(*a*) Relative innocence ending in *Sin* in *Adam*, whose transgression developed a death-working principle.

(b) Awakened conscience and *Promise* in *Abraham*.
(c) Imputable transgression and *Law* in *Moses*.
(d) Free justification and *Gospel* in *Christ*, whose righteousness developed a new life-working principle. The Law of Moses had shown the need of this, and it fulfilled the Promise to Abraham. In Christ the Law found both its accomplishment and its conclusion, in one word, its "end" (Rom. x. 4), as He Himself indicated (Matt. xi. 13).

For its relation to the Gospel, work out this summary.

The *Law* was negative, particular, complex, preparatory, temporary, and easy to act up to, in that it controlled *deeds*. It uttered precepts and commands, requiring works and saying, "Thou shalt love," "Do and live" (Deut. iv. 1).

The *Gospel* is positive, general, simple, final, eternal, and hard to act up to, in that it controls *motives*. It utters principles and sanctions, requires faith, and says, "God so loved," "Live and do" (Rom. viii. 2-4).

The moral Law still binds us, not as the condition of our acceptance before God, but as an evidence of our acceptance by God before men.

The relation of Judaism to Christianity is not that of error to truth, but of the bud to the flower, of the child to the man, of the dawn to the day, of the acorn which perishes when it has germinated to the oak which it has produced. "Tear up the Jewish root, and the Christian branch will perish," thought Titus when he took Jerusalem. In reality its Fall settled the Judaic controversy; separated Christians from Jews finally in the eyes of the heathen; cut the cords which bound the new faith to a local habitation, and enabled it to become worldwide. In S. John's writings Jew and Gentile stand undistinguished in the same fold.

Why did Titus desire to destroy Christianity? For in Acts, which records twelve separate persecutions that S. Paul suffered from the Jews (1 Thess. ii. 14-16) we see the Roman power protecting him from his own compatriots; the heathen indifferent, curious, tolerant, and docile, but only hostile on those rare occasions when fears for their worldly interests were roused. In ancient days worship of other gods by Gentiles had been recognised if not actually permitted (Deut. xxix. 25, 26). But later on the prophets call on all men to worship one God only (Jer. xvi. 19-21). And when the Gentiles found that Christianity always and everywhere claimed to be not only *a* religion, but the one true religion, they resented this claim. In 64 the First of Ten heathen Persecutions of the Church broke out, and thenceforth the Empire was at war with the Church until A.D. 313. See Blunt's "Christian Church during the First Three Centuries," chap. viii. (Murray, 6s.).

Israel's religion had never before won other nations or saved Israel from ruin; Gentile wisdom had proved powerless to arrest decay of all forms of belief, and universal depravity of morals. Yet 1900 years ago, from the midst of Jewish weakness and Gentile uncleanness (Job xiv. 4), there sprang a new thing irresistibly mighty, and not only clean but cleansing, which has been the salt of the earth ever since. Secular history seeks to account for this in vain. We know that the new principle of life which made this marvellous change possible was the indwelling Spirit of God working through the Church of the Living Jesus.

II. Books to be Read.

(See "Oxford Helps," § xv.)

Save for the remaining chapters of the Acts, our reading this term is wholly of the two greatest authors of the Apostolic age, S. Paul and S. John, with one of whom we now make our first acquaintance. Poetry is not an element that we commonly recognise in the New Testament. But besides the parallelism in many of our Lord's discourses, the poetical structure of some of His parables, and such rhythmical outpourings as Rom. viii. 29-39, xi. 33-6; 1 Cor. xiii. 1-8, xv. 35-58; 2 Cor. vi. 3-10; James v. 1-6, it contains one whole book, which is in the highest sense poetry, viz., the Apocalypse.

Acts xv.—xxviii. tells of the Gospel's progress westward from its cradle in Jerusalem to Rome, the capital of the world, and dwells, with all the minute accuracy of a contemporary historian and eye-witness, upon those parts of S. Paul's career during which S. Luke was his companion. It breaks off suddenly at the eve of the Neronian persecution, concerning which it would have been unsafe to speak freely, and we must glean the events of the last thirty-four years of our period from less complete records. The keynote of Acts xv.—xxviii. is *The Gentiles are fellow-heirs and fellow-partakers of the promise.*

S. Paul's thirteen Epistles fall into four groups, and should always be read in their chronological order. Six were written to Europe (viz., three to Macedonia, two to Achaia, and one to Italy), three to Asia Minor, and four to individuals. Of the churches S. Paul addresses, five had been founded by him. (1 Cor. v. 9; 2 Cor. x. 9; Col. iv. 16; 2 Thess. iii. 17, indicate that he may have written other letters not preserved.) As a rule, his Epistles consist of six parts: (*a*) Solemn Salutation; (*b*) Expression of Thankfulness for God's work in the church addressed; (*c*) Religious Doctrine; (*d*) Practical Exhortation; (*e*) Personal Details and Greetings. (*f*) Autograph Benediction as a mark of authenticity. (The notes at the end, which R.V. omits, are very late, and in some cases evidently erroneous.) But we misunderstand the Epistles if we try to reduce them to regular subdivisions as so many set treatises on abstract doctrine. Clause by clause they were dictated to his children in the faith, as he sat stitching the coarse tent cloth, and wondrous thoughts of things Divine were welling up within him. From his heart to their hearts, and to our hearts, he speaks, with all the tenderness and all the familiarity of personal intercourse, and in these living utterances of a living man the expositions of truth are incidental. Each thought leads on to the next, not by a process of elaborate reasoning, but by a natural association of ideas. There is in them not formal system, but spontaneous coherence and sequence. Each Epistle should be looked at apart from the rest. Each should be read swiftly at a sitting, as well as studied in detail, that its general purpose and character may be duly apprehended.

FIRST GROUP.—*The Advent Epistles*, written at Corinth in 52, and addressed to a Macedonian Church, whose religion was practical and straightforward. Hence they are the simplest of all in their matter and manner, and deal with Christian life rather than Christian doctrine. Their subject is the Second Coming of Christ, and our preparation in patience and watchfulness for it. Undue curiosity as to the time of the end is discouraged.

1 *Thessalonians* was occasioned by Timothy's return with cheering news of Thessalonian steadfastness. Its tone is very sweet and consolatory. S. Paul commends the Church as a whole, admonishes the sinful, comforts the sorrowful, and concludes with general exhortation. Its keynote is *The Coming of our Lord Jesus with all His saints*.

2 *Thessalonians* was occasioned by the erroneous inferences which had been drawn from the former letter. The Advent must be unexpected, but it may not be near. Its keynote is *The Revelation of the Lord Jesus with the angels of His power*. S. Paul's favourite trilogy of Faith, Hope, and Love pervades both epistles.

SECOND GROUP.—The *Anti-Judaic Epistles*, written in 57 and 58, in the midst of physical and mental trials which have left deep traces on their style. Their subject is Individual Christian Life, God's Grace and our Faith. Compared with Macedonian, Achaian religion was more enlightened, but more conceited and of lower type morally.

1 *Corinthians*, written in Ephesus at the Passover of 57, was occasioned by a letter asking questions as to marriage, things offered to idols, spiritual gifts, public worship, collections, and the Resurrection. S. Paul shows that there may be love and unity where there are different opinions, and that practical details of life should be decided by eternal principles. Its keynote is *Take heed, be steadfast, and let all ye do be done in love*.

2 *Corinthians*, written at Philippi (?), is in two parts. Ch. i.—ix., occasioned by a cheering account of the church from Titus, whose keynote is *Transient light affliction and eternal weight of glory*; ch. x.—xiii., occasioned by news of a fresh attack upon S. Paul's authority, and written in a sterner and more sorrowful tone, whose keynote is *In nothing behind the very chiefest Apostles*. Of all the Epistles this is the one in which we see deepest into S. Paul's heart.

Galatians, written at Corinth in 58 (?), was occasioned by news that the Galatians were forsaking the freedom of Christ for the bondage of Moses. It is "a trumpet note of defiance to the Pharisees of Christianity." It falls into three parts of two chapters each, personal, historical, and practical, and its keynote is *Neither circumcision nor uncircumcision, but a new creature.*

Romans, written at Corinth in 58 in expectation of visiting the capital, fills the central place in S. Paul's writings, both chronologically and doctrinally, and contains the sum of his theology, dealing in the largest and most general way with the universality of sin and the universality of grace. Galatians is like a rough sketch for it. Its keynote is *The revelation of the Righteousness of God*; and we may sum up its main argument thus : "The Gospel is the power of God unto salvation because it contains the revelation of a righteousness. This is needed because God's wrath is upon sin, and all, both Jews and Gentiles, have sinned (i.—iii. 20). God offers man a salvation, whose freeness the Old Testament illustrates and vindicates, whose effects, as we ourselves know, are immediate, progressive, and ultimate. It is a reversal of the Fall, a lifting up of the individual life above sin ; a complete deliverance from sin and its consequences (iii. 21—viii.). The relation of this Gospel to the Jew is a sorrowful story, but it involves no injustice on God's part, and will be gloriously compensated hereafter (ix.—xi.). The practical results of this Gospel should be dedication of ourselves to God, devotion to duty in all the relations of life, in submission to authority, love, toleration, conscientiousness, in one word, in imitation of Christ (xii.—xv.)." Or we may say the Epistle shows the dealings with men of God the Father (i.—iii. 20), God the Son (iii. 21—vii.), God the Holy Ghost (viii.) ; or see, as its dominating ideas, Faith (iii.—vii.), Hope (viii.), and Love (xii. xiv.). Faith, which links God's righteousness and man's justification, is mentioned some sixty times. Those who know something of Greek can have no more helpful guide to the understanding of Romans and of S. Paul's Epistles generally than Dean Vaughan's edition of its Greek text with notes (Macmillan, 7s. 6d.).

THIRD GROUP.—*The Anti-Gnostic Epistles*, all written at Rome in 63. They deal with loftier and more mysterious themes than the earlier ones, and show throughout thought enriched and ripened, and growth both in grace and wisdom. Their subject is Corporate Christian Life, and Christ as God and Man.

Philippians, occasioned by the visit of Epaphroditus, and written to a church which seems to have been to S. Paul what the household of Bethany was to his Master, falls, like Galatians, into personal, doctrinal, and practical sections Its keynote is *Press on and rejoice always*.

Colossians, occasioned by the return of Onesimus, combats error. Its keynote is *Christ is the Head of the Church, and in Him dwelleth all the fulness of the Godhead*.

Philemon, written and sent together with Colossians, forms "the practical manifesto of Christianity against the horrors and iniquities of slavery." Its keynote is *No longer as a bondman, but as a brother beloved*.

Ephesians, which may have been a circular letter to all the Asiatic churches (i. 1, R.V. margin), builds up truth. Its keynote is *The Church is Christ's Body, the fulness of Him that filleth all in all*. It may be called the Epistle of the Ascension.

FOURTH GROUP.—*The Pastoral Epistles*, manuals of practical discipline rather than expositions of doctrine. They have not the depth and grandeur of the earlier epistles, their purpose being wholly different. Their subject is the Work of the Ministry, Being and Doing. The trilogy of Faith, Hope, and Love again becomes prominent.

1 *Timothy*, written from Macedonia in 65 or 66, has least structural unity of all the epistles. Its keynote is *Teach healthful words, and the doctrine which is according to godliness*.

Titus, written from Macedonia in 66, has for keynote *Those who are God's must be godly*.

2 *Timothy*, written from his Roman prison in 67 to implore his best-beloved disciple to come to him quickly, contains S. Paul's last brave and tender words, and its keynote is *Through the cross to the crown*.

The three Epistles of S. John were probably written at Ephesus during his last years. 1 *John* is addressed to the Church generally, and especially to Gentile Christians in Asia Minor. Its recurring thoughts are Light, Life, Truth, Abiding, and above all Love ; and its keynote is *Eternal Life through the Incarnation of the Eternal Word*.

2 *John*, one of the three private letters in the New Testament which illustrate Christian intercourse rather

than Christian doctrine, is addressed to a lady of uncertain name and abode, with her children. This fact in itself indicates the new value attached to womanhood and childhood in Christ. Its keynote is *Love in truth and truth in love*.

3 *John* is addressed to a hospitable Christian who bore the common name of Gaius. Its keynote is *Imitate not the evil, but the good*. The use of the word "friends" in the last clause is peculiar to S John. Comp. John xi. 11, xv. 14, 15.

All that S. John teaches might be inferred from S. Paul's writings, but the last of the Apostles sums up Divine revelation in a clear and final exposition of loftiest truth, which transcends the controversies of earlier days. The Judaic question has fallen into the background; and S. John opposes those subsequent heresies which all began and ended with denial of the doctrine that Christ is truly God and truly Man, by showing forth truth rather than combatting error. He makes three great declarations about God. God is Light, God is Love, God is Righteous. He expresses our Christian privileges through three conceptions brought out through a threefold metaphor. (*a*) That of Righteousness from the law court, looking at Christ as the Righteous One (1 John ii. 1, 29). (*b*) That of Sonship from the household, looking at Christ as the Son (1 John iii. 1, 8). (*c*) That of Sanctification from the Temple, looking at Christ as the Holy One sacrificed (1 John iii. 3, 5, i. 7). He uses *eternal*, not in antithesis to *temporal*, but to *seen*. He speaks of eternal life, not as that which shall be, but as that which *is* for all believers.

Revelation. That this is a work by S. John of special value and importance, forming a fit climax to the whole Word of God, is certain. Its exact date and its meaning are far less easily determined. Internal evidence connects it with two startling and most important events, the first great outbreak of Heathen Persecution by Nero in 64, when all the world hated the Christians on the false charge that the Christians hated all the world; and the Fall of the Jewish Nation (66—70). Those who had lived through the anguish and tumult of that time, and seen its awful bloodshed, would find more than poetic metaphor in such passages as Rev. xiv. 19, 20. If written then it is S. John's earliest work. But external evidence connects it with the Second Persecution of the Church by Domitian in 96, and some of its pictures of judgment seem drawn from the eruption of Vesuvius in 79, which must have made an even deeper and wider impression than Uzziah's earthquake of old (Amos i. 1). In any case, S. John's Gospel, in which we find the deepest teaching of the whole Bible, was doubtless later than the Apocalypse; yet our Cycle most fitly completes its revolution with this New Testament counterpart of Daniel. For (*a*) Its new Heavens and Earth, its Paradise, and River, and Tree of Life, its gold and pearl and precious stones, its Bridegroom and Bride carry us back to the first pages of revelation, and show how God's will regarding man, though thwarted for a time, will be gloriously fulfilled to all eternity. (*b*) It is the last magnificent development of divinely inspired prophecy. (*c*) It possesses at once the unity of a great poem, and the gorgeousness of a dream, and thus closes the diapason with a transcendent note of music. (*d*) It gathers up all the rest of the Bible in its allusions, and looks furthest into the future. (*e*) "The Revelation of Jesus Christ" (that is the correct name of a book often ignorantly called "The Revelations of John") is the last gift of the glorified Saviour to His Church. Old Testament witness beforehand, New Testament preparatory prophecy, Christ's own witness to Himself on earth, and the Apostolic witness to Him later on, are all consummated by His final witness to Himself from Heaven. Its keynote is *The revelation of the Risen Christ as the Lord God.*

Rev. i. 19 is a table of contents for the whole book. Ch. i. refers to the Past, chs. ii., iii. to the Present. Chs. iv.—xxii. contain visions certainly past as visions when S. John described them, and certainly prefiguring things that were Future to him. The question is how far are they future for us? Here interpreters of three different schools come forward.

(*a*) The *Preterists*, who point to the word "shortly" in Rev. i. 1, and say that they have been fulfilled in the past. Sodom is Jerusalem, Babylon is heathen Rome; and the book finds its great and sufficient theme in the downfall of these two cities which had drunk so deeply of the blood of the saints. Just as Daniel's "vile person" was Antiochus Epiphanes, so Nero, to whom divine honours were blasphemously paid, is the Beast out of the Sea, and the Beast out of the earth (evidently the same as the False Prophet) is probably Simon Magus. The Sun-clad Woman is the Primitive Church in its flight to Pella. The earliest commentators favour this interpretation, and a general expectation that the world would end in A.D. 1000 sprang out of dating the 1000 years of Rev. xx. 4 from the foundation of the Church.

(*b*) The *Presentists*, or Historical School, who say that they are being fulfilled in the present, that Revelation is a synopsis of anticipated history, either of the whole world or of the Church. This view is not much more than 600 years old, and the greatest diversity exists among its exponents as to the application of details, and the point we have now reached chronologically.

(*c*) The *Futurists*, who say that they are to be fulfilled in the future. Between ch. iii. and ch. iv. there is a gap of at least 1800 years. These interpreters have generally been few in number, but they have had representatives in all ages.

Without attempting to judge between the three views, one or two principles may be laid down for those students of Scripture who do not undertake to be authoritative exponents of it.

(1) The Apocalypse is a book of *signs*, and the use of similar signs elsewhere will be our best key to them. We must be consistent in our explanations. A dried-up river is more possible than a woman riding a seven-headed beast. We are not therefore to regard one as literal and the other as figurative.

(2) No book is so saturated with Old Testament allusion. Hence the Old Testament meanings of the various things alluded to must be reckoned with.

(3) Our own century and continent are large to us out of proportion to their real size. Hence those whose knowledge of other ages and regions is limited rashly assert that the Apocalypse is full of the events of to-day.

(4) "Divine prophecies," says Bacon, "have steps and

grades of fulfilment through divers ages." Just as Old Testament prophecies had primary reference to David and ultimate reference to Christ, so S. John's visions were for his own generation, and referred to events of his own age in the first instance. This does not exclude the possibility of a wider reference to ages yet to come.

(5) Study of the history of the first century will to some extent unravel the primary reference. The ultimate reference must remain more or less dim until all is fulfilled.

(6) Meanwhile the preciousness and sacredness of the book lie deeper than either. Whatever its details mean, it enunciates two things unmistakably. (*a*) As "a Christian philosophy of history," it shows that the affairs of men in all ages and places are governed by God. (*b*) It also shows that although falsehood and evil are potent, truth and goodness will prove omnipotent in the world which a good God made. Christ will triumph. Those who hate Him will perish, those who love Him will be unspeakably blest. Could the persecuted Church, feeble, despised, and opposed by both the "religious" and the secular world, have met her foes without the spiritual tonic of this Divine encouragement?

III. PERIODS AND DATES.

That Claudius expelled the Jews from Rome in A.D. 52, that Festus became Procurator in A.D. 60, and that Nero's persecution of the Christians took place in A.D. 64, are the only fixed points from which we can calculate the chronology of these 46 years. We may fairly think of S. John's life as closing with the first Christian century, but the actual dates assigned to its close vary from 89 to 120. For the details of S. Paul's journeys see "Oxford Helps," §§ xxiv. and xxv., and refer again to the lists of rulers on p. 228.

(1) A.D. 51 to Pentecost 54 (3 years). From the Conference at Jerusalem to S. Paul's last return to Antioch. *S. Paul's Second Journey.* **Acts xv.—xviii. 17; 1 Thessalonians; 2 Thessalonians; Acts xviii. 18-22.**

(2) A.D. 54 to Pentecost 58 (4 years). From S. Paul's last return to Antioch to his Imprisonment. *St. Paul's Third Journey.* **Acts xviii. 23—xix. 20;**

1 Corinthians; Acts xix. 21—xx. 1; 2 Corinthians; Acts xx. 2; Galatians; Romans; Acts xx. 3—xxiii.

(3) A.D. 58—63 (5 years). From S. Paul's Imprisonment to his Liberation. *S. Paul's Captivity at Cæsarea and Rome.* Acts xxiv.—xxviii.; Philippians; Colossians; Philemon; Ephesians.

(4) A.D. 63—67 (4 years). From S. Paul's Liberation to his Martyrdom. *S. Paul's Fourth Journey.* 1 Timothy; Titus; 2 Timothy.

(5) A.D. 67—97 (30 years). From S. Paul's Martyrdom to the close of the New Testament Canon. *The Last of the Apostles.* 1, 2, 3, John; Revelation.

IV. GEOGRAPHY.

(See "Oxford Helps," Maps X., XI., XII.)

Jerusalem, whose church S. Peter founded, became the first metropolis of Christianity, and these five visits paid to it by S. Paul form useful landmarks in his history. (1) Alone in A.D. 40 to see Peter (Gal. i.); (2) with Barnabas in 44 to bring his collection (Acts xi. 30); (3) with Barnabas in 51 to report upon the evangelisation of the Gentiles; (Acts xv.); (4) with Silas and Timothy in 54 to salute the church and keep Pentecost (Acts xviii.); (5) with Luke, Aristarchus, Timothy, Trophimus, and others in 58 to keep Pentecost and bring his collection (Acts xxi.). The extension of the Church from Jerusalem through three different areas, orthodox, heterodox and heathen, is sketched in our Lord's very last words on earth, which are an outline of all subsequent Church history (Acts i. 8).

Antioch, whose church S. Barnabas and S. Paul founded, the third city in the Roman Empire, became the second metropolis of Christianity and the mother church of all the Gentile churches. In his first journey S. Paul went to Cyprus and Asia Minor, in his second he re-visited Syria and Asia Minor, and just half-way through his whole Christian career entered Europe, where Philippi and Thessalonica in Macedonia and Corinth in Achaia became the great centres of Christianity. In his third journey he re-visited Asia Minor and Greece, but spent most of his time at *Ephesus*, whose church he founded, which became the third metropolis of Christianity. Here S. John completed the work of the Apostles, and from its church the Church of England ultimately traces her descent. Then from Cæsarea, Roman capital of Palestine, "Paul the prisoner" was brought to *Rome*, the capital of the whole empire, which became the fourth metropolis of Christianity. Its fifth metropolis was *Alexandria*, second city in the empire, whose church, probably founded by S. Mark, has Apollos for its chief New Testament representative. More than two centuries later, *Constantinople*, the first city which was Christian from its foundation, became the sixth metropolis of Christianity. In its greatness that of Ephesus was merged; and omitting Ephesus these five cities became the seats of the five patriarchates round which early ecclesiastical history groups itself.

All the countries which Acts ii. 9-11 enumerates in their exact geographical order had Christian churches planted in them by the end of the first century. In Palestine, besides the church of Jerusalem, where Simeon, the Lord's brother, presided over a feeble remnant, we hear of churches in Lydda, Joppa, Sharon, Cæsarea, and Samaria; and of Syrian churches in Tyre, Ptolemais, Antioch, and Damascus. In Asia Minor, where we perceive greatest mixture of race in narrowest compass, where Jewish faith, Greek culture, and Roman power all influenced the original inhabitants, churches grew apace, and were some of them old enough to have lost their first love when the Beloved Disciple presided in their midst. There were churches in Cyprus (whose ancient church still preserves its independence through an almost unique history), Macedonia, Achaia, Crete, Illyricum, and Dalmatia, for all of which S. Paul himself had laboured fervently.

From Rome the Gospel had spread westward, ever following the course of the sun, to Spain and Gaul; it had also reached Carthage and Egypt and Ethiopia in the south; and in the east Armenia, Persia, Parthia, Arabia, and perhaps India; beginning in most cases in the synagogue, and spreading from Jew and proselyte to heathen. For in those days every Christian was a missionary, and wherever he went throughout the empire he was received as a brother by humble little companies of fellow-believers. The "Barbarians" outside the empire had not yet been reached, but there were Christians in regions too distant to contain a church, and Christian influences slowly quickening and purifying human life in all its phases in regions which no Christian had yet reached. The story is repeating itself to-day in not a few of "the uttermost parts of the earth"; and now, as then, we know that the issue is certain and glorious.

V. HEROES.

Keynotes { *S. Paul*, Psalm cxvi. 10, 16 (A.V.).
{ *S. John*, Dan. x. 8, 9, 18, 19.

Among Israel's many great men three stand out pre-eminent as her greatest—viz., Moses, of Levi, the founder of her religion and polity; David, of Judah, the founder of her everlasting monarchy; and *S. Paul*, of Benjamin, the chief builder of the Church, in which both her religion and her monarchy are to find their highest realisation. Imagine for a moment the Bible deprived of the Pentateuch, the Psalms, and the Epistles of S. Paul, and you will to some extent estimate the importance of these three. The commanding personality of the last dominates all our reading this term; he occupies 17 out of the 28 chapters of the first Church history, and writes 13 out of the 27 books of the New Testament. He was the first and greatest of missionaries to foreign parts, the Christian who did the grandest life-work for Christ on record, the man who received from Christ's own lips the most ample and splendid commission human being was ever honoured with (Acts xxvi. 16-18). How many events there were in his life of which we know nothing may be gathered from 2 Cor. xi., yet "there is scarce one other person of history," says Dean Vaughan, "so familiarly known to us, Cicero perhaps —perhaps Napoleon—I could scarcely name a third." A great spiritual convulsion cleft his career in twain, when "Saul the Pharisee" became "Paul the Bondservant of Jesus Christ." In a moment he turned, not from an irreligious to a religious life, not from an immoral to a moral life but from a conscientious and honoured antagonism against Christ to a conscientious and passionate devotion for Christ that cost him everything most men hold dear. God revealed His Son to him, Christ apprehended him, that is the only reasonable explanation of this sudden and absolute change. Rightly understood, the story of his "wonderful conversion" checks doubt as to the possibility or reality of conversion to God; it also checks glib talk about conversion as if it meant no more than external reformation, or change of religious opinion, or strong spasm of feeling. And although his conversion was instantaneous, and his knowledge of Christ direct and all-convincing, his public testimony to the truth was preceded by three years of solitary thought and prayer (Gal. i. 17, 18), spent in that wilderness where Moses was taught of God, and where perhaps Christ, as true Man, stood the test of temptation. A pupil of Gamaliel and member of the Sanhedrin, a native of Tarsus, and a Roman citizen, he had been influenced by the religious enlightenment of the Jews, the intellectual sovereignty of the Greeks, and the political supremacy of the Romans, and so became a highly trained instrument in God's hands. For 30 years a Christian, for 27 years a missionary, by his unflinching endurance of keenest temptation, sorrow, and persecution, he not only gave proof of the reality of his conversion, but of the power and reality of the Gospel to which he had been converted. The man who had amplest opportunity and strongest inducement to disprove the Resurrection of Christ, had it been a delusion or an imposture (as some try to assume), sacrificed all to witness to it as a great fact. And this witness is mighty in our days as well as in his.

Notice also that he is, of all missionaries, the most representative, for he dealt with all sorts and conditions of men, bigoted Pharisee, sceptical Sadducee, time-serving Herodian, serious Jew, trifling Greek, practical Roman, dreamy Oriental, and impulsive Barbarian. And his work was done in face of obstacles from without and from within that would have baffled most men. What his thorn (or stake) in the flesh actually was we cannot know certainly, but careful comparison of Acts xxiii. 5; Gal. iv. 12-16, vi. 17, 11 (R.V.); 1 Cor. ii. 3; 2 Cor. iv. 10, v. 4, vii. 5, x. 1, 10; Col. i. 24, indicates that it was an acute form of Oriental ophthalmia, which renders the sufferer blind and helpless, and is at once painful and disfiguring. If he were indeed liable to such a malady, he would be unusually dependent upon companionship; and like Jeremiah, he was surrounded by a group of devoted followers and friends, each of whom deserves separate study.

We owe S. Paul three debts of the first magnitude:— (1) The emergence of Christianity from Judaism; (2) the planting of the Gospel in what is now *the* Christian continent; (3) the shaping of Christian theology, in works whose renewed study has again and again brought renewed spiritual life to different ages and different sons of the Church. How little he himself knew what his consecrated genius was achieving! How little can we judge his missionary successors by what they seem to their own generation to accomplish!

S. John's piety, like that of Samuel, ripened by gradual stages without violent break, from the day that he followed Jesus, as a young and ardent disciple of the Baptist, to the day when he was carried in extreme old age into the church at Ephesus to preach his last sermon, "Little children, love one another," to a new generation in the new age which he had lived to see. His calm, certain, didactic style differs widely from the enthusiastic argumentation of S. Paul. His power of righteous indignation, and that bold faithfulness which brought him only of the Twelve to the foot of the Cross, show that he is most inadequately represented by the feminine-looking youthful S. John of mediæval art.

The first age of the Church's history exhibits three types of the Apostolate reflected in three successive phases of that history. A prism analyses the one brightness into three distinct hues, so the one faith is seen, to our no small advantage, through three individualities. S. Peter, the founder, looking back to the past, dwells on Hope and Christian practice, and is reflected in the Mediæval Church. S. Paul, the propagator, looking at the present, dwells on Faith and Christian doctrine, and is reflected in the Church of the Reformation. S. John, the consummator, looking far into the future, dwells on Love and Christian experience, and foreshadows a type yet to come.

This chapter has dealt wholly with men hitherto.

Women there are in Old Testament history of striking character and great influence, but the mention of "the women" in Acts i. 14 inaugurates a new order of things. Never did any woman directly oppose Christ. Women ministered to Him (Luke viii. 2, 3 ; Matt. xxvii. 55) and spake of Him (Luke ii. 38 ; John iv. 39 ; Matt. xxviii. 5, 7). Women were last at His cross and first at His tomb, and when He rose He appeared twice to women ere He appeared to any man. Woman's true exaltation must be traced to and can only be rightly recognised in connexion with Him who deigned to be born of a virgin ; and the large and fruitful share which women from the first took in the highest work of the Church calls upon us to note heroines as well as heroes henceforth.

VI. THE COMING ONE.

"Christ shall appear a second time to them that wait for Him, unto salvation."—Heb. ix. 28.

Each term we have seen the Hope of the Promise broadening and brightening, and it was not until the God-sent Deliverer had come and gone that inspired pens could sum up all that He was and all that He had done. Again and again history has shown that a creed based upon the idea that Christ was merely the wisest and best of men, who died a martyr's death, is powerless over men's hearts and quickly vanishes away. If Christianity is to be more than a vague sentiment or a dead morality, it must be founded upon three foundation truths concerning Him. All have been taught at all times by the Catholic Church, but all have not always been equally prominent :—

(*a*) His Resurrection. "God raised Him" was the keynote of S. Peter's teaching (Acts ii. 32), the first great startling witness to the world (Acts xxv. 19).

(*b*) His Crucifixion. "He gave Himself for us" was the keynote of S. Paul's teaching (1 Cor. ii. 2). And He had Himself clearly alluded to His atoning work, saying that He would and could be a Ransom for the remission of sins, because He was both Human and Divine (Matt. xx. 28, xxvi. 28, 63, 64).

(*c*) His Incarnation. "He became flesh" was the keynote of S. John's teaching (John i. 14; 1 John iv. 2, 3). The Church is only now entering upon her full heritage in this glorious truth of the Divine Man and Incarnate God, and never has it seemed of such paramount importance as it seems to-day.

Christ Incarnate, Crucified, Risen, reversing the order of time, these truths were successively insisted upon; and there is yet a fourth truth at once earliest and latest of all: Christ Ascended and Coming Again (1 Cor. xvi. 22, R.V.). We end as we began our consideration of the Coming One by looking out into the future. The Old Testament Hope has been fulfilled; our "living Hope" in the New Testament has yet to be fulfilled. We stand, as S. Paul so often shows, between the epiphany of His grace in the past, and the epiphany of His glory in the future, and find a motive power for the present in both (Titus ii. 11-13, R.V.).

Four events, each twofold, in that future of the world's history which we sometimes wrongly regard as an absolutely blank page, have been revealed to us (Rev. i. 1-3).

(*a*) Christ will come for His saints to receive His own to Himself (1 Thess. iv.). Christ will come with His saints to be seen and known of all men (2 Thess. i.; Rev. i. 7).

(*b*) There will be a first resurrection of those who are His, and a second resurrection of the rest of mankind (Rev. xx.).

(*c*) Christ will judge His saints that they may be rewarded according to their works (2 Cor. v. 9, 10). Christ will judge the whole world (Rev. xx.).

(*d*) Christ will reign a thousand years over the earth (Rev. xx.). Christ will reign for ever over the universe (Rev. xi. 15).

Four names are given to this great group of events in the New Testament: (1) That Day (2 Thess. i. 10), the Great Day (Jude 6), or the Day of God (2 Peter iii. 12), or the Day of the Lord (1 Thess. v. 2), or the Day of Jesus Christ (Phil. i. 6), or the Day of our Lord Jesus (2 Cor. i. 14). (2) The Coming (or Presence) of Christ, used seventeen times in all, and especially in the Epistles to the Thessalonians. (3) The Appearing (or Epiphany) of Christ used seven times in the Pastoral Epistles, and not elsewhere. (4) The End or Consummation of all things (1 Peter iv. 7).

Nothing less will solve all problems and abolish all evils, will carry out those purposes of God which for a while were thwarted, will bring about our individual satisfaction and perfection, and the perfection and happiness of the world Christ came to redeem, than this "one far-off divine event, To which the whole creation moves." Unhappily controversy and speculation have been imported into the whole subject to such an extent that many Christians are not a little hindered and troubled in its study, and others doubt that the second Advent will be literal. But most of the arguments against a literal second Coming of Christ are equally applicable to His first Coming, which certainly was literal. A merely figurative coming would contradict the "again" of John xiv. 3, and the emphatic "in like manner" of Acts i. 11.

And as the Jews were blamed for not being better prepared by prophecy for the First Coming, so may we be blamed, if we do not discern in part that which has still to be fully revealed. As usual, the fulfilled prophecy of the Old Testament is the best key to the unfulfilled prophecy of the New Testament.

VII. GOD'S REVELATION OF HIMSELF TO MAN.

Legend says that the Apostles, ere they dispersed from Jerusalem twelve years after the Ascension, assembled to shape the Apostles' Creed as an authoritative statement of Christian doctrine. The fact underlying this tale is that from earliest times there was definite teaching of the leading mysteries of the faith, and before truth was fully expounded in the New Testament, terse summaries of it, as keys to Scripture and safeguards against error, were current in the Church. We are not to regard them as human attempts to define Divine mysteries, but as formulating truth which God had already revealed. The earliest examples of them are Acts viii. 37; 1 Cor. xv. 3-7; Heb. vi. 1, 2; 1 Tim. iii. 16, and the "faithful sayings" of the Pastoral Epistles. Two creeds are now recognised throughout the whole Church. *The Apostles' Creed*, whose substance can be traced back to earliest times, originating in the baptismal profession, and still used for the testing and instructing of catechumens. *The Nicene Creed*, shaped in 325 at the First General Council, and used as a fuller and deeper exposition of truth for testing and instructing communicants. The Western, but not the Eastern Church, adds for the last 1100 years to these *the Athanasian Creed*, a masterly exposition, for the teacher, of the doctrines of the Trinity and of the Incarnation.

The doctrine of the Trinity cannot be explained to our natural faculties (though nature illustrates it in our own threefold being, 1 Thess. v. 23); and the Scriptures contain no formal expression of it. For there was much that Christ Himself could not say till He had risen, much that the Apostles only learned slowly under the Spirit's guidance as they looked back to His earthly and up to His heavenly life. But all the following passages imply it, just as Gen. i. implies without stating the existence of God: Acts vii. 55, x. 38; Rom. i. 4; 2 Cor. xiii. 14; 2 Thess. iii. 5 (comp. Rom. v. 5); Eph. ii. 18, iii. 14, 16, 17, iv. 4-6; 1 Peter i. 2; Rev. i. 4, 5. Notice also that the Creeds fix our attention not on what we are and should do, but on what Christ is and has done (contrast Luke xviii. 11 and Heb. xii. 2), and that God, Three in One, is revealed to us, not in His absolute Being, but in His relation to ourselves. Some bond of union among men connecting each with all through something higher than themselves has, in all ages, been the need of the human heart, but no age has felt and expressed that need so strongly as our own. So acknowledged the intelligent artizan, who was uttering some well-worn cavil at the doctrine of the Trinity, to one of our bishops lately. The bishop silenced his cavil, and won him to holier and truer thought of God by translating that abstract theological mystery into language he could comprehend, thus: "The doctrine of the Trinity expresses three things, the Fatherhood of God, the Brotherhood of God, the Mateship of God."

What is this new relation of God to men of which the Christian revelation speaks? We may put the matter briefly thus. Unless thought is wholly drowned in pleasure and excitement or worldly care, every man is conscious of two things—(*a*) That apart from *vice* whereby we wrong ourselves, and *crime* whereby we wrong others, there is also in us *sin* whereby we wrong God. (*b*) That this sin is unnatural, *i.e.*, is not part of God's law for man, but a bondage whence we would fain be delivered, and whence no outward religious rites and no good resolutions can really deliver us. So we are led to seek and to find a Saviour in Christ.

How does Christ save? He bore, say some, as my Substitute, all the punishment that I deserved to bear. God, like a judge who arbitrarily allows an innocent man to endure the sentence that a criminal has incurred, setting the criminal free, has thus been reconciled to me, and will take me to heaven if I believe that Christ has done this. This too common but most inadequate setting forth of the gospel illustrates it by the imaginary act of a human judge who is guilty of a double outrage upon justice. But righteousness demands righteousness, and cannot accept mere punishment instead. The Scriptural view (as careful students of S. Paul's Epistles especially will see for themselves) is this: Christ, as my Representative, assumed that humanity which He had originally created in His own image, conquered where Adam fell, and by enduring death condemned sin, and saved sinners by uniting them to Himself. Thus He reconciled, not God to me, but me to God, who in His wondrous love had given His Son for us men and for our salvation. He died, and I died in Him, and must therefore reckon myself dead to sin. He lives, and I live in Him, and must therefore live unto righteousness. He gave Himself up for me, and I must therefore give myself up to Him, not by mere intellectual assent to a doctrine, but by personal trust in a personal Saviour. I strive, not upwards *to* salvation, but onwards *from* salvation, not to win heaven for myself, but because He has won it for me "by His precious blood-shedding," and calls upon me and can enable me to walk worthy of what He has done.

From its opening assertion of a Divine Creator, to its closing cry heavenwards of a definite faith and certain hope in a Divine Redeemer, the Bible makes a wondrous ascent. Starting from the being of God and the spiritual nature of man, it leads us up, not through vague propositions, but through historical verities, to that unfathomable revelation of God in Christ which is the key to the understanding of all nature and all history. We still, it is true, know only in part. But instead of mourning over the limitations of our knowledge, should we not rather rejoice that we have an inexhaustible creed and an unsearchable God? (Rom. xi. 33-6.)

VIII. Man's Relation to God in Worship.

Christ left the preservation and propagation of the truth He taught in the hands of the Society which He formed, a body of men all united to each other because they were each united by a real spiritual tie to God, *in* the world, but not *of* the world, extending to all races, all times, and all countries. Acts i. 1 strikes the keynote of the whole history of the Church by representing its work as the continuation of Christ's own. Its power depended on His abiding Presence (Matt. xxviii. 20; John xiv. 18). It witnessed to His truth in four ways which we take chronologically.

(*a*) By its two Sacraments, which are not only rites of entrance and of continued membership to Christians, but ever-recurring declarations to the world of their faith (1 Tim. vi. 12; 1 Cor. xi. 26).

(*b*) By its sacred Seasons. Easter and Pentecost seem to have passed straight into the Church from Judaism, their new significance gradually superseding their old (1 Cor. v. 7, 8; Acts xx. 16). The Lord's Day as a weekly festival of the Resurrection also replaced the Sabbath (Acts xx. 7; Rev. i. 10). That weekly celebration of the Holy Communion was the primitive rule, is suggested by the New Testament, and shown clearly in a recently discovered treatise called "The Teaching of the Twelve Apostles," which is probably the next oldest Christian writing.

(*c*) By the New Testament Scriptures, written by some of its members, and gathered up and preserved as a divinely inspired book by the whole Church.

(*d*) By the Creeds, and by the various liturgical forms which grew up.

In some ages, Christians have been content to listen only to the spoken testimony of the Church without verifying her teaching, each for himself, from the Bible. Then truth has been exaggerated or mutilated, and error has grown apace. In other ages, Christians have been content to listen only to the written testimony of the Bible, saying, "My religion is a matter between God and my own soul, and concerns no one else. What I take to be the meaning of His word is the measure of all truth." Then divisions have sprung up, and internal dissensions have weakened the Church's power for good. Each man, it is true, is directly responsible to God and spiritually free. But each as a Christian is also member of a corporate body. The Church, as the "witness and keeper of Holy Writ" (Article XX.), testifies to the inspiration of Scripture; Scripture attests the truth of what the Church teaches. We must not separate these testimonies. The communion of the Church and the study of the Word are both needed, and beyond and above both we must learn, through the teaching of the Holy Spirit, from the Living Christ Himself. And so we arrive at the threefold evidence of Christianity. (*a*) The personal experience of Christians (John ix. 25; 2 Cor. iv. 13). (*b*) The New Testament Scriptures, which have just come victoriously through fifty years of the ablest and keenest hostile criticism to which any book was ever subjected. (*c*) The unbroken chain of living witnesses, ever lengthening and ever widening with the ages, whose daily worship for more than 1860 years has borne witness to a history for whose truth hundreds, nay millions, have been ready to vouch with their lives. What stronger or more varied authentication could any statements have?

For the regulation of worship, the maintenance of truth, and the preservation of unity, provision was made from the first for a succession of authorised teachers (2 Tim. ii. 2). Regular Christian worship grew out of attendance at the daily services of the Temple (Acts iii.), and there are many traces of it in the New Testament (Acts ii. 42, iv. 24, xiii. 3, xx. 7; 1 Cor. xiv.; Heb. x. 25). The first difference of opinion that arose was settled at the first synod of the Church (Acts xv.). The various Christian communities were federated into one Catholic Church, and although sects dropped off it from time to time, it continued one in intercommunion until 1054. But the notion that the Apostolic Church was ideally perfect in knowledge and practice is most misleading and discouraging. Like other kingdoms, Christ's Kingdom contained both loyal and disloyal subjects, and from the very first the wheat and tares grew together, discriminated only by God. Church history includes some of the saddest and most disappointing as well as some of the most glorious pages ever penned. Turbulent self-conceit, rancorous party strife, grave moral delinquencies, unstable quest of novel teachings, Judaising apostasy (see Galatians) Antinomian error (see Rom. vi.), Gnostic heresies (see Colossians), meet us again and again in the New Testament; and the Pastoral Epistles show that in little more than one generation there were many mere professors as well as true Christians in the Church.

Yet a benumbed and moribund past had given place to a future full of hope and glory, which has become our present. By A.D. 100 the faith of Christ had been firmly established among the three great civilisations of the world, Greek, Roman, and Jewish. Men say the age of miracles is now over. In reply we ask them to look at what is going on to-day in many parts of the Mission Field at home and abroad. There they are not content with *studying* Christian evidence; they *make* it. For there the miracle of changed human hearts and lives, which Christ reckoned the greatest of all, still takes place, through the all-subduing power of His Spirit (John xiv. 12). And remembering that the Church has only within the last century really attempted to carry out systematically her "marching orders" (Matt. xxviii. 19, 20), we recognise that we are only on the threshold of the possibilities of Christianity. The Chronological Scripture Cycle deals with time, but it ends, as it began, in eternity (Rev. xiii. 8; 1 Cor. xv. 28).

IX. QUESTIONS.

(See pp. 13, 18.)

[Questions VII., X., XVI., XVII., and XXV. may be answered with help of any books.]

I. What do you know of S. Paul's father, and of his kinsfolk, also of his education and social position? Quote two passages in which he is called "our beloved." (8.)

II. Make a list of fourteen places at which S. Paul *founded* churches, and a list of churches to which he wrote. (8.)

III. Enumerate the seven occasions on which he was enlightened or encouraged by a vision of the Lord or of His angel. (7.)

IV. How often did he suffer shipwreck, and how often was he opposed and persecuted by heathen? (3.)

V. Make a list of his seven recorded sermons, noting when, where, to whom, and with what result each was spoken, and indicating very briefly its leading thought. (28.)

VI. Fill in the statement of Acts xx. 1, 2 by a brief narrative of S. Paul's movements drawn from 2 Corinthians. (6.)

VII. Would you justify or condemn S. Paul's conduct as described in Acts xxiii. 3, 6? (6.)

VIII. What were the objects of the collection S. Paul made, and what motives does he urge upon contributors to it? (7.)

IX. What allusions are there in S. Paul's Epistles to the soldier that guarded him? (4.)

X. Give three passages in which S. Paul quotes Christ's own words spoken before His Ascension, and three in which he quotes from Greek authors. (6.)

XI. "Faithful is the saying." Quote all the passages that begin thus, and show their doctrinal significance. (5.)

XII. Find some references to the Mosaic *ritual*, and to Greek and Roman usages and customs in S. Paul's Epistles. (12.)

XIII. Name—(*a*) The only church for which S. Paul has no commendation. (*b*) The only church for which he has no reproof. (*c*) The only church to which he does not call himself an Apostle. (*d*) The only church to which he sends his love. (*e*) The only church from which he accepted personal gifts. (*f*) The three Epistles that contain no clear Old Testament quotations. (*g*) The Epistles whose salutation adds "mercy" to "grace and peace." (*h*) The only mention of S. John by S. Paul. (*i*) The only mention of S. Paul outside his own Epistles and Acts. (10.)

XIV. Construct a life of Christ from the Epistles of S. Paul. (24.)

XV. Summarise S. Paul's teaching as to—(*a*) Tolerance; (*b*) Sectarian designations from personal names; (*c*) Conscience. (9.)

XVI. Is there any contradiction between the teaching of S. Paul and S. James concerning Faith and Works? (9.)

XVII. "By grace have ye been saved" (Eph. ii. 5). "Which are being saved" (1 Cor. i. 18). "Now is salvation nearer to us than when we first believed" (Rom. xiii. 11). How can S. Paul consistently make these three statements simultaneously of the same class of people? (6.)

XVIII. "We stand," "We walk," "Filled with," "Built up." Illustrate by quotations S. Paul's use of these four metaphors. (12.)

XIX. "Neither circumcision nor uncircumcision availeth, but . . ." Quote S. Paul's three conclusions to this sentence, and illustrate his characteristic teaching that blessing does not depend upon the privileges we enjoy, but upon the use we make of those privileges. (5.)

XX. Illustrate 1 Cor. xi. 1 by showing how S. Paul, as a follower of Christ, gave evidence both in word and deed of—(*a*) Courage; (*b*) Patience; (*c*) Humility; (*d*) Long-suffering; (*e*) Self-denial; (*f*) Self-discipline; (*g*) Self-abnegation; (*h*) Unworldliness; (*i*) Single-heartedness; (*j*) Laboriousness; (*k*) Conscientiousness; (*l*) High aspirations; (*m*) Patriotism; (*n*) Considerateness and courtesy; (*o*) Enthusiasm; (*p*) Passionate Devotion; (*q*) Prayerfulness; (*r*) Submission to God's will; (*s*) Zeal for God's glory; (*t*) Intense love to God and man. (20.)

XXI. Find in the Church History of the New Testament fulfilments of the prophecies in Matt. x. 19, 23, xxiv. 12; John xvi. 2; and of the promises in John xiv. 26 and xvi. 13. (6.)

XXII. Briefly sketch the early history of the Church of Ephesus, as told in the New Testament. (10.)

XXIII. Give examples of the following callings from the Acts and Epistles:—(1) Governor or Procurator; (2) Deputy or Proconsul; (3) Chancellor of the Exchequer; (4) Treasurer, *i.e.*, fiscal city officer; (5) Chief Captain, *i.e.*, Colonel; (6) Centurion, *i.e.*, Captain; (7) Judge; (8) Barrister;

(9) Doctor; (10) Silversmith; (11) Coppersmith; (12) Tentmaker; (13) Tanner; (14) Bondservant. (14.)

XXIV. "We know that ... if (or because)...." Trace this statement through 1 John, giving its contexts. (10.)

XXV. What do you understand by these expressions, as used in the New Testament?—Faith, Justification, Grace, Mystery, Church, Bishop, Elder, Deacon, Saint, Anathema. (20.)

XXVI. Make a list of the names and titles given to our Lord by S. Paul and S. John. (25.)

XXVII. Mention, in alphabetical order, noting the abode of each, 28 Christian women referred to in the Acts and Epistles. (28.)

XXVIII. Give, in tabular form, an epitome of the messages to the Seven Churches (Rev. ii., iii.), showing in each:—(a) The Lord's attributes; (b) His commendation; (c) His reproof; (d) His warning of judgment; (e) The enemies He notes; (f) His exhortation; (g) His promise to him that overcometh. (21.)

XXIX. Enumerate the eleven Songs in the Apocalypse, and write out the seven Beatitudes it contains. (9.)

XXX. The imagery and phraseology of the Apocalypse are borrowed throughout from the Old Testament. Illustrate this by references, especially to the Pentateuch, Ezekiel, and Daniel. (15.)

XXXI. What do you know of the following?—Antipas, Demas, Diotrephes, Epaphroditus, Mnason, Onesiphorus, Silvanus, Tertius. How many of the name of Titus and of Gaius can you discriminate? (20.)

XXXII. Give references for the following:—(a) "They are worthy" (twice). (b) "Mighty in the Scriptures." (c) "Measuring themselves by themselves." (d) "Dwelling in the things which he hath seen." (e) "Supposing that godliness is a way of gain." (f) "It behoved the Christ to suffer." (g) "Who emptied Himself." (h) "He died for all." (i) "That He might have mercy upon all." (j) "On whom we have set our hope." (k) "I press on toward the goal." (l) "The life which is life indeed." (m) "Sin is lawlessness." (n) "Apart from the law sin is dead." (o) "The world through its wisdom knew not God." (p) "Everything that is made manifest is light." (q) "Light shall shine out of darkness." (*r*) "Be not weary in well-doing." (*s*) "Through love be servants one to another." (*t*) "Follow after things which make for peace." (*u*) "Judge nothing before the time." (*v*) "Let each man prove his own work." (*w*) "Comforted each of us by the other's faith." (*x*) "I have kept the faith." (*y*) "He shall spread His tabernacle over them." (*z*) "At home with the Lord." (27.)

For *Second Series* of Questions, see p. 309.

L'ENVOY.

WHAT next? is the question with which we have ended each term's work. No one who has really entered into the enjoyment of our three years' Bible study will wish merely to drop it now. Two determinations will rather be formed. First, since our course is not a straight line but a *Cycle* (or wheel that returns into itself), to read the whole Bible again systematically. If our first reading was delightful and instructive, our second cannot fail to prove even more delightful and instructive. For we are dealing with the one inexhaustible Book.

Secondly, to continue the history of the Church which we have just begun. Many things in the New Testament would be explained, many disputes upon which the energies of Christians now waste themselves would cease to exist, if we rightly linked the New Testament story of that first of all the Christian ages of which we are heirs, with the story of this latest age, which is at once so interesting and so difficult, because we ourselves are part of it. The history of the 1800 years that lie between them explains the transition from the one to the other. There is a Church History Class in the College by Post; and all can read up the subject for themselves in such works as Smith's "Students' Ecclesiastical History" (Murray, 7s. 6d.), or Cutts' "Turning Points of General Church History" (S.P.C.K., 5s.).

QUESTIONS. SECOND SERIES.

(See p. 14.)

[Throughout books may be freely consulted for all the questions except Question XXXII. The maximum of marks for each Paper is 400, the maximum for each question is added to it.]

FIRST TERM.

I. Find seven Scriptural metaphors expressing the excellence of the Word of God. (14.)

II. What portions of the Bible were composed by women? (4.)

III. Which three of the Twelve Tribes furnished authors for the largest number of books in the Bible? State approximately the number to be attributed to each. (18.)

IV. Mention all those parts of the Old Testament whose authors are not certainly known. (10.)

V. Name any created things existing before God said "Let there be light," and any intelligent creatures of whose creation we have no record in Genesis. (4.)

VI. Can we prove from Scripture that the "days" of the Creation were 24 hours long? (5.)

VII. Enumerate the most remarkable nations descended from each of the three sons of Noah. (15.)

VIII. Show from the study of Abraham's life what great facts about God he had firmly grasped. (9.)

IX. Account for the statement in Rom. ix. 13 by contrasting the characters of Jacob and Esau as shown in their personal history and in the spiritual teaching connected with them. (Remember that "Esau is Edom.") (15.)

X. Point out the difference in origin and meaning of

"Jacob" and "Israel," and illustrate this difference from the contrasted use of these terms in the Prophets. (15.)

XI. Show how each of the Twelve Tribes fulfilled, in geographical position and history, Jacob's words about their ancestors. (24.)

XII. Make a list of the passages which enumerate *all* the sons of Jacob, or *all* the tribes named after them. (14.)

XIII. "Ye meant evil, but God meant it for good." Give other instances of this Divine overruling in Bible history. (6.)

XIV. Name *eight* children of Heth mentioned in the Bible. What is known concerning the origin, conquests, and migrations of the Hittites? (12.)

XV. Enumerate *fourteen* kings of Egypt named in Scripture. Briefly summarise the intercourse between Egypt and the Chosen People throughout their history. (20.)

XVI. Sum up, in two or three sentences, each of the sixteen speeches forming the colloquy of Job iii.—xxv., showing the progress of the argument throughout. (32.)

XVII. Discuss fully the meaning of each of the three signs described in Exod. iv. 2-9. (12.)

XVIII. Explain the things alluded to in the following passages :—Gen. xxxi. 30, xli. 42 ; Heb. xi. 21 ; Exod. viii. 26. (12.)

XIX "I have sinned." Quote instances of this confession in Scripture, distinguishing those which marked a satisfactory repentance from the rest. (9.)

XX. Name the day and hour that the Exodus began. What were the Egyptians doing while the Israelites were departing ? (2.)

XXI. Consider the historical origin and purpose of the two national ordinances of Circumcision and the Passover. What light do they throw upon the two Christian Sacraments ? (20.)

XXII. Reconcile Exod. iv. 10 and Acts vii. 22 ; also Exod. xxiv. 10 and 1 Tim. vi. 16. (6.)

XXIII. Was the Manna a natural product ? (4.)

XXIV. Tabulate the events that took place between Passover and Pentecost, 1491. (10.)

XXV. "The Blood of the Covenant." Quote the two Old Testament and five New Testament passages where this phrase occurs, showing how they explain each other. (10.)

XXVI. Name six places called after events that took place in them. (6.)

XXVII. Illustrate Heb. ix. 11, 12 by expounding the typical meaning of each of the eight parts of Aaron's garb as enumerated in Lev. viii. 7-9. (16.)

XXVIII. Tabulate the events that took place between Pentecost 1491 and Passover 1490. (10.)

XXIX. Work out with New Testament references the typical meaning of any *one* of the events between Passover 1491 and Passover 1490. (4.)

XXX. Note all the facts and incidents concerning the Patriarchs and Moses for a knowledge of which we are indebted *solely* to the Psalms, Acts, and Hebrews. (12.)

XXXI. Each of these phrases occurs both in Genesis or Exodus, and in the New Testament. (Slight variations are indicated by italics.) Give two references to each :—
(*a*) "Blessing I will bless thee." (*b*) "God rested on the seventh day." (*c*) "Man became a living soul." (*d*) "They shall be one flesh." (*e*) "The tree of life in the midst of the *garden*." (*f*) "Be *thou* perfect." (*g*) "The elder shall serve the younger." (*h*) "The earth is the Lord's." (*i*) "*Your* lamb without blemish." (*j*) "The *people* which *Thou hast* purchased." (*k*) "I will be *to you a* God." (*l*) "I will give *thee* rest." (24.)

XXXII. Give references for the following :—(*a*) "What is this thou hast done?" (*b*) "I will do this thing that thou hast spoken." (*c*) "The thing that thou doest is not good." (*d*) "Wherein have I sinned against thee?" (*e*) "God is great, and we know Him not." (*f*) "I have waited for Thy salvation." (*g*) "My life shall behold the light." (*h*) "Fear not, for God hath heard." (*i*) "The people believed and worshipped." (*j*) "Thou hast saved our lives." (*k*) "The Lord hath blessed me for thy sake." (*l*) "He knoweth the way that I take." (*m*) "God did send me." (*n*) "There will I meet with thee." (*o*) "I know it, my son." (*p*) "And the boys grew." (*q*) "He lieth under the lotus trees." (*r*) "He shall be as a wild ass." (*s*) "Thou art much mightier than we." (*t*) All the men are dead which sought thy life." (*u*) "Wilt thou go with this man?" (*v*) Show them the work that they must do." (*w*) "They turned trembling one to another." (*x*) "I shall die in my nest." (*y*) "Hating unjust gain." (*z*) "He maketh peace." (26.)

SECOND TERM.

I. Which of the five sacrifices ordained in Lev. i.—vii. seem to have been instituted for the first time at Sinai? (4.)

II. After what events were the sacrifices ordained in Lev. xvi. and Num. xix. appointed? Describe them. What light is thrown upon their unique character by the New Testament? (10.)

III. Name *eight* notable periods of 40 years and *eight* periods of 40 days in the Bible. (16.)

IV. Tabulate the events that took place between the Feasts of Passover and Tabernacles, 1490. (15.)

V. Under what circumstances were two men stoned in the Wilderness? (4.)

VI. Had Korah, the son of Izhar, any descendants? (4.)

VII. Write a brief life of Aaron, giving dates and places of his birth and death, and of the chief incidents in his career. (18.)

VIII. Summarise in about twelve sentences the three parts of Balaam's prophecy. (12.)

IX. Make a list of all the nations mentioned in Deuteronomy. What inferences as to the date of this book does the catalogue suggest? (14.)

X. Note the facts and incidents mentioned in Deuteronomy only. (15.)

XI. Find eighteen New Testament quotations from Deuteronomy. In how many of these is the book referred to Moses? (18.)

XII. Quote some memorable instances of obedience to the command in Deut. xii. 2, 3. (12.)

XIII. "Be pitiful" (tender-hearted, R.V.). Illustrate S. Peter's exhortation from the injunctions in the Mosaic Law concerning (*a*) aliens, (*b*) the young and helpless, (*c*) dumb creatures. (12.)

XIV. Consider how far the curses of Deut. xxviii. 15-68 have come upon and overtaken Israel during the last 2500 years. (15.)

XV. "Thy Thummim and thy Urim." What were these, and how often are they mentioned in Scripture? (8.)

XVI. Enumerate the occasions on which "The Angel of the Lord" was seen of men. Who was this Being? (15.)

XVII. What New Testament references are there to the Shechinah or manifested Glory of God? (5.)

XVIII. Seven tribes are likened to beasts. Name them and their symbols. (7.)

XIX. Give the R.V. equivalents of the following:—
(*a*) "Tabernacle of the congregation." (*b*) "Meat offering." (*c*) "Trespass offering." (*d*) "Curious girdle." (*e*) "Bonnets." (*f*) "Badgers' skins." (*g*) "Fowls that creep." (*h*) "Scape goat." (*i*) "Unicorn." (*j*) "Giants." (*k*) "Groves." (*l*) "Observe times." (12.)

XX. Trace the progress in Israel's national character, which was the result of their 40 years' experience in the Wilderness. (8.)

XXI. State the period of time covered by each of these books:—*Exodus, Leviticus, Numbers, Deuteronomy, Joshua*. (5.)

XXII. Compare Psalm xc. with the personal experience of Moses as described in the Pentateuch. (9.)

XXIII. Give the name of Joshua's grandfather. Sketch the course of the successive campaigns by which Joshua made the Israelites masters of Palestine. (12.)

XXIV. Enumerate the Cities of Refuge, stating in whose portion each was, and mentioning any historical incidents connected with it. To whom did these cities belong? What is their typical significance? Name a murderer who met his death at one of them. (24.)

XXV. Write a short history of Jericho, city of palm trees, from B.C. 1451 to A.D. 30. (10.)

XXVI. How many cities were assigned to Kohath, Gershon, and Merari respectively? What was the consequent geographical position of each of the three Levite tribes? (6.)

XXVII. Give the exact meaning and origin (if you can) of these terms:—Canaan, Palestine, the Holy Land, Galilee

Sharon, Jordan, Suph, Arabah, the Hinder Sea, the Brook of Egypt. (20.)

XXVIII. What events are connected in this term's reading with the following places?—Baal-tamar, Bezek, the Fords of Jordan, Hazeroth, Kibroth-Hattaavah, Massah, Mosera, Shittim, Taberah, the brook Zered. (10.)

XXIX. Specify which of the original inhabitants of Canaan were left in each tribe's portion, with the places of their abode. (14.)

XXX. Illustrate from Old Testament history the difference between *choosing* what is right and merely *desiring* what is right. (10.)

XXXI. Find *twelve* Moabites and *nine* Ammonites mentioned in the Bible, and sketch the relations of Moab and Ammon to Israel throughout their history. (30.)

XXXII. Give references for the following:—(*a*) "A Syrian ready to perish." (*b*) "One of his chosen men." (*c*) "The day thou stoodest before the Lord." (*d*) "The goodwill of Him that dwelt in the bush." (*e*) "March on with strength." (*f*) "Cut down for thyself there." (*g*) "Vex them not nor contend with them." (*h*) "He shall dwell alone." (*i*) "Ye shall know the revoking of My promise." (*j*) "He will not fail thee." (*k*) "Thou shalt eat and be full." (*l*) "Because ye sanctified Me not." (*m*) "That there be no plague." (*n*) "As I have done, so God hath requited me." (*o*) "I pray Thee, let me go over." (*p*) "Lo, I am come unto thee." (*q*) "To destroy the moist with the dry." (*r*) "That man perished not alone in his iniquity." (*s*) "The word is very nigh unto thee." (*t*) "He shall write him a copy of this law." (*u*) "He left nothing undone." (*v*) "Aaron held his peace." (*w*) "They became servants to do taskwork." (*x*) "They proclaimed peace unto them." (*y*) "They spake no more of going up against them." (*z*) "Thou hast lacked nothing." (26.)

THIRD TERM.

I. Briefly contrast the characters and careers of Gideon and Samson. (12.)

II. Find *five* allusions in Judges to previous events in Israel's history. (5.)

III. Consider Samuel as (*a*) a servant of God, (*b*) a prophet, (*c*) a patriot, (*d*) a statesman. (12.)

IV. Name *four* men who owed their names to the sorrowful circumstances of their birth. (4.)

V. Find *four* Amalekites mentioned in the Bible. What is known of the origin and abode of this people? Quote the earliest and latest allusions to them. (12.)

VI. Give with references the refrain of a song which is quoted thrice and referred to once in the Scriptures. (3.)

VII. Consider carefully the causes that led to the rejection of Saul. (10.)

VIII. Who killed one of Goliath's brothers? What do we know of his kinsfolk? (2.)

IX. Give as many Old Testament illustrations as you can of 1 Cor. i. 26-9. (10.)

X. Find *twelve* Philistines mentioned in the Bible. Name three false gods worshipped by the Philistines, and connect some historical incident with each of their five cities. (24.)

XI. What is known of the origin and national character of the Philistines? Sketch their relations to Israel throughout. (20.)

XII. May we infer from Scripture that the dead can manifest themselves to the living and communicate with them? (3.)

XIII. Give references in the Psalter and elsewhere to passages where God is called "our" or "my" (1) "Salvation," (2) "Health," (3) "Life," (4) "Strength," (5) "Hope," (6) "Refuge," (7) "Portion," (8) "Inheritance," (9) "Praise," (10) "Song," (11) "Joy," (12) "Glory." (12.)

XIV. Which of the High Priests enumerated in 1 Chron. vi. 3-15 are mentioned elsewhere? Can you name any Præ-Captivity High Priests omitted in this list? (10.)

XV. What do you know of Azel, Beerah, the Hagrites, and Saraph? (8.)

XVI. Name two notable citizens of Anathoth. (2.)

XVII. Write a brief life of Abner. (10.)

XVIII. State the exact number of priests and Levites that brought the Ark up to Mount Zion. (4.)

XIX. Gather up twenty-five allusions in the Psalter to

Jerusalem as (a) the Holy City, abode of God, or (b) the Royal City, abode of the King. (25.)

XX. "The Lord's Anointed," "My Anointed," "Thine Anointed." Where does this phrase first occur, and of what persons is it used? Give its New Testament equivalent. (12.)

XXI. Discriminate *two* places named Aphek, Aroer, Bethlehem, Bethshemesh, Carmel, Gibeah, Hebron, Mizpah, Ramah, and Ramoth. (20.)

XXII. "The Lord hath put away thy sin." Quote *nine* metaphors through which the completeness of this Divine putting away is expressed in Scripture. (18.)

XXIII. Would you condemn or justify David's conduct with regard to (1) Saul, (2) Achish, (3) Shimei? (9).

XXIV. Mention *six* Old Testament women living between B.C. 1500 and B.C. 1000 who were married more than once. (6.)

XXV. Give instances of sickness being sent as an exemplary punishment for flagrant sin. Show that sickness is not always a judgment on the sufferer. (14.)

XXVI. Name a common edible brought to a prophet in his old age who had brought it to others in his youth. (3.)

XXVII. "I will do it, (a) For My own sake, (b) For My servant's sake." Give instances of this Divine principle of action. (12.)

XXVIII. Distinguish between Abiezer and Ahiezer; Abijah and Ahijah; Abimelech and Ahimelech; Abinoam and Ahinoam; Adonibezek and Adonizedek; Amos and Amoz; Buz and Buzi; Elah and Eli; Eleazar and Eliezer; Gedaliah and Gemariah; Gershom and Gershon; Hosea and Hoshea; Joab and Joah; Korah and Kohath. (28.)

XXIX. Knowledge of God is light and ignorance of God is darkness. Trace this image in the Psalter and elsewhere. (20.)

XXX. Each of the following queries refers to a different tribe:—(1) Whose warriors were bold as lions and fleet as roes? (2) Whose warriors jeoparded their lives unto the death? (3) Whose warriors were not of double heart? (4) Whose warriors proved in battle the power of the prayer of faith? (5) Whose warriors were noted for a physical peculiarity mentioned thrice? (6) Which of the Ten Tribes extended their borders by conquest over Philistines and Amalekites after the other tribes had gone into captivity? (7) Which was the least warlike tribe? (8) Which produced men who had understanding of the times? (9) Which is more than once rebuked for pride? (10) Which led Israel in sin? (11) To which were Joshua's only recorded words of blessing spoken? (12) To which was the privilege of teaching given as the reward of faithfulness. (13) To which was the gift of song given in the largest measure? (26.)

XXXI. Explain exactly what is meant by *Redemption*. Trace this metaphor throughout the Bible. (18.)

XXXII. Give references for the following:—(*a*) "The bread of the mighty." (*b*) "As the man is, so is his strength." (*c*) "The war was of God." (*d*) "God is a righteous Judge." (*e*) "By Him actions are weighed." (*f*) "He hath redeemed my soul." (*g*) "Deliver us, and we will serve Thee." (*h*) "What shall be his work?" (*i*) "What do these Hebrews here?" (*j*) "Whose son is this youth?" (*k*) "Who am I, O Lord God?" (*l*) "I know that Thou delightest in me." (*m*) "The records are ancient." (*n*) "There is none like that." (*o*) "The covetous contemneth the Lord." (*p*) "These men be too hard for me." (*q*) "The land was wide and quiet and peaceable." (*r*) "Shall the sword devour for ever?" (*s*) "Rebuke the wild beast of the reeds." (*t*) "Thou shalt be turned into another man." (*u*) "The Lord hath made Himself known." (*v*) "He hath wrought with God this day." (*w*) "Blessed be thy wisdom." (*x*) "Glad with joy in Thy presence." (*y*) "They ministered with song." (*z*) "In His temple everything saith, Glory." (26.)

FOURTH TERM

I. Elucidate all the historical and geographical allusions in Psalm cxxxiii. (6.)

II. What is the exact meaning etymologically of the words *Satan* and *Devil*? Does either occur in the plural? Trace the use of both in Old and New Testament, distinguishing "devil" from "demon." (18.)

III. Make a list of the names or descriptive titles of the Tabernacle and the Temple which bring out their purpose and character. (25.)

IV. State precisely the contents of the Ark (*a*) in the Tabernacle, (*b*) in the First Temple. (3.)

V. Name five great warriors who dedicated the spoil won in battle to the repair of the Temple. (2.)

VI. What became of the treasures in the storehouse named in 1 Chron. xxvi. 15? (2.)

VII. "The shadow of Thy wings." Give the probable origin of this metaphor, and quote *six* passages in the Psalter, and *six* elsewhere in which it occurs. (14.)

VIII. Name *five* Phœnicians and *four* Phœnician cities mentioned in Scripture, noting the earliest and latest allusions to Tyre. What false gods did the Phœnicians worship? (12.)

IX. Sketch the relations of Israel to Phœnicia throughout her history, and account for the contrast presented to her relations with the Philistines. (15.)

X. Illustrate Psalm xlv. 6 by giving *six* references in the Psalms, *nine* in the Prophets, *four* in Revelation, and *six* elsewhere in the New Testament to the Throne of God. (25.)

XI. Name three sons of Abraham who married Egyptian princesses. (3.)

XII. Mention three women who rode on camels, and two men who rode on mules. Give some other Biblical references to both animals. (10.)

XIII. What inferences as to the scenery and physical characteristics of Palestine might be drawn from Hebrew literature generally? (10.)

XIV. Quote passages that allude to the *ant*, the *bee*, the *gnat*, the *moth*, and the *spider*. (5.)

XV. Quote ten passages in Proverbs enforcing the fifth commandment. (5.)

XVI. Each of the things mentioned in Prov. vi. 16-19 is characterised elsewhere in Proverbs as an abomination to the Lord. Give references. (7.)

XVII. Find sixteen aphorisms which occur more than once in Proverbs. (16.)

XVIII. What has Proverbs to say of wives and of

widows; of a gracious, a wise, and a virtuous woman; and of a contentious, an indiscreet, and an odious woman? (10.)

XIX. Illustrate Prov. xxii. 6 by a short essay on the principles and methods of education in Israel. (10.)

XX. Where do the Scriptures allude to *figs, dates, melons, pomegranates, almonds, nuts, cucumbers, lentiles,* and *honeycomb*? (18.)

XXI. What conclusions as to the authorship of Ecclesiastes may be derived from a careful consideration of the book itself? (8.)

XXII. Briefly summarise the argument of each of its four sections. (12.)

XXIII. Give instances of persons who with few religious privileges were blest and made a blessing; and of persons who in the midst of many privileges forfeited blessings that might have been theirs. (8.)

XXIV. Discriminate *two* persons named Ahab, Amaziah, Deborah, Enoch, Ezra, Gad, Hoshea, Iddo, Ishmael, Jehu, Job, Joel, Jonadab, Jonah, Jotham, Levi, Manasseh, Micah, Nadab, Nathan, Noah, Obadiah, Phinehas, Shallum, and Zephaniah. (50.)

XXV. Consider carefully the causes, immediate and remote, which led to the revolt of the Ten Tribes. (8.)

XXVI. "The light of Thy countenance." To what past and future manifestations of God would an Israelite have referred this phrase? Note all the passages where it occurs. (12.)

XXVII. Sketch the history of King Asa, and discuss his character. (6.)

XXVIII. Give Biblical examples of temptation resisted and yielded to, illustrating 1 Cor. x. 13 and James i. 14. (10.)

XXIX. Can we reconcile 2 Sam. xxiv. 24 and 1 Chron. xxi. 25, 1 Kings iv. 26 and 2 Chron. ix. 25, 1 Kings xvi. 8 and 2 Chron. xvi. 1? (6.)

XXX. (1) Man is *ready* to halt and perish. (2) God is *ready* to pardon and save. (3) God can make us *ready* to (*a*) speak for Him, (*b*) work for Him, (*c*) die for Him. Give at least one reference for each of these assertions. (12.)

XXXI. Each of the following queries refers to a different tribe:—(1) Whose portion contained Jerusalem? (2) Whose portion became the abode of two dauntless reformers separated by nine centuries? (3) In whose portion did our Lord dwell longest? (4) In whose portion did He preach and work most? (5) In whose portion were two mourning mothers made suddenly joyful? (6) Which tribe is omitted in Deut. xxxiii.? (7) Which is omitted in 1 Chron. iv.—viii., and Rev. vii.? (8) Which was Judah's rival throughout? (9) Which contributed most largely to the Bible? (10) Of which was it said "Let his men be few"? (11) Of which was it said "He shall be great"? (12) Of which do we twice find representatives faithfully worshipping at Jerusalem? (13) From which were all the high priests, save Aaron, descended? (26.)

XXXII. Give references for the following:—(*a*) "A discreet counsellor." (*b*) "A thousand years twice told." (*c*) "I will make known my words unto you." (*d*) "That they may know My service." (*e*) "The knowledge of the Holy One is understanding." (*f*) "As well the small as the great, the teacher as the scholar." (*g*) "He shall die for lack of instruction." (*h*) "One sinner destroyeth much good." (*i*) "The righteous is a guide to his neighbour." (*j*) "My hand was stretched out in the night." (*k*) "Let thine eyes look right on." (*l*) "I am sent to thee with heavy tidings." (*m*) "The wicked earneth deceitful wages." (*n*) "I hated life." (*o*) "A flattering mouth worketh ruin." (*p*) "Well is it with the man that dealeth graciously." (*q*) "He that despiseth his neighbour is void of wisdom." (*r*) "Our shield belongeth unto the Lord." (*s*) "Victory is of the Lord." (*t*) "It is the gift of God." (*u*) "Give me neither poverty nor riches." (*v*) "The Lord gave them rest." (*w*) "This is My resting place for ever." (*x*) "The Lord searcheth all hearts." (*y*) "I have trusted in the Lord without wavering." (*z*) "That we may seek him with thee." (26).

FIFTH TERM.

I. Sketch the relations between the kingdoms of Israel and Judah from 976 to 770. (15.)

II. Name two persons who did not see death, and nine who were raised from the dead. (6.)

III. Give instances from Kings and Chronicles of recognition of laws in the Pentateuch. (6.)

IV. Whose descendants avenged the murder of Zechariah, son of Jehoiada? (2.)

V. Find *ten* Syrian kings and *twelve* other Syrians mentioned in the Bible. Name *eight* Syrian cities. What do we know of the gods of the Syrians? (32.)

VI. Sketch the relations between Israel and Syria throughout their history. (15.)

VII. Name a successor of Jeroboam I. whose prayer God answered. (2.)

VIII. Find a parallel in the Psalter for every verse of Jonah's prayer. (9.)

IX. Note the chief illustrations in Amos from natural objects and agricultural pursuits. (6.)

X. Explain Amos iv. 5 by quoting two New Testament statements of the meaning of leaven. (2.)

XI. Elucidate the historical allusions in Amos i. 3, 9, ii. 4, iii. 14, iv. 2. (10.)

XII. Illustrate Amos iii. 8 by naming two princes, one farmer, three shepherds, six priests, and six Levites whom God called to be prophets. (18.)

XIII. Sketch the history of the schools of the Prophets from Samuel to the Captivity. (10.)

XIV. Find twelve allusions to Egypt in Hosea. (6.)

XV. Trace out carefully the ever-recurring tendency to idolatrous worship of God among the descendants of Rachel who "stole the teraphim." (10.)

XVI. Investigate the other causes which led to the downfall of the kingdom of Israel. (8.)

XVII. "A vine out of Egypt." Trace the typical use of the vine throughout the Bible. (8.)

XVIII. Explain the historical allusions in Micah i. 5, 10, 13, ii. 5, iii. 11, iv. 8, 13, vii. 14. (16.)

XIX. Discriminate *three* persons named Azariah, Hananiah, Jeremiah, Joshua, Micaiah, Saul, Shemaiah, Zechariah, and Zedekiah. (27.)

XX. Make a list of incidents peculiar to the books of Samuel and Kings and to the two books of Chronicles, bringing out the characteristic differences of these two historical works. (15.)

XXI. Find three allusions to Hezekiah outside Kings, Chronicles, and Isaiah. (3.)

XXII. Illustrate S. Paul's great declaration of the solidarity of humanity (Rom. xiv. 7) by giving instances in which (*a*) one man's faithfulness has saved a people, (*b*) one man's unfaithfulness has destroyed a people. (8.)

XXIII. Explain Chiun, Huzzab, Nehushtan, Rahab (Isa. xxx.), Siccuth your King, the tax of Moses (2 Chron. xxiv.). (12.)

XXIV. Note how recently discovered monuments illustrate and confirm the following passages : 2 Kings xvi. 7-9, xviii. 7, 14, 33, 34, xix. 28, 32. (10.)

XXV. Illustrate Isa. xxvi. 9 by collecting passages that speak of man seeking God. (8.)

XXVI. Distinguish the following places :—Baalah and Baalath, Bethel and Bether, Besor and Bezer, Cush and Cuth, Elam and Elath, Etam and Etham, Gaza and Gezer, Hachilah and Havilah, Hor and Horeb, Kadesh and Kedesh, Lachish and Laish, Moreh and Moriah, Nob and Noph, Seba and Sheba, Shenir and Shinar, Sin and Zin. (32.)

XXVII. Make a list of persons to whom or of whom it is said that God would be or was with them. (8.)

XXVIII. Point a contrast between ancient and modern Oriental women by Biblical instances of women (*a*) cooking, (*b*) sewing, (*c*) buying and selling, (*d*) writing letters, (*e*) building, (*f*) succouring the needy, (*g*) rescuing the imperilled, (*h*) giving counsel about public affairs, (*i*) ruling, (*j*) teaching, (*k*) praying, (*l*) prophesying. (12.)

XXIX. God (*a*) cares for the poor, (*b*) blesses those who aid them, (*c*) judges those who oppress them. Illustrate by quotations, especially from the Psalms and Prophets. (10.)

XXX. Name twelve men and three women of the tribe of *Benjamin*, and six men and six women of *Manasseh*. (27.)

XXXI. Name a general, two judges, and three idolaters of the tribe of *Ephraim* ; three rulers, a prophet, and an oppressed subject of *Issachar* ; two rulers and a prophet of *Zebulon* ; a ruler and an artificer of *Dan* ; three sinners of *Reuben* ; a ruler of *Naphtali*, and an idolater of *Simeon*. (21.)

XXXII. Give references for the following :—(*a*) "Written among the living." (*b*) "A brand plucked out of the burning." (*c*) "The Lord saw the affliction of Israel." (*d*) "His eyes observe the nations." (*e*) "God saw their works." (*f*) "I will never forget any of their works." (*g*) "They dealt faithfully." (*h*) "Like people, like priest." (*i*) "Your eyes the prophets, and your heads the seers." (*j*) "Ye trample upon the poor." (*k*) "Forgive them not." (*l*) "I would not look toward thee nor see thee." (*m*) "How shall Jacob stand?" (*n*) "They shall see Thy zeal for the people." (*o*) "Though I would redeem them." (*p*) "(He) made them sin a great sin." (*q*) "He had sackcloth within upon his flesh." (*r*) "The meadows by the Nile . . . shall become dry." (*s*) "I am thy servant and thy son." (*t*) "By the strength of my hand I have done it." (*u*) "Is thine heart right?" (*v*) "On whom dost thou trust?" (*w*) "Have we made thee of the king's counsel?" (*x*) "Sheep that no man gathereth." (*y*) "Thou hast increased their joy." (*z*) "Wait on thy God continually." (26.)

SIXTH TERM.

I. Compare and contrast the four Reformations in Judah's history with regard to the Reformers, the abuses reformed, and the results. (12.)

II. Which would you reckon the six most important battles in Israel's history? (6.)

III. Describe six memorials of Israel's past history which a traveller through Palestine might have seen before the Captivity. (6.)

IV. Make as complete a list as possible of those who formed in Jeremiah's days (*a*) the heathen party of the princes and nobles, (*b*) the great body of the sacerdotal and prophetic order. Note the chief offences with which both parties are charged by Jeremiah and Ezekiel. (12.)

V. Contrast the political position of Jeremiah with that of Isaiah. (5.)

VI. Find twelve parallels between Zephaniah and Jeremiah. (12.)

VII. Briefly indicate the meaning of the six parables in Jeremiah. (12.)

VIII. "I swear by Myself," or, "by My Name." Find seven passages in which God uses these words. (7.)

IX. Summarise the dialogue with which the book of Habakkuk opens. (4.)

X. For what lawful and unlawful purposes was the Valley of Hinnom used? Note all the Old Testament allusions to it and to them, and find twelve New Testament passages containing the Greek form of its name. (20.)

XI. Write a concise history of the kingdom Nimrod founded. Does the Assyrian character as delineated by the Hebrew prophets correspond with the Assyrian character as portrayed by the monuments? (14.)

XII. Note passages in six prophets referring to Assyria and Nineveh; and consider how far their predictions have been fulfilled. (12.)

XIII. Name some women in Bible history whose personal influence for good or for evil was very great. (6.)

XIV. Make a chronological list of passages in the Psalter and the Prophets from which the Jews might have learned the lesson enforced by our Lord in Matt. ix. 13. (8.)

XV. Mention two Ethiopians whose piety met with a great and unexpected reward. What promises to Ethiopia does Scripture contain, and to whom might they be applied now? (4.)

XVI. Had the exiles in Babylon any intercourse with Jerusalem during the reign of Zedekiah? (2.)

XVII. Where are the Chosen People called Jeshurun, Hephzibah, God's flock, God's hosts, God's armies, God's assembly or God's congregation, God's inheritance, God's peculiar treasure? (9.)

XVIII. Summarise Ezekiel xx.—xxii. (8.)

XIX. Give references for each of the five similes—wind, water, fire, oil, and dew—under which the operations of the Holy Spirit are spoken of, indicating the significance of each. (15.)

XX. What evidence is there as to the religious and political condition of North and South Palestine and of the exiles in Egypt immediately after the Captivity? (6.)

XXI. Discriminate *two* places named Antioch, Bethany, Cæsarea, Gilgal, Kir, Luz, Rimmon, Succoth, Sion. (18.)

XXII. Note how recently discovered monuments illustrate and confirm the following passages: Hab. ii. 12; 2 Chron. xxxiii. 10, 11; Isa. xlvii. 6 (R.V.). (6.)

XXIII. Illustrate Isa. xliii. 1 by quoting as many instances as you can of men and women whom the Lord or His angelic messengers addressed by name. (15.)

XXIV. Make a list of Old Testament saints upon whom God "put His name" by being known as their God. (5.)

XXV. Summarise Isa. xlix.—lvii. (14.)

XXVI. Illustrate Isa. xlix. 7 and Isa. lxiii. 1 by citing *ten* passages where we are told that God is *faithful*, and *twelve* where we are told that God is *able*. (22.)

XXVII. Are there any traces in the Old Testament of a definite belief in "the Resurrection of the body and the life everlasting"? (8.)

XXVIII. Illustrate Isa. lvii. 3, 4 and Isa. lxv. 23 by giving Biblical examples of (*a*) godly children of godly parents, (*b*) ungodly children of ungodly parents, (*c*) godly children of ungodly parents, (*d*) ungodly children of godly parents. (16.)

XXIX. Make a list of forty men of *Judah* who were memorable for goodness, valour, or wisdom; and of eighteen who were infamous for their evil deeds. (58.)

XXX. Distinguish between Mahlah and Mahlon, Medad and Medan, Mesha and Meshach, Naamah and Naaman, Obed and Oded, Rezin and Rezon, Shaphan and Shaphat, Sheba and Sheva, Shimea and Shimei, Uriah and Urijah, Uzzah and Uzziah, Vashti and Vashni, Zebul and Zebah, Zillah and Zilpah. (28.)

XXXI. Quote some prophecies that mention definite periods of time that were in the future for the prophet who uttered them. (4.)

XXXII. Give references for the following :—(*a*) "Israel My glory." (*b*) "The dearly beloved of My soul." (*c*) "Thou shalt not be forgotten of Me." (*d*) "I will strengthen thee for good." (*e*) "The oaths to the tribes were a sure word." (*f*) "In the latter days ye shall understand it." (*g*) "The joyous city that dwelt carelessly." (*h*) "A land that is very far off." (*i*) "The land whereunto their soul longeth to return." (*j*) "We are weary and have no rest." (*k*) "How long shall it yet be?" (*l*) " I will satisfy My fury." (*m*) " I poured out their life blood." (*n*) " The earth was waste and void." (*o*) " He created it not a waste." (*p*) " Ye have dealt deceitfully against your own souls." (*q*) " Thy doom is come unto thee." (*r*) " Thou hast had thy way." (*s*) " He shook the arrows to and fro." (*t*) " We will denounce him." (*u*) " This shall they have for their pride." (*v*) " He humbled himself greatly." (*w*) " Cursed be he that doeth the work of the Lord negligently." (*x*) " Yet will I gather others to him beside his own." (*y*) " That they may all call upon the name of the Lord." (*z*) " Then answered I and said, Amen." (26.)

SEVENTH TERM.

I. " I the Lord have spoken it." Find twelve passages in Ezekiel where this phrase or an equivalent phrase occurs. (12.)

II. Illustrate Ezek. xxxiv. 11, 12 by collecting passages which speak of God seeking man. (10.)

III. Which idolatrous nations received the most signal proofs of the Deity of Jehovah. (12.)

IV. Why did Daniel refuse the King's meat? (2.)

V. Trace the successive stages in Nebuchadnezzar's knowledge of the true God. (6.)

VI. Do secular historians or the monuments enable us to identify the four royal persons mentioned in Dan. iv.? (8.)

VII. Note all the Old Testament prophecies concerning Babylon and the Chaldeans. Consider the symbolical use of Babylon. (20.)

VIII. Sketch the relations between Babylon and Assyria, and between Babylon and Israel throughout their history. (20.)

IX. Find episodes in Daniel which illustrate Matt. vi. 33, xviii. 20 ; 1 John v. 4 ; Luke xii. 8 ; 1 Peter i. 11. (5.)

X. Discriminate four Gentile decrees for the restoration of the Jews, giving the date and purpose of each. (8.)

XI. Show by quotation chiefly from the Psalter how true *satisfaction* may be found. (10.)

XII. Of what ancient hostilities was the persistent enmity met with by the restored Jews a revival? (6.)

XIII. "The fear of the Jews." Where does this phrase occur, and what are its various contexts? (4.)

XIV. Mention the only Old Testament book that does not name God, and the only New Testament book that does not name Christ. Show how each recognises God or Christ notwithstanding. (4.)

XV. What do you know of Ezra's personal history? How far does his ancestry account for his piety and influence? (9.)

XVI. Enumerate the epistles of the Old Testament, noting the author, date, and theme of each. (8.)

XVII. What do you know of the following?—Arioch, Bigthan, Geshem, Jahaziah, Jarib, Melzar, Shemaiah, Tatnai, Tobiah, Zeresh. (20.)

XVIII. Illustrate Zech. ix. 9 by showing that the ass is the most prominent animal throughout Israel's history. (15.)

XIX. Explain Horonite, Nethinim, Ophel, Purim, Solomon's servants, Tirshatha. (12.)

XX. Name seven Old Testament prophetesses. (7.)

XXI. What are the favourite metaphors and similes in the Psalter to express (a) God's righteousness, (b) God's wrath, (c) man's frailty, (d) slander, (e) the prosperity of the righteous? (20.)

XXII. Show from internal evidence that Malachi belongs to the later, not the earlier period of the Restoration. (4.)

XXIII. Illustrate Mal. ii. 7 by showing what the priesthood had done for the preservation of the knowledge and worship of God in Judah. (10.)

XXIV. What evidence is there that the priests exercised judicial functions? (6.)

XXV. Make a chronological table of the three groups of Old Testament prophets, approximately indicating the length of time during which each prophesied, showing which were each other's contemporaries, and naming the chief nations concerning whom each prophesied. (32.)

XXVI. On whom were the three last curses of the Old Testament pronounced? (3.)

XXVII. Make a list of faithful and unfaithful servants in Scripture, indicating which were slaves. (10.)

XXVIII. How often does each of these prayers occur in

Psalm cxix. ?—(*a*) Remember me, (*b*) Hear me, (*c*) Seek me, (*d*) Save me, (*e*) Redeem me, (*f*) Deliver me, (*g*) Consider me, (*h*) Help me, (*i*) Quicken me, (*j*) Strengthen me, (*k*) Teach me, (*l*) Give me understanding. (12.)

XXIX. Find fifteen books no longer extant to which the Old Testament refers. (15.)

XXX. Make a list of twenty-six famous and six infamous *Levites*. (32.)

XXXI. Mark off by horizontal lines twenty-one inches to represent the centuries from B.C. 2000 to A.D. 100. Indicate by perpendicular lines (*a*) the periods named on p. 169, (*b*) the duration of the united monarchy, (*c*) of the monarchies of Judah and Israel, (*d*) of the Captivity, (*e*) of the Assyrian, Babylonian, Persian, Grecian, and Roman Empires, (*f*) of the priesthoods of the houses of Eleazar and Ithamar, (*g*) of the First and Second Temple. (32.)

XXXII. Give references for the following:—(*a*) "The bread of heaven." (*b*) "The day of small things." (*c*) "A time of much rain." (*d*) "Ivory inlaid in boxwood." (*e*) "The house which a great King of Israel builded." (*f*) "Whose are all thy ways?" (*g*) "They have laid their swords under their heads." (*h*) "Thou shalt surely fall before him." (*i*) "They have overthrown me wrongfully." (*j*) "Woe worth the day!" (*k*) "They conspired to cause confusion therein." (*l*) "Brought to silence in the midst of the sea." (*m*) "He was a faithful man." (*n*) "He shall magnify himself in his heart." (*o*) "Every one unto his work." (*p*) "As thou hast said, so must we do." (*q*) "O Lord, shine forth." (*r*) "That we should have discernment in Thy truth." (*s*) "The sum of Thy word is truth." (*t*) "Make crowns." (*u*) "I am the son of Thine handmaid." (*v*) "I will accept you." (*w*) "From this day will I bless you." (*x*) "When I shall be sanctified in you." (*y*) "All the peoples have seen His glory." (*z*) "The Lord is there." (26.)

EIGHTH TERM.

I. Trace the influence of Isaiah's writings upon John the Baptist. (9.)

II. Give references for all the sayings of the Baptist about Christ, and of Christ about the Baptist. (9.)

III. Note in chronological order all the events and incidents in Old Testament history to which our Lord alludes. (20.)

IV. Does Scripture warrant us in anticipating a future literal restoration of Israel to their own land? (10.)

V. Give the occasion, date, and chief incidents of each of Christ's recorded visits to Jerusalem. (21.)

VI. Which miracle of healing did Christ repeat oftenest? Which class of His miracles is unparalleled among miracles wrought by others? (4.)

VII. "According to your faith." Elucidate this by showing that some of His miracles were instantaneous, and others more or less gradual. (6.)

VIII. In which of His miracles did He seek human co-operation? What is the significance of His doing this? (6.)

IX. Illustrate Acts ii. 22 by showing from Scripture (*a*) that miraculous manifestations are not necessarily of Divine origin, (*b*) that Christ's miracles were evidences of His Divine mission rather than of His Divine nature. (10.)

X. After which of His miracles did the people glorify God? (7.)

XI. Illustrate Dr. Westcott's remark that S. Mark more than any other evangelist records the effect produced on others by the Lord's working. (24.)

XII. Contrast the parables of the *Minæ* and of the *Talents*, of the *Great Supper* and of the *Marriage Feast*. Account for their characteristic differences by pointing out the circumstances under which each was spoken. (8.)

XIII. Give two references to each of twenty-four sayings of Christ which occur in more than one context. (24.)

XIV. "As He said," Matt. xxviii. 6. Note all the occasions here referred to. (5.)

XV. Harmonise Matt. ix. 17 and xiii. 52, Luke ix. 50 and xi. 23, John v. 31 and viii. 14. (9.)

XVI. Enumerate all the sayings and incidents of Christ's ministry which reveal Him as "a Light to lighten the Gentiles." (10.)

XVII. "The Spirit of the Lord is upon me." Consider this aspect of the character and work of Christ. (10.)

XVIII. Quote a verse in which the Father, the Son, and the Holy Ghost are each referred to twice. (2.)

XIX. "The higher and holier the teacher in the eyes of other men, the unworthier is he in his own eyes." Give Biblical instances of this, and point out one noteworthy exception to it. (12.)

XX. Enumerate all the persons by whom and all the occasions on which Christ was acknowledged to be the Son of God. (12.)

XXI. Prove from Scripture, without reference to the writings of S. John, that Christ is "very God of very God." (10.)

XXII. From the private interviews with Christ, which are recorded in the Gospels, illustrate His patient condescension, also the importance He attaches to individual influence upon individuals. (9.)

XXIII. Mention by name thirty men and ten women who believed in Christ before His Ascension. (40.)

XXIV. Sketch the growth of opposition to Christ during the three and a half years of His ministry, and show how it influenced His teaching and action. (20.)

XXV. Quote the various accusations brought against Him by His enemies. Which did He refute, and which did He tacitly accept? (12.)

XXVI. Name (a) one who knew the exact age he would attain, (b) one who knew the manner of his death years before he died, (c) two who received Divine assurance of their personal salvation, (d) the only one of Christ's followers to whom lasting earthly fame was promised. (5.)

XXVII. Trace out in S. John's Gospel how Christ reveals Himself as the One having Life in Himself and giving Life to men. (12.)

XXVIII. What personal details can we glean of the authors of the Synoptical Gospels? (12.)

XXIX. Summarise the external and internal evidence for attributing the fourth Gospel to the Apostle John. (12.)

XXX. Sketch the life of S. Peter and discuss his character. (12.)

XXXI. Illustrate James v. 16 by giving twelve Old Testament instances of answered intercessory prayer. (12.)

XXXII. Give references for the following:—(a) "My Son, My Chosen." (b) "A new teaching." (c) "The things concerning the Kingdom of God." (d) "For a testimony unto all the nations." (e) "Making no distinction." (f) "The multitude welcomed Him." (g) "Ye know nothing at all." (h) "Certain which set all others at nought." (i) "Is it not for this cause that ye err?" (j) "Because they were not united by faith with them that heard." (k) "On some have mercy who are in doubt." (l) "Having forgotten the cleansing." (m) "They stood still, looking sad." (n) "He was much perplexed." (o) "God is one." (p) "All live unto Him." (q) "No word from God shall be void of power." (r) "Therefore do these powers work in him." (s) "On whom ye have set your hope." (t) "Ye are Christ's." (u) "Be ye free from the love of money." (v) "Keep yourselves from all covetousness." (w) "Be not anxious." (x) "Watch ye at every season." (y) "Looking for the Kingdom of God." (z) "Sanctify in your hearts Christ as Lord." (26.)

NINTH TERM.

I. Give the occasion, date, and chief incidents of each of S. Paul's recorded visits to Jerusalem. (15.)

II. Note in chronological order twenty-five events and incidents in Old Testament history to which S. Paul alludes. (25.)

III. Write a concise biography of S. Paul's dearest friend. Is he mentioned in S. John's writings? (15.)

IV. "He shall bear witness of Me." Quote twelve passages bearing out the above statement in this term's reading. (12.)

V. What are the three objects of Christian *ambition* which S. Paul puts before the Thessalonians, Corinthians, and Romans? (See R.V. margin.) (3.)

VI. Illustrate 1 Cor. iv. 1, 2 by tracing the metaphor of stewardship throughout the New Testament. (14.)

VII. Illustrate Gal. v. 22, 23 from the earliest chapters of Church history. (12.)

VIII. Quote all the passages in which S. Paul speaks of giving thanks for and praying for those to whom he writes, and in which he asks their prayer for himself. To which churches and individuals is he silent on this subject? (25.)

IX. In reference to subsequent uses of the phrase, consider all S. Paul's references to "the cross." (8.)

X. Summarise the argument of the Epistle to the Ephesians. (12.)

XI. "I am not able," "I am able." Trace out, especially in S. Paul's Epistles, the two ideas of weakness in self and strength in Christ. (12.)

XII. Examine the significance throughout the Bible of the act of laying on of hands. (10.)

XIII. Give Scriptural instances of conscience (*a*) awakened, (*b*) enlightened, (*c*) perverted, (*d*) seared. (8.)

XIV. What New Testament characters and incidents are connected with Ashdod, Damascus, Egypt, Gaza, Joppa, Kidron, Salem, Sharon, Sychar, Tyre, and Sidon? What Old Testament mention is there of Olivet? (12.)

XV. "The end of your *faith*, even the salvation of your souls" (1 Peter i. 9). "By *hope* were we saved" (Rom. viii. 24). "Every one that *loveth* is begotten of God" (1 John iv. 7). Harmonise these three statements. (12.)

XVI. Consider generally our gain in having different aspects of the same truths presented to us in the writings of different Apostles. (10.)

XVII. What do you know of the Churches of Thyatira and Antioch in Syria? (10)

XVIII. Illustrate 1 John iv. 8 by a list of the objects of God's love that are expressly named in Scripture. (12.)

XIX. Name the twenty-one sevenfold things mentioned in the Apocalypse. (21.)

XX. "He that openeth" (Rev. iii. 7). Where are we told of the Lord opening (*a*) the eyes, (*b*) the ears, (*c*) the understanding, (*d*) the heart, (*e*) the mouth? (6.)

XXI. "The Lamb of God." Examine the historical origin and doctrinal significance of this title. (10.)

XXII. Find seven references in the Apocalypse and elsewhere to God's Book of Life. (7.)

XXIII. Find three allusions in the Psalter to the River of God. (3.)

XXIV. "An unfallen creature may proclaim the Gospel as a *herald*; only a redeemed creature can testify from personal experience to the Gospel as a *witness.*" Illustrate, especially from the writings of S. Luke and S. John. (12.)

XXV. Trace throughout the Bible (*a*) the Divine call to salvation, "*Come,*" (*b*) the Divine call to service, "*Go.*" (15.)

XXVI. What light does the Old Testament throw upon these expressions: "The middle wall of partition," "The place called Har-Magedon"? (6.)

XXVII. Make a list from the whole Bible of "things which God hath prepared." (12.)

XXVIII. Name all the books of the Bible that contain explicit internal evidence as to their authorship. (12.)

XXIX. Give five Old Testament references to "*Sheol,*" eleven New Testament references to "*Hades,*" and three New Testament references to "*Paradise.*" Expound the meanings of these words as shown by their derivations. (24.)

XXX. Quote seven New Testament passages bearing upon the present condition of those who "have departed this life in God's faith and fear." (7.)

XXXI. Do any of the following occur in the Bible? If not, where do they occur, or of what texts are they misquotations?—(*a*) "Assurance of salvation." (*b*) "Justification by faith." (*c*) "Hope full of immortality." (*d*) "Not lost, but gone before." (*e*) "A reason for the faith that is in you." (*f*) "In the world, but not of the world." (*g*) "In the midst of life we are in death." (*h*) "His end was peace." (*i*) "Charity begins at home." (*j*) "Money is the root of all evil." (*k*) "Spare the rod and spoil the child." (*l*) "God tempers the wind to the shorn lamb." (12.)

XXXII. Give references for the following:—(*a*) "There is no distinction" (twice). (*b*) "Teachers of that which is good." (*c*) "Helpers of your joy." (*d*) "Giving no occasion of stumbling in anything." (*e*) "The uncertainty of riches." (*f*) "I would have you to be free from cares." (*g*) "All things are yours." (*h*) "Encourage the faint-hearted." (*i*) "Complete the doing also." (*j*) "I have found no works of thine fulfilled." (*k*) "Worse than an unbeliever." (*l*) "I speak this to move you to shame." (*m*) "Hold such in honour." (*n*) "Not knowing God, ye were in bondage."

(*o*) " We desire to hear of thee what thou thinkest." (*p*) " The earth was lightened with his glory." (*q*) " Try your own selves." (*r*) " Approved in Christ." (*s*) " That thy progress may be manifest unto all." (*t*) " Manifest throughout the whole prætorian guard." (*u*) " The patience and the faith of the saints." (*v*) " In all the world bearing fruit and increasing." (*w*) " God's own possession." (*x*) " For whom Christ died." (*y*) " And such we are." (*z*) " Remember Jesus Christ." (26.)

THE END.

GENERAL INDEX.

(The pages given are those on which either the book itself or its subject-matter is dealt with.)

	PAGES		PAGES
Genesis	19-35.	The Psalms	45, 66, 67, 84, 85, 104, 105, 126, 127, 147, 170-212.
Exodus	20, 23-35 39, 40, 50.		
Leviticus	43, 44, 50-55.		
Numbers	41-46, 49, 53.	The Proverbs	82-84, 89
Deuteronomy	43, 45, 49, 53.	Ecclesiastes	83, 84.
		The Song of Songs	81, 82, 89.
Joshua	41-50.	Isaiah	52, 102-105, 109-113, 122, 123, 127, 130-132.
Judges	42-46, 55, 61, 62, 65, 66, 68.		
Ruth	42, 44, 46, 50.		
1 Samuel	61-64, 66, 68-74.	Jeremiah	119-121, 123-132, 139, 140.
2 Samuel	62, 64, 66-68, 70-74.	Lamentations	125, 127, 131.
		Ezekiel	124-127, 131, 132, 143, 147, 152, 153.
1 Kings	79, 80, 84-91, 96-100, 104, 107, 108, 112.		
		Daniel	143, 144, 147-155, 165-167.
2 Kings	96-100, 104-110, 113, 114, 118-121, 126-128, 132, 133.	Hosea	101, 104, 111, 113.
		Joel	102, 104, 111, 112.
1 Chronicles	64-66, 69-74, 84.	Amos	101, 104, 111, 112.
2 Chronicles	64, 65, 79, 80, 84-91, 96-100, 104, 105, 108-110, 118-121, 126-128, 132, 133, 147.	Obadiah	124, 127, 131, 132.
		Jonah	100, 101, 104, 106, 110, 112.
		Micah	103, 104, 111, 113.
Ezra	140-142, 144, 146-152.	Nahum	103, 105, 113.
Nehemiah	144, 147, 151, 152.	Habakkuk	123, 126, 130, 131, 132.
Esther	141, 144, 145, 147, 148, 156.	Zephaniah	123, 126, 130, 132.
Job	21-23, 28, 31.	Haggai	145, 147, 153, 154.

GENERAL INDEX.

	PAGES
Zechariah	145, 147, 153, 154, 157.
Malachi	146, 147, 153, 154.
The Apocrypha	164-169.
S. Matthew	218-221, 227-240, 244-277.
S. Mark	218-222, 227-240, 244-277.
S. Luke	218-222, 227-240, 244-277.
S. John	218-222, 227-240, 244-277.
The Acts	223, 227, 234, 238, 239, 278-284, 291-300, 302, 304.
Romans	284, 286, 292, 301.
1 Corinthians	284, 285, 292.
2 Corinthians	284, 285, 292.
Galatians	284, 285, 292.
Ephesians	284, 286, 287, 292.
Philippians	284, 286, 287, 292.
Colossians	284, 286, 287, 292.
1 Thessalonians	284, 285, 291, 292.
2 Thessalonians	284, 285, 291, 292.
1 Timothy	284, 287, 292.
2 Timothy	284, 287, 292.
Titus	284, 287, 292.
Philemon	284, 287, 292.
Hebrews	50-53, 224, 226, 227.
James	223-225, 227.
1 Peter	223-225, 227.
2 Peter	223-225, 227.
1, 2, 3 John	287, 288, 292.
Jude	223-225, 227.
Revelation	288-292.

INDEX TO THE PSALMS.

(The Arabic numerals are those assigned to the Psalms on pp. 179–212.)

Psalm		No.	Psalm		No.
Psalm	I.	76	Psalm	XXXVII.	64
"	II.	34	"	XXXVIII.	40
"	III.	61	"	XXXIX.	41
"	IV.	62	"	XL.	43
"	V.	45	"	XLI.	42
"	VI.	39	"	XLII.	83
"	VII.	20	"	XLIII.	84
"	VIII.	2	"	XLIV.	105
"	IX.	33	"	XLV.	74
"	X.	46	"	XLVI.	95
"	XI.	10	"	XLVII.	96
"	XII.	47	"	XLVIII.	97
"	XIII.	9	"	XLIX.	87
"	XIV.	48	"	L.	79
"	XV.	26	"	LI.	37
"	XVI.	23	"	LII.	16
"	XVII.	21	"	LIII.	49
"	XVIII.	35	"	LIV.	19
"	XIX.	3	"	LV.	55
"	XX.	29	"	LVI.	11
"	XXI.	30	"	LVII.	15
"	XXII.	58	"	LVIII.	17
"	XXIII.	4	"	LIX.	8
"	XXIV.	25	"	LX.	31
"	XXV.	12	"	LXI.	60
"	XXVI.	66	"	LXII.	50
"	XXVII.	54	"	LXIII.	53
"	XXVIII.	67	"	LXIV.	51
"	XXIX.	5	"	LXV.	102
"	XXX.	68	"	LXVI.	103
"	XXXI.	59	"	LXVII.	104
"	XXXII.	38	"	LXVIII.	36
"	XXXIII.	93	"	LXIX.	57
"	XXXIV.	13	"	LXX.	44
"	XXXV.	18	"	LXXI.	106
"	XXXVI.	63	"	LXXII.	73

		No.			No.
Psalm	LXXIII.	88	Psalm	CXII.	90
"	LXXIV.	107	"	CXIII.	139
"	LXXV.	100	"	CXIV.	140
"	LXXVI.	101	"	CXV.	141
"	LXXVII.	81	"	CXVI.	142
"	LXXVIII.	22	"	CXVII.	143
"	LXXIX.	108	"	CXVIII.	144
"	LXXX.	98	"	CXIX.	150
"	LXXXI.	80	"	CXX.	118
"	LXXXII.	82	"	CXXI.	119
"	LXXXIII.	94	"	CXXII.	120
"	LXXXIV.	85	"	CXXIII.	122
"	LXXXV.	121	"	CXXIV.	123
"	LXXXVI.	71	"	CXXV.	124
"	LXXXVII.	99	"	CXXVI.	125
"	LXXXVIII.	86	"	CXXVII.	77
"	LXXXIX.	92	"	CXXVIII.	78
"	XC.	1	"	CXXIX.	110
"	XCI.	91	"	CXXX.	109
"	XCII.	131	"	CXXXI.	70
"	XCIII.	132	"	CXXXII.	75
"	XCIV.	126	"	CXXXIII.	65
"	XCV.	133	"	CXXXIV.	128
"	XCVI.	134	"	CXXXV.	129
"	XCVII.	135	"	CXXXVI.	130
"	XCVIII.	136	"	CXXXVII.	117
"	XCIX.	137	"	CXXXVIII.	28
"	C.	138	"	CXXXIX.	69
"	CI.	24	"	CXL.	6
"	CII.	111	"	CXLI.	7
"	CIII.	112	"	CXLII.	14
"	CIV.	113	"	CXLIII.	52
"	CV.	114	"	CXLIV.	127
"	CVI.	115	"	CXLV.	72
"	CVII.	116	"	CXLVI.	145
"	CVIII.	32	"	CXLVII.	146
"	CIX.	56	"	CXLVIII.	147
"	CX.	27	"	CXLIX.	148
"	CXI.	89	"	CL.	149

www.ingramcontent.com/pod-product-compliance
Lightning Source LLC
Chambersburg PA
CBHW030307240426
43673CB00040B/1087